D1242314

INTRODUCTION TO PROBABILISTIC AUTOMATA

Computer Science and Applied Mathematics

A SERIES OF MONOGRAPHS AND TEXTBOOKS

Editor
Werner Rheinboldt
University of Maryland

Hans P. Künzi, H. G. Tzschach, and C. A. Zehnder
NUMERICAL METHODS OF MATHEMATICAL OPTIMIZATION: WITH ALGOL
AND FORTRAN PROGRAMS, CORRECTED AND AUGMENTED EDITION, 1971

Azriel Rosenfeld
PICTURE PROCESSING BY COMPUTER, 1969

James Ortega and Werner Rheinboldt
ITERATIVE SOLUTION OF NONLINEAR EQUATIONS IN
SEVERAL VARIABLES, 1970

A. T. Berztiss
DATA STRUCTURES: THEORY AND PRACTICE, 1971

Azaria Paz
INTRODUCTION TO PROBABILISTIC AUTOMATA, 1971

In preparation

David Young
ITERATIVE SOLUTION OF LARGE LINEAR SYSTEMS

Ann Yasuhara
RECURSIVE FUNCTION THEORY AND LOGIC

INTRODUCTION TO PROBABILISTIC AUTOMATA

Azaria Paz

*Department of Computer Sciences
and Mathematics
Israel Institute of Technology
Haifa, Israel*

1971

Academic Press

New York and London

ACADEMIC PRESS, INC.
111 Fifth Avenue, New York, New York 10003

United Kingdom Edition published by
ACADEMIC PRESS, INC. (LONDON) LTD.
Berkeley Square House, London W1X 6BA

LIBRARY OF CONGRESS CATALOG CARD NUMBER: 74-137627

PRINTED IN THE UNITED STATES OF AMERICA

To My Parents Moshe and Rachel
and to My Brother Israel

Contents

Preface

Probabilistic automata have been studied in the literature from different (although related) points of views. An approach emerging from information theory was initiated by Shannon and Weaver in their classical book as early as 1948. Later, in 1958, a (somewhat vague) definition of a probabilistic automata was given by Ashby in a semipopular book. The theory began its real development only in the early sixties when scientists from different parts of the world introduced probabilistic automata as a natural generalization for deterministic automata of different types.

Almost every book on automata theory published in the past few years contains some parts devoted to probabilistic automata (see, e.g., Harrison, 1965; Booth, 1967; Salomaa, 1969; Starke, 1969; Arbib, 1969; Carlyle, 1969). This seems to prove that there is growing interest in this new and fast developing area of research. This is a first attempt to devote a book to probabilistic automata and related topics, an attempt based on the assumption that the theory considered is already mature enough to deserve a book of its own.

The book is intended to serve both as a monograph and as a textbook and, as such, is augmented with a large collection of exercises distributed among the various sections. Some exercises are necessary for understanding the following sections; others, which the author considers to be hard, are marked with an asterisk. For the convenience of the reader, a section containing answers and hints to selected exercises is given at the end of the book. A collection of open problems as well as an exhaustive bibliography are included for the benefit of those readers who may wish to continue research in the area.

The choice of topics presented and their extent is, of course, subjective, and the author wishes to express his apologies to those who may feel that their work has not been covered thoroughly enough (after all, a first book in a new area is a first trial in a sequence of trials and errors).

The book emerged from a two-quarter course given during two consecutive years at the Department of Electrical Engineering and Computer Sciences, University of California, Berkeley. Some parts of the book have also been presented in a course given at the Department of Mathematics, Technion, Haifa, Israel. While the first chapter of the book is engineering oriented, the other two chapters are mathematically oriented. The interdependency between the two parts is weak, and they can be presented separately and independently. Only some theorems in Section C of Chapter II depend on the first chapter. The only prerequisites assumed for being able to follow the material in this book are: finite automata theory, e.g., Harrison (1965), Booth (1967), Salomaa (1969), Arbib (1969); linear algebra and matrices, e.g., MacDufee (1964), Thrall and Tornheim (1957), Gantmacher (1959); elementary probability theory, e.g., Feller (1957), and some mathematical maturity.

Acknowledgments

The author wishes to express his deep gratiude to the Department of Electrical Engineering and Computer Sciences, University of California, Berkeley under the auspices of which the main bulk of this book has been prepared during two consecutive years and to the Department of System Sciences, University of California, Los Angeles which provided him with ideal working conditions during two consecutive summers. The author is also indebted to many friends, colleagues, and students who helped to improve the exposition and the material in the book, especially to J.W. Carlyle from UCLA, and L.A. Zadeh, M.A. Harrison, and A. Gill from University of California, Berkeley. Finally I wish to thank my wife Erella for her permanent encouragement and patience.

Abbreviations

Notation

X, Σ, Y, Δ	input and output alphabets, xix
Σ	partition over set of states S, 117
x, σ	elements in X and Σ, respectively, xix
y	element in Y, xix
λ or e	empty word, xix
$X^*, \Sigma^*, Y^*, \Delta^*$	set of all words over X, Σ, Y, Δ, respectively, xix
U, V, E, L	subsets of words, xix
u, v	elements of X^*, Y^*, respectively, xix
x	element of Σ^*, 158
ϕ	empty set, xix
Π	multiplication sign, xxi
$\Rightarrow$	implication sign, xxi
$\Leftrightarrow$	equivalence sign, xxi
ε	is an element of, xxii
Ω	sample space, xix
$\{ \ \}$	unordered set brackets, xix
$(\ )$	ordered set brackets, xix
$P, [a_{ij}] = A$	matrix notation, xix
ξ, ξ_i	vector notation, xix
ξ_i, ξ_{ij}	element of vector ξ or ξ_i, respectively, xix
$\lvert A \rvert$	determinat of matrix A, 121
$\lvert S \rvert$	number of elements in the set S, xix
$C(A)$	convex closure of the rows of A, 140
$\gamma(P)$	matrix functional, 70
$\lvert \ \rvert, \lVert \ \rVert$	matrix funtionals, 69
$d(p), \delta(p)$	matrix functionals, 68
A^T, ξ^T	transpose of matrix or vector A, ξ, respectively, xx
η	column vector of ones, 3, xx
η^F	final column vector, 146
s_i	degenerate stochastic vector, xx
$\mathscr{P}_n$	set of stochastic n-dimensional vectors, xx

$\operatorname{int}(V)$, $\operatorname{relint}(V)$, $\operatorname{aff}(V)$	Interior, relative interior, and affine closure of V, xx
$\sup(a_i)$, $\inf(a_i)$	supremum and infimum of sequence (a_i), xxi
aRb	a is related by relation R to b, xxii
$a \equiv b \pmod{c}$	a is congruent to c modulo c, xxii
a^+, a^-	positive and negative truncation, 68
$A + B$	direct sum of two matrices, 25, 101
$A \times B$	Kronecker product of two matrices, 101
$A \times B$	Kronecker product of two PAs,
$A(x)$	matrix associated with input x, 80
$A(v\vert x)$	matrix associated with input–output pair (x, y), 1
$A(v\vert u)$	matrix associated with input–output pair (u, v), 3
$\eta(v\vert u)$	final vector associated with input output (u, v), 3
$A(\sigma, l)$	successor set of states, 91
$\pi(v\vert u)$	initial vector associated with input–output pair (u, v), 3
$P_\pi(v\vert u)$	probability associated with input–output pair (u, v), 3
$\bar{\pi}(v, u)$	transition vector associated with pair, 4
$_m p_{ij}$	transition probability at time m, xxiv
K^M	K-matrix for machine M, 19
H^M	H-matrix for machine M, 20
$G^{(M,\pi)}$	G-matrix for initiated machine M, 21
J^M	J-matrix for machine M, 30
$h^M(\xi)$	point in $C(H^M)$ associated with vector ξ, 33
$\mathscr{S}(m)$, $\mathscr{S}$	Column vector spaces, 19
$A_{\sigma_i \sigma_j}$	block of A corresponding to $\sigma_i \sigma_j$, 117
η_{σ_i}	subvector of η corresponding to σ_i, 117
π_{σ_i}	subvector of π corresponding to σ_i, 117
$P(v_1 \ldots v_k; v_1' \ldots v_1')$	compound sequence matrix, 118
H_{mn}	product of stochastic matrices, 73
$\mathscr{P}(X, Y)$	set of input output–output relations, 55
$\mathscr{F}^M$	set of functions induced by machine M, 25
$M > M'$	machine M covers machine M', 29
E_g	generalized event, 135
$r(E_g)$	rank of generalized event, 135
$T(f, \lambda)$, $T(A, \lambda)$	cutpoint event, 153
$T_{\neq}(A, \lambda)$	exclusive cutpoint event, 171
$(S, X, Y, \{A(y\vert x)\})$	stochastic sequential machine, 1
$(S, \{A(\sigma)\})$	Markov on system, 80
(π, S, A)	homogeneous Markov chain, 117
Γ, Γ^n	graph associated with Markov chain, 85

Preliminaries

A. NOTATIONS

The following notations are used throughout unless otherwise stated:

X or Σ denotes an *input* alphabet with individual elements (symbols) x and σ respectively. Sequences of symbols X or Σ are called *words* or *tapes* and are denoted by u (when X is the alphabet) or x (when Σ is the alphabet). Y or Δ denotes an *output* alphabet with individual elements y or σ respectively. *Words* (or *tapes*) over Y or Δ are denoted by v or y respectively. The set of all words [including the *empty* word denoted by λ or e] over X (or Σ or Y or Δ) is denoted by X^* (or Σ^* or Y^* or Δ^* respectively). Subsets of words over a given alphabet are called *events* or *languages* and are denoted by U or V or E. If $x = \sigma_1 \cdots \sigma_k$ and $x' = \sigma_1' \cdots \sigma_j'$ are words then xx' is the word $xx' = \sigma_1 \cdots \sigma_k \sigma_1' \cdots \sigma_j'$ and the operation is called concatenation ($x\lambda = \lambda x = x$); x^k denotes the word $\overbrace{xx \cdots x}^{k}$. If U and U' are languages, then $UU' = \{xx' : x \in U, x' \in U'\}$ and $U^k = \{x^k : x \in U\}$. $\varnothing$ denotes the empty language [$U\varnothing = \varnothing U = \varnothing$]. Other set theoretic equations between languages are denoted as usual. $l(u)$ denotes the *length* of the word u [the number of symbols in the word u], (u, v) denotes a pair of words of the *same length*, $u \in X^*$ and $v \in Y^*$; $l(u, v)$ denotes the common length of u and v. If S is a set, then $|S|$ denotes the number of elements in S. The brackets ( ) are used generally for enclosing an ordered set, the brackets { } are used generally for enclosing an unordered set. The notation $[a_{ij}]$ is used for denoting a *matrix* whose elements are a_{ij}. $\xi = (\xi_i)$ or $\xi_i = (\xi_{ij})$ denotes a *vector* ξ

or ξ_i whose elements are ξ_i or ξ_{ij} respectively. The superscript T over a vector or a matrix [ξ^{T} or A^{T}] denotes the transpose of the vector or the matrix. η denotes a column vector all the entries of which are equal to 1 and whose dimension will depend on the context. A vector is called *substochastic* if all its entries are nonnegative and the sum of its entries is ≤ 1; if the sum is $= 1$, then the vector is called *stochastic*. The set of all n-dimensional stochastic vectors is denoted by $\mathscr{P}_n$. A matrix is called *substochastic* or *stochastic* if it is square and all its rows are substochastic or stochastic correspondingly. A matrix is called *constant* if all its rows are equal one to the other. The vector $(0, \ldots, 1, \ldots, 0)$, where the 1 is in the ith place and the dimension depends on the context, is called a degenerate *stochastic* vector and is denoted by the notation $\bar{s}_i$. The usual notation $\mathrm{Pr}(A|B)$ is used to denote the conditional probability of the event A given that B. If $\bar{x}_1, \ldots, \bar{x}_n$ are point vectors, then the combination $\sum \lambda_i \bar{x}_i$ is a *convex combination* of them if (λ_i) is a stochastic vector. The notation $\mathrm{conv}(\bar{x}_1, \ldots, \bar{x}_n)$ stands for the convex closure of the set $\{\bar{x}_1, \ldots, \bar{x}_n\}$. The set of point vectors $\{\bar{x}_1, \ldots, \bar{x}_n\}$ is linearly independent if the set of vectors $\{\bar{x}_2 - \bar{x}_1, \ldots, \bar{x}_n - \bar{x}_1\}$ is linearly independent. A *simplex* is a set of points which can be represented as the convex closure of a set of linearly independent point vectors. A set of points is *convexly independent* if no point in the set is a convex combination of the other points in the set. A *convex polyhedron* is a set of points which can be represented as the convex closure of a finite set of convexly independent points. If V is a convex polyhedron and $W \subset V$ [W is a subset of V], then W is a *face* of V if the linear closure of W [notation: aff W] has no points in common with the convex closure of $V - W$ [the set of points which are in V but not in W]. The *interior* of a convex polyhedron V [notation: int V] is the set of all points in V except the points on the faces of V which differ from V, the *relative interior* of V [notation: relint V] is the set of all points of V except its vertices. Two functions are equal if they have the same domain and agree on it. The term *machine* is used for devices which have both inputs and outputs, the term *automaton* is used for devices with input only [the output is represented directly by the internal states] and the term *acceptor* is used for automata, or machines which are used for discriminating between words over a given alphabet. Superscripts are used for discriminating between different machines (automata, acceptors) and are omitted if context is clear.

B. SOME ANALYTICAL LEMMAS

The following analytical lemmas are assumed.

Lemma 2.1: Let $\{a_n\}$ and $\{b_n\}$ be nondecreasing sequences of real numbers such that $a_i \leq b_i$ for all i with $\lim_{i \to \infty} a_i = a$, $\lim_{i \to \infty} b_i = b$ [including the case where

a and/or b is equal to ∞). Then $a \leq b$. If $a < b$, then there is a natural number N such that for all $j \geq N$ and all i the inequality $a_i < b_j$ holds.

Corollary 2.2: If $a_i \leq M$ for some real number M and all i, then also $a \leq M$. If $a > M$ for some real number M, then there is a i_0 with $a_i > M$ for all $i \geq i_0$.

Lemma 2.3: Let $\{a_{mn}\}$ be a double sequence, nondecreasing with regard to both m and n. Then $\lim_{m \to \infty} \lim_{n \to \infty} a_{mn} = \lim_{n \to \infty} \lim_{m \to \infty} a_{mn}$ [including the case where the limit has infinite value].

Definition: Let (a_i) be a set of real numbers, $\sup_i (a_i)$ is defined as the number $\bar{a}$ such that $a_i \leq \bar{a}$ for all i and for any $\epsilon > 0$ there is n such that $a_n \geq a - \epsilon$; $\inf_i (a_i)$ is the number $\underline{a}$ such that $\underline{a} \leq a_i$ for all i and for all $\epsilon > 0$ there is n such that $a_n \leq \underline{a} + \epsilon$ [$\bar{a}$ or $\underline{a}$ can assume the values $+\infty$ or $-\infty$ also].

Lemma 2.4: If (a_i) and (b_i) are two sets of numbers such that $a_i \leq b_i$ for all i, then $\bar{a} \leq \bar{b}, \underline{a} \leq \underline{b}$. Moreover if $a_i \leq M$ for some real number M and all i, then $\bar{a} \leq M$ and similarly if $a_i \geq M$ for all i, then $\underline{a} \geq M$.

The notation $\prod_{i=1}^{\infty} a_i$ stands for the infinite product of a sequence of numbers (a_i) and is equal to $\lim_{n \to \infty} \prod_{i=1}^{n} a_i$ [provided that the limit exists and including the case where the limit equals ∞].

The product $\prod_{i=1}^{\infty} a_i$ converges if there is m with $a_i > 0$ for $i \geq m$ and $\lim_{n \to \infty} \prod_{i=m}^{n} a_i$ exists and is finite.

Lemma 2.5: Let $\{a_i\}$ be a sequence of numbers $a \leq a_i \leq 1$. If $\sum_{i=1}^{\infty} a_i$ diverges, then $\prod_{i=j}^{\infty} (1 - a_i)$ converges to zero for any j.

Lemma 2.6: Let (a_i) be a sequence of numbers, $0 \leq a_i$. If $\sum_{i=1}^{\infty} a_i < \infty$, then the product $\prod_{i=1}^{\infty} (1 + a_i)$ converges.

C. SOME ALGEBRAIC PRELIMINARIES

The notation $A \Rightarrow B$ is used for *implication* ("statement A implies statement B"]; $A \Leftrightarrow B$ means that statement A is *equivalent* to statement B; $a \in A$ means that *a is an element of A* and $\{a : A\}$ stands for the set of all elements a satisfying the property A. The *Cartesian* product of two sets A and B is defined as $A \times B = \{(a, b) : a \in A, b \in B\}$.

A (binary) *relation* between the sets A and B [including the case where $B = A$] is a subset of $A \times B$. If R denotes a relation and $(a, b) \in R$ we shall denote this also by the notation aRb. A relation R between A and A ("over A") is

1. *Reflexive* if aRa for every $a \in A$.
2. *Symmetric* if $aRb \Rightarrow bRa$.
3. *Transitive* if aRb and $bRc \Rightarrow aRc$.

A relation satisfying all the three properties above is called an *equivalence* relation.

Any equivalence relation R over a set A induces a partition of the set A into subsets A_i such that $A_i \cap A_j \neq \varnothing$ if $i = j$, $\cup A_i = A$ and aRb if and only if both a and b are in the same subset A_i for some i. The subsets A_i as above are called *equivalence classes* of R. If the number of different equivalence classes induced by a relation R over a set A is finite, then the relation R is of *finite index*. Let A be a set with an operation $\circ : A \times A \to A$ and a relation R over A.

   1. R is *right invariant* if aRb implies that for any c, $a \circ c\ R\ b \circ c$.
   2. R is *left invariant* if aRb implies that for any c, $c \circ a\ R\ c \circ b$.
   3. R is a *congruence* relation if it is an equivalence relation and it is both left and right invariant.

Let a, b, c be integers then $a \equiv b$ mod c ["a is congruent to b modulo c"] means that c is a factor of $a - b$. Congruence modulo an integer c has the following properties:

Lemma 3.1: If $a \equiv b$ mod c and $a' \equiv b'$ mod c then $a + a' \equiv b + b'$ mod c and $aa' \equiv bb'$ mod c.

We conclude this section with two lemmas concerning operations between infinite [countable] stochastic matrices.

Lemma 3.2: The set of countable stochastic matrices is closed under matrix multiplication.

Lemma 3.3: Multiplication of countable stochastic matrices is associative.

D. PROBABLISTIC PRELIMINARIES

Consider a physical experiment such as tossing a coin, matching a deck of cards, observing the life-span of radioactive atoms, etc. The set of all possible outcomes of such an experiment is called a *sample space*. The elements of a sample space are called *sample points* and aggregates of sample points or subsets of the sample space are called *events*. In what follows we shall concern ourselves only with finite or countable sample spaces [i.e., sample spaces containing finitely many or at most a countable number of elements].

The set of all events over a sample space [including the empty set—to be denoted by $\varnothing$—and the whole space considered as an event—to be denoted by Ω] is closed under countable intersection and union, and under complementation with regard to Ω. The set of all events as above with the operations of union, intersection, and complementation is sometimes called a *σ-algebra* [see Feller (1966)].

A *probability measure* p over a σ-algebra $\mathscr{A}$ as defined above is a function p from $\mathscr{A}$ into the interval $[0, 1]$ of real numbers such that:

1. $p(A) \geq 0$ is defined for all A in $\mathscr{A}$.
2. $p(\Omega) = 1$.
3. If $\{A_n\}_1^\infty$, is a countable set of nonoverlapping or disjoint events in $\mathscr{A}$, then $p\{\cup_{n=1}^\infty A_n\} = \sum_{n=1}^\infty p(A_n)$.

It is easy to show that (1)–(3) above imply:

4. $p(\varnothing) = 0$.
5. $p(\Omega - A) = 1 - p(\Omega)$.

A *random variable* is a function from the sample space into the real numbers. Under the assumption that the sample space is at most countable, no restriction is placed on such a function.

Example: The physical experiment: Tossing a coin 100 times. The sample space: All 2^{100} possible outcomes. A sample point: The coin falls "heads" all the 100 times. An event: The coin falls "tails" for 50 consecutive times. A probability measure over Ω: If $\omega \in \Omega$ is a sample point such that the coin falls heads m times and it falls tails $100 - m$ times then $p(\omega) = p^m q^{100-m}$ where $0 \leq p \leq 1, 0 \leq q \leq 1, p + q = 1$, p and q are real numbers. If A is an event, then $p(A) = \sum_{\omega \in A} p(\omega)$. A random variable over Ω: Let $x(\omega)$ be the function $x(\omega) = $ the number of "heads" in the sample point ω, then $x(\omega)$ is a random variable.

Given a σ-algebra, a probability measure, and a random variable over it, a related *distribution function* from the real numbers to the interval $[0, 1]$ is defined as follows: Let A_t be the event $A_t = \{\omega : x(\omega) \leq t\}$. Then the distribution function is the function $F(t) = p(A_t)$. Sometimes the notation $p(x(\omega) \leq t)$ is used for $p(A_t)$, and the notation $p(x(\omega) = t)$ is used for $p(B_t)$ where B_t is the event $\{\omega : x(\omega) = t\}$.

Given a σ-algebra and a probability measure over it, the *conditional probability* $p(A|B)$ [read: the probability of A given that B where A and B are events] is defined as $p(A|B) = p(A \cap B)/p(B)$. The intuitive meaning of the above definition is as follows: If it is given that the event B occurred, then the sample space reduces to the points in B, and the event A reduces to the event $A \cap B$ so that $p(A|B)$ is the proportion of the weight of the event $A \cap B$ to the weight of the event B [usually $p(A)$ is interpreted as the proportion of the weight of A to the weight of the whole space Ω which is equal to 1].

Given two random variables x and y over a σ-algebra and a probability measure over it, one can define the following function

$$p(x = t | y = u) = \frac{p(x = t \wedge y = u)}{p(y = u)} \tag{*}$$

where, $x = t \wedge y = u$ is the event $\{\omega : x(\omega) = t \wedge y(\omega) = u\}$. The random variables are said to be *independent* if

$$p(x = t \,|\, y = u) = p(x = t)$$

i.e., the information that $y(\omega) = u$ does not change the probability of $x(\omega) = t$. It follows from formula (∗) that if x and y are independent [or more generally, if A and B are independent events, i.e., $p(A|B) = p(A)$], then

$$p(x = t \wedge y = u) = p(x = t|y = u) \cdot p(y = u) = p(x = t) \cdot p(y = u)$$

More generally, if A and B are independent events then

$$p(A \cap B) = p(A) \cdot p(B)$$

Let $x_0, x_1, \ldots$ be a sequence of random variables such that for any m

$$p(x_m = j | x_0 = n_0, x_1 = n_1, \ldots, x_{m-1} = i) = p(x_m = j | x_{m-1} = i)$$

i.e., the random variable x_m depends on the random variable x_{m-1} but not on the previous ones. Such a system is called a Markov chain. We shall consider only finite or countable Markov chains, i.e., Markov chains over a sample space containing finitely many or a countable number of elements.

Any Markov chain can be represented in the following model: The sample space is represented by a finite or a countable number of vertices: the random variable x_i represents the position of a moving point at time $t = i$; $p(x_i = j)$ is the probability that the point will be at the vertex v_j at time $t = i$ and $p(x_m = j | x_{m-1} = i)$ is the probability that the point will be at vertex v_j at time $t = m$ provided that it has been at vertex i at time $t = m - 1$.

As the process is assumed to be Markov we have that

$$p(x_m = j | x_{m-1} = i) = p(x_m = j | x_0 = n_0, \ldots, x_{m-1} = i)$$

and we shall use, for the above probability, the notation $_m p_{ij}$.

If $_m p_{ij} = _n p_{ij}$ for any natural numbers m and n, then the Markov chain is called *homogeneous* and it is called *nonhomogeneous* otherwise. As the values $_m p_{ij}$ are independent of m in the first case, we shall use the notation p_{ij} for that case. It is tacitly assumed throughout that the Markov chains considered are *discrete*, i.e., the transitions from state to state occur at discrete intervals of time.

The probabilities $_m p_{ij}$ can be arranged in a matrix form and such a matrix is called *stochastic* or *Markov*. Clearly any Markov matrix $[_m p_{ij}]$ has the property that $0 \leq {_m p_{ij}} \leq 1$ and $\sum_j p_{ij} = 1$ which stems from the fact that system represented by the matrices $[_m p_{ij}]$ evolves in time and it must enter some state at time $t = m + 1$ if it has been in state i at time m where the term "state" is used for denoting a point in the sample space.

Examples:

1. Sequential deterministic machine with possible errors.

2. A slot machine: the static position of the dials represent the states. In this case the $_mp_{ij}$ are generally independent of m.

3. Suppose some person is ill with probability p_0 [the probability of him being healthy is $q_0 = 1 - p_0$]. After swallowing a specific medicine he may change state [there are two states, representing illness and healthiness] the probability of the transition from state i to state j at time m being $_mp_{ij}$ depending on the medicine swallowed at time m.

EXERCISES

1. Prove all tthe lemmas given without proof in the preceding sections.

2. Prove that the set of $n \times n$ stochastic matrices are a monoid under matrix multiplication [i.e., the set of stochastic $n \times n$ matrices is closed under multiplication and the unit $n \times n$ matrix is stochastic].

3. Let $P(m) = [_mp_{ij}]$ be the transition probabilities matrix at time m of a given Markov chain. Denote $\prod_{i=1}^n P(i) = [p_{ij}^{(n)}]$, prove that $p_{ij}^{(n)}$ is the probability that the process will go to state j beginning from state i after n steps.

4. A stochastic matrix P is called *constant* if all its rows are equal. Prove: If P is constant stochastic and Q is stochastic [of the same order], then PQ is constant stochastic and $QP = P$. [Thus $P^2 = P$ which means that stochastic constant matrices are idempotent.]

5. Let P be a stochastic matrix such that there is an integer k_0 with P^{k_0} constant. Prove that in this case, for all $m > k_0$, $P^m = P^{k_0}$.

6. If $\pi = (\pi_i)$ is a vector such that $\sum \pi_i = t$ and P is a stochastic matrix [of the same order], then the sum of the entries of the vector πP is also equal to t.

7. Prove: If P and Q are finite stochastic matrices such that $PQ = I$, then both P and Q are degenerate. [A stochastic matricx is *degenerate* if all its entries are either 0 or 1.]

8. Prove, by an example, that Exercise 7 above is not true in the infinite case unless it is required that both P and Q have nonzero elements only.

Chapter I

Stochastic Sequential Machines

INTRODUCTION

In this chapter we introduce various mathematical models of stochastic sequential machines (SSMs) and provide motivation for these models. Methods for synthesizing SSMs from their mathematical models are given. Various concepts of equivalence and coverings for SSMs are introduced and studied. Some decision problems and minimization-of-states problems induced by the above concepts are investigated and a procedure is formulated for constructing a minimal state SSM equivalent to a given one. The last part of this chapter in devoted to stochastic input–output relations and their representatibility by SSMs.

A. THE MODEL

1. Definitions and Basic Relations

Definition 1.1: A stochastic sequential machine (SSM) is a quadruple $M = (S, X, Y, \{A(y|x)\})$ where S, X, and Y are finite sets [the internal states, inputs, and outputs respectively], and $\{A(y|x)\}$ is a finite set containing $|X| \times |Y|$ square matrices of order $|S|$ such that $a_{ij}(y|x) \geq 0$ for all i and j, and

$$\sum_{y \in Y} \sum_{j=1}^{|S|} a_{ij}(y|x) = 1 \qquad \text{where} \quad A(y|x) = [a_{ij}(y|x)]$$

Interpretation: Let π be any $|S|$-dimensional vector. If the machine begins with an initial distribution π over the state set S and is fed sequentially with a word $u = x_1 \cdots x_k$, it prints the word $v = y_1 \cdots y_k$ and moves on to the next state. The transition is controlled by the matrices $A(y|x)$ where $a_{ij}(y|x)$ is the probability of the machine going to state s_j and printing the symbol y, given it had been in state s_i and fed with the symbol x.

Examples:

a. Any deterministic sequential machine with faulty elements which may cause errors in transition from state to state is an SSM.

b. Consider a psychological [or physical] experiment such that a sequence of stimuli [inputs] is applied to an animal [or to a physical system]. The system, assumed to have a finite number of possible internal states [which may or may not be observable], responds with a sequence of outputs and undergoes successive changes of its internal state. Transition is generally not deterministic, nor is the relationship between inputs and outputs.

c. A finite-state communication channel (Shannon, 1948) transmitting symbols from a source alphabet X, the symbols received belonging to an output alphabet Y. The channel may assume a finite number of states and is specified by a conditional probability function $p(y, s_j|s_i, x)$, interpreted as the probability of the output symbol received being y and of the channel remaining in state s_j, given the channel is in state s_i and the input symbol x is transmitted. Such a communication channel is readily described by an SSM.

d. Consider a situation where a pursuer is following a moving object (Zadeh, 1963), with both capable of assuming a finite number of positions [states]. Assume also that the motion of the pursuer is characterized by a conditional probability distribution $p_{ij}(x)$ (which denotes the probability of the pursuer moving to state j from state i on application of x) where x is one of several controls (inputs) available to the pursuer. As for the object, assume that it does not seek to evade the pursuer [the alternative case can be dealt with in a similar way] and that its motion is governed by a probability distribution q_{kl} [which denotes the probability of the object moving to state l from state k]. The combined system can be described by an SSM with set of states S equal to that of all pairs (i, k) with i referring to the pursuer and k to the object; the set of inputs X is that of all controls available to the pursuer; the set of outputs is identified here with that of states, and the transition function is given by

$$a_{(ik),(jl)}(x) = p_{ij}(x)\, q_{kl}$$

[It is tacitly assumed that the random variables controlling the pursuer and the object are mutually independent.] In this setup the problem of the pursuer is to find a minimal sequence of inputs which takes the composite system from its initial state to an "interception" state.

Let M be an SSM. Let $A(v|u)$ be defined as

$$A(v|u) = [a_{ij}(v|u)] = A(y_1|x_1)\,A(y_2|x_2)\cdots A(y_k|x_k) \qquad (1)$$

It follows from the interpretation of the values $a_{ij}(y|x)$ that $a_{ij}(v|u)$ is the probability of the machine going to state s_j and printing the word v, having been in state s_i and fed sequentially the word u. This assertion is clearly true for $l(v, u) = 1$, since in this case $(v, u) = (y, x)$ for some y and x. Assuming now that the assertion is true for $l(v, u) = k - 1$, we have, by the notation (1) above, that

$$a_{ij}(vy|ux) = \sum_k a_{ik}(v|u)a_{kj}(y|x) \qquad (2)$$

and the right-hand side of (2) is, by elementary rules of probability, the probability of the machine going to state s_j and printing the word vy, having been in state s_i and fed sequentially the word ux. The assertion is thus proved true for any pair (v, u) with $l(v, u) \geq 1$ by induction. For $l(v, u) = l(\lambda, \lambda) = 0$, we define $A(\lambda|\lambda) = I$, the $|S|$-dimensional unity matrix, meaning that with probability 1 there is no change in the internal state of the machine and no output emerges if no input is fed.

Notation: η denotes a column vector with all entries equal to 1, and with dimension equal to the number of states of the machine to which it is related.

Definition 1.2: Given a machine M and an input–output pair of words (v, u), the vector $\eta(v|u)$ is defined as

$$\eta(v|u) = A(v|u)\eta \qquad (\eta(\lambda|\lambda) = I\,\eta = \eta) \qquad (3)$$

Interpretation: The ith entry in vector $\eta(v|u)$ consists in summation of all entries in the ith row of matrix $A(v|u)$, and is therefore the probability of the machine printing the word v [and moving to some state], having been in state s_i and fed the word u.

It follows from (3) and (1) that

$$\eta(vy|ux) = A(vy|ux)\eta = A(v|u)A(y|x)\eta = A(v|u)\eta(y|x) \qquad (4)$$

Similarly,

$$\eta(yv|xu) = A(y|x)\,\eta(v|u) \qquad (5)$$

Definition 1.3: Let π be a [probabilistic] initial distribution vector over the states of a given machine M, and let (v, u) be any input–output pair of words. The vector $\pi(v|u)$ and the function $p_\pi(v|u)$ are defined as

$$\pi(v|u) = \pi A(v|u) \qquad (\pi(\lambda|\lambda) = \pi I = \pi) \qquad (6)$$

$$p_\pi(v|u) = \pi\eta(v|u) \qquad (= \pi(v|u)\eta) \qquad (7)$$

It follows by elementary rules of probability and from the interpretation of $\eta(v|u)$ that $p_\pi(v|u)$ is the probability of the machine printing the word v when started with initial distribution π over its states and fed with the word u. Similarly, $\pi_i(v|u)$, the ith entry of the vector $\pi(v|u)$, is the probability of the machine printing the word v and moving to state s_i when started with initial distribution π over its states and fed the word u. The following equalities are easily verified:

$$p_\pi(v_1v_2|u_1u_2) = \pi\eta(v_1v_2|u_1u_2) = \pi A(v_1v_2|u_1u_2)\eta$$
$$= \pi A(v_1|u_1)A(v_2|u_2)\eta = \pi(v_1|u_2)\eta(v_2|u_2) \qquad (8)$$

Note that $\pi(v|u)$ need not be a stochastic vector, as there may be several output words v, with positive probability, corresponding to a given input word u. Let $\bar{\pi}(v, u)$ be the vector whose ith entry is the probability of the machine moving to state s_i given that the machine started with initial distribution π over its states, the input has been u, and the output v. It follows that

$$\bar{\pi}_i(v, u) \cdot p_\pi(v|u) = \pi_i(v|u) \qquad (9)$$

To prove this relation, we rewrite it in the form: Pr [final state s_i|output v, input u, initial distribution π] · Pr [output v|input u, initial distribution π] = Pr [final state s_i, output v|input u, initial distribution π].

It follows from (9) that

$$\bar{\pi}_i(v, u) = \begin{cases} \pi_i(v|u)/p_\pi(v|u) & \text{if} \quad p_\pi(v|u) \neq 0 \\ \text{undefined} & \text{otherwise} \end{cases}$$

If $p_\pi(v|u) \neq 0$, then $\bar{\pi}(v, u)$ is a probabistic vector; moreover, in this case we also have the relation

$$p_\pi(vv_1|uu_1) = p_\pi(v|u)\, p_{\bar{\pi}(v,u)}(v_1|u_1) \qquad (10)$$

since, using (8), (6), (7), and (9) we get

$$p_\pi(vv_1|uu_1) = \pi(v|u)\eta(v_1|u_1)$$
$$= \pi(v|u)\eta\, \frac{\pi(v|u)}{\pi(v|u)\eta}\, \eta(v_1|u_1)$$
$$= \pi(v|u)\eta\, \bar{\pi}(v, u)\, \eta(v_1|u_1)$$
$$= p_\pi(v|u)p_{\bar{\pi}(v,u)}(v_1|u_1)$$

as required. If $p_\pi(v|u) = 0$, we define $p_\pi(vv_1/uu_1) = 0$ for any input–output pair of words (v_1, u_1).

Example 1: Let $M = (S, X, Y, \{A(y|x)\})$ with $X = \{0, 1\}$, $Y = \{a, b\}$, $S = \{s_1, s_2\}$, and

$$A(a|0) = \begin{bmatrix} \frac{1}{2} & 0 \\ 0 & \frac{1}{2} \end{bmatrix}, \qquad A(b|0) = \begin{bmatrix} \frac{1}{4} & \frac{1}{4} \\ \frac{1}{2} & 0 \end{bmatrix}$$

$$A(a|1) = \begin{bmatrix} 0 & \frac{1}{2} \\ 0 & 0 \end{bmatrix}, \qquad A(b|1) = \begin{bmatrix} \frac{1}{2} & 0 \\ \frac{1}{2} & \frac{1}{2} \end{bmatrix}$$

and let $\pi = (\frac{1}{4}\ \frac{3}{4})$ be an initial distribution for M. It is easily verified that

$$A(ab|00) = A(a|0)\,A(b|0) = \begin{bmatrix} \frac{1}{8} & \frac{1}{8} \\ \frac{1}{4} & 0 \end{bmatrix}$$

$$\eta(ab|00) = A(ab|00)\,\eta = \begin{bmatrix} \frac{1}{8} & \frac{1}{8} \\ \frac{1}{4} & 0 \end{bmatrix} \begin{pmatrix} 1 \\ 1 \end{pmatrix} = \begin{pmatrix} \frac{1}{4} \\ \frac{1}{4} \end{pmatrix}$$

$$\pi(ab|00) = \pi A(ab|00) = (\frac{1}{4}\ \frac{3}{4}) \begin{bmatrix} \frac{1}{8} & \frac{1}{8} \\ \frac{1}{4} & 0 \end{bmatrix} = (\frac{7}{32}\ \frac{1}{32})$$

$$p_\pi(ab|00) = \pi(ab|00)\eta = \frac{1}{4}$$

$$\bar{\pi}(ab,00) = \pi(ab|00)/p_\pi(ab|00) = (\frac{7}{8}\ \frac{1}{8})$$

Similarly,

$$\pi(a|0) = (\frac{1}{8}\ \frac{3}{8}), \qquad p_\pi(a|0) = \frac{1}{2}$$

$$\bar{\pi}(a,0) = (\frac{1}{4}\ \frac{3}{4}), \qquad p_{\bar{\pi}(a,0)}(b|0) = \frac{1}{2}$$

so that

$$p_\pi(a|0)p_{\bar{\pi}(a,0)}(b|0) = \frac{1}{2}\,\frac{1}{2} = \frac{1}{4} = p_\pi(ab|00)$$

in accordance with (10).

Note the difference between $\pi(ab|00)$ and $\bar{\pi}(ab,00)$. The first vector is not probabilistic, and the values in it are the probabilities of the machine entering the first (second) state and printing the output ab, given that the input is 00 and the initial distribution is π. However, this input and initial distribution may also have other outputs (ba or bb or aa) with positive probability, In the vector $\bar{\pi}(ab,00)$, both the input and the output are assumed in advance.

EXERCISES

1. Let M be as in Example 1 and $\pi = (0\ 1)$, an initial distribution for M.

   a. Find: $A(v|u)$, $\eta(v|u)$, $\pi(v|u)$, $\bar{\pi}(v,u)$, $p_\pi(v|u)$ with $v = bb$ and $u = 10$.

   b. The same with $v = ab, u = 10$; in this case, compute also the value $p_\pi(aba|100)$. Discuss your results.

2. Show that every deterministic sequential machine of the Mealy type can be represented as an SSM as given in Definition 1.1.

3. Give an algorithm for recursive construction of any vector of the form $\eta(v|u)$ for a given machine.

4. For a given machine M and a given initial distribution π, prove that the vector $\sum_v \pi(v|u)$ is probabilistic for any given input u (summation over all possible outputs v having the same length as u).

5. For the machine given in Example 1, find:

   a. the value $q(b|001, ab) = $ the probability of the next output being b, given that the input 00 resulted in the output *ab* and the input 1 was fed next,

    b. the value $r(b|001) = $ the probability of the final output being *b*, after the input 001 is fed.

6. Give three reasons why the following quadruple is not an SSM:

$$M = (S, X, Y, \{A(y|x)\}) \qquad \text{with} \quad S = \{s_1, s_2\}$$

$$X = \{0, 1\}, \qquad Y = \{a, b\}$$

$$A(a|0) = \begin{bmatrix} \frac{1}{4} & 0 \\ 0 & \frac{1}{4} \end{bmatrix}, \qquad A(b|0) = \begin{bmatrix} 0 & \frac{3}{4} \\ 1 & 0 \end{bmatrix}$$

$$A(a|1) = \begin{bmatrix} 0 & -\frac{1}{2} \\ \frac{1}{2} & \frac{1}{4} \end{bmatrix}, \qquad A(b|1) = \begin{bmatrix} 1\frac{1}{4} & \frac{1}{4} \\ \frac{1}{4} & 0 \end{bmatrix}$$

2. Moore, Mealy, and Other Types of SSMs

In the preceding section, we described an SSM parallel to the Mealy-type deterministic sequential machine. The Moore-type machine also has a stochastic version which will be described below.

Definition 2.1: A Moore-type SSM is a quadruple $M = (S, X, Y, \{A(x)\}, \Lambda)$ where S, X, and Y are as in Definition 1.1, $\{A(x)\}$ is a finite set containing $|X|$ square *stochastic* matrices of order $|S|$ and Λ a deterministic function from S into Y.

    Interpretation: In accordance with the interpretation following Definition 1.1, the value $a_{ij}(x)\,[A(x) = [a_{ij}(x)]]$ is the probability of the machine moving from state s_i to s_j when fed the symbol x. When entering state s_j, the machine prints the symbol $\Lambda(s_j) \in Y$.

    Let $A(u)$ be defined as

$$A(u) = [a_{ij}(u)] = A(x_1)\,A(x_2)\cdots A(x_k) \qquad (A(\lambda) = I) \qquad (11)$$

It follows from the above interpretation that $a_{ij}(u)$ is the probability of the machine moving from state s_i to s_j when fed the word u. [The proof of this assertion, along the same lines as for the corresponding assertion in the preceding section, is left to the reader.] The output word v depends on the sequence of states through which the machine passed when scanning the input word u. It is worth noting here that, as in the deterministic case, there is a basic difference (inplicit in the definitions) between Moore-type and Mealy-type machines. For the latter, the output depends on the input and the current state, and is intuitively associated with the transition; thus $p_\pi(\lambda|\lambda) = \pi I\eta = \pi\eta = 1$, since no output emerges when there is no input. By contrast, the output of a Moore-type machine depends on the next state and is intuitively associated with a state; thus $p_\pi(\lambda|\lambda) = 0$ and there is a time difference of one stroke between the beginning of the output sequences of the two types. Disregarding the empty input–output sequence, equivalence between the two types can be defined as follows:

Definition 2.2: Two machines M and M' are state-equivalent if to every state s_i of M there corresponds a state s_j of M', and vice versa, such that $p_{s_i}^M(v|u) = p_{s_j}^{M'}(v|u)$ for every input–output pair (v, u) with $l(v, u) \geq 1$.

Let M be an SSM of Moore-type $M = (S, X, Y, \{A(x)\}, \Lambda)$. Define an SSM M' of Mealy-type as follows: $M' = (S, X, Y, \{A'(y|x)\})$ where S, X, and Y are as in M, but the entries of the matrices $A'(y|x) = [a'_{ij}(y|x)]$ are defined by

$$a'_{ij}(y|x) = \begin{cases} a_{ij}(x), & \text{if } y = \Lambda(s_j) \\ 0, & \text{otherwise} \end{cases}$$

It is left as an exercise to show that the machines M and M' are state-equivalent.

Let M be a Mealy-type SSM, $M = (S, X, Y, \{A(y|x)\})$. Define an SSM M' of the Moore type as follows: $M' = (S', X, Y, \{A'(x)\}, \Lambda)$ where X and Y are as in M; S' is the cartesian product $S \times Y$; the ($|S| \cdot |Y|$-dimensional) matrices $A'(x)$ are defined as

$$\begin{bmatrix} A(y_1|x) & A(y_2|x) & \cdots & A(y_k|x) \\ A(y_1|x) & & \cdots & A(y_k|x) \\ \vdots & & & \vdots \\ A(y_1|x) & & \cdots & A(y_k|x) \end{bmatrix}$$

where $y_1, \ldots, y_k$ is the sequence of symbols in Y; finally, Λ is the function $\Lambda(s_i, y) = y$ for all i. It is left to the reader to show that the machines M and M' are state-equivalent.

Inasmuch as every Moore-type SSM has a Mealy-type equivalent and vice versa, either type will be used at convenience for proving properties of machines in general.

It is easy to see that the above definitions of Moore and Mealy types generalize the corresponding definitions of deterministic machines. On the other hand, since the stochastic machines are more elaborate in structure than deterministic machines, further generalized definitions are possible. Consider, for example, the following:

Definition 2.3: An output-independent SSM is one such that the matrices $A(y|x)$ can be written in the form $A(y|x) = I(y|x) A(x)$ where the $A(x)$ are stochastic, and $I(y|x)$ are diagonal matrices with $\sum_y I(y|x) = I$ ($=$ the $|S|$-dimensional unit matrix).

The interpretation of this definition is as follows: Let $a'_i(y|x)$ be the ith diagonal entry in $I(y|x)$, and $a''_{ij}(x)$ the (i, j)th entry in $A(x)$; then $a_{ij}(y|x)$ is given by

$$a_{ij}(y|x) = a_i'(y|x)a_{ij}''(x) \tag{12}$$

If $a_i'(y|x)$ is interpreted as the probability of the output being y if the input is x and the current state i, and $a_{ij}''(x)$ as the probability of next state being s_j if the current state is s_i and the input x, then (12) means that the two random variables are mutually independent, that is, the next state of the machine is independent of its output for a given current state and input.

It is clear that the output-independent machines as defined in Definition 2.3 provide another generalization of deterministic Mealy-type machines. On the other hand, the two generalizations are not equivalent. We will show now that although every output-independent machine is an SSM, the converse is not always true.

Lemma 2.1: If M is an output-independent machine, then for any degenerate initial distribution $\bar{s}_i$ the value $P_{\bar{s}_i}(yv|xu)/P_{\bar{s}_i}(y|x)$ does not depend on y, provided $P_{\bar{s}_i}(y|x) \neq 0$.

Proof: Let $a_i'(y|x)$ be the ith diagonal entry of $I(y|x)$, then $a_i'(y|x) = \bar{s}_i I(y|x)\eta$ and

$$\bar{s}_i I(y|x) = a_i'(y|x)\bar{s}_i = \bar{s}_i I(y|x)\eta \, \bar{s}_i$$

But

$$\bar{s}_i A(y|x)\eta = \bar{s}_i I(y|x) A(x)\eta = \bar{s}_i I(y|x)\eta$$

$A(x)$ is stochastic, so that $A(x)\eta = \eta$. Combining these equalities, we have

$$p_{\bar{s}_i}(yv|xu) = \bar{s}_i A(y|x) A(v|u)\eta$$
$$= \bar{s}_i I(y|x) A(x) A(v|u)\eta = \bar{s}_i I(y|x)\eta \, \bar{s}_i A(x) A(v|u)\eta$$
$$= \bar{s}_i A(y|x)\eta \, \bar{s}_i A(x) A(v|u)\eta = p_{\bar{s}_i}(y|x) \, \bar{s}_i A(x) A(v|u)\eta$$

or

$$\frac{P_{\bar{s}_i}(yv|xu)}{P_{\bar{s}_i}(y|x)} = \bar{s}_i A(x) A(v|u)\eta$$

and the right-hand side does not depend on y.

Example 2: Let M be the SSM with $S = \{s_1, s_2\}$, $X = \{a\}$, $Y = \{0, 1\}$, and

$$A(0|a) = \begin{bmatrix} \frac{1}{4} & \frac{1}{6} \\ \frac{1}{6} & \frac{1}{3} \end{bmatrix}, \qquad A(1|a) = \begin{bmatrix} \frac{1}{2} & \frac{1}{12} \\ \frac{1}{3} & \frac{1}{6} \end{bmatrix}$$

Assume also that the initial distribution is $\bar{s}_1 = (1\ 0)$. Then

$$P_{\bar{s}_1}(0|a) = (1\ 0) \begin{bmatrix} \frac{1}{4} & \frac{1}{6} \\ \frac{1}{6} & \frac{1}{3} \end{bmatrix} \begin{bmatrix} 1 \\ 1 \end{bmatrix} = \frac{5}{12}$$

$$P_{\bar{s}_1}(00|aa) = (1\ 0) \begin{bmatrix} \frac{1}{4} & \frac{1}{6} \\ \frac{1}{6} & \frac{1}{3} \end{bmatrix}^2 \begin{bmatrix} 1 \\ 1 \end{bmatrix} = \frac{3}{16}$$

$$p_{s_1}(1|a) = (1\ 0) \begin{bmatrix} \frac{1}{2} & \frac{1}{12} \\ \frac{1}{3} & \frac{1}{6} \end{bmatrix} \begin{bmatrix} 1 \\ 1 \end{bmatrix} = \frac{7}{12}$$

$$p_{s_1}(10|aa) = (1\ 0) \begin{bmatrix} \frac{1}{2} & \frac{1}{12} \\ \frac{1}{3} & \frac{1}{6} \end{bmatrix} \begin{bmatrix} \frac{1}{4} & \frac{1}{6} \\ \frac{1}{6} & \frac{1}{3} \end{bmatrix} \begin{bmatrix} 1 \\ 1 \end{bmatrix} = \frac{1}{4}$$

thus

$$\frac{P_{s_1}(00|aa)}{P_{s_1}(0|a)} = \frac{3/16}{5/12} = \frac{9}{20}$$

and

$$\frac{P_{s_1}(10|aa)}{P_{s_1}(1|a)} = \frac{1/4}{7/12} = \frac{3}{7}$$

The two values are not equal, hence the given machine is not output independent.

Another Mealy-type SSM can be defined by requiring that the entries in the matrices $I(y|x)$ be either 0 or 1, and another Moore-type SSM by assuming that the function Λ in Definition 2.2 is probabilistic [see Exercises 6 and 7 at the end of this section].

EXERCISES

1. Find a Moore-type machine which is equivalent to the machine in Example 1.

2. Given the Moore-type machine $M = (S, X, Y, \{A(x)\}, \Lambda)$ with $S = \{s_1, s_2\}$, $X = \{0, 1\}$, $Y = \{a, b\}$,

$$A(0) = \begin{bmatrix} \frac{1}{2} & \frac{1}{2} \\ 0 & 1 \end{bmatrix}, \qquad A(1) = \begin{bmatrix} 1 & 0 \\ \frac{1}{2} & \frac{1}{2} \end{bmatrix}$$

and $\Lambda(s_1) = a$, $\Lambda(s_2) = b$, find an equivalent Mealy-type machine.

3. Prove that the interpretation of $A(x)$ and (11) implies that $a_{ij}(u)$ is the probability of the machine moving from state s_i to s_j when fed the word u.

4. Prove that every Mealy-type machine has an equivalent Moore-type machine and vice versa, using the construction given in the text.

5. For the machine given in problem above, compute the following values:
   a. $p_{s_1}(abb|010)$
   b. $q(a|011, bb)$
   c. $r(a|1101)$
[For the definition of q and r, see Exercise 5 in Section 1.]

6. Consider the following:

Definition: An SSM is of the Mealy-type with probabilistic output if the matrices $A(y|x)$ can be written in the form $A(y|x) = A(x) I(y)$, $A(x)$ being stochastic and $I(y)$ diagonal matrices with $\sum_{y \in Y} I(y) = I$.

Show that, under proper interpretation, the output of such a machine is a [probabilistic] function of the next state and independent of the transition imposed on the current state by the input.

7. Show that Example 2 can be represented as a Mealy-type SSM with probalistic output.

3. Synthesis of Stochastic Machines

In the two methods for synthesizing stochastic sequential machines presented below, the machines are assumed to be of the Moore-type.

a. Method 1

Method 1 is illustrated in Figure 1. Let $M = (S, X, Y, \{A(x)\}, \Lambda)$ be a machine, Z an auxiliary alphabet with $|S| = n$ symbols, and $p(s_i, x)$ an independent information source emitting the symbol $z_j \in Z$ with probability $a_{ij}(x)$.

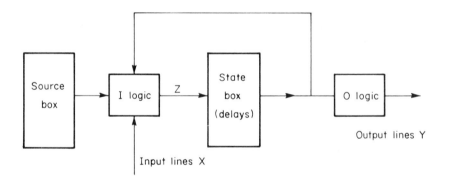

Figure 1. Schematic representation of a network synthesizing an SSM.

The source box emits all sources $p(s_i, x)$, each of them through a separate line. The box marked "*I* Logic" is a combinatorial network whose output is that emitted by source $p(s_i, x)$ if the feedback input is s_i and the X input is x. The "state box" is a combination of delays (or flip–flops) representing the states of the machine. If the input to this box is z_i, the delays are set so as to represent the state s_i, the feedback being a signal representing the current state of the machine. Finally, the "0 logic" box is a combinatorial gate simulating the function Λ.

It is clear that the above diagram synthesizes the given machine. It follows from the construction that pr[next state s_j|current state s_i input x] = pr[I logic output z_j|current state s_i, input x] = pr[z_j| the source emits $p(s_j, x)$] = $a_{ij}(x)$ as required.

The procedure above involves synthesis of combinatorial networks with or without feedback, and construction of information sources with prescribed probability distributions, for which the reader is referred to Harrison (1965), Hartmanis and Stearns (1966), or McCluskey (1965), and to Gill (1962b, 1963), Sheng (1965), Tsersvadze (1963), or Warfield (1965) respectively. It will now be shown that the procedure can be simplified by means of the following lemma.

Lemma 3.1: Any $m \times n$ stochastic matrix A can be expressed in the form $A = \sum p_i U_i$ where $p_i > 0$, $\sum p_i = 1$, and U_i are degenerate stochastic matrices (with entries either zero or one), and the number of matrices U_i in the expansion is at most $m(n - 1) + 1$.

Proof: Let $A = [a_{ij}]$, $U_1 = [u'_{ij}]$ is a degenerate stochastic matrix such that

$$u_{ij} = \begin{cases} 1 & \text{if} \quad a_{ij} \text{ is the first maximal element in the } i\text{th row of } A \\ 0 & \text{otherwise} \end{cases}$$

Let p_1 be the value $p_1 = \min_i \max_j a_{ij}$; then clearly $A - p_1 U_1$ is a matrix with nonnegative entries. Moreover, $A_1 = [1/(1 - p_1)][A - p_1 U_1]$ is a stochastic matrix (for the sum of entries in any row of $A - p_1 U_1$ equals $1 - p_1$) with more zero entries than the original matrix A, and $A = p_1 U_1 + (1 - p_1)A_1$. The procedure is now repeated for A_1 as the new A, represented in the form $A_1 = p_2 U_2 + (1 - p_2)A_2$ with A_2 again stochastic with less zeros than A_1. In this manner at most $m(n - 1)$ steps yield a matrix A_k in the form of a degenerate stochastic matrix U_k. The required expansion is thus found with at most $m(n - 1) + 1$ matrices U_k.

Example 3: Let A be the matrix

$$A = \begin{pmatrix} \frac{1}{2} & \frac{1}{4} & \frac{1}{4} \\ \frac{1}{2} & 0 & \frac{1}{2} \\ \frac{1}{4} & \frac{1}{4} & \frac{1}{2} \end{pmatrix}$$

then

$$U_1 = \begin{pmatrix} 1 & 0 & 0 \\ 1 & 0 & 0 \\ 0 & 0 & 1 \end{pmatrix}, \qquad p_1 = \tfrac{1}{2}$$

hence,

$$A_1 = \begin{bmatrix} 0 & \frac{1}{2} & \frac{1}{2} \\ 0 & 0 & 1 \\ \frac{1}{2} & \frac{1}{2} & 0 \end{bmatrix}, \qquad U_2 = \begin{bmatrix} 0 & 1 & 0 \\ 0 & 0 & 1 \\ 1 & 0 & 0 \end{bmatrix}, \qquad p_2 = \tfrac{1}{2}$$

$$A_3 = \begin{bmatrix} 0 & 0 & 1 \\ 0 & 0 & 1 \\ 0 & 1 & 0 \end{bmatrix} = U_3$$

And the resulting resolution is

$$A = \tfrac{1}{2}U_1 + \tfrac{1}{2}[\tfrac{1}{2}U_2 + \tfrac{1}{2}U_3] = \tfrac{1}{2}U_1 + \tfrac{1}{4}U_2 + \tfrac{1}{4}U_3$$

Note that although the above example is a square matrix, this requirement is not essential and the procedure works for any stochastic matrix.

We now apply Lemma 3.1 to the procedure. To this end, let A be the stochastic matrix whose rows are the probabilistic distribution vectors $p(s_i, x)$, i.e., A has $|S| \times |X|$ rows and $|S|$ columns, and can be expressed in the form $A = \sum_{i=1}^{t} p_i U_i$ according to the lemma. Let $W = \{w_1, \ldots, w_t\}$ be an auxiliary alphabet with t symbols, one for each matrix U_i in the expansion of A, and let p be a single information source over W emitting the symbol w_i with probability p_i.

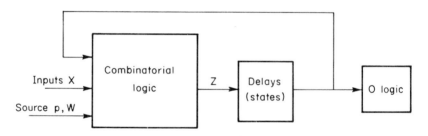

Figure 2. Simplified network for an SSM.

The combinatorial logic is constructed so that its output is z_j for input (x_l, w_m, s_k) if and only if the entry of matrix U_m in the row corresponding to (s_k, x_l) and in the column corresponding to s_j equals one (notation: $u^m_{(k,l),j} = 1$); the state box and the 0-logic are as in Figure 1. We have that pr(next state $s_j|$ current state s_k, input x_l) = pr(W-input is w_m with $u^m_{(k,l)j} = 1$) = $\sum p_m$ where the summation is over all m with $u^m_{(k,l),j} = 1$. This sum, however, equals the corresponding entry in A which is $p_j(s_k, x_l)$ as required.

Example 4: Let $M = (S, X, Y, \{A(x)\}, \Lambda)$ be an SSM with $S = \{0, 1\} = X = Y$, $\Lambda\{0\} = 1$, $\Lambda(1) = 0$, and

$$A(0) = \begin{bmatrix} \frac{1}{2} & \frac{1}{2} \\ \frac{1}{4} & \frac{3}{4} \end{bmatrix}, \qquad A(1) = \begin{bmatrix} \frac{2}{3} & \frac{1}{3} \\ \frac{1}{2} & \frac{1}{2} \end{bmatrix}$$

then $A = [p_j(s_k, x_l)]_{s_j, s_k \in S; x_l \in X}$ or,

$$A = \begin{bmatrix} \frac{1}{2} & \frac{1}{2} \\ \frac{1}{4} & \frac{3}{4} \\ \frac{2}{3} & \frac{1}{3} \\ \frac{1}{2} & \frac{1}{2} \end{bmatrix}$$

Applying the resolution of Lemma 3.1, we get

$$A = \tfrac{1}{2} \begin{bmatrix} 1 & 0 \\ 0 & 1 \\ 1 & 0 \\ 1 & 0 \end{bmatrix} + \tfrac{1}{4} \begin{bmatrix} 0 & 1 \\ 1 & 0 \\ 0 & 1 \\ 0 & 1 \end{bmatrix} + \tfrac{1}{6} \begin{bmatrix} 0 & 1 \\ 0 & 1 \\ 1 & 0 \\ 0 & 1 \end{bmatrix} + \tfrac{1}{12} \begin{bmatrix} 0 & 1 \\ 0 & 1 \\ 0 & 1 \\ 0 & 1 \end{bmatrix}$$

thus $W = \{w_1, w_2, w_3, w_4\}$ and $p = (\frac{1}{2}, \frac{1}{4}, \frac{1}{6}, \frac{1}{12})$. Encoding the symbols in W as 00, 01, 10, 11 respectively we get the transition table, Table I. Now using the

Table I Transition Table for the machine in Example 4.

w	x	(current)	s (next)	Output
00	0	0	0	1
00	0	1	1	0
00	1	0	0	1
00	1	1	0	0
01	0	0	1	1
01	0	1	0	0
01	1	0	1	1
01	1	1	1	0
10	0	0	1	1
10	0	1	1	0
10	1	0	0	1
10	1	1	1	0
11	0	0	1	1
11	0	1	1	0
11	1	0	1	1
11	1	1	1	0

Karanaugh map method or other methods we obtain a network which synthesizes the given SSM, as shown in Figure 3.

b. Method 2

Given the machine $M = (S, X, Y, \{A(x)\}, \Lambda)$, expand all matrices $A(x)$ in the form $A(x) = \sum_i p_i^x U_i^x$ using Lemma 3.1. Assuming that the above expansions all have the same matrix U in the ith place for all i [i.e., the values p_i^x, but not

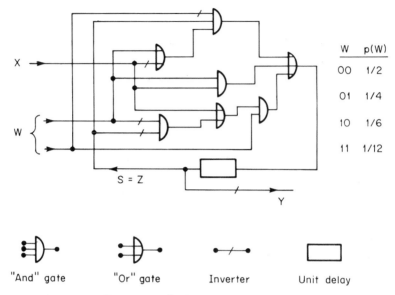

W	p(W)
00	1/2
01	1/4
10	1/6
11	1/12

"And" gate   "Or" gate   Inverter   Unit delay

Figure 3. Realization of transition Table I.

the matrices U_i^x, depend on x], the restriction on p_i^x is weakened to $p_i^x \geq 0$. [This is possible because there are only a finite number of different matrices of the form U_i^x and some zero-valued p_i^x may be added if necessary to meet the requirements.] Let Z be an auxiliary alphabet with q symbols, where $q = \max_i$ [there exists $x \in X$ such that $p_i^x \neq 0$ in the expansion of $A(x)] \leq (n-1)^n$.

We define the deterministic Moore-type sequential machine $\mathcal{M}$ as follows: $\mathcal{M} = (S, Z, Y, \delta, \Lambda)$, where S, Y, and Λ are the same as in M, Z is the auxiliary alphabet as specified above, and δ is the function defined by

$$\delta(s_i, z_k) = s_j \qquad \text{if} \quad u_{ij}^k = 1 \tag{13}$$

where $U_k = [u_{ij}^k]$ [by construction, $U_k^x = U_k$ does not depend on x.] Finally, let $p(x)$ be an independent information source over Z such that the probability of z_i being emitted by $p(x)$ is p_i^x. Consider now Figure 4. The source box here emits all sources $p(x)$, each of them through a separate line. The I-logic is a combinatorial gate whose output is that emitted by source $p(x)$ if the X input is x.

It is easily seen that the above diagram is a realization of M (the states of M being identified with those of $\mathcal{M}$), for if the current state of $\mathcal{M}$ is s_i, then its next state is s_j only if the input is z_k and $\delta(s_i, z_k) = s_j$ or $u_{ij}^k = 1$ [see Eq. (13)]. But the probability of the input being z_k is p_k^x, depending on the input symbol x of M. Therefore, pr(next state of $\mathcal{M}$ s_j|current state of $\mathcal{M}$ s_i) = $\sum p_k^x u_{ij}^k = a_{ij}(x)$ by the construction of the matrices U_k.

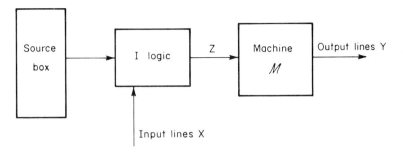

Figure 4. Schematic representation of a network synthesizing an SSM according to second procedure.

As in the preceding procedure, the above construction can be further simplified by using Lemma 3.1 again and resolving, accordingly, the stochastic matrix A whose rows are the distributions $p(x)$. The resulting diagram will be as in Figure 5.

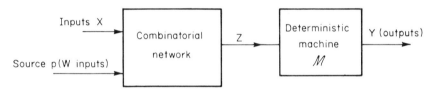

Figure 5. Simplification of network in Figure 4.

Since the simplification follows the same course as in the preceding case, the details are left to the reader.

Example 5: Let M be the same SSM as in Example 4. The second procedure will be used.

$$A(0) = \tfrac{1}{2}\begin{bmatrix} 1 & 0 \\ 0 & 1 \end{bmatrix} + \tfrac{1}{4}\begin{bmatrix} 0 & 1 \\ 1 & 0 \end{bmatrix} + 0\begin{bmatrix} 1 & 0 \\ 1 & 0 \end{bmatrix} + \tfrac{1}{4}\begin{bmatrix} 0 & 1 \\ 0 & 1 \end{bmatrix}$$

$$A(1) = \tfrac{1}{6}\begin{bmatrix} 1 & 0 \\ 0 & 1 \end{bmatrix} + 0\begin{bmatrix} 0 & 1 \\ 1 & 0 \end{bmatrix} + \tfrac{1}{2}\begin{bmatrix} 1 & 0 \\ 1 & 0 \end{bmatrix} + \tfrac{1}{3}\begin{bmatrix} 0 & 1 \\ 0 & 1 \end{bmatrix}$$

Thus $p(0) = (\tfrac{1}{2}, \tfrac{1}{4}, 0, \tfrac{1}{4})$ and $p(1) = (\tfrac{1}{6}, 0, \tfrac{1}{2}, \tfrac{1}{3})$. Let $A = \begin{bmatrix} p(0) \\ p(1) \end{bmatrix}$, then

$$A = \tfrac{1}{2}\begin{bmatrix} 1 & 0 & 0 & 0 \\ 0 & 0 & 1 & 0 \end{bmatrix} + \tfrac{1}{4}\begin{bmatrix} 0 & 1 & 0 & 0 \\ 0 & 0 & 0 & 1 \end{bmatrix}$$

$$+ \tfrac{1}{6}\begin{bmatrix} 0 & 0 & 0 & 1 \\ 1 & 0 & 0 & 0 \end{bmatrix} + \tfrac{1}{12}\begin{bmatrix} 0 & 0 & 0 & 1 \\ 0 & 0 & 0 & 1 \end{bmatrix}$$

Let $Z = \{z_1, z_2, z_3, z_4\}$, $W = \{w_1, w_2, w_3, w_4\}$ and assigning $z_1 \to 00 \leftarrow w_1$, $z_2 \to$ $01 \leftarrow w_2$, $z_3 \to 10 \leftarrow w_3$, $z_4 \to 11 \leftarrow w_4$.

Table II Transition table for the machine in Example 5.

w	x	z	z	s (current)	s (next)	y
00	0	00	00	0	0	1
00	1	10	00	1	1	0
01	0	01	01	0	1	1
01	1	11	01	1	0	0
10	0	11	10	0	0	1
10	1	00	10	1	0	0
11	0	11	11	0	1	1
11	1	11	11	1	1	0
Combinatorial network				Machine $\mathscr{M}$		

The combinatorial network and the machine $\mathscr{M}$ are given in the transition tables, Table II. The synthesis of the machine M is given in the network in Figure 6.

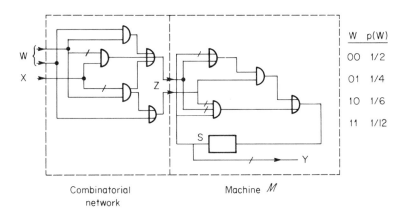

W	p(W)
00	1/2
01	1/4
10	1/6
11	1/12

Figure 6. Realization of Transition Table II.

c. Comparison of Methods

The methods given above are obviously not exhaustive. Another alternative with the SSM in its Mealy-type form is as follows: The matrices $A(y|x)$ are arranged in the form of a single matrix

$$A = \begin{bmatrix} A(y_1|x_1) & \cdots & A(y_k|x_1) \\ & \vdots & \\ A(y_1|x_m) & \cdots & A(y_k|x_m) \end{bmatrix}$$

where $Y = y_1, \ldots, y_k$ and $X = x_1, \ldots, x_m$. A is stochastic and can be resolved according to Lemma 3.1, after which the process is continued along the same lines as in the original procedure (details are left to the reader).

In the deterministic case the most common measure of complexity of a machine is the number of its states; it is evident, however, from the above considerations that other factors (such as the number of gates in the resulting network or its type), should also be taken into consideration.

For example, the degree of simplicity of the network is governed not only by the realization method used, but also by the assignments prescribed for the state variables and inputs (both original and auxiliary). Still another likely factor is the number of symbols in the auxiliary alphabet W appearing in all the above methods as a random source with prescribed probabilities for each symbol. It is easily seen that from this viewpoint the first method is preferable, since by it. Lemma 3.1 is applied to a matrix A with $|X| \times |S|$ rows and $|S|$ columns, so that $|W| \leq (|S| - 1)(|X| \times |S|) + 1$, whereas by the second method the lemma is first applied to the matrices $A(x)$; since there are at most $(|S| - 1)^{|S|}$ deterministic stochastic matrices, the auxiliary alphabet Z has at most that many symbols, and the resulting matrix A has $|X|$ rows and at most $(|S| - 1)^{|S|}$ columns. Resolution of the resulting matrix A yields

$$|W| \leq ((|S| - 1)^{|S|} - 1)|X| + 1$$

a much higher bound than in the first case, which proves our claim.

EXERCISES

1. Given the SSM, $M = (S, X, Y, \{A(x)\}, \Lambda)$ with $S = \{s_1, s_2, s_3\}$, $X = \{0, 1\}$, $Y = \{a, b\}$,

$$A(0) = \begin{bmatrix} \frac{1}{3} & \frac{2}{3} & 0 \\ 0 & \frac{1}{4} & \frac{3}{4} \\ \frac{1}{2} & 0 & \frac{1}{2} \end{bmatrix}, \qquad A(1) = \begin{bmatrix} \frac{3}{4} & 0 & \frac{1}{4} \\ \frac{1}{4} & \frac{3}{4} & 0 \\ \frac{1}{4} & \frac{1}{8} & \frac{5}{8} \end{bmatrix}$$

and $\Lambda(s_1) = \Lambda(s_2) = b$, $\Lambda(s_3) = a$, give a synthesis of M using the first method.

2. As above, using the second method.

3. Prove that if $\{A_i\}$ is a set of stochastic matrices and (p_i) is a probabilistic vector of dimension equal to the number of matrices in the set, then $\sum p_i A_i$ is a stochastic matrix.

4. Let M_1 and M_2 be machines over the same input alphabet $X = \{x_1, x_2\}$ and output alphabet $Y = \{0, 1\}$ respectively. Let the transition matrices be

$$M_1(0|x_1) = \begin{bmatrix} 0 & \frac{1}{3} & \frac{2}{3} \\ 0 & \frac{1}{6} & \frac{1}{3} \\ 0 & \frac{1}{12} & \frac{1}{6} \end{bmatrix}, \qquad M_1(1|x_1) = \begin{bmatrix} 0 & 0 & 0 \\ 0 & \frac{1}{2} & 0 \\ \frac{1}{4} & 0 & \frac{1}{2} \end{bmatrix}$$

$$M_1(0|x_2) = \begin{bmatrix} \frac{1}{12} & \frac{7}{24} & \frac{25}{36} \\ \frac{1}{90} & \frac{2}{15} & \frac{16}{45} \\ \frac{1}{36} & 0 & \frac{2}{9} \end{bmatrix}, \qquad M_1(1|x_2) = \begin{bmatrix} 0 & 0 & 0 \\ \frac{1}{360} & \frac{177}{360} & \frac{1}{180} \\ 0 & \frac{3}{4} & 0 \end{bmatrix}$$

$$M_2(0|x_1) = \begin{bmatrix} 0 & \frac{1}{3} & \frac{1}{6} & \frac{1}{2} \\ 0 & \frac{1}{6} & 0 & \frac{1}{3} \\ 0 & \frac{1}{12} & 0 & \frac{1}{6} \\ 0 & \frac{1}{12} & \frac{1}{6} & 0 \end{bmatrix}, \qquad M_2(1|x_1) = \begin{bmatrix} 0 & 0 & 0 & 0 \\ \frac{1}{6} & 0 & 0 & \frac{1}{3} \\ \frac{1}{6} & \frac{1}{4} & \frac{1}{3} & 0 \\ \frac{1}{6} & \frac{1}{4} & 0 & \frac{1}{3} \end{bmatrix}$$

$$M_2(0|x_2) = \begin{bmatrix} 0 & \frac{1}{3} & \frac{7}{12} & \frac{1}{12} \\ 0 & \frac{1}{6} & 0 & \frac{1}{3} \\ 0 & \frac{1}{12} & \frac{1}{6} & 0 \\ 0 & \frac{1}{12} & 0 & \frac{1}{6} \end{bmatrix}, \qquad M_2(1|x_2) = \begin{bmatrix} 0 & 0 & 0 & 0 \\ \frac{1}{6} & 0 & \frac{1}{4} & \frac{1}{12} \\ \frac{1}{4} & 0 & \frac{1}{3} & \frac{1}{6} \\ \frac{1}{4} & 0 & \frac{1}{6} & \frac{1}{3} \end{bmatrix}$$

Transform M_1 and M_2 into Moore-type machines and find the random distribution over W according to the second method. Show that although $|S^{M_1}| < |S^{M_2}|$, $|W^{M_1}| > |W^{M_2}|$.

5. Prove that if some of the input lines of a deterministic sequential machine are induced by a random independent source, the resulting machine is an SSM.

6. Work out in detail the construction of the network in Figure 6 according to the second method.

7. As above using the method described in Subsection 3,d.

4. Bibliographic Notes

Subsections 1 and 2 of Section A are based on the work of Carlyle (1961) with additions and examples suggested by Rabin (1963), Zadeh (1963b), Starke (1965) and Salomaa (1968). Subsection 3 is based in part on the work of Nieh and Carlyle (1968), Cleave (1962) and Davis (1961). Some additions in this section are new and the synthesis procedure suggested in Subsection 3d is due to Carlyle (private communication). Further reference: Booth (1964, 1965, 1967), Gill (1962-b, 1963), Harrison (1965) Hartmanis and Stearns (1966), McCluskey (1965), Sheng (1965), Sklansky and Kaplan (1963), Tsertsvadze (1963), and Warfield (1965).

B. STATE THEORY AND EQUIVALENCE

1. Set K^M and Matrix H^M

From this section on the machines to be considered are of the Mealy type unless otherwise specified.

Definition 1.1: Given a machine M, K^M denotes the ordered infinite set

$$K^M = (\eta^M(\lambda|\lambda) \cdots \eta^M(y|x) \cdots \eta^M(v|u) \cdots)$$

such that all vectors of the form $\eta^M(v|u)$ for all pairs (v, u) are in the set and the order is induced by some fixed lexicographic order on the pairs (v, u). $K^M(m)$ denotes the ordered subset of K^M such that $\eta^M(v|u) \in K^M(m)$ implies that $l(v, u) \leq m$ and the order in $K^M(m)$ is the same as in K^M. $[K^M]$ denotes the [infinite] matrix whose ith column is the ith element of K^M.

Let $\mathscr{S}(m)$ be the linear space spanned by vectors in $K^M(m)$ ($\mathscr{S}$ denotes the space spanned by all vectors in K^M.) Then rank $\mathscr{S}(i) \leq$ rank $\mathscr{S}(j)$ if $i \leq j$, and rank $\mathscr{S}(m) \leq n = |S|$ for $m = 0, 1, \ldots$. Furthermore, it is readily seen that if $\mathscr{S}(i) \equiv \mathscr{S}(i + 1)$ for some i, then $\mathscr{S}(i) \equiv \mathscr{S}(i + j)$ for $j = 1, 2, \ldots$. To prove this assertion, we observe that

$$\eta \in \mathscr{S}(i + 2) \Rightarrow \eta = \sum a_k \eta(v_k|u_k) \quad \text{and} \quad l(v_k, u_k) \leq i + 2$$
$$\Rightarrow \eta = \sum a_k A((y_k|x_k)\eta(v_k{}'|u_k{}') \quad \text{and} \quad l(v_k{}', u_k{}') \leq i + 1$$
$$\Rightarrow \eta = \sum_k a_k A(y_k|x_k) \sum_j b_j \eta(v_k'|u_{kj}')$$

and

$$l(v_{kj}', u_{kj}') \leq i \qquad (\text{for} \quad \mathscr{S}(i) \equiv \mathscr{S}(i + 1))$$

so that

$$\eta = \sum_k \sum_j b_j a_k A(y_k|x_k)\eta(v_{kj}'|u_{kj}') = \sum_k \sum_j b_j a_k \eta(v_{kj}''|u_{kj}'')$$

and $l(v_{kj}'', u_{kj}'') \leq i + 1$. Thus, $\eta \in \mathscr{S}(i + 1) \equiv \mathscr{S}(i)$ and the assertion follows.

The above considerations show that there exists an integer m such that

$$1 = \text{rank } \mathscr{S}(0) < \text{rank } \mathscr{S}(1) < \cdots < \text{rank } \mathscr{S}(m) = \text{rank } \mathscr{S}(m + 1)$$
$$= \text{rank } \mathscr{S}(m + 2) = \cdots = \text{rank } \mathscr{S} \leq n$$

also implying that $m \leq n - 1$.

It is thus possible to find a set of linearly independent vectors in $K^M(n - 1)$ such that any vector in K^M is a linear combination of these vectors.

Definition 1.2: Let $\eta_1, \ldots, \eta_m$ be a set of vectors having the following properties:
1. η_1 is the vector $\eta(\lambda|\lambda)$.

2. $\eta_1, \ldots, \eta_m$ are the first vectors in K^M(in order of the vectors in it) which are linearly independent and span the whole set.

The matrix H^M is defined as

$$H^M = [\eta_1, \eta_2, \ldots, \eta_m] = [h_{ij}], \qquad i = 1, \ldots, n, \quad j = 1, \ldots, m \leq n$$

Thus, H^M is such that $h_{ij} = 1$, for $i = 1, 2, \ldots, n$; $0 \leq h_{ij} \leq 1$ for all i and j; the vectors η_i are elements of K^M and linearly independent, and any vector of the form $\eta(v|u)$ is a linear combination of them; finally, the rank of H^M is $m \leq n$.

In the sequel, when referring to the rank of a machine M, we refer to that of its H^M matrix.

Example 6: If the matrices of a single-input two-output machine M are

$$A^M(y_1)\begin{bmatrix} \frac{1}{4} & 0 & \frac{1}{4} \\ 0 & 0 & 0 \\ \frac{3}{8} & 0 & \frac{3}{8} \end{bmatrix}, \qquad A^M(y_2) = \begin{bmatrix} 0 & \frac{1}{2} & 0 \\ 0 & 1 & 0 \\ 0 & \frac{1}{4} & 0 \end{bmatrix}$$

then its H^M matrix is

$$H^M = \begin{bmatrix} 1 & \frac{1}{2} \\ 1 & 0 \\ 1 & \frac{3}{4} \end{bmatrix}$$

Straightforward computation shows that by multiplying any of the matrices $A(y_1)$ or $A(y_2)$ by any of the column vectors of H^M [which are a subset of $K^M(1)$], we have a new vector linearly dependent on the columns of H^M. It follows that $\mathscr{S}(1) \equiv \mathscr{S}(2)$ ($\equiv \mathscr{S}$), which proves that the given matrix H^M has all the required properties.

EXERCISES

1. Construct a step-by-step algorithm for finding a matrix H^M for a given machine M.

2. Find an H^M matrix for the machine whose matrices are

$$A(y_1|x_1) = \begin{bmatrix} \frac{2}{9} & 0 & \frac{4}{9} & 0 \\ \frac{2}{9} & 0 & \frac{4}{9} & 0 \\ \frac{1}{9} & 0 & \frac{2}{9} & 0 \\ \frac{1}{9} & 0 & \frac{2}{9} & 0 \end{bmatrix}, \qquad A(y_2|x_1) = \begin{bmatrix} \frac{1}{6} & 0 & 0 & \frac{1}{6} \\ \frac{1}{6} & 0 & 0 & \frac{1}{6} \\ \frac{1}{3} & 0 & 0 & \frac{1}{3} \\ \frac{1}{3} & 0 & 0 & \frac{1}{3} \end{bmatrix}$$

$$A(y_1|x_2) = \begin{bmatrix} 0 & \frac{1}{2} & 0 & \frac{1}{2} \\ 0 & 0 & 0 & 0 \\ 0 & \frac{1}{8} & 0 & \frac{1}{8} \\ 0 & \frac{3}{8} & 0 & \frac{3}{8} \end{bmatrix}, \qquad A(y_2|x_2) = \begin{bmatrix} 0 & 0 & 0 & 0 \\ \frac{1}{3} & \frac{1}{3} & \frac{1}{3} & 0 \\ \frac{1}{4} & \frac{1}{4} & \frac{1}{4} & 0 \\ \frac{1}{12} & \frac{1}{12} & \frac{1}{12} & 0 \end{bmatrix}$$

3. Given a matrix $H^M = [h_{ij}]$ such that $h_{ij} = 1$ for all i, $0 \le h_{ij} \le 1$, and all its columns are linearly independent vectors, show that a machine M can be constructed effectively such that the given matrix H is its H^M matrix.

4. Find a machine M whose H^M matrix is

$$H^M = \begin{bmatrix} 1 & \frac{1}{2} & \frac{1}{4} \\ 1 & 1 & 1 \\ 1 & 0 & 0 \\ 1 & \frac{1}{3} & \frac{2}{3} \end{bmatrix}$$

5. Let M be a machine and π an initial distribution for M. Define the ordered set of row vectors $G^{(M,\pi)} = (\bar{\pi}(\lambda, \lambda), \ldots, \bar{\pi}(y, x), \ldots, \bar{\pi}(v, u), \ldots)$, such that all vectors of the form $\bar{\pi}(v, u)$ for all pairs (v, u) are in the set [if for some pair (v, u) the vector $\bar{\pi}(v, u)$ is not defined, then set $\bar{\pi}(v, u) = \bar{\pi}(\lambda, \lambda)$ for this input–output pair], and the order is induced by fixed lexicographic order on the pairs (v, u). Show that a matrix $G^{(M,\pi)} = [g_{ij}^M]$ can be found effectively such that its first row is $\bar{\pi}(\lambda, \lambda)$, $0 \le g_{ij} \le 1$ for all i and j, all its rows are linearly independent vector elements of $G^{(M,\pi)}$, and any vector of the form $\bar{\pi}(v, u)$ is a linear combination of the rows of $G^{(M,\pi)}$.

6. Construct a step-by-step algorithm for finding a matrix $G^{(M,\pi)}$ for a given machine and a given initial distribution π.

7. Find the matrix $G^{(M,\pi)}$ for the machine whose matrices are as in Exercise 2, with distribution $\pi = (\frac{1}{4}, \frac{1}{2}, \frac{1}{4}, 0)$.

2. Equivalence and Minimization of States

Definition 2.1: Let π and ρ be two initial distributions for a given machine. π and ρ are called *k-equivalent* distributions if the functions $p_\pi(v|u)$ and $p_\rho(v|u)$ [see (7)] have the same values for all pairs (v, u) such that $l(v, u) \le k$. π and ρ are called *equivalent* distributions if the functions $p_\pi(v|u)$ and $p_\rho(v|u)$ have the same values for all pairs (v, u). We are now able to prove the following theorem:

Theorem 2.1: Two distributions π and ρ for a given machine are equivalent if and only if they are $(n - 1)$-equivalent, where n is the number of states of the machine.

Proof: The "only if" part of the theorem is trivial. Assume now that the condition of the theorem holds, i.e., $p_\pi(v|u) = p_\rho(v|u)$ for all pairs (v, u) with $l(v, u) \le n - 1$. This implies that $\pi\eta(v|u) = \rho\eta(v|u)$ for all pairs (v, u) with $l(v, u) \le n - 1$, so that $\pi H^M = \rho H^M$. [The columns of H^M are, by construction, of the form $\eta(v|u)$ with $l(v, u) \le n - 1$.] Let (v, u) be any input–output pair, then $\eta(v|u) = \sum a_i \eta_i$ where the η_i's are the columns of H^M. It follows that

$$p_\pi(v|u) = \pi\eta(v|u) = \pi \sum a_i\eta_i = \sum a_i\pi\eta_i$$
$$= \sum a_i\rho\eta_i = \rho \sum a_i\eta_i = \rho\eta(v|u) = p_\rho(v|u) \quad \blacksquare$$

Corollary 2.2: Two initial vectors π and ρ for a given machine M are equivalent if and only if $\pi H^M = \rho H^M$.

Remark: An interesting geometrical interpretation of the above theorem and corollary derives from the following considerations.

Let

$$H^M = \begin{bmatrix} 1 & 0 \\ 1 & 1 \\ 1 & \frac{1}{2} \end{bmatrix}$$

for some machine M, and consider Figure 7. The set of all possible distribution

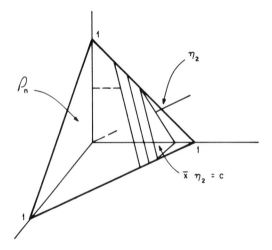

Figure 7. Geometrical interpretation of distribution equivalence.

vectors for M is represented by the simplex $\mathscr{P}_n$. Any point $\bar{x}$ on the simplex satisfies the equation $\bar{x}\eta_1 = 1$, $x_i \geq 0$. Any point $\bar{x}$ also satisfying the equation $\bar{x}\eta_2 = c$ for some real number c, must lie on the intersection of the simplex with the plane $\bar{x}\eta_2 = c$. The equivalence classes of initial distributions are therefore represented by parallel segments in the simplex, and their number is infinite.

Let M be a machine and let $\xi_i(y|x)$ be the ith row (assumed to be a nonzero row) in the matrix $A(y|x)$. Let ξ' be a substochastic vector with the property $\xi_i(y|x)H^M = \xi'H^M$, and let M' be a machine derived from M by replacing the row $\xi_i(y|x)$ of $A(y|x)$ with the row ξ'. We have the following:

Theorem 2.3: The machines M and M' as above are state-equivalent.

Proof: It suffices to prove that the equality

$$\eta^M(v|u) = \eta^{M'}(v|u) \tag{14}$$

holds for any pair (v, u). If the pair of symbols (y, x) does not appear in (v, u), then (14) holds trivially, for nothing is changed in the matrix $M'(v|u)$. Assume now that the pair of symbols (y, x) apears only once in (v, u), i.e., $(v, u) = (v_1 y v_2, u_1 x u_2)$ where y does not appear in v_1 or v_2 and x does not appear in u_1 or u_2. Then

$$\eta^M(v|u) = \eta^M(v_1 y v_2 | u_1 x u_2) = A^M(v_1|v_2)A^M(y|x)\eta^M(v_2|u_2)$$

By the definition of M', we have that $A^M(y|x)H^M = A^{M'}(y|x)H^M$, so that $A^M(y|x)\eta^M(v_2|u_2) = A^{M'}(y|x)\eta^M(v_2|u_2)$ as $\eta^M(v_2|u_2)$ is a linear combination of the column of H^M. It follows that

$$\eta^M(v|u) = A^M(v_1|u_1)A^{M'}(y|x)\eta^M(v_2|u_2)$$
$$= A^M(v_1|u_1)A^{M'}(y|x)\eta^{M'}(v_2|u_2) = \eta^{M'}(v|u)$$

The theorem follows since the above argument is readily extended by induction to the general case.   ∎

Theorem 2.4: Let M be an n-state machine such that two rows of H^M are identical. Then an $(n-1)$-state machine M^* can be effectively constructed such that M and M^* are state-equivalent (see Definition A.2.2).

Proof: Let ξ be a row in a matrix $A(y|x)$ of M. Assume that the rows j and k of H^M are identical, then the coefficients of ξ_j and ξ_k in the summation $\sum \xi_i h_{iq}, q = 1, 2, \ldots, m$ are also identical. Replace the vector ξ in $A(y|x)$ with a new vector ξ', such that $\xi_k' = 0, \xi_j' = \xi_j + \xi_k$, and $\xi_i' = \xi_i$, otherwise. Then,

$$\sum \xi_i h_{iq} = \xi_1 h_{1q} + \cdots + (\xi_j + \xi_k)h_{jq} + \cdots + 0 h_{kq}$$
$$+ \cdots + \xi_m h_{mq} = \sum \xi_i' h_{iq}$$

with $q = 1, 2, \ldots, m$ or $\xi H = \xi' H$. The resulting machine M' is therefore state-equivalent to the original machine M by the previous theorem, but the kth columns in all matrices of M' are zero columns. Let M^* be the system derived from M' by deleting all kth rows and kth columns in the matrices of M'. M^* is clearly an $(n-1)$-state machine, for deletion of the zero columns of the matrices of M' does not affect the relations $\sum_{y \in Y} \sum_j a_{ij}^{M'}(y|x) = 1$; moreover, M^* is state-equivalent to M' by the correspondence

$$s_j^{M'} \rightarrow s_j^{M^*} \leftarrow s_k^{M'} \quad \text{and} \quad s_i^{M'} \rightarrow s_i^{M^*} \quad \text{for } k \neq i \neq j$$

This follows from the fact that

$$p_{s_j}^{M'}(v|u) = \bar{s}_j \eta^{M'}(v|u) = \bar{s}_k \eta^{M'}(v|u)$$

[the jth and kth entries in any column of $H^{M'}$ are identical, hence this holds also for any vector of the form $\eta^{M'}(v|u)]$, and $p_{s_j}^{M^*}(v|u) = p_{s_j}^{M'}(v|u)$ by construction. The theorem follows by the transitivity of state equivalence. ∎

Definition 2.2: A machine M is in reduced form if no two rows of H^M are identical [i.e., no two of its states are equivalent]. The following corollary is a direct consequence of Definition 2.2 and Theorem 2.4.

Corollary 2.5: Every machine M has a reduced-form state-equivalent machine.

Definition 2.3: An initiated stochastic sequential machine (ISSM) is an SSM combined with a fixed initial distribution.

Definition 2.4: Two ISSMs (M, π) and (M^*, π^*) are *k-equivalent* if $p_{\pi}^{M}(v|u) = p_{\pi^*}^{M^*}(v|u)$ for all pairs (v, u) with $l(v, u) \leq k$. They are equivalent if the above equality holds for all pairs (v, u).

Definition 2.5: A state s_i of an ISSM (M, π), is accessible if there exists an input–output pair (v, u) [the pair (λ, λ) included] such that $\pi_i(v|u) \neq 0$.

Definition 2.6: An ISSM is connected if all its states are accessible.

Theorem 2.6: If s_i is an accessible state of an ISSM (M, π), then there exists an input–output pair (v, u) with $l(v, u) \leq |S| - 1$ such that $\pi_i(v|u) \neq 0$.

Proof: If s_i is accessible by an input–output pair (v, u) such that $l(v, u) = m$, then there exists a sequence of states of length $m + 1, s_1, s_2, \ldots, s_{m+1}$ such that s_1 corresponds to a nonzero entry in π, $s_{m+1} = s_i$, and there is a positive probability of transition by the corresponding input–output pair from one state in the sequence to the next. If $m > |S| - 1$, then the graph connecting that sequence of states contains a loop which can be reduced to yield a shorter input–output pair (v', u') by which s_i is accessible. Proceeding in this way, an input–output pair (v, u) with $l(v, u) \leq |S| - 1$ can be found by which s_i is accessible.

Remark: It follows from the above theorem that the set of accessible states of a given ISSM (M, π) is the set of states corresponding to nonzero entries in all vectors $\pi(v|u)$ where $l(v, u) \leq |S| - 1$. A practical method for determining the accessible states of (M, π) is thus available.

Theorem 2.7: Every ISSM has an equivalent connected ISSM.

Proof: We first observe that if s_j is not an accessible state, then the jth entry in π is necessarily zero, so that the vector π' derived from π by deleting that entry is a stochastic vector. We note next that if s_j is not accessible and, for some pair (y, x), $a_{ij}(y|x) > 0$, then s_i is not accessible either. Given an ISSM, (M, π), let (M', π') be the initiated machine such that:

a. π' is derived from π by deleting all entries corresponding to nonaccessible states.

b. The matrices of (M', π') are derived from the matrices of (M, π) by deleting all rows and columns corresponding to nonaccessible states. It is clear that

(M', π') is the required ISSM because, by the previous remarks, if a deleted column has nonzero entries, then all rows corresponding to these entries are also deleted, so that the resulting matrices have the property that $\sum_{y \in Y} M'(y|x)$ is a stochastic matrix, as required. ∎

Definition 2.7: Let A and B be two square matrices of order r and s respectively. The matrix

$$A \dotplus B = \begin{bmatrix} A & 0 \\ 0 & B \end{bmatrix}$$

of order $r + s$ is called their direct sum, and has the following properties:

a. If A and B are stochastic matrices, then so is $A \dotplus B$.
b. $(A_1 \dotplus B_1)(A_2 \dotplus B_2) = A_1 A_2 \dotplus B_1 B_2$ (provided the pairs A_1 and A_2, B_1 and B_2, are each of the same order).

These properties are readily verified.

Definition 2.8: Let $M = (S, X, Y, \{A(y|x)\})$ and $M' = (S', X', Y', \{A'(y|x)\})$ be two SSMs. The machine $M \dotplus M' = (S \cup S', X, Y, \{A(y|x) \dotplus A'(y|x)\})$ is called their direct sum.

Theorem 2.7: Two ISSMs (M, π) and (M', π') are equivalent if and only if they are $(|S| + |S'| - 1)$-equivalent.

Proof: The "only if" part of the theorem is trivial. Assume now that the condition of the theorem holds. Let M^* be the direct sum $M \dotplus M'$ and let p and p' be the $(|S| + |S'|)$-dimensional vectors

$$p = (\pi_1, \ldots, \pi_{|S|}, 0, \ldots, 0), \qquad p' = (0, \ldots, 0, \pi_1', \ldots, \pi_{|S'|}')$$

where

$$\pi = (\pi_1, \ldots, \pi_{|S|}) \qquad \text{and} \qquad \pi' = (\pi_1', \ldots, \pi_{|S'|}').$$

Then it is readily seen that $p_\pi^M(v|u) = P_p^{M^*}(v|u)$ and $p_{\pi'}^{M^*}(v|u) = P_{p'}^{M^*}(v|u)$. Therefore, assuming that (M, π) and (M', π') are $(|S| + |S'| - 1)$-equivalent, we have that $p_{p'}^{M^*}(v|u) = p_{\pi'}^{M'}(v|u) = p_p^M(v|u) = p_p^{M^*}(v|u)$ for all pairs (v, u) with $l(v, u) \leq |S| + |S'| - 1$. Thus p and p' are $(|S| + |S'| - 1)$-equivalent distributions for M^*. The theorem now follows, using Theorem 2.1, and bearing in mind that M^* has $|S| + |S'|$ states. ∎

Notation: For a given machine M, $\mathscr{F}^M$ denotes the set of all functions $\mathscr{F}^M = \{p_\pi^M : \pi \in \mathscr{P}_n\}$.

Definition 2.9: Two machine M and M' are equivalent if $\mathscr{F}^M \equiv \mathscr{F}^{M'}$. In other words, for every distribution π there is a distribution π' and vice versa such that (M, π) and (M', π') are equivalent ISSMs.

Remarks

1. It is readily seen that $\mathscr{F}^M$ is closed under convex combinations. To show this, we observe that if $\rho = (\rho_i) \in \mathscr{P}_n$, then

$$\sum_i \rho_i p_{\pi i}(v|u) = \sum_i \rho_i(\pi^i \eta(v|u)) = \sum_i \rho_i \sum_j \pi_j{}^i \eta_j(v|u)$$

$$= \sum_j \sum_i \rho_i \pi_j{}^i \eta_j(v|u) = \sum_j \rho_j' \eta_j(v|u) = p_{\rho'}(v|u)$$

where $\rho_j' = \sum_i \rho_i \pi_j{}^i$ and therefore $\rho' = (\rho_j') \in \mathscr{P}_n$.

2. By $p_\pi(v|u) = \sum_i \pi_i p_{s_i}(v|u)$, we have that the set $\mathscr{F}^M$ is the convex closure of the set of functions $\{p_{\bar{s}_1}, p_{\bar{s}_2}, \dots, p_{\bar{s}_n}\} = \mathscr{F}_s{}^M$. [A function of the form $p_{\bar{s}_i}$ will be called an *extremal function*.]

3. In terms of the sets $\mathscr{F}^M$, state equivalence of two machines M and M' signifies that $\mathscr{F}_s{}^M \equiv \mathscr{F}_s{}^{M'}$, hence [by the previous remarks] state equivalence implies equivalence. The converse, however, is not true, for the elements of $\mathscr{F}_s{}^M$ [or of $\mathscr{F}_s{}^{M'}$] need not be convexly independent. [A set is convexly independent if no element of the set is a convex combination of the other elements].

4. The following two conditions, are equivalent for two machines M and M':
(a) $\mathscr{F}^M \equiv \mathscr{F}^{M'}$
(b) $\mathscr{F}_s{}^M \subset \mathscr{F}^{M'}$ and $\mathscr{F}_s{}^{M'} \subset \mathscr{F}^M$
The proof is left to the reader.

Theorem 2.8: Let M be an n-state machine such that some row of H^M is a convex combination of the other rows. Then there exists an $(n-1)$-state machine M' equivalent to M.

Proof: Let $h_1, \dots, h_n$ be the rows of H^M, and assume that $h_i = \sum_{j \neq i} a_j h_j$ $(a_j) \in \mathscr{P}_n$ and $a_i = 0$. Thus, $\mathrm{conv}(h_1, \dots, h_n) = \mathrm{conv}(h_1, \dots, h_{i-1}, h_{i+1}, \dots, h_n)$. Let ξ be any nonzero row vector in any matrix of M, then $\xi / \sum \xi_i$ is a vector in $\mathscr{P}_n$, so that $\sum_j (\xi_j / \sum_i \xi_i)h_j \in \mathrm{conv}(h_1, \dots, h_n) = \mathrm{conv}(h_1, \dots, h_{i-1}, h_{i+1}, \dots, h_n)$. It follows that there exists a vector $\rho \in \mathscr{P}_n$ and $\rho_i = 0$ with $\sum_j (\xi_j / \sum_i \xi_i)h_j = \sum_{i \neq j} \rho_j h_j$. Thus, $\xi H^M = (\sum \xi_i)\rho H^M$, and replacing the vectors ξ in the matrices of M with the corresponding vectors $(\sum \xi_i)\rho$, we have a state-equivalent machine M (see Theorem 2.3) such that the ith columns in all its matrices are zero columns. M and M' are therefore equivalent machines (see Remark 3 above). Let (M', π) be an ISSM derived from M'. By the same argument as above, we find that there exists a vector $\pi' \in \mathscr{P}_n$ with $\pi_i' = 0$ such that (M', π) is equivalent to (M', π'). Now the state s_i for (M', π') is not accessible, hence there exists an equivalent ISSM, (M^*, π^*) with $(n-1)$ states only, by Theorem 2.7. The theorem follows by the transitivity of equivalence.

Definition 2.10: A machine M is in minimal-state form, if the set of row vectors in H^M is convexly independent.

Corollary 2.9: Every machine M has an equivalent minimal-state from machine M'.

Example: Let M be a machine with one input and two output symbols, defined by the matrices.

$$A(y_1|x) = \begin{bmatrix} \frac{1}{4} & 0 & 0 & \frac{1}{4} \\ 0 & 0 & 0 & 0 \\ \frac{1}{2} & 0 & 0 & \frac{1}{2} \\ \frac{1}{4} & 0 & 0 & \frac{1}{4} \end{bmatrix}, \qquad A(y_2|x) = \begin{bmatrix} \frac{1}{2} & 0 & 0 & 0 \\ 1 & 0 & 0 & 0 \\ 0 & 0 & 0 & 0 \\ \frac{1}{2} & 0 & 0 & 0 \end{bmatrix}$$

$$H^M = \begin{bmatrix} 1 & \frac{1}{2} \\ 1 & 0 \\ 1 & 1 \\ 1 & \frac{1}{2} \end{bmatrix}$$

The first and last rows of H^M are identical, hence the machine can be reduced to the state-equivalent machine M' [which is in reduced form] as described in the text, with

$$A'(y_1|x) = \begin{bmatrix} \frac{1}{2} & 0 & 0 \\ 0 & 0 & 0 \\ 1 & 0 & 0 \end{bmatrix}, \qquad A'(y_2|x) = \begin{bmatrix} \frac{1}{2} & 0 & 0 \\ 1 & 0 & 0 \\ 0 & 0 & 0 \end{bmatrix}$$

$$H^{M'} = \begin{bmatrix} 1 & \frac{1}{2} \\ 1 & 0 \\ 1 & 1 \end{bmatrix}$$

The first row of $H^{M'}$ is a convex combination of the other two, so that M' is state-equivalent to M'', with

$$A''(y_1|x) = \begin{bmatrix} 0 & \frac{1}{4} & \frac{1}{4} \\ 0 & 0 & 0 \\ 0 & \frac{1}{2} & \frac{1}{2} \end{bmatrix}, \qquad A''(y_2|x) = \begin{bmatrix} 0 & \frac{1}{4} & \frac{1}{4} \\ 0 & \frac{1}{2} & \frac{1}{2} \\ 0 & 0 & 0 \end{bmatrix}, \qquad H^{M''} = H^{M'}$$

Now let $\pi = (\pi_1\, \pi_2\, \pi_3)$ be any distribution for M'', then

$$\pi^* = (0 \ \pi_2 + \tfrac{1}{2}\pi_1 \ \pi_3 + \tfrac{1}{2}\pi_1)$$

has the property $\pi H^{M''} = \pi^* H^{M''}$, so that π and π^* are equivalent vectors. But the first state is not accessible in (M'', π^*), hence M'' is equivalent to M^* [a connected and minimal-state form machine] with

$$M^*(y_1|x) = \begin{bmatrix} 0 & 0 \\ \frac{1}{2} & \frac{1}{2} \end{bmatrix}, \qquad M^*(y_2|x) = \begin{bmatrix} \frac{1}{2} & \frac{1}{2} \\ 0 & 0 \end{bmatrix}$$

Remark: Given a reduced machine M, in order to find its minimal-state form equivalent machine M' one must be able to find the (unique) set of convexly independent [external] vectors among the row vectors of H^M. This problem can be solved by linear programming methods [e.g., Vajda (1961)]. Clearly, a vector $h_i{}^M$ is a convex combination of the other row vectors of H^M if there exists a solution to the following linear programming problem: Find a vector $x = (x_1, \ldots, x_n)$ such that $\sum_{j \neq i} x_j = 1$, $x_i = 0$, $x_j \geq 0$ for all j and $xH^M = h_i{}^M$. Some of the extremal rows of H^M can, however, be found by simpler methods [see Exercises 7, 8, and 9 below].

EXERCISES

1. Find the reduced form and minimal-state form machine equivalent to the one defined by the matrices

$$A(y_1|x) = \begin{bmatrix} \frac{1}{4} & \frac{1}{4} & \frac{1}{4} & 0 \\ \frac{1}{6} & \frac{1}{6} & \frac{1}{6} & 0 \\ \frac{1}{6} & \frac{1}{6} & \frac{1}{6} & 0 \\ \frac{1}{12} & \frac{1}{12} & \frac{1}{12} & 0 \end{bmatrix}, \qquad A(y_2|x) = \begin{bmatrix} 0 & 0 & \frac{1}{8} & \frac{1}{8} \\ 0 & 0 & \frac{1}{4} & \frac{1}{4} \\ 0 & 0 & \frac{1}{4} & \frac{1}{4} \\ 0 & 0 & \frac{3}{8} & \frac{3}{8} \end{bmatrix}$$

Find a distribution π, equivalent to the distribution $(\frac{1}{4} \frac{1}{2} \frac{1}{8} \frac{1}{8})$ for the above machine and such that $\pi = (\pi_1 \, \pi_2 \, \pi_3 \, \pi_4)$ and $\pi_2 = \pi_3 = 0$.

2. Construct an algorithm for finding the set of all nonaccessible states of a given ISSM.

3. Prove the relations (a) and (b) after Definition 2.7.

4. Prove the assertion in Remark 4.

5. Let $f_1, \ldots, f_k$ be functions. Prove that $f_i \in \text{conv}(f_1, \ldots, f_k)$ implies that $f_i \in \text{conv}(f_1, \ldots, f_{i-1}, f_{i+1}, \ldots, f_k)$, unless f_i is an extremal function.

6. Prove that the relation $\text{conv}(\mathscr{F}_s{}^M) = \text{conv}(\mathscr{F}_{s'}{}^{M'})$ for two given minimal-state form machine implies that $\mathscr{F}_s{}^M = \mathscr{F}_{s'}{}^{M'}$, with the following consequences:

    a. All minimal-state form equivalent machines are state-equivalent and have the same number of states.

    b. If M and M' are equivalent machines and M is minimal-state form, then $|S| \leq |S'|$.

7. Prove that if a row in some H^M has an entry which is maximal or minimal in the corresponding column, then that row is extremal (i.e., is not a convex combination of other rows).

8. Let d_i be the value $d_i = \sum_j (h_{ij}{}^M)^2$ for a given row $h_i{}^M$ in a matrix H^M. Prove that the rows corresponding to the maximal d_i values are extremal.

9. Let $h_i{}^M$ be an extremal row in a matrix H^M, and let d_{ij} be the value $d_{ij} = \sum_k (h_{ik} - h_{jk})^2$ where h_j is some other row of H^M. Prove that the rows h_j corresponding to maximal d_{ij} values are extremal.

10. Find a set of extremal column vectors in the matrix ($(H^M)^T$ denotes the transpose of H^M).

$$(H^M)^{\mathrm{T}} = \begin{bmatrix} 1 & 1 & 1 & 1 & 1 & 1 \\ 0 & \frac{3}{4} & \frac{1}{3} & \frac{2}{3} & \frac{1}{5} & \frac{2}{5} \\ \frac{1}{2} & \frac{1}{4} & \frac{1}{3} & \frac{1}{4} & \frac{3}{4} & \frac{1}{3} \end{bmatrix}$$

11*. Let L be a linear space over the real numbers and a an arbitrary fixed element of L. The set of elements $\{y: y = x + a, x \in L\}$ is called a translate of L or a flat. Prove that

a. A set of points in n-dimensional space, which is closed under convex combination of its points, is a flat.

b. Let $\mathscr{P}_n^-$ be the flat (hyperplane) $\mathscr{P}_n^- = \{\pi = (\pi_1, \ldots, \pi_n): \sum \pi_i = 1\}$, and M an n-state SSM. Define an equivalence relation over $\mathscr{P}_n^-$ induced by M which is right-invariant and such that $\mathscr{P}_n^-$ is decomposed by this equivalence relation into a cartesian product of two flats, the elements of the first flat being the equivalence classes of the defined equivalence.

3. Covering Relations

Definition 3 1: Let M and M^* be two SSMs. The machine M covers the machine $M^*(M \geq M^*)$ if $\mathscr{F}^M \supseteq \mathscr{F}^{M^*}$.

Theorem 3.1: The following four conditions are equivalent:

a. $M \geq M$.

b. There exists a stochastic matrix B such that $B\eta^M(v|u) = \eta^{M^*}(v|u)$ for all pairs (v, u) (i.e., $B[K^M] = [K^{M^*}]$).

c. There exists a stochastic matrix B such that

$$BA^M(y|x)\eta^M(v|u) = A^{M^*}(y|x)B\eta^M(v|u)$$

for all pairs (v, u) and all pairs (y, x).

d. There exists a stochastic matrix B such that

$$BA^M(y|x)H^M = A^{M^*}(y|x)BH^M$$

Proof: (a) $\Longleftrightarrow$ (b): Assume that (a) holds. Then
Let $\eta^{M^*}(v|u)$ be a vector in K^{M^*}, then

$$\eta^{M^*}(v|u) = \begin{bmatrix} p_{\hat{s}_1}^{M^*}(v|u) \\ \vdots \\ p_{\hat{s}_{n*}}^{M^*}(v|u) \end{bmatrix} = \begin{bmatrix} p_{\pi^{(1)}}^M(v|u) \\ \vdots \\ p_{\pi^{(n*)}}^M(v|u) \end{bmatrix}$$

$$= \begin{bmatrix} \pi^{(1)}\eta^M(v|u) \\ \vdots \\ \pi^{(n*)}\eta^M(v|u) \end{bmatrix} = \begin{bmatrix} \pi^{(1)} \\ \vdots \\ \pi^{(n*)} \end{bmatrix} \eta^M(v|u) = B\eta^M(v|u)$$

where $p^M_{\pi_{(i)}}$ is the function in $\mathscr{F}^M$ equal to $p_{\tilde{s}_i}{}^{M^*}$ in $\mathscr{F}^{M^*}$ and B the matrix whose rows are the vectors $\pi^{(i)}$. Thus (a) implies (b). Assume now that (b) holds and let $p^{M^*}_{\pi^*}$ be any function in $\mathscr{F}^{M^*}$ Let π be the distribution $\pi = \pi^* B$; then, for all pairs (v, u), we have

$$p^M_\pi(v|u) = \pi \eta^M(v|u) = \pi^* B \eta^M(v|u) = \pi^* \eta^{M^*}(v|u) = p^{M^*}_{\pi^*}(v|u)$$

Thus $\mathscr{F}^M \supseteq \mathscr{F}^{M^*}$ and (b) implies (a).

(b) $\Leftrightarrow$ (c): Assume that (b) holds, and consider Figure 8. It follows directly

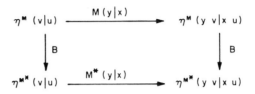

Figure 8. Mapping B from M to M^*.

from this diagram that (b) implies (c). We now prove by induction on the length of pairs (v, u), that (c) implies (b). For $l(v, u) = 0$ the implication is trivial, as both $\eta^M(\lambda, \lambda)$ and $\eta^{M^*}(\lambda, \lambda)$ have all their entries equal to 1, and therefore for any stochastic matrix B of suitable dimention $B\eta^M(\lambda, \lambda) = \eta^{M^*}(\lambda, \lambda)$. Assuming that the equality $B\eta^M(v|u) = \eta^{M^*}(v|u)$ holds for some pair (v, u) with $l(v, u) = k$ and (c), we have that

$$B\eta^M(yv|xu) = BA(y|x)\eta^M(v|u) = A^{M^*}(y|x)B\eta^M(v|u)$$
$$= A^{M^*}(y|x)\eta^{M^*}(v|u) = \eta^{M^*}(yv|xu)$$

as necessary. The implication is thus proved.

(c) $\Leftrightarrow$ (d): That (c) implies (d) is trivial, as the columns of H^M are vectors of the form $\eta^M(v|u)$. The converse is also obvious as any vector of the form $\eta^M(v|u)$ is a linear combination of the columns of H^M. ∎

Definition 3.2: Given two machines $M \geq M^*$, J^{M^*} is the matrix whose columns are vectors in K^{M^*} which are related to the same input–output pairs as the columns in H^M.

Theorem 3.2: Let $M \geq M'$ be two machines such that rank $M =$ rank M', then there exists a stochastic matrix B such that $BH^M = H^{M^*}$. Furthermore, if $\eta^M(v|u) = \sum_{i=1}^m a_i \eta_i{}^M$ (the $\eta_i{}^M$s being the columns of H^M) is a vector in K^M and $\eta^{M^*}(v|u) = \sum_{i=1}^m b_i \eta_i{}^{M^*}$ the corresponding vector in K^{M^*}, then $a_i = b_i$ for $i = 1, 2, \ldots, m$.

Proof: Let B be the matrix in condition (b) of Theorem 3.1. Then $J^{M^*} = BH^M$. Denote the columns of H^M by $\eta_1, \ldots, \eta_m$ and the corresponding columns of J^{M^*} by $\eta_1{}^*, \ldots, \eta_m{}^*$. Finally, let $\eta^M(v|u)$ be any vector in K^M. Then

$$\eta^M(v|u) = \sum_{i=1}^{m} a_i \eta_i \qquad (15)$$

this implies that

$$\eta^{M^*}(v|u) = B\eta^M(v|u) = \sum a_i B\eta_i = \sum a_i \eta_i^* \qquad (16)$$

Thus any vector in K^{M^*} is a linear combination of the columns of J^{M^*} and therefore, since M and M^* have a common rank, rank J^{M^*} = rank H^{M^*} = rank H^M. Furthermore, the columns in H^{M^*} must be columns in J^{M^*} (in the same order). If this is not true, then let $\eta^{M^*}(v_0|u_0)$ be the first column in H^{M^*} which is not a column in J^{M^*}. The corresponding vector $\eta^M(v_0|u_0)$ in K^M is, by definition, not in H^M, hence it is a linear combination of vectors in H^M preceding the vector $\eta^M(v_0|u_0)$ in K^M. This would imply by (16) that $\eta^{M^*}(v_0|u_0)$, a column of H^{M^*}, is a linear combination of other columns of H^{M^*}, contrary to the properties of H^{M^*}. Thus the columns of H^{M^*} are a subset of those of J^{M^*}. Now this subset cannot be proper, for rank H^M = number of columns in H^M = number of columns in J^{M^*} = rank J^{M^*} = rank H^{M^*} = number of columns in H^{M^*}. The second part of the theorem is an immediate consequence of the first part and of relations (15) and (16) above. ∎

Theorem 3.3: Let M and M^* be two equivalent SSMs with n and n^* states respectively. Then rank M = rank M^*, conv$(h_1^M, \ldots, h_n^M)$ = conv$(h_1^{M^*}, \ldots, h_{n^*}^{M^*})$(where h_i^M and $h_i^{M^*}$ are the ith rows in H^M and H^{M^*} respectively), and there are stochastic matrices B and B^* such that $H^{M^*} = BH^M$ and $H^M = B^* H^{M^*}$.

Proof: $M \cong M^*$ implies that $M \geq M^*$ and $M^* \geq M$. By Theorem 3.1, there exist stochastic matrices B and B^* such that $\eta^{M^*}(v|u) = B\eta^M(v|u)$ and $\eta^M(v|u) = B^* \eta^{M^*}(v|u)$ for all pairs (v, u). This implies that rank $M^* \geq$ rank $M \geq$ rank M^*, or rank M^* = rank M. By Theorem 3.2, $H^{M^*} = BH^M$ and $H^M = B^* H^{M^*}$, signifying that every row of H^M is a convex combination of rows of H^{M^*} and vice versa, or, conv$(h_1^M, \ldots, h_n^M)$ = conv$(h_1^{M^*}, \ldots, h_{n^*}^{M^*})$. ∎

Theorem 3.4: Let M and M^* be two state-equivalent machines with n and n^* states respectively. Then $\{h_1^M. \ldots, h_n^M\} = \{h_1^{M^*}, \ldots, h_{n^*}^{M^*}\}$.

Proof: The entries in the ith row of H^M are values of an extremal function $p_{s_i}^M \in \mathscr{F}_S^M$ for some input–output pairs $(\lambda, \lambda), (v_1, u_1), \ldots, (v_{m-1}, u_{m-1})$. As M is state-equivalent to M^*, it follows from Remark 3 on p. 26 that $\mathscr{F}_S^M = \mathscr{F}_S^{M^*}$ so that there exists an extremal function $p_{s_j}^{M^*} \in \mathscr{F}_{S^*}^M$ equal to $p_{s_i}^M$. The entries in the ith row of H^M are therefore equal to those of the jth row of the matrix J^{M^*} whose columns are $\eta^{M^*}(\lambda|\lambda), \eta^{M^*}(v_1|u_1), \ldots, \eta^{M^*}(v_{m-1}|u_{m-1})$. Now, state-equivalence implies equivalence and therefore, by the previous theorem, $J^{M^*} = H^{M^*}$ so that there exists a row in H^{M^*}, the jth row, identical with the ith row in H^M. The proof is completed by reversing the argument. ∎

Theorem 3.5: Let M and M^* be two state-equivalent and *reduced* machines with n and n^* states respectively, then $n = n^*$; the rows of H^M are a permutation of the rows of H^{M^*}; and, if $A^M(y|x)$ and $A^{M^*}(y|x)$ are corresponding matrices of M and M^* respectively, then $A^M(y|x)H^M = A^{M^*}(y|x)H^{M^*}$ up to a permutation of rows.

Proof: It follows by definition that no two rows of H^M and no two rows of H^{M^*} are identical (the machines are reduced). By the previous theorem $\{h_1^M, \ldots, h_n^M\} = \{h_1^{M^*}, \ldots, h_n^{M^*}\}$. Combining these facts, we have that $n = n^*$ and the ordered set of rows of H^M is a permutation of the ordered corresponding set of rows of H^{M^*}. If the states of M^* are properly ordered, then the equality $H^M = H^{M^*}$ holds and, as the machines are state-equivalent and the equivalence is one-to-one, we have that $\eta^M(v|u) = \eta^{M^*}(v|u)$ for all pairs (v, u). By (5), $A^{M^*}(y|x)H^{M^*} = A^M(y|x)H^{M^*}$. The theorem is thus proved. ∎

Theorem 3.6: Let M and M^* be two equivalent minimal state form machines with n and n^* states respectively, then

   a. $n = n^*$.
   b. M is state-equivalent to M^*.
   c. The corresponding matrices $A^M(y|x)$ and $A^{M^*}(y|x)$ satisfy the relation $A^M(y|x)H^M = A^{M^*}(y|x)H^{M^*}$ up to a permutation of rows.
   d. There exist permutation matrices B and B^* such that $H^M = B^* H^{M^*}$ and $H^{M^*} = BH^M$.

Proof: By Theorem 3.3, since M and M^* are equivalent, we have that conv $(h_1^M, \ldots, h_n^M) = \text{conv}(h_1^{M^*}, \ldots, h_{n^*}^{M^*})$. By definition, points $h_1^M, \ldots, h_n^M$ are the vertices of the polyhedron $\text{conv}\{h_1^M, \ldots, h_n^M\}$ and points $h_1^{M^*}, \ldots, h_{n^*}^{M^*}$ those of $\text{conv}\{h_1^{M^*}, \ldots, h_{n^*}^{M^*}\}$. As the set of vertices of a polyhedron is uniquely determined by the polyhedron, we have that $\{h_1^M, \ldots, h_n^M\} = \{h_1^{M^*}, \ldots, h_{n^*}^{M^*}\}$. M and M^* being minimal-state form, they are also reduced-form, so that all points in either set on both sides of the above equality are distinct. Thus $n = n^*$ and M is state-equivalent to M^*. Properties (c) and (d) now follow from the previous theorem. ∎

Corollary 3.7: Let M and M^* be two equivalent machines such that M is a minimal-state form machine. Then $n \leq n^*$.

Proof: The set $\{h_1^M, \ldots, h_n^M\}$ is the unique set of vertices of the polyhedron $\text{conv}(h_1^M, \ldots, h_n^M) = \text{conv}(h_1^{M^*}, \ldots, h_{n^*}^{M^*})$, and the number of vertices of a polyhedron is the smallest number of points such that their convex closure spans the whole polyhedron. ∎

Remark: Compare the above theorem and corollary with Exercise 6 in the previous section.

We now consider the uniqueness problem for reduced-form and minimal-state form machines.

Definition 3.3: If H^M is a matrix related to a machine M and ξ is a row sub-stochastic nonzero vector of suitable dimension, then $h^M(\xi)$ is the point $(\xi/\sum \xi_i)H^M$ in conv$(h_1, \ldots, h_m)$. The vector ξ is *simplicial*, if $h^M(\xi)$ is a point on a face of conv$(h_1, \ldots, h_m)$ which is a simplex.

Definition 3.4: Two machines M and M' are *isomorphic* if they are equal up to a permutation of states.

Theorem 3.8: Let M be a reduced-form machine. There exists a reduced form machine M^* which is state-equivalent but not isomorphic to M if and only if there exists a row $\xi(y|x)$ in a matrix $A^M(y|x)$ which is not simplicial.

Proof: Assume first that all the rows in the matrices $A^M(y|x)$ are simplicial. If M^* is reduced and state-equivalent to M, then by Theorem 3.5, $A^M(y|x)H^M = A^{M^*}(y|x)H^{M^*}$ for all pairs (y, x) up to a proper rearrangement of states. Since the rows of $A^M(y|x)$ are simplicial, this is possible only if $A^M(y|x) = A^{M^*}(y|x)$, for an interior point of a simplex has a unique representation as a combination of its vertices. Thus M is isomorphic to M^*. Assume now that there is a row $\xi(y|x)$ in a matrix $A^M(y|x)$ which is not simplicial. This means that $h(\xi(y|x)) = \sum \alpha_i h_i$, where the h_i corresponding to nonzero coefficients α_i are not a simplex. This implies, by a classical theorem on convex bodies (see Exercise 5 at the end of this section), that there exists a set of coefficients (β_i) not identical to (α_i), such that the combination $\sum \beta_i h_i$ is convex and equals $\sum \alpha_i h_i$. Thus there exists a substochastic vector ρ not identical to $\xi(y|x)$ and such that $\xi(y|x)H^M = \rho H^M$. Let M^* be a machine derived from M by replacing the vector $\xi(y|x)$ in $A(y|x)$ with the vector ρ. By Theorem 2.3, M and M^* are state-equivalent, but M^* is not isomorphic to M by construction. ∎

Assume now that two equivalent machines M and M^* are in minimal-state form. Then they are also in reduced form and state-equivalent [Theorem 3.6]. This observation leads to the following corollary.

Corollary 3.9: Let M be a minimal-state form machine. There exists a minimal state form machine M^* which is equivalent but not isomorphic to M if and only if there exists a row $\xi(y|x)$, in a matrix $A(y|x)$ of M, which is not simplicial.

It follows from the above theorem and corollary that the uniqueness of the reduced or minimal-state form of a machine M is conditional on the nature of the points $h^M(\xi(y|x))$, where $\xi(y|x)$ is a row in a matrix $A^M(y|x)$. To find the nature of these points, we must be able to extract from the set of points $(h_1{}^M, \ldots, h_n{}^M)$ (denoted by V throughout this subsection) all subsets W such that conv(W) is a face of (V). This done, we have to decide whether the faces conv(W) are simplexes or not. A decision procedure for these questions is based on a theorem stated below. [The reader is referred to Grunbaum (1968) for proof of the first part of the theorem.]

Let M and H^M be a machine and its corresponding H matrix, assumed to be of dimension $n \times m$. With H^M we associate a new matrix $\bar{H}^M$ such that the columns of $\bar{H}^M$ form a basis for the null-space of the space spanned by the columns of H^M. Clearly $\bar{H}^M$ is an $n \times (n - m)$ matrix. Let $\bar{V}$ be the set of rows of $\bar{H}^M$ [considered as points in $(n - m)$-space]. Let $N' = (i_1, \ldots, i_k)$ be a subset of the set of integers $N = (1, \ldots, n)$. $V(N')$ denotes the set $V(N') = (h_{i_1}, \ldots, h_{i_k})$ and similarly $\bar{V}(N') = (\bar{h}_{i_1}, \ldots, \bar{h}_{i_k})$, where $\bar{V} = (\bar{h}_1, \ldots, \bar{h}_n)$. Finally, $V - W$ stands for the set $V(N - N')$ where $W = V(N')$.

Definition 3.5: The set of points conv(W) $=$ conv($V(N')$) is a *coface* of conv (V) if and only if conv($V - W$) is a face of conv(V). [We shall say, alternatively, that W is a coface of V.]

Theorem 3.9: $W = V(N')$ is a coface of V if and only if either $W = \phi$ or **0** is in the relative interior of $\bar{V}(N')$. [The whole polyhedron is considered as a face of itself.] A face $V(N') = W$ of V is a simplex if and only if the set of its vertices is linearly independent.

Remark: It is clear that the criteria used in this theorem are decidable and effectively checkable by straightforward linear programming methods. Note also that the second part of the theorem is a trivial consequence of the definitions.

EXERCISES

1. Let M be a reduced machine such that all entries in its matrices are either 0 or 1 (i.e., M is deterministic). Prove that M is also in minimal-state form.

2. Prove: If M is a reduced deterministic SSM, then no SSM M^* such that $M^* \geq M$ has fewer states than M.

3. Prove: Let M and M^* be two state-equivalent machines such that the mapping between the states of M and those of M^* is one-to-one, then for every pair (y, x), $A^M(y|x)H^M = A^{M^*}(y|x)H^M$, and $A^{M^*}(y|x)H^{M^*} = A^M(y|x)H^{M^*}$ up to a permutation of rows.

4. Prove: $M^* \geq M$ if and only if $\mathscr{F}_S{}^M \supseteq \mathscr{F}^{M^*}$.

5. The following is Radon's classical theorem on convex bodies:

Theorem: Each set of $n + 2$ or more points in n-dimensional space can be subdivided into two disjoint sets whose convex closures have a common point.

On the basis of this theorem, prove that for any row $\xi(y|x)$ in a matrix $A(y|x)$ which is not simplicial, there exists a substochastic vector not identical to $\xi(y|x)$, with $h(\xi(y|x)) = h(\rho)$.

6. Prove: Let M be a machine. Construction of a reduced form by merging equivalent states yields resultant machines which may be nonisomorphic only if there exists two rows $\xi_i(y|x) \neq \xi_j(y|x)$ in a matrix $A(y|x)$ which are not simplicial and such that $h(\xi_i(y|x)) = h(\xi_j(y|x))$ and the states s_i and s_j are equivalent.

7. Prove: Let M be a machine. Construction of a minimal-state form equivalent machine yields resultant machines which may be nonisomorphic only if

there are two rows $\xi_i(y|x) \neq \xi_j(y|x)$ in a matrix $A(y|x)$ which are not simplicial and such that $h(\xi_i(y|x)) = h(\xi_j(y|x))$, the states s_i and s_j are equivalent and $h_i(= h_j)$ is a vertex of conv$(h_1, \ldots, h_n)$.

Note: Is "h_i is a vertex of conv$(h_1, \ldots, h_n)$" a necessary condition? Explain.

8. Let H^M be the matrix

$$
H^M = \begin{bmatrix}
1 & \frac{1}{2} & \frac{1}{2} & \frac{1}{2} \\
1 & \frac{1}{2} & 0 & \frac{1}{2} \\
1 & 0 & 0 & \frac{1}{2} \\
1 & 0 & \frac{1}{2} & \frac{1}{2} \\
1 & 0 & 0 & 1
\end{bmatrix}
$$

Find the faces of conv$(h_1, \ldots, h_5)$ for the above matrix, and also which faces are simplexes.

9. Consider the following:

Definition: A machine M is observer/state-calculable if there exists a function $f: S \times X \times Y \to S$ such that $a_{ij}(y|x) = 0$ if $s_j \neq f(s_i, x, y)$. Accordingly, such a machine has at most one nonzero element in each row of its matrices. What corollaries derive from Theorem 3.8 and Corollary 3.9 when applied to it?

10. Prove that the vertices of a polyhedron are uniquely determined by the polyhedron.

11. Prove that any machine of rank 2 has an equivalent two-state, minimal-state form, machine.

12. Prove that the covering relation is transitive.

4. Decision Problems

Theorem 4.1: Let $M \geq M^*$ be two machines, and let B be any stochastic matrix such that $BH^M = J^{M^*}$. Then $B\eta^M(v|u) = \eta^{M^*}(v|u)$ for all pairs (v, u).

Proof: By Theorem 3.1 ($M \geq M^*$) there exists a stochastic matrix B' such that $B'\eta^M(v|u) = \eta^{M^*}(v|u)$, in particular $B'H^M = J^{M^*}$. Thus $B'H^M = J^{M^*} = BH^M$, so that the rows of B considered as distributions for M are equivalent to the corresponding rows of B'. It follows that $B\eta^M(v|u) = B'\eta^M(v|u) = \eta^{M^*}(v|u)$ for all pairs (v, u), and the theorem is proved. ∎

Corollary 4.2: Let M and M^* be machines. If for *some* stochastic matrix B, such that $BH^M = J^{M^*}$, the condition $BA^M(y|x)H^M = A^{M^*}(y|x)BH^M$ does not hold for all pairs (y, x), then $M \not\geq M'$.

Proof: It is implicit in the proof of Theorem 3.1 that the matrix B satisfying the relation (b) satisfies also the relation (d). Using the previous theorem, we conclude that if $M \geq M^*$ and $BH^M = J^{M^*}$, then B must satisfy the relation (b) in Theorem 3.1. The corollary is thus proved. ∎

Corollary 4.3: Let M and M^* be machines. $M \geq M^*$ if and only if there exists a stochastic matrix B satisfying the conditions $BH^M = J^{M^*}$, and for any such B the condition (d) of Theorem 3.1 is satisfied.

Corollary 4.4: Given two machines M and M^*, it is decidable whether $M \geq M^*$.

Proof: There exist algorithms for finding the matrices H^M and J^{M^*}. Using the preceding corollary, we see that if a stochastic matrix B such that $BH^M = J^{M^*}$ does not exist, then $M \not\geq M$, and this question can be answered with the aid of linear programming methods. If such a B does exist, it is again obtainable by linear programming methods. Finally, with B found, if and only if the relation (d) in Theorem 3.1 holds for it, then $M \geq M^*$. The corollary is thus proved. ∎

Corollary 4.5: Given two machines M and M^*, it is decidable whether $M \equiv M^*$.

Proof: $M \equiv M^*$ if and only if $M \geq M^*$ and $M^* \geq M$. ∎

EXERCISES

1. Given two machines M and M^*, formulate a decision procedure for finding whether $M \geq M^*$ based on Theorem 2.7.

2. Given two machines M and M^*, formulate a decision procedure for finding whether $M \equiv M^*$, based on the fact that $M \equiv M^*$ implies that rank $M =$ rank M^*, on Theorem 3.2, and on Corollary 4.3.

3. Let M and M^* be the machines whose defining matrices are

$$A^M(0|0) = \begin{bmatrix} \frac{1}{4} & \frac{1}{4} & 0 \\ \frac{5}{16} & \frac{5}{16} & 0 \\ 0 & 0 & 0 \end{bmatrix}, \qquad A^M(1|0) = \begin{bmatrix} 0 & \frac{1}{2} & 0 \\ 0 & \frac{3}{8} & 0 \\ 0 & 1 & 0 \end{bmatrix}$$

$$A^M(0|1) = \begin{bmatrix} 0 & 0 & 0 \\ 0 & \frac{5}{16} & \frac{5}{16} \\ 0 & \frac{1}{4} & \frac{1}{4} \end{bmatrix}, \qquad A^M(1|1) = \begin{bmatrix} \frac{1}{2} & 0 & \frac{1}{2} \\ \frac{3}{16} & 0 & \frac{3}{16} \\ \frac{1}{4} & 0 & \frac{1}{4} \end{bmatrix}$$

$$A^{M^*}(0|0) = \begin{bmatrix} \frac{5}{16} & \frac{1}{8} & \frac{1}{16} \\ \frac{5}{8} & \frac{1}{4} & \frac{1}{8} \\ 0 & 0 & 0 \end{bmatrix}, \qquad A^{M^*}(1|0) = \begin{bmatrix} \frac{1}{8} & \frac{1}{4} & \frac{1}{8} \\ 0 & 0 & 0 \\ \frac{1}{4} & \frac{1}{2} & \frac{1}{4} \end{bmatrix}$$

$$A^{M^*}(0|1) = \begin{bmatrix} 0 & 0 & 0 \\ \frac{1}{4} & \frac{3}{8} & \frac{3}{8} \\ \frac{1}{8} & \frac{3}{16} & \frac{3}{16} \end{bmatrix}, \qquad A^{M^*}(1|1) = \begin{bmatrix} \frac{1}{2} & 0 & \frac{1}{2} \\ 0 & 0 & 0 \\ \frac{1}{4} & 0 & \frac{1}{4} \end{bmatrix}$$

Check for $M \geq M^*$ and $M^* \geq M$.

5. Minimization of States by Covering, Problem I

In the preceding section, we have seen that any machine can be reduced to an equivalent reduced-form or minimal-state-form machine. We now consider further reduction of the number of states of a minimal-state-form machine. The following problems are considered:

Problem I: Find an n^*-state machine M^* such that $M^* \geq M$ and $n^* < n$.
Problem II: Find an n^*-state machine M^* such that $M \geq M^*$ and $n^* < n$.
Problem III: Let (M, π) be an initiated machine; find an initiated machine (M^*, π^*) such that $(M, \pi) \cong (M^*, \pi^*)$ and $n^* < n$.

A solution to Problem I yields a machine capable of realizing more functions than the original and with fewer states, and a solution to Problem II a machine less general than the original and again with fewer states. [The need for considering the latter problem is due to the fact that there are cases in which it alone has a solution.] In Problem III we seek a minimal-state realization of a particular function defined by a given machine.

We have proved in Section 3 [Theorem 3.1] that $M^* \geq M$ holds for two machines M^* and M, if and only if there exists a stochastic matrix B^* such that

$$B^* \eta^{M^*}(v|u) = \eta^M(v|u) \qquad \text{for all pairs} \quad (v, u) \tag{17}$$

or, equivalently, such that

$$B^* A^{M^*}(y|x) H^{M^*} = A^M(y|x) B^* H^{M^*} \tag{18}$$

If M is given and an answer to Problem I sought for it without additional information on M^*, (17) or (18) are of little use, as the matrix H^{M^*} is not known. On the other hand, one may begin the search for a solution by assuming that rank $M^* = $ rank M. If this is the case, then using Theorem 3.2, we know that a matrix B^* satisfying (17) must also satisfy $B^* H^{M^*} = H^M$. Since only H^M is given, one may begin with any H^{M^*} matrix such that

$$\text{conv}(h_1^{M^*}, \ldots, h_{n^*}^{M^*}) \supseteq (h_1^M, \ldots, h_n^M) \qquad \text{and} \quad n^* < n \tag{19}$$

[since B^* is stochastic, (19) is necessary], and try to reconstruct M^* according to (18). The following algorithm ensues:

Step 1: Assume rank $M = $ rank M^*, and find any matrix H^{M^*} satisfying (19).

Step 2: Find a matrix B^* satisfying

$$B^* H^{M^*} = H^M \tag{20}$$

Step 3: Solve (18) for $A^{M^*}(y|x)$, subject to the condition that the matrices $A^{M^*}(y|x)$ be nonnegative.

If all steps prove effective, the algorithm yields a solution to Problem I. In some other cases it may provide a definite negative answer as to the existence of a solution. Unfortunately, it has many shortcomings in the general case, and these are considered in the following comments on its three steps.

Step 1: The equality rank $M^* =$ rank M has not been proved to be a necessary assumption. In other words failure to find a solution to Problem I under this assumption does not mean that no solution exists. On the other hand, no counterexample has been found to-date for proving that the situation $M^* \geq M$, $n^* < n$, rank $M^* >$ rank M, and no $M^+ \geq M$ with $n^+ < n$ and such that rank $M^+ =$ rank M may occur, but here no method is available for finding a covering machine M^*. There is, however, at least one case which necessitates the above assumption, namely that of rank $M = n - 1$ [see Exercise 1 in this section].

Still another shortcoming of the first step is that it involves another problem to which no general solution is known (although solutions are available for some particular cases), namely: Given a polyhedron within the positive unit cube, find another polyhedron within the cube with fewer vertices and covering the given polyhedron.

Step 2: With a matrix H^{M^*} assumed, there may exist an infinity of matrices B^* satisfying (20), obtainable by linear-algebra methods, but we need not check all of them. To ascertain whether the assumed H^{M^*} actually leads to a covering machine as required, it suffices to check a single B^* satisfying (20), and if step 3 fails here, this signifies that the assumed H^{M^*} is unsuitable. This follows from Corollary 4.2 and Theorem 3.2. [The reader is advised to attempt a detailed proof.]

Step 3: Under the assumption that rank $M =$ rank M^*, the matrix B^* found in Step 2 is a transformation which perserves the rank of the row space of H^{M^*} and thus has a (nonstochastic) left inverse B such that $BB^* H^{M^*} = H^{M^*}$. Multiplying both sides of (18) by B, we have $BB^* A^{M^*}(y|x)H^{M^*} = BA^M(y|x)B^* H^{M^*}$. Thus one can write the matrix BB^* in the form $BB^* = I + N$, where I is the n^*-dimensional unity matrix and $NH^{M^*} = 0$. Let η be any column vector which is a linear combination of the columns of H^{M^*}, then $N\eta = 0$. However, since all columns of the matrix $A^{M^*}(y|x)H^{M^*}$ are linear combinations of the columns of H^{M^*}, $BB^* A^{M^*} H^{M^*} = (I + N)A^{M^*} H^{M^*} = A^{M^*} H^{M^*}$ and the following equation results

$$A^{M^*}(y|x)H^{M^*} = BA^M(y|x)B^* H^{M^*} \tag{21}$$

Solving Eq. (21) for $A^{M^*}(y|x)$ [all other matrices are known], subject to the restriction that $A^{M^*}(y|x)$ are nonnegative matrices, provides the answer to our problem. The system (21), subject to the above restriction is readily reduced to a set of linear programming problems. Failure to find a nonnegative solution to (21) indicates that the chosen matrix H^{M^*} is unsuitable and a fresh start is called for.

It is thus seen that the above three step procedure is not an algorithm in the ordinary sense, for even in the case where the assumption that rank M = rank M^* is justified there still may be an infinity of H^{M^*} matrices satisfying (19) which may serve as starting point for Step 1.

Example 7: Let M be a five state machine $[X = \{0, 1\}, Y = \{0, 1, 2\}]$

$$A(0|0) = \begin{bmatrix} 0 & \frac{1}{2} & 0 & 0 & 0 \\ 0 & \frac{1}{2} & 0 & 0 & 0 \\ 0 & 0 & 0 & 0 & 0 \\ 0 & 0 & 0 & 0 & 0 \\ 0 & 0 & 0 & 0 & 0 \end{bmatrix}, \quad A(1|0) = \begin{bmatrix} 0 & 0 & 0 & 0 & 0 \\ 0 & 0 & 0 & 0 & 0 \\ 0 & \frac{1}{4} & 0 & \frac{1}{4} & 0 \\ 0 & \frac{1}{4} & 0 & \frac{1}{4} & 0 \\ 0 & 0 & 0 & 0 & 0 \end{bmatrix}$$

$$A(2|0) = \begin{bmatrix} 0 & 0 & 0 & \frac{1}{2} & 0 \\ 0 & 0 & 0 & \frac{1}{2} & 0 \\ 0 & 0 & 0 & \frac{1}{2} & 0 \\ 0 & 0 & 0 & \frac{1}{2} & 0 \\ 0 & 0 & 0 & 0 & 1 \end{bmatrix}, \quad A(0|1) = \begin{bmatrix} \frac{1}{2} & 0 & 0 & 0 & 0 \\ 0 & 0 & 0 & 0 & 0 \\ 0 & 0 & 0 & 0 & 0 \\ \frac{1}{2} & 0 & 0 & 0 & 0 \\ 0 & 0 & 0 & 0 & 0 \end{bmatrix}$$

$$A(1|1) = \begin{bmatrix} 0 & 0 & 0 & 0 & 0 \\ \frac{1}{4} & 0 & \frac{1}{4} & 0 & 0 \\ \frac{1}{4} & 0 & \frac{1}{4} & 0 & 0 \\ 0 & 0 & 0 & 0 & 0 \\ 0 & 0 & 0 & 0 & 0 \end{bmatrix}, \quad A(2|1) = \begin{bmatrix} 0 & 0 & \frac{1}{2} & 0 & 0 \\ 0 & 0 & \frac{1}{2} & 0 & 0 \\ 0 & 0 & \frac{1}{2} & 0 & 0 \\ 0 & 0 & \frac{1}{2} & 0 & 0 \\ 0 & \frac{1}{2} & 0 & 0 & \frac{1}{2} \end{bmatrix}$$

An H^M matrix for this machine is

$$H^M = \begin{bmatrix} 1 & \frac{1}{2} & \frac{1}{2} & \frac{1}{2} \\ 1 & \frac{1}{2} & 0 & \frac{1}{2} \\ 1 & 0 & 0 & \frac{1}{2} \\ 1 & 0 & \frac{1}{2} & \frac{1}{2} \\ 1 & 0 & 0 & 1 \end{bmatrix} \begin{matrix} h_1 \\ h_2 \\ h_3 \\ h_4 \\ h_5 \end{matrix}$$

As the first coordinate of the h_is is always 1, one may use a three-dimensional subspace (again with first coordinate 1). The geometrical representation is given in Figure 9.

Since rank $M = 4 = n - 1$, we have here that any covering machine M^* with fewer states has the same rank (see Exercise 1, Section 5) and four states. The figure shows that the only possible choice, in this case, for H^{M^*} is

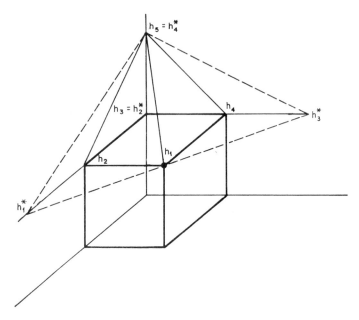

Figure 9. Geometrical interpretation of H^M.

$$H^{M^*} = \begin{bmatrix} 1 & 1 & 0 & \frac{1}{2} \\ 1 & 0 & 0 & \frac{1}{2} \\ 1 & 0 & 1 & \frac{1}{2} \\ 1 & 0 & 0 & 1 \end{bmatrix} \begin{matrix} h_1^* \\ h_2^* \\ h_3^* \\ h_4^* \end{matrix}$$

and the matrix B^* satisfying (20)

$$B^* = \begin{bmatrix} \frac{1}{2} & 0 & \frac{1}{2} & 0 \\ \frac{1}{2} & \frac{1}{2} & 0 & 0 \\ 0 & 1 & 0 & 0 \\ 0 & \frac{1}{2} & \frac{1}{2} & 0 \\ 0 & 0 & 0 & 1 \end{bmatrix}$$

Let us now try to solve (18) for $A^{M^*}(1|0)$, replacing all other matrices in that equation with the above ones. This yields $(B^* H^{M^*} = H^M)$

$$\begin{bmatrix} \frac{1}{2} & 0 & \frac{1}{2} & 0 \\ \frac{1}{2} & \frac{1}{2} & 0 & 0 \\ 0 & 1 & 0 & 0 \\ 0 & \frac{1}{2} & \frac{1}{2} & 0 \\ 0 & 0 & 0 & 1 \end{bmatrix} A^{M^*}(1|0) H^{M^*} = \begin{bmatrix} 0 & 0 & 0 & 0 & 0 \\ 0 & 0 & 0 & 0 & 0 \\ 0 & \frac{1}{4} & 0 & \frac{1}{4} & 0 \\ 0 & \frac{1}{4} & 0 & \frac{1}{4} & 0 \\ 0 & 0 & 0 & 0 & 0 \end{bmatrix} \begin{bmatrix} 1 & \frac{1}{2} & \frac{1}{2} & \frac{1}{2} \\ 1 & \frac{1}{2} & 0 & \frac{1}{2} \\ 1 & 0 & 0 & \frac{1}{2} \\ 1 & 0 & \frac{1}{2} & \frac{1}{2} \\ 1 & 0 & 0 & 1 \end{bmatrix}$$

The first, second, and fifth rows on the right-hand side are zero rows. As for the left-hand side, assuming that a nonnegative matrix $A^{M^*}(1|0)$ satisfying the above equation exists, it is seen that the first and third rows of $A^{M^*}(1|0)H^{M^*}$ are zero rows [contributing to formation of the first row on the right-hand side]; the first and second rows of $A^{M^*}(1|0)H^{M^*}$ must be zero rows [contributing to the formation of the second row on the right-hand side]; finally the fourth row of $A^{M^*}(1|0)H^{M^*}$ is a zero row [being identical to the fifth row on the right-hand side]. Thus all rows of $A^{M^*}(1|0)H^{M^*}$ must be zero rows, but this is impossible as there are nonzero rows on the right-hand side. The conclusion is that there is no machine M^* convering M with less than five states, although rank $M = 4$.

Example 8: Let M be a four state machine $[X = Y = \{0, 1\}]$,

$$A(0|0) = \begin{bmatrix} \frac{1}{4} & \frac{1}{4} & 0 & 0 \\ 0 & 0 & 0 & 0 \\ \frac{3}{8} & \frac{3}{8} & 0 & 0 \\ \frac{1}{4} & \frac{1}{4} & 0 & 0 \end{bmatrix}, \qquad A(1|0) = \begin{bmatrix} \frac{1}{4} & 0 & \frac{1}{4} & 0 \\ \frac{1}{2} & 0 & \frac{1}{2} & 0 \\ \frac{1}{8} & 0 & \frac{1}{8} & 0 \\ \frac{1}{4} & 0 & \frac{1}{4} & 0 \end{bmatrix}$$

$$A(0|1) = \begin{bmatrix} 0 & 0 & 0 & 0 \\ 0 & 0 & \frac{1}{4} & \frac{1}{4} \\ 0 & 0 & \frac{1}{4} & \frac{1}{4} \\ 0 & 0 & \frac{3}{8} & \frac{3}{8} \end{bmatrix}, \qquad A(1|1) = \begin{bmatrix} 0 & \frac{1}{2} & 0 & \frac{1}{2} \\ 0 & \frac{1}{4} & 0 & \frac{1}{4} \\ 0 & \frac{1}{4} & 0 & \frac{1}{4} \\ 0 & \frac{1}{8} & 0 & \frac{1}{8} \end{bmatrix}$$

and H^M matrix for this M is

$$H^M = \begin{bmatrix} 1 & \frac{1}{2} & 0 \\ 1 & 0 & \frac{1}{2} \\ 1 & \frac{3}{4} & \frac{1}{2} \\ 1 & \frac{1}{2} & \frac{3}{4} \end{bmatrix} \begin{matrix} h_1 \\ h_2 \\ h_3 \\ h_4 \end{matrix}$$

As rank $M = 3 = n - 1$, a covering machine M^* with fewer states must have the same rank and three states. The geometrical representation of this H^M is shown in Figure 10, and it is seen that the only possible choice for H^{M^*} is

$$H^{M^*} = \begin{bmatrix} 1 & \frac{1}{2} & 0 \\ 1 & 0 & \frac{1}{2} \\ 1 & 1 & 1 \end{bmatrix}$$

Using this H^{M^*}, two possible matrices B^* and B are found as

$$B^* = \begin{bmatrix} 1 & 0 & 0 \\ 0 & 1 & 0 \\ \frac{1}{2} & 0 & \frac{1}{2} \\ 0 & \frac{1}{2} & \frac{1}{2} \end{bmatrix}, \qquad B = \begin{bmatrix} 1 & 0 & 0 & 0 \\ 0 & 1 & 0 & 0 \\ 0 & -1 & 0 & 2 \end{bmatrix}$$

Using these matrices and (21) the machine M^* is found

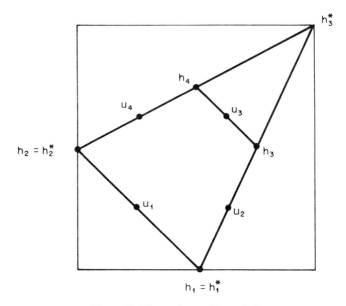

Figure 10. Illustration to Example 8.

$$A^{M^*}(0|0) = \begin{bmatrix} \frac{1}{4} & \frac{1}{4} & 0 \\ 0 & 0 & 0 \\ \frac{1}{2} & \frac{1}{2} & 0 \end{bmatrix}, \qquad A^{M^*}(1|0) = \begin{bmatrix} \frac{3}{8} & 0 & \frac{1}{8} \\ \frac{3}{4} & 0 & \frac{1}{4} \\ 0 & 0 & 0 \end{bmatrix}$$

$$A^{M^*}(0|1) = \begin{bmatrix} 0 & 0 & 0 \\ \frac{1}{8} & \frac{1}{8} & \frac{1}{4} \\ \frac{1}{4} & \frac{1}{4} & \frac{1}{2} \end{bmatrix}, \qquad A^{M^*}(1|1) = \begin{bmatrix} 0 & \frac{3}{4} & \frac{1}{4} \\ 0 & \frac{3}{8} & \frac{1}{8} \\ 0 & 0 & 0 \end{bmatrix}$$

By construction, $M^* \geq M$, and M^* has only three states.

EXERCISES

1. Let $M^* \geq M$ be machines with n^* and n states respectively, and such that $n^* < n$. Prove that rank $M \leq$ rank $M^* < n$, hence rank $M = n - 1$ implies rank $M =$ rank M^*.

2. Let $M^* \geq M$ be as in Exercise 1, let m^* and m be their respective ranks and B^* the matrix satisfying (17) for these machines. Prove that

   a. $m \leq m^* \leq m + n^* -$ rank $B^* \leq n^* < n$, hence if rank $B^* = n^*$, then $m^* = m$.

   b. $m \leq$ rank $B^* \leq m + n^* - m \leq n^*$.

Hint: Use Sylvester's inequalities and (17).

OPEN PROBLEMS

a. Answer the following decision problem, or prove that it is not decidable:

Given a machine M, does there exist a machine M^* with fewer states than M and such that $M^* \geq M$?

b. If the problem under (a) is decidable, then construct a finite algorithm for finding a machine $M^* \geq M$ with $|S^{M^*}| < |S^M|$, whenever such a machine M^* exists.

c. Construct an algorithm for finding all solutions to the following problem:

Given two convex polyhedra V_1 and V_2 such that V_1 covers V_2 [i.e., the vertices of V_2 are convex combinations of those of V_1], find a third polyhedron V_3, with a minimal *number of vertices*, which covers V_2 and is covered by V_1.

6. Minimization of States by Covering—Problem II

This section deals with the problem of finding a machine M^* covered by a given machine M and with fewer states.

Replacing M^* with M in (18), we have

$$BA^M(y|x)H^M = A^{M^*}(y|x)BH^M \tag{22}$$

Since M is given and so are H^M and $A^M(y|x)$, Problem II appears to be simpler in the sense that (22) can be used without any a priori assumption as to the rank of M^*. Thus one can assume any stochastic matrix B having fewer rows than columns and try to solve (22) in terms of $A^{M^*}(y|x)$ [for all pairs (y, x)] subject to the restriction that the matrices $A^{M^*}(y|x)$ be nonnegative.

If no solution exists for a given B, another is assumed and so on. The drawback here is that their number is infinite, and no means has been found to date for solving the problem [or deciding that no solution exists] on the basis of a finite number of checks.

Definition 6.1: If H^M is the matrix H associated with a machine M and A any nonnegative matrix of suitable dimension, then $h^M(A)$ is the set of all nonzero vectors of the form $h^M(A_i)$, A_i denoting the ith row of A [see Definition 3.3].

The following theorem is a geometrical interpretation of (22), enabling us to check whether or not a chosen matrix B provides a solution to our problem.

Theorem 6.1: Let M be a machine. There exists a machine $M^* \leq M$ with $n^* < n$ states if and only if there exists a stochastic $n^* \times n$ matrix B such that

$$\bigcup_{(y,x)} h^M(BA^M(y|x)) \subset \text{conv } h^M(B) \tag{23}$$

A machine M^* as above can be constructed effectively if a matrix B satisfying (23) is given,

Proof: Assume first that $M \geq M^*$ with $n^* < n$. Then (22) is satisfied by some $n^* \times n$ stochastic matrix. Let $\xi = (\xi_1, \ldots, \xi_n)$ be any nonzero row in $A^{M^*}(y|x)$ and $\zeta = (\zeta_1, \ldots, \zeta_n)$ the corresponding row of $BA^M(y|x)$ on the left-hand side of (22). All entries in the first column of H^M are 1 and, since B is a stochastic matrix, so are all entries in the first column of BH^M. Thus $\zeta H^M = \xi BH^M \Rightarrow \sum \zeta_i = \sum \xi_i \Rightarrow (\zeta/\sum \zeta_i) H^M = (\xi/\sum \xi_i) BH^M$.

Now $\xi/\sum \xi_i$ is a probabilistic vector, hence $(\xi/\sum \xi_i)BH^M$ is a convex combination of the rows of BH^M, or $(\xi/\sum \xi_i)BH^M \in \text{conv } h(B)$. On the other hand, $(\zeta/\sum \zeta_i) H = h(\zeta)$ by definition, so that $\cup_{(y,x)} h(BA^M(y|x)) \subseteq \text{conv } h(B)$.

Assume now that there exists an $n^* \times n$ stochastic matrix B satisfying (23); then any row vector in the left-hand side of (23) is a convex combination of the points in $h^M(B)$. Those vectors [on the left-hand side] are of the form $\alpha\zeta H^M$, where α is a normalizing constant and ζ is a row in a matrix $BA^M(y|x)$ for some pair (y, x). We thus have

$$\alpha\zeta H^M = \pi BH^M \qquad (24)$$

where π is a stochastic vector.

It is readily seen that (22) is satisfied if the matrices $A^{M^*}(y|x)$ are defined as follows:

a. If a row in $BA^M(y|x)$ is a zero row, then so is the corresponding row in $A^{M^*}(y|x)$.

b. Let ζ be a nonzero row in $BA^M(y|x)$, then the corresponding row in $A^{M^*}(y|x)$ is $(1/\alpha)\pi$, where π and α are as in (24) the theorem is thus proved.   ∎

Corollary 6.2: Let M be an n-state machine of rank m. Let $h_1^*, \ldots, h_{n^*}^*$ be a set of $n^* < n$ points in m-dimensional space, such that

$$\underset{(y,x)}{\cup} h^M(A^M(y|x)) \subset \text{conv}(h_1^*, \ldots, h_{n^*}^*) \subset \text{conv}(h_1, \ldots, h_n) \qquad (25)$$

then there exists an n^*-state machine $M^* \leq M$ and M^* can be effectively constructed if the points $h_1^*, \ldots, h_{n^*}^*$ are given.

Proof: Let B be the stochastic $n^* \times n$ matrix such that

$$BH^M = \begin{bmatrix} h_1^* \\ \vdots \\ h_{n^*}^* \end{bmatrix}$$

Since $\text{conv}(h_1, \ldots, h_{n^*}^*) \subset \text{conv}(h_1, \ldots, h_n)$, B can be found effectively. For any stochastic matrix B, it is true that

$$\underset{(y,x)}{\cup} h^M(BA^M(y|x)) \subset \text{conv}(\underset{(y,x)}{\cup} h^M(A^M(y|x)))$$

so that, for the above B we have

$$\bigcup_{(y,x)} h^M(BA^M(y|x)) \subset \operatorname{conv}(\bigcup_{(y,x)} h^M(A^M(y|x)))$$

$$\subset \operatorname{conv}(h_1^*, \ldots, h_{n^*}^*) = \operatorname{conv} h^M(B)$$

by the definition of B.

Equation (23) of Theorem 6.1 is thus verified for the above matrix B, and the corollary follows.

A particular case of the above corollary would be when the points $(h_1^*, \ldots, h_{n^*}^*)$ are a subset of the points $(h_1, \ldots, h_n)$. In this case B would be a degenerate stochastic matrix. We therefore also have the following:

Corollary 6.3: Let M be an n-state machine. If there exists a subset $(h_1^*, \ldots, h_{n^*}^*)$ of the set of points $(h_1, \ldots, h_n)$ such that

$$\bigcup_{(y,x)} h^M(A^M(y|x)) \subset \operatorname{conv}(h_1^*, \ldots, h_{n^*}^*) \tag{26}$$

then an n^*-state machine $M^* \leq M$ can be constructed effectively.

The above corollaries may help in solving our problem in some particular cases. On the other hand, the following remarks are in order:

1. The conditions specified in the corollaries are only sufficient conditions, and a solution to the covering problem may exist even if the conditions do not hold for a given machine (see Exercise 1 at the end of this section).

2. While the conditions of Corollary 6.3 are decidable (prove this fact), this is not known to be true for those of Corollary 6.2. In fact the latter involve the unsolved problem mentioned on p. 38.

Example 8 (continued)

We shall show, using a procedure based on Theorem 6.1, that there exists no machine $M^* \leq M$ with $n^* < 4$ states, where M is the machine in Example 8. This will show that the second covering problem is nontrivial in the sense that a solution is not always available.

We first arrange the set $\bigcup_{(y,x)} h^M(A^M(y|x))$ in tabular form (Table III) where $s_1, \ldots, s_4$ are the states of M, and $h_1, \ldots, h_4$ the rows of H^M; if a row corre-

Table III Distribution of the set $\bigcup_{(y,x)} h^M(A^M(y|x))$ according to states and matrices in $\{A^M(y|x)\}$

T	$h^M(A^M(0\|0))$	$h^M(A^M(1\|0))$	$h^M(A^M)(0\|1))$	$h^M(A^M(1\|1))$
s_1	$\frac{1}{2}(h_1 + h_2)$	$\frac{1}{2}(h_1 + h_3)$	0	$\frac{1}{2}(h_2 + h_4)$
s_2	0	$\frac{1}{2}(h_1 + h_3)$	$\frac{1}{2}(h_3 + h_4)$	$\frac{1}{2}(h_2 + h_4)$
s_3	$\frac{1}{2}(h_1 + h_2)$	$\frac{1}{2}(h_1 + h_3)$	$\frac{1}{2}(h_3 + h_4)$	$\frac{1}{2}(h_2 + h_4)$
s_4	$\frac{1}{2}(h_1 + h_2)$	$\frac{1}{2}(h_1 + h_3)$	$\frac{1}{2}(h_3 + h_4)$	$\frac{1}{2}(h_2 + h_4)$

sponding to s_i in some matrix $A^M(y|x)$ is a zero row, then the corresponding entry in the table is zero. Let B be any stochastic matrix with $m \leq 3$ rows. The table T', corresponding to the set $\cup_{(y,x)} h^M(BA^M(y|x))$, has only m rows. A nonzero entry in a column of T' will be a convex combination of the nonzero entries in the corresponding column of T. [This follows from the definitions.] Since all nonzero entries in a column of T are identical, any convex combination of them results in an entry having the same value as the combined entries. We shall consider two cases:

a. The matrix B [which has $m \leq 3$ rows] has nonzero entries in two, three, or all of its columns. The entries in the rows of T' are, in this case, convex combinations of the corresponding entries in at least two rows of T, hence, T' has nonzero entries in all its columns, which are identical to the nonzero entries in the corresponding columns of T. This implies that

$$|\underset{(y,x)}{\cup} h^M(BA^M(y|x))| = \text{number of different nonzero entries in } T'$$

$$= \text{number of different nonzero entries in } T$$

$$= |\underset{(y,x)}{\cup} h^M(A^M(y|x))|$$

On the other hand, since B has $m \leq 3$ rows, we have that the set $h^M(B)$ has at most three different points. It is seen in Figure 10, where the points in the set $\cup_{(y,x)} h^M(A^M(y|x))$ are denoted by $u_1, \ldots, u_4$, that (23) cannot be satisfied, since the set $u_1, \ldots, u_4$ cannot be covered by a convex closure of three points only, inside $\text{conv}(h_1, \ldots, h_n)$.

b. If the matrix B has nonzero entries in one column only, then the table T' has nonzero entries in at least three columns. In this case the set $\cup_{(y,x)} h^M(BA^M(y|x))$ contains three of the four points $u_1, \ldots, u_4$ at least. On the other hand, the set $\cup_{(y,x)} h^M(BA^M(y|x))$ contains only one point, since B has only one nonzero column, and (23) cannot be satisfied in this case either.

Example 9: Let M be the four-state machine $(X = Y = \{0, 1\})$

$$A(0|0) = \begin{bmatrix} \frac{1}{4} & \frac{1}{8} & \frac{1}{8} & 0 \\ \frac{3}{8} & \frac{3}{16} & \frac{3}{16} & 0 \\ \frac{1}{4} & \frac{1}{8} & \frac{1}{8} & 0 \\ 0 & 0 & 0 & 0 \end{bmatrix} \qquad A(1|0) = \begin{bmatrix} 0 & \frac{1}{4} & \frac{1}{4} & 0 \\ 0 & \frac{1}{8} & \frac{1}{8} & 0 \\ 0 & \frac{1}{4} & \frac{1}{4} & 0 \\ 0 & \frac{1}{2} & \frac{1}{2} & 0 \end{bmatrix}$$

$$A(0|1) = \begin{bmatrix} 0 & 0 & 0 & 0 \\ 0 & \frac{1}{8} & \frac{1}{8} & \frac{1}{4} \\ 0 & \frac{3}{16} & \frac{3}{16} & \frac{3}{8} \\ 0 & \frac{1}{8} & \frac{1}{8} & \frac{1}{4} \end{bmatrix} \qquad A(1|1) = \begin{bmatrix} \frac{1}{2} & 0 & 0 & \frac{1}{2} \\ \frac{1}{4} & 0 & 0 & \frac{1}{4} \\ \frac{1}{8} & 0 & 0 & \frac{1}{8} \\ \frac{1}{4} & 0 & 0 & \frac{1}{4} \end{bmatrix}$$

A matrix H^M for this machine is

$$H^M = \begin{bmatrix} 1 & \frac{1}{2} & 0 \\ 1 & \frac{3}{4} & \frac{1}{2} \\ 1 & \frac{1}{2} & \frac{3}{4} \\ 1 & 0 & \frac{1}{2} \end{bmatrix} \begin{matrix} h_1 \\ h_2 \\ h_3 \\ h_4 \end{matrix}$$

Figure 11 shows the sets $(h_1, \ldots, h_4)$ and $\cup_{(y,x)} h^M(A^M(y|x)) = (u_1, \ldots, u_4)$.

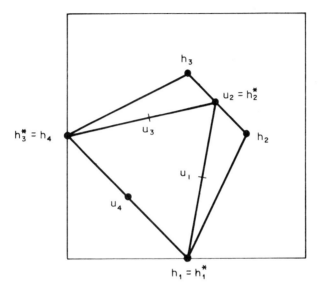

Figure 11. Illustration to Example 9.

The reader is advised to compute these points and verify that their position in the figure is correct. It is seen that the choice $h_1{}^* = h_1$, $h_2{}^* = u_2$, $h_3{}^* = h_4$ satisfies the condition of Corollary 6.2.

The resulting matrix B is

$$B = \begin{bmatrix} 1 & 0 & 0 & 0 \\ 0 & \frac{1}{2} & \frac{1}{2} & 0 \\ 0 & 0 & 0 & 1 \end{bmatrix}$$

and the resulting machine M^* is [The reader is advised to verify the results by actual computation.]

$$A^{M^*}(0|0) = \begin{bmatrix} \frac{1}{4} & \frac{1}{4} & 0 \\ \frac{5}{16} & \frac{5}{16} & 0 \\ 0 & 0 & 0 \end{bmatrix}, \qquad A^{M^*}(1|0) = \begin{bmatrix} 0 & \frac{1}{2} & 0 \\ 0 & \frac{3}{8} & 0 \\ 0 & 1 & 0 \end{bmatrix}$$

$$A^{M^*}(0|1) = \begin{bmatrix} 0 & 0 & 0 \\ 0 & \frac{5}{16} & \frac{5}{16} \\ 0 & \frac{1}{4} & \frac{1}{4} \end{bmatrix}, \qquad A^{M^*}(1|1) = \begin{bmatrix} \frac{1}{2} & 0 & \frac{1}{2} \\ \frac{3}{16} & 0 & \frac{3}{16} \\ \frac{1}{4} & 0 & \frac{1}{4} \end{bmatrix}$$

EXERCISES

1. Show that there exists a machine $M^* \leq M$ with $n^* = 4$, where M is the machine in Example 7. Hint: Use the matrix

$$B = \begin{bmatrix} 1 & 0 & 0 & 0 & 0 \\ 0 & 1 & 0 & 0 & 0 \\ 0 & 0 & 1 & 0 & 0 \\ 0 & 0 & 0 & 1 & 0 \end{bmatrix}$$

Note: Show that the machine M in Example 7 with the matrix B above, does not satisfy the condition of Corollary 6.2.

2. Is the configuration $M^* \leq M \leq M^+$ with $n^* < n > n^+$ possible? Hint: Solve covering Problem I for the machine in Example 9.

3. Let M be the (deterministic) four-state machine $[X = \{0, 1, 2\}, Y = \{0, 1\}]$

$$A(0|0) = \begin{bmatrix} 1 & 0 & 0 & 0 \\ 1 & 0 & 0 & 0 \\ 1 & 0 & 0 & 0 \\ 0 & 0 & 0 & 0 \end{bmatrix}, \quad A(0|1) = \begin{bmatrix} 1 & 0 & 0 & 0 \\ 1 & 0 & 0 & 0 \\ 0 & 0 & 0 & 0 \\ 0 & 0 & 0 & 0 \end{bmatrix}$$

$$A(1|0) = \begin{bmatrix} 0 & 0 & 0 & 0 \\ 0 & 0 & 0 & 0 \\ 0 & 0 & 0 & 0 \\ 1 & 0 & 0 & 0 \end{bmatrix}, \quad A(1|1) = \begin{bmatrix} 0 & 0 & 0 & 0 \\ 0 & 0 & 0 & 0 \\ 1 & 0 & 0 & 0 \\ 1 & 0 & 0 & 0 \end{bmatrix}$$

$$A(0|2) = \begin{bmatrix} 1 & 0 & 0 & 0 \\ 0 & 0 & 0 & 0 \\ 0 & 0 & 0 & 0 \\ 0 & 0 & 0 & 0 \end{bmatrix}, \quad A(1|2) = \begin{bmatrix} 0 & 0 & 0 & 0 \\ 1 & 0 & 0 & 0 \\ 1 & 0 & 0 & 0 \\ 1 & 0 & 0 & 0 \end{bmatrix}$$

a. Find an H^M for this machine, and show that it is a reduced-form (and minimal state form) machine.

b. Show that there exists an n^*-state machine $M^* \leq M$ with $n^* < n$ states [compare Exercise 2, Section 3].

4. Let M be a machine $[X = \{0, 1\}, Y = \{0, 1, 2\}]$

$$A(0|0) = \begin{bmatrix} 0 & \frac{1}{2} & 0 & 0 & 0 \\ 0 & \frac{1}{2} & 0 & 0 & 0 \\ 0 & 0 & 0 & 0 & 0 \\ 0 & 0 & 0 & 0 & 0 \\ 0 & 0 & 0 & 0 & 0 \end{bmatrix}, \quad A(1|0) = \begin{bmatrix} 0 & 0 & 0 & 0 & 0 \\ 0 & 0 & 0 & 0 & 0 \\ 0 & 0 & 0 & \frac{1}{2} & 0 \\ 0 & 0 & 0 & \frac{1}{2} & 0 \\ 0 & 0 & 0 & 0 & 0 \end{bmatrix}$$

$$A(2|0) = \begin{bmatrix} 0 & 0 & 0 & 0 & \frac{1}{2} \\ 0 & 0 & 0 & 0 & \frac{1}{2} \\ 0 & 0 & 0 & 0 & \frac{1}{2} \\ 0 & 0 & 0 & 0 & \frac{1}{2} \\ \frac{1}{2} & 0 & \frac{1}{2} & 0 & 0 \end{bmatrix}, \qquad A(0|1) = \begin{bmatrix} \frac{1}{2} & 0 & 0 & 0 & 0 \\ 0 & 0 & 0 & 0 & 0 \\ 0 & 0 & 0 & 0 & 0 \\ \frac{1}{2} & 0 & 0 & 0 & 0 \\ 0 & 0 & 0 & 0 & 0 \end{bmatrix}$$

$$A(1|1) = \begin{bmatrix} 0 & 0 & 0 & 0 & 0 \\ 0 & 0 & \frac{1}{2} & 0 & 0 \\ 0 & 0 & \frac{1}{2} & 0 & 0 \\ 0 & 0 & 0 & 0 & 0 \\ 0 & 0 & 0 & 0 & 0 \end{bmatrix}, \qquad A(2|1) = A(2|0)$$

a. Find a matrix H^M for this machine and show that it is minimal-state form, strongly connected, has equivalent strongly connected nonisomorphic machines, and its rank is smaller than its number of states.

b. Show that no machine M^* exists with less than five states and such that $M^* \geq M$ or $M^* \leq M$.

5. Consider the following.

Definition: A sequential pseudostochastic machine is a quadruple $M = (S, X, Y, \{A(y|x)\})$ where all elements in the quadruple are as in Definition 1.1, but the entries in the matrices $A(y|x)$ may be negative, positive, or zero.

a. Prove the following

Theorem: Let M be an n-state machine of rank $m < n$. There exists a pseudostochastic sequential machine M^* with m states such that M and M^* are equivalent, (equivalence being defined in the usual way).

b. Find the four-state pseudomachine equivalent to the one defined in Exercise 4 above.

OPEN PROBLEM

a. Answer the following decision problem, or prove that it is not decidable:

Given a machine M, does there exist a machine M^* with fewer states than M and such that $M^* \leq M$?

b. If the problem under (a) is decidable, then construct a finite algorithm for finding a machine $M^* \leq M$ with $|S^{M^*}| < |S^M|$ whenever such a machine M^* exists.

7. Minimization of States by Covering—Problem III

In this section, Problem III [i.e., that of finding an initiated machine (M^*, π^*) having a minimal number of states and equivalent to a given initiated machine (M, π)] is reduced to the two problems considered in the previous sections.

Let (M, π) be a given initiated machine as in Exercise 5, Section 1, we can construct a matrix $G^{(M,\pi)}$ whose rows are of the form $\bar{\pi}(v, u)$ for some pairs (v, u) and linearly independent, and any vector of the form $\bar{\pi}(v, u)$ is a linear combination of them. We shall now prove the following:

Theorem 7.1: Given an initiated machine (M, π) and a machine M^*, there exists a stochastic vector π^* such that $(M, \pi) = (M^*, \pi^*)$ if and only if there exists a stochastic matrix B^* such that

$$B^*[K^{M^*}] = G^{(M,\pi)}[K^M] \tag{27}$$

Proof: Assume first that (27) is satisfied, and let π^* be the first row in B^*. Then, since the first row of $G^{(M,\pi)}$ is π, we have that the first entry in a column of the form $G^{(M,\pi)}\eta^M(v|u)$ on the right-hand side equals $p_\pi^M(v|u)$. The corresponding value on the left-hand side is the first entry in the column $B^*\eta^{M^*}(v|u)$ which equals $p_{\pi^*}^{M^*}(v|u)$, so that $(M, \pi) = (M^*, \pi^*)$. Assume now that there exists a vector π^* such that $(M^*, \pi^*) = (M, \pi)$ then $\pi^*[K^{M^*}] = \pi[K^M]$. This implies that $\pi^* A^{M^*}(v|u)[K^{M^*}] = \pi A^M(v|u)[K^M]$, since the columns of the matrix $A^M(v|u)[K^M]$ are a subset of the columns of K^M and those of $A^{M^*}(v|u)[K^{M^*}]$ are the corresponding columns in $[K^{M^*}]$. But any row vector π in $G^{(M,\pi)}$ is of the form $a\pi A^M(v|u)$, where a is a normalizing constant, hence for any such vector there exists a corresponding vector $a\pi^* A^{M^*}(v|u) = \bar{\pi}^*$ such that $\bar{\pi}^*[K^{M^*}] = \bar{\pi}[K^M]$. The matrix B^* whose rows are the vectors $\bar{\pi}^*$ corresponding to $\bar{\pi}$ of $G^{(M,\pi)}$ satisfies (27), and the theorem is proved. ∎

Theorem 7.1 above reduces the third problem to one of finding a machine M^* having fewer states than the given initiated machine (M, π), and such that the relation

$$B^*[K^{M^*}] = [K^{(M,\pi)}] \tag{28}$$

holds for some stochastic matrix B^*, where $[K^{(M,\pi)}]$ denotes the matrix $G^{(M,\pi)}[K^M]$. For tackling this problem, a relation similar to (18), which is equivalent to (28) can be derived.

Let $H^{(M,\pi)}$ be a matrix having the following properties:

1. The columns of $H^{(M,\pi)}$ are columns of $[K^{(M,\pi)}]$.

2. The columns of $H^{(M,\pi)}$ are linearly independent, and any column in $[K^{(M,\pi)}]$ is a linear combination of them.

3. The columns of $H^{(M,\pi)}$ are the first columns of $[K^{(M,\pi)}]$ satisfying 1 and 2 above.

Clearly, the columns of $H^{(M,\pi)}$ can be chosen from those of the form $\eta^{(M,\pi)}(v|u) = G^{(M,\pi)}\eta(v|u)$ with $l(v, u) \leq n - 1$. To prove this, we note that any column in $[K^{(M,\pi)}]$ has the form

$$G^{(M,\pi)}\eta^M(v|u) = G^{(M,\pi)} \sum a_i \eta_i^M = \sum a_i G^{(M,\pi)}\eta_i^M$$

where η_i^M are the columns of H^M and a_i constants. It follows that the matrix $H^{(M,\pi)}$ can be effectively constructed.

Denote by $H^{(M,\pi)}(y|x)$ the matrix such that its ith column is $\eta^{(M,\pi)}(yu|xv)$ if the ith column of $H^{(M,\pi)}$ is $\eta^{(M,\pi)}(u|v)$; likewise, $K^{(M,\pi)}(y|x)$ and $[K^M(y|x)]$. We seek a matrix $\Delta(y|x)$ such that

$$\Delta(y|x)[K^{(M,\pi)}] = [K^{(M,\pi)}(y|x)] \tag{29}$$

But Eq. (29) is satisfied by any matrix $\Delta(y|x)$ satisfying also

$$G^{(M,\pi)}A(y|x)H^M = \Delta(y|x)G^{(M,\pi)}H^M \tag{30}$$

for if $\Delta(y|x)$ satisfies (30), then

$$[K^{(M,\pi)}(y|x)] = G^{(M,\pi)}[K^M(y|x)] = G^{(M,\pi)}A(y|x)[K^M]$$
$$= \Delta(y|x)G^{(M,\pi)}[K^M] = \Delta(y|x)[K^{(M,\pi)}]$$

by definition, and bearing in mind that the columns of $[K^M]$ are linear combinations of the columns of H^M.

Now Eq. (30) has at least one solution [there may be more], being satisfied by any matrix $\Delta(y|x)$ satisfying also

$$G^{(M,\pi)}A(y|x) = \Delta(y|x)G^{(M,\pi)} \tag{31}$$

Eq. (31) has a (unique) solution, for the rows of the matrix on its left-hand side $G^{(M,\pi)}A(y|x)$ are by the definition of $G^{(M,\pi)}$ linear combinations of the rows of the latter, and these are linearly independent.

Using the above definitions and a method similar to that used in the proof of Theorem 3.1, one can prove the following:

Theorem 7.2: Given an initiated machine (M, π) with n states, there exists an initiated machine (M^*, π^*) with $n^* < n$ states and such that $(M, \pi) = (M^*, \pi^*)$ if and only if there exists an n^*-state machine M^* and an $n^* \times n^*$ stochastic matrix $(n^* < n)$ B^* satisfying the relation

$$B^* A^{M^*}(y|x)H^{M^*} = \Delta^{(M,\pi)}(y|x)B^* H^{M^*} \tag{32}$$

The proof of this theorem is left to the reader. Theorem 7.2 reduces the third problem to the first covering problem [with $H^{(M,\pi)}$ replacing H^M], so that all considerations in Section 5 are valid here. Since no general procedure is available for solving the first problem, the above theorem, together with Section 5, yields solutions to the third problem only in particular cases.

We shall therefore also consider some additional approaches, based on Section 6.

Theorem 7.3: Let $M \geq {}^{\backprime}M^*$ be two machines with $B[K^M] = [K^{M^*}]$, and π a distribution for M such that $h^M(\pi) \in \text{conv } h^M(B)$. Then, there exists a distribution π^* for M^* such that $(M, \pi) = (M^*, \pi^*)$.

Proof: Since $h^M(\pi) \in \text{conv } h^M(B)$, there exists π^* such that $\pi H^M = \pi^* B H^M$. Hence π and $\pi^* B$ are equivalent vectors for the machine M, so that $\pi \eta^M(v|u) = \pi^* B \eta^M(v|u)$ for all pairs (v, u). It follows that

$$p_\pi^M(v|u) = \pi \eta^M(v|u) = \pi^* B \eta^M(v|u) = \pi^* \eta^{M^*}(v|u) = p_{\pi^*}^{M^*}(v|u)$$

for all pairs (v, u), and the theorem follows. ∎

Corollary 7.4: Let (M, π) be an initiated machine with n states. There exists an initiated machine (M^*, π^*) with $n^* < n$ states and such that $(M, \pi) = (M^*, \pi^*)$ if either condition 1, 2, or 3, as well as condition 4, holds:

1. There exists a stochastic $n^* \times n$ matrix B such that

$$\bigcup_{(y, x)} h^M(BA^M(y|x)) \subset \text{conv } h^M(B)$$

2. There exists a set of n^* points $h_1^*, \ldots, h_{n^*}^*$ in m-dimensional space ($m = \text{rank } H^M$) such that

$$\bigcup_{(y, x)} h^M(A^M(y|x)) \subset \text{conv}(h_1^*, \ldots, h_{n^*}^*) \subset \text{conv}(h_1, \ldots, h_n)$$

3. There exists a subset $h_1^*, \ldots, h_{n^*}^*$ of the set of points $h_1, \ldots, h_n$ such that

$$\bigcup_{(y, x)} h^M(A^M(y|x)) \subset \text{conv }(h_1^*, \ldots, h_{n^*}^*)$$

4. Let B be as under condition (1) if that condition is satisfied, or otherwise a matrix defined by

$$BH^M = \begin{bmatrix} h_1^* \\ \vdots \\ h_{n^*}^* \end{bmatrix}$$

if either condition (2) or (3) is satisfied. Then $h^M(\pi) \in \text{conv } h^M(B)$.

Proof: By Theorems 7.3 and 7.1 and Corollaries 6.2 and 6.3.

Example 10: Let (M, π) be an initiated machine $[X = Y = \{0, 1\}], \pi = (\frac{1}{8}\ 0\ \frac{7}{8}\ 0)$

$$A(0|0) = \begin{bmatrix} 0 & 0 & 0 & 0 \\ \frac{1}{2} & \frac{1}{2} & 0 & 0 \\ \frac{1}{2} & \frac{1}{2} & 0 & 0 \\ 0 & 0 & 0 & 0 \end{bmatrix}, \qquad A(1|0) = \begin{bmatrix} \frac{1}{4} & \frac{1}{4} & \frac{1}{2} & 0 \\ 0 & 0 & 0 & 0 \\ 0 & 0 & 0 & 0 \\ \frac{1}{4} & \frac{1}{4} & \frac{1}{2} & 0 \end{bmatrix}$$

$$A(0|1) = \begin{bmatrix} 0 & 0 & 0 & 0 \\ 0 & 0 & 0 & 0 \\ \frac{1}{4} & 0 & \frac{1}{2} & \frac{1}{4} \\ \frac{1}{4} & 0 & \frac{1}{2} & \frac{1}{4} \end{bmatrix}, \qquad A(1|1) = \begin{bmatrix} \frac{1}{2} & 0 & 0 & \frac{1}{2} \\ \frac{1}{2} & 0 & 0 & \frac{1}{2} \\ 0 & 0 & 0 & 0 \\ 0 & 0 & 0 & 0 \end{bmatrix}$$

A matrix H^M for this machine is

$$H^M = \begin{bmatrix} 1 & 0 & 0 \\ 1 & 1 & 0 \\ 1 & 1 & 1 \\ 1 & 0 & 1 \end{bmatrix}$$

The points in $\cup_{(y,x)} h(A(y|x))$ are $(\frac{1}{2}, 0)$, $(\frac{3}{4}, \frac{1}{2})$, $(\frac{1}{2}, \frac{3}{4})$, and $(0, \frac{1}{2})$ (first coordinate omited), $h(\pi) = (\frac{7}{8}, \frac{7}{8})$.

The second and fourth conditions of Corollary 7.6 are satisfied if we choose $h_1^* = (\frac{1}{2}, 0)$, $h_2^* = (1, 1)$ and $h_3^* = (0, \frac{1}{2})$. [The reader is advised to draw an illustrating sketch.]

The resulting matrix B is

$$B = \begin{bmatrix} \frac{1}{2} & \frac{1}{2} & 0 & 0 \\ 0 & 0 & 1 & 0 \\ \frac{1}{2} & 0 & 0 & \frac{1}{2} \end{bmatrix}$$

and the required initiated machine is found to be: $\pi^* = (\frac{1}{12}\ \frac{5}{6}\ \frac{1}{12})$,

$$A^{M^*}(0|0) = \begin{bmatrix} \frac{1}{2} & 0 & 0 \\ 1 & 0 & 0 \\ 0 & 0 & 0 \end{bmatrix}, \qquad A^{M^*}(1|0) = \begin{bmatrix} \frac{1}{4} & \frac{1}{4} & 0 \\ 0 & 0 & 0 \\ \frac{1}{2} & \frac{1}{2} & 0 \end{bmatrix}$$

$$A^{M^*}(0|1) = \begin{bmatrix} 0 & 0 & 0 \\ 0 & \frac{1}{2} & \frac{1}{2} \\ 0 & \frac{1}{4} & \frac{1}{4} \end{bmatrix}, \qquad A^{M^*}(1|1) = \begin{bmatrix} 0 & 0 & 1 \\ 0 & 0 & 0 \\ 0 & 0 & \frac{1}{2} \end{bmatrix}$$

The reader is advised to verify the results by actual computation.

EXERCISES

1.a. Find the matrices $G^{(M,\pi)}$, $H^{(M,\pi)}$ and $\Delta^{(M,\pi)}(y|x)$ for all pairs (y, x) where (M, π) is as in Example 10.

1.b. Find a three-state initiated machine (M^+, π^+) equivalent to (M, π) in Example 10 and different from (M^*, π^*) there, using a procedure based on Theorem 7.2.

1.c. Show that the third condition of Corollary 7.4 does not hold for Example 10.

2. Prove that if $(M^*, \pi^*) \sim (M, \pi)$, then the number of states of M^* is not smaller than rank $H^{(M,\pi)}$.

3. Give a proof of Theorem 7.2.

4. Consider the following machine $[X = Y = \{0, 1\}]; \pi = (\frac{1}{4}\ \frac{1}{4}\ \frac{1}{4}\ \frac{1}{4})$,

$$A(0|0) = \begin{bmatrix} 0 & 0 & 0 & 0 \\ 0 & \frac{1}{2} & 0 & \frac{1}{2} \\ \frac{1}{2} & 0 & \frac{1}{2} & 0 \\ 0 & 0 & 0 & 0 \end{bmatrix}, \qquad M(0|1) = \begin{bmatrix} 0 & 0 & 0 & 0 \\ 0 & 0 & 0 & 0 \\ 0 & \frac{1}{4} & \frac{1}{2} & \frac{1}{4} \\ 0 & \frac{1}{4} & \frac{1}{2} & \frac{1}{4} \end{bmatrix}$$

$$M(1|0) = \begin{bmatrix} 0 & \frac{1}{2} & 0 & \frac{1}{2} \\ 0 & 0 & 0 & 0 \\ 0 & 0 & 0 & 0 \\ \frac{1}{2} & 0 & \frac{1}{2} & 0 \end{bmatrix}, \qquad M(1|1) = \begin{bmatrix} 0 & \frac{1}{4} & \frac{1}{2} & \frac{1}{4} \\ 0 & \frac{1}{4} & \frac{1}{2} & \frac{1}{4} \\ 0 & 0 & 0 & 0 \\ 0 & 0 & 0 & 0 \end{bmatrix}$$

Show that the third and fourth conditions of Corollary 7.4 apply to this machine, and find a two-state initiated machine (M^*, π^*) equivalent to (M, π).

5. Same as 4, but $\pi = (\frac{1}{4}, 0, \frac{1}{4}, \frac{1}{2})$ and (M^*, π^*) has three states. Is further reduction of states possible in this case?

6. Consider the initiated machine (M, π) whose defining matrices are

$$A(0|0) = \begin{bmatrix} 1 & 0 & 0 & 0 \\ 1 & 0 & 0 & 0 \\ 0 & 0 & 0 & 0 \\ 0 & 0 & 0 & 0 \end{bmatrix}, \qquad A(1|0) = \begin{bmatrix} 0 & 0 & 0 & 0 \\ 0 & 0 & 0 & 0 \\ 0 & 1 & 0 & 0 \\ 0 & 1 & 0 & 0 \end{bmatrix}$$

$$A(0|1) = \begin{bmatrix} 0 & 0 & 1 & 0 \\ 0 & 0 & 0 & 0 \\ 0 & 0 & 1 & 0 \\ 0 & 0 & 0 & 0 \end{bmatrix}, \qquad A(1|1) = \begin{bmatrix} 0 & 0 & 0 & 0 \\ 0 & 0 & 0 & 1 \\ 0 & 0 & 0 & 0 \\ 0 & 0 & 0 & 1 \end{bmatrix}$$

and $\pi = (1\ 0\ 0\ 0)$.

Show that rank $H^{(M,\pi)} = 3$, but there exists no initiated machine (M', π') equivalent to (M, π) with fewer than four states.

OPEN PROBLEMS

a. Answer the following decision problem, or prove that it is not decidable:

Given an initiated machine (M, π), does there exist an initiated machine (M^*, π^*) with fewer states than (M, π) and such that $(M, \pi) \sim (M^*, \pi^*)$?

b. If the problem under (a) is decidable, then construct a finite algorithm for finding an initiated machine $(M^*, \pi^*) \sim (M, \pi)$ with $|S^{M^*}| < |S^M|$ whenever such an initiated machine (M^*, π^*) exists.

8. Bibliographical Notes

The basis for the material in Chapter I.B is to be found in Carlyle (1961, 1965, 1967). Many additions, clarifications and simplifications are due to Bacon (1966), Even (1965), Ott (1966a, 1966b) and Paz (1967a, c). Linear-algebra methods, on which the material in some subsections is based, were used previously by Blackwell and Koopmans (1957) and Gilbert (1959) for Markov chains, and by Youval (Perles *et al.*, 1963) for finite automata. Some of the exercises are based on the work of Even (1965), Bukharaev (1968) and Ott (1966a, b). Additional reference: Dantig (1963).

C. INPUT–OUTPUT RELATIONS

1. Definitions and Basic Properties

Definition 1.1: *A probabilistic input–output* relation is a function $p(v|u)$ whose domain is the set of all pairs (v, u) of input–output sequences (of equal length) over respective finite input and output alphabets X and Y, whose range is the interval $[0, 1]$, and subject to the restrictions:

1. $p(\lambda|\lambda) = 1$
2. $\sum_y p(vy|ux) = p(v|u)$ for all $x \in X$, the summation is over all $y \in Y$

Throughout this section the term "relation" refers to a probabilistic input–output relation unless otherwise specified.

Remark: Note that (1) and (2) in Definition 1.1 imply that

3. $\sum_y p(y|x) = 1$ for all $x \in X$

Definition 1.2: An initial segment of length n of a relation p (denoted by $[p]_n$) is the part of p which corresponds to input–output pairs of length not exceeding n. Any relation p with $[p]_n$ as its initial segment is a completion of $[p]_n$.

Notation: $\mathscr{P}(X, Y)$ denotes the class of all relations over the input and output alphabets X and Y.

Definition 1.3: The left-hand derivate of a relation $p \in \mathscr{P}(X, Y)$ with respect to the pair (u', v') [denoted by $p_{[u',v']}$] is the function

$$p_{[u',v']}(v|u) = \begin{cases} \dfrac{p(v'v|u'u)}{p(v'|u')}, & \text{if } p(v'|u') > 0 \\ \text{the zero function}, & \text{otherwise} \end{cases}$$

Theorem 1.1: The class $\mathscr{P}(X, Y)$ has the following properties:

1. If p is a finite convex combination of function in $\mathscr{P}(X, Y)$ such that $p = \sum_{i=1}^{n} \lambda_i p_i$, $\sum_{i=1}^{n} \lambda_i = 1$, $\lambda_i \geq 0$, $i = 1, 2, \ldots, n$, and (x, y) a pair such that $\sum \lambda_i p_i(y|x) \neq 0$, then $p_{[x,y]} = \sum \mu_i p_{i[x,y]}$ where $\mu_i = \lambda_i p_i(y|x)/\sum \lambda_i p_i(y|x)$, so that $\sum \mu_i = 1$ and $\mu_i \geq 0$ for $i = 1, 2, \ldots, n$.

2. If (x^1, y^1) and (x^2, y^2) are two pairs and $p \in \mathscr{P}(X, Y)$ is a relation such that $p(y^1|x^1) \neq 0$ and $p(y^1 y^2|x^1 x^2) \neq 0$, then $(p_{[x^1,y^1]})_{[x^2,y^2]} = p_{[x^1 x^2, y^1 y^2]}$.

3. The class $\mathscr{P}(X, Y)$ is closed under convex combinations of its elements.

4. If $p \in \mathscr{P}(X, Y)$, and (x, y) is a pair such that $p(y|x) \neq 0$, then $p_{[x,y]} \in \mathscr{P}(X, Y)$.

Proof: (1): Under the given conditions, we have that

$$p_{[x,y]}(v|u) = \frac{\sum \lambda_i p_i(yv|xu)}{\sum \lambda_i p_i(y|x)} = \sum \mu_i \frac{p_i(yv|xu)}{p_i(y|x)} = \sum \mu_i p_{i[x,y]}$$

2. It follows from the definition that

$$(p_{[x^1,y^1]})_{[x^2,y^2]}(v|u) = \frac{p_{[x^1,y^1]}(y^2 v|x^2 u)}{p_{[x^1,y^1]}(y^2|x^2)}$$

$$= \frac{p(y^1 y^2 v|x^1 x^2 u)/p(y^1|x^1)}{p(y^1 y^2|x^1 x^2)/p(y^1|x^1)}$$

$$= \frac{p(y^1 y^2 v|x^1 x^2 u)}{p(y^1 y^2|x^1 x^2)} = p_{[x^1 x^2, y^1 y^2]}(v|u)$$

Proof of properties (3) and (4) is left to the reader.

Relations induced by stochastic sequential machines are characterized by

Theorem 1.2: Let $p_1, \ldots, p_n$ be a finite set of functions in $\mathscr{P}(X, Y)$. There exists an n-state machine M such that $p_i = p_{s_i}{}^M$ if and only if for every i, and for every pair (x, y) such that $p_i(y|x) \neq 0$, the function $p_{i[x,y]}$ is a convex combination of the functions p_i.

Proof: The "only if" part is straightfoward and its proof is left to the reader. Assume now that the conditions of the theorem hold. If there exists a machine M such that $p_i = p_{s_i}{}^M$, then $p_i(y|x) = p_{s_i}{}^M(y|x) = \bar{s}_i A^M(y|x)\eta$ and

$$p_{i[x,y]}(v|u) = \frac{p_{s_i}{}^M(yv|xu)}{p_{s_i}{}^M(y|x)} = \frac{\bar{s}_i A^M(y|x)\eta^M(v|u)}{\bar{s}_i A^M(y|x)\eta}$$

$$= \frac{\sum_j a_{ij}(y|x) \cdot p_{s_j}{}^M(v|u)}{\sum_j a_{ij}(y|x)} = \frac{\sum_j a_{ij}(y|x)p_j(v|u)}{\sum_j a_{ij}(y|x)}$$

Thus the machine M must satisfy the equations

$$\sum_j a_{ij}^M(y|x) = p_i(y|x) \tag{33}$$

$$p_{i[x,y]}(v|u) = \frac{\sum_j a_{ij}(y|x)p_j(v|u)}{\sum_j a_{ij}(y|x)} \tag{34}$$

But we also have by the conditions of the theorem that

$$p_{i[x,y]}(v|u) = \sum_{j=1}^n \lambda_{ij}p_j(v|u) \tag{35}$$

Combining the three equations, we have

$$\sum_j \lambda_{ij}p_j(v|u) = \sum_j a_{ij}(y|x)p_j(v|u)/p_i(y|x) \tag{36}$$

or

$$p_i(y|x)\sum_j \lambda_{ij}p_j(v|u) = \sum_j a_{ij}(y|x)p_j(v|u) \tag{37}$$

A possible but not necessarily unique solution to (37) is

$$a_{ij}(y|x) = p_i(y|x)\lambda_{ij} \tag{38}$$

Let M be the machine whose defining matrices are given by (38). We now prove by induction that for this machine, $p_{s_i}{}^M = p_i$ as required:

1. It follows by construction that $p_{s_i}{}^M(y|x) = p_i(y|x)$, $i = 1, 2, \ldots, n$.

2. Assume that $p_{s_i}^M(v|u) = p_i(v|u)$ for all i and all pairs (v, u) with $l(u, v) \leq k$, and let (u, v) be any such pair; then

$$p_{s_i}^M(yv|xu) = \sum_j a_{ij}(y|x)p_{s_j}^M(v|u) = \sum_j a_{ij}(y|x)p_j(v|u)$$

and the latter by (37) and (35), equals

$$p_i(y|x)p_{i[x,y]}(v|u) = p_i(y|x)\frac{p_i(yv|xu)}{p_i(y|x)} = p_i(yv|xu)$$

where $l(xu, yv) = k + 1$. Thus $p_{s_i}^M = p_i$, and the proof is complete.

Corollary 1.3: Let $p \in \mathscr{P}(X, Y)$ be a relation. If the set of all nonzero derivates of p is finite and contains n different relations, then there exists an n-state machine M such that $p = p_{s_i}^M$.

Proof: Let $p, p_{[u^1,v^1]}, \ldots, p_{[u^{n-1},v^{n-1}]}$ be the set of all nonzero different derivates (including p itself which is the derivate with respect to the pair (λ, λ)) of p. Then, any other nonzero derivate of p is included in this set, hence the conditions of Theorem 1.2 hold. ∎

Remark: In Section B3, Exercise 9, we introduced the definition of an observer/state-calculable machine. These machines have at most one nonzero element in each row of their matrices. Now it is readily shown that if M is such a machine and $p_{s_i}^M$ is considered as a relation in $\mathscr{P}(X, Y)$ for the appropriate X and Y, then this relation has only a finite number of nonzero different derivates. To prove this claim, we note first that

$$p_{\bar{s}_i[x,y]}^M(v|u) = \frac{p_{\bar{s}_i}^M(yv|xu)}{p_{\bar{s}_i}^M(y|x)} = p_{(\bar{s}_i(x,y))}^M(v|u)$$

by (10) (Section A,1), and therefore the number of different nonzero relations of the form $p_{\bar{s}_i[u,v]}^M$ equals that of nonzero vectors of the form $\bar{s}_i(u, v)$. If M is an observer/state-calculable machine, then by the definitions any vector of the form $\bar{s}_i(v|u) = \bar{s}_i A^M(v|u)$ has at most one nonzero entry. Thus any nonzero vector of the form $\overline{\bar{s}_i(u, v)}$, which is $\bar{s}_i(v|u)$ multiplied by a normalizing constant, is a stochastic degenerate vector and there exists only a finite number such vectors. Furthermore, a closer look at Corollary 1.3 above and its proof shows that the machine M in that corollary can be chosen to be observer/state-calculable, for the states of M are identified with the derivates $p, p_{[u^1,v^1]}, \ldots, p_{[u^{n-1},v^{n-1}]}$ and the transition between these states is deterministic. We thus have the following characterizing:

Theorem 1.4: Let $p \in \mathscr{P}(X, Y)$ be a relation. If and only if the set of nonzero derivates of p is finite, then there exists an observer/state-calculable machine M such that $p = p_{\bar{s}_1}^M$.

Another corollary to Theorem 1.2 is:

Corollary 1.5: Let $p \in \mathscr{P}(X, Y)$ be a relation. There exists a machine M and an initial vector π for M such that $p = p_\pi^M$ if and only if there exists a finite set of functions $p_1, \ldots, p_n$ in $\mathscr{P}(X, Y)$ such that $p \in \mathrm{conv}(p_1, \ldots, p_n)$, and for every i, and every pair (x, y) such that $p_i(y|x) \neq 0$, also $p_{i[x,y]} \in \mathrm{conv}(p_1, \ldots, p_n)$.

The proof if straightforward and is included in the exercises below.

EXERCISES

1. Prove properties (3) and (4) in Theorem 1.1.

2. Prove Corollary 1.5.

3. Prove the "only if" part of Theorem 1.2.

2. Compound Sequence Matrix

Definition 2.1: Let $(u_1, v_1), (u_2, v_2), \ldots, (u_n, v_n), (u_1', v_1'), (u_2', v_2'), \ldots, (u_n', v_n')$ be a set of $2n$ pairs of sequences and $p \in \mathscr{P}(X, Y)$ a relation. The matrix

$$P = [p(v_i v_j'|u_i u_j')]$$

is then called a *compound sequence matrix*, and its determinant a *compound sequence determinant*.

Definition 2.2: The rank $r(p)$ of a relation p is the maximum among the ranks of all compound sequence matrices which can be formed from p, or $+\infty$ if no such maximum exists.

Corollary 2.1: If $p \in \mathscr{P}(X, Y)$ is a relation such that $p = p_\pi^M$ for some machine M and some distribution π, then $r(p) = \text{rank}\,(M, \pi)$.

Proof: Let $_P(M, \pi)$ be a compound sequence matrix for p_π^M. Any entry in $_P(M, \pi)$ has the form $p_\pi^M(v_i v_j'|u_i u_j') = \pi(v_i|u_i)\eta(v_j'|u_j')$ so that the matrix $_P(M, \pi)$ can be written in the form $_P(M, \pi) = G'H$, where G' is the matrix whose rows are the vectors $\pi(v_i|u_i)$ and H the matrix whose columns are the vectors $\eta(v_j'|u_j')$. Let G be the matrix whose rows are the vectors $\bar{\pi}(u_i|v_i)v$ corresponding to $\pi(v_i|u_i)$ in G'. Since the rows in G' differ from those in G by a multiplicative constant, obviously rank $G' = $ rank G, so that rank $p^{(M,\pi)} = $ rank (GH). It follows that

$$\text{rank}\,p = \text{rank}\,p_\pi^M = \max\,{}_P(M, \pi)\,\text{rank}\,{}_P(M, \pi) = \max_{G,H}\,\text{rank}\,(GH)$$

$$= \text{rank}\,(G^{(M,\pi)}H^M) = \text{rank}\,H^{(M,\pi)} = \text{rank}\,(M, \pi)$$

(See Section B.7 for the definitions). ∎

Lemma 2.2: Let p be a relation of finite rank n, and P a compound sequence matrix for p of rank n. Another compound sequence matrix P', also of rank n, can be found such that the pairs (u_1, v_1) and (u_1', v_1') in the sequence defining P' satisfy

$$(\lambda, \lambda) = (u_1, v_1) = (u_1', v_1') \tag{39}$$

Proof: Let $(u_1, v_1), \ldots, (u_n, v_n), (u_1', v_1'), \ldots, (u_n', v_n')$ be the sequence defining P, and $(u, v), (u', v')$ any two input–output pairs. The following determinant then equals zero

$$\begin{vmatrix} & & p(v_1 v'|u_1 u') \\ P & & \vdots \\ & & p(v_n v'|u_n u') \\ p(vv_1'|uu_1') \ldots p(vv_n'|uu_n') & & p(vv'|uu') \end{vmatrix} = 0 \tag{40}$$

since P is a regular compound sequence matrix of maximal possible rank n. Substituting $u = v = u' = v' = \lambda$ in (40) and expanding about the last column, we obtain ($p(\lambda|\lambda) = 1$) that $|P| + \sum \alpha_i |P_i| = 0$ where the α_i are numerical constants and P_i is derived from P by replacing the ith row with $p(v_1'|u_1') \cdots p(v_n'|u_n')$. Thus one of the P_i is a regular matrix and P in (40) can be replaced with P_i. Using the same argument for the new determinant (40), expanding this time about the last row, we find that there exists a regular matrix $(P_i)^j$ derived from P_i by replacing its jth column with

$$p(v_1|u_1)$$
$$\vdots$$
$$p(v_n|u_n)$$

We thus have a regular matrix $(P_i)^j$ derived from P by replacing (u_i, v_i) and (u_j', v_j') with the pair (λ, λ). Appropriate reordering of rows and columns yields a compound sequence matrix with the required properties. ∎

EXERCISES

1. Prove that any relation p of rank 1 has the property
$$p(vv'|uu') = p(v|u)p(v'|u').$$
2. Prove that the set of relations of finite rank $\leq n$ is closed under convex combinations of its elements.

3. Prove that the set of relations of finite rank $\leq n$ is closed under left derivation.

4. Show that Theorem 1.2 can be refined as follows.

Theorem: Let $p_1, \ldots, p_n$ be a finite set of relations in $\mathscr{P}(X, Y)$. There exists an n-state machine M such that $p_i = p_{s_i}^M$ if and only if for every i rank $p_i \leq n$, and for every i and every pair (x, y) such that $p_i(y|x) \neq 0$, the segment $[p_{i[x,y]}]_{2n-1}$ is a convex combination of the segments $[P_i]_{2n-1}$.

5. Refine Corollary 1.5 using Exercise 4 above.

3. Representability of Relations by Machines

Expanding the determinant in (40) about its last column, we obtain

$$p(vv'|uu') = \sum_{i=1}^{n} a_i(v|u)p(v_i v_i'|u_i u') \qquad (41)$$

where the $a_i(v|u)$ are functions of the entries of matrix P and of the values $p(vv_j'|uu_j')$. Replacement of v, v', u, u' with $v_i v, v' v_j', u_i u, u' u_j'$ respectively in (41) yields

$$p(v_i vv' v_j'|u_i uu' u_j') = \sum_{k=1}^{n} a_k(v_i v|u_i u)p(v_k v' v_j'|u_k u' u_j') \qquad (42)$$

or, in matrix form,

$$P(vv'|uu') = A(v|u)P(v'|u') \qquad (43)$$

where

$$P(v|u) = [P(v_i vv_j'|u_i uu_j')] \quad \text{and} \quad A(v|u) = [a_j(v_i v|u_i u)] \qquad (44)$$

$(P(\lambda|\lambda) = P$ and $A(\lambda|\lambda) = I = $ the identity matrix.) In particular, we have

$$P(v|u) = A(v|u)P \qquad (45)$$

and

$$P(y|x) = A(y|x)P \quad \text{or} \quad A(y|x) = P(y|x)P^{-1} \qquad (46)$$

Thus if P (which is regular) and $P(y|x)$ are given, $A(y|x)$ is obtainable from (46). Substitution of (45) on both sides of (43), with the common (regular) matrix P cancelled out, yields

$$A(vv'|uu') = A(v|u)(v'|u') \qquad (47)$$

The above formulas lead to the following

Theorem 3.1: Given a compound sequence regular matrix P of maximal rank n for a relation p. A pseudostochastic sequential machine M with n states (see Exercise 5, Section B,6) and an initial distribution π can be found effectively, such that $p = p_\pi{}^M$.

Proof: Using Lemma 2.2, construct another compound sequence matrix P' satisfying (39). Compute the matrices $A(y|x)$, using (46). [It is assumed that the matrices $P'(y|x)$ are available.] Let Q be any regular matrix of order n such that $Q\eta$ equals the first column of P and the first row of Q is nonnegative [which implies that it is a probabilistic vector, as the 1, 1 entry in P is 1]. Define

$$A^M(y|x) = Q^{-1}A(y|x)Q \qquad (48)$$

and $\pi = $ the first row of Q.

Let M be the pseudomachine whose matrices are $A^M(y|x)$ with initial distribution π. Then by (47) we have that

$$A^M(v|u) = Q^{-1}A(v|u)Q$$

hence, $P_\pi{}^M(v|u) = \pi A^M(v|u)\eta = \pi Q^{-1}A(v|u)Q\eta = \bar{s}_1 A(v|u)P_1$, with P_1 denoting the first column of $P[\pi Q^{-1} = \bar{s}_1 = (1\ 0\ \cdots\ 0)$, as π is the first row of Q by construction]. But $A(v|u)P = P(v|u)$ by (45), hence $A(v|u)P_1$ is the first column of $P(v|u)$, so that $P_\pi{}^M(v|u) = \bar{s}_1 A(v|u)P_1 = \bar{s}_1 P_1(v|u) = $ the 1, 1 entry in $P(v|u) = p(v|u)$ as required. ∎

Theorem 3.2: Let p be a relation of finite rank $\leq n$ such that the values $p(v|u)$ are recursively computable. [In other words, $p(v|u)$ with $l(v, u) = k$ is obtainable effectively from the values $p(v'|u')$ with $l(v', u') \leq k - 1$.] Then a regular compound sequence matrix of order n can be formed from a segment $[p]_{2n-2}$ of p.

Proof: If p is a relation of finite rank $\leq n$ then by definition there exists a regular compound sequence matrix of maximal rank $\leq n$ for P. By Theorem 3.1 there exists a pseudomachine M with $\leq n$ states and a distribution π such that $p = p_\pi{}^M$. Recalling the construction of matrices H^M [Section B,1] and $G^{(M,\pi)}$ [Exercise 5, Section B.1] we see that it is not affected by the fact that M is a pseudomachine. Thus H^M and $G^{(M,\pi)}$ exist for a pseudomachine M such that the values $p_{\bar{s}_i}{}^M(v|u)$ in the former and $p_\pi{}^M(v|u)$ in the latter correspond to pairs of length $\leq n - 1$, and rank $G^{(M,\pi)}H^M = $ rank $H^{(M,\pi)} \leq n$. But the entries in $H^{(M,\pi)}$ are of the form

$$\bar{\pi}(v, u)\eta^M(v'|u') = a\pi(v|u)\eta^M(v'|u') = ap_\pi{}^M(vv'|uu')$$

where a is a normalizing constant depending only on the row $\bar{\pi}(v, u)$ of $G^{(M,\pi)}$ and $l(vv'|uu') \leq 2n - 2$. The required matrix P can thus be derived from the above $H^{(M,\pi)}$, which is regular for pseudomachines [prove this fact!], by division of its rows by an appropriate constant. ∎

Corollary 3.3: Let p be a relation satisfying the conditions of Theorem 3.2. A pseudostochastic machine M with $\leq n$ states and an initial distribution can then be found effectively such that $p = p_\pi{}^M$.

Proof: By Theorem 3.1 and 3.2. ∎

Corollary 3.4: Let p be a relation satisfying the conditions of Theorem 3.2. Then its segment $[p]_{2n-1}$ uniquely determines the whole relation.

Proof: The initiated pseudomachine (M, π) such that $p = p_\pi{}^M$ is determined by $[p]_{2n-1}$, as the required compound sequence determinant P is obtainable from $[p]_{2n-2}$ and the matrices $A(y|x)$ [see (46)] depend on P and $P(y|x)$, which can be derived from $[p]_{2n-1}$ by (44).

Corollary 3.5: Let p be a relation of finite rank n satisfying the conditions of Theorem 3.2. If there exists a true initiated machine (M, π) with n states and $p = p_\pi{}^M$, then there exist also a compound sequence determinant P of rank n for p and a nonsingular matrix Q such that $A^M(y|x) = Q^{-1}A(y|x)Q$ where $A(y|x)$ is defined as in (46).

Proof: Under the assumptions, P may be chosen as the matrix $P^{(M,\pi)}$ defined in the proof of Corollary 2.1. Thus $P = P^{(M,\pi)} = G^{(M,\pi)}H^M$. [See definitions in the proof of Corollary 2.1] and

$$A(y|x)G'^{(M,\pi)}H^M = A(y|x)P = P(y|x) = G'^{(M,\pi)}A^M(y|x)H^M$$

As M has n states and $p_\pi{}^M$ is of rank n, $H^{(M,\pi)}$ has n independent columns and n rows. Thus $H^{(M,\pi)}$ together with $G'^{(M,\pi)}$ and H^M are regular matrices, implying that $(G'^{(M,\pi)})^{-1}A(y|x)G'^{(M,\pi)} = A^M(y|x)$ as required. ∎

Example 11: Consider the relation (assumed to be of rank 2) in the following table (X is a single-symbol alphabet and is omitted):

v	λ	0	1	00	01	10	11	000	001	010	011	$\cdots$
$p(v)$	1	$\frac{3}{10}$	$\frac{7}{10}$	$\frac{1}{4}$	$\frac{1}{20}$	$\frac{7}{20}$	$\frac{7}{20}$	$\frac{3}{40}$	$\frac{7}{40}$	$\frac{1}{40}$	$\frac{1}{40}$	$\cdots$

Setting $u_1 = \lambda, u_2 = 0, u_1' = \lambda, u_2' = 1$, we have

$$P = \begin{bmatrix} 1 & \frac{7}{10} \\ \frac{3}{10} & \frac{1}{20} \end{bmatrix}$$

which is a regular matrix of rank 2. Proceeding as in Theorem 3.1 we have

$$P(0) = \begin{bmatrix} \frac{3}{10} & \frac{1}{20} \\ \frac{1}{4} & \frac{7}{40} \end{bmatrix}, \qquad P(1) = \begin{bmatrix} \frac{7}{10} & \frac{7}{20} \\ \frac{1}{20} & \frac{1}{40} \end{bmatrix}, \qquad P^{-1} = \begin{bmatrix} -\frac{5}{16} & -\frac{35}{8} \\ \frac{15}{8} & \frac{25}{4} \end{bmatrix}$$

$$A(0) = P(0)P^{-1} = \begin{bmatrix} 0 & 1 \\ \frac{1}{4} & 0 \end{bmatrix}, \qquad A(1) = P(1)P^{-1} = \begin{bmatrix} \frac{7}{16} & \frac{7}{8} \\ \frac{1}{32} & \frac{1}{16} \end{bmatrix}$$

There are many possible alternatives for matrix Q. One such choice is

$$Q = \begin{bmatrix} \frac{4}{5} & \frac{1}{5} \\ \frac{4}{10} & -\frac{4}{10} \end{bmatrix}$$

so that

$$Q^{-1} = \begin{bmatrix} \frac{5}{8} & \frac{5}{4} \\ \frac{5}{2} & -5 \end{bmatrix}$$

and finally

$$A^M(0) = Q^{-1}A(0)Q = \begin{bmatrix} \frac{1}{2} & 0 \\ 0 & -\frac{1}{2} \end{bmatrix}$$

$$A^M(1) = Q^{-1}A(1)Q = \begin{bmatrix} \frac{1}{2} & 0 \\ \frac{3}{2} & 0 \end{bmatrix}$$

$\pi = (\frac{4}{5}, \frac{1}{5})$ and $(M, \pi) = P$. Verification is left to the reader.

Let p be a relation. If there exists an initiated (pseudo-) machine (M, π) such that $p = p_\pi{}^M$, then (M, π) is said to represent p and p to be representable by a (pseudo-) ISSM.

We are now able to sum up the situation as to the representability of relations.

a. The following theorem is readily proved for the general case:

Theorem 3.6: A given relation p is representable by a pseudo-ISSM if and only if p is of finite rank.

The "if" part is meaningless unless it is specified how the relation is "given." It is therefore assumed that it is given such that the values $p(v|u)$ are recursively computable [as in Theorem 3.2].

b. If a relation is given as above and known to be of finite rank, then it is also known to be representable. Still, so long as no bound is set on that rank, the latter cannot be computed, nor can a representation be found for it [see Exercise 5 at the end of this section].

c. If a relation is given and a bound set on its rank, then using Corollary 3.3, a representation can be effectively found for it, but the result is, in general, an initiated pseudomachine (with number of states equal to the rank of the relation).

d. Given a relation p which is known to be of finite rank $\leq n$, no effective answer is known as to whether p is representable by a *true* ISSM. This last problem can be further subdivided as follows:

Given a relation p of rank n, is p representable by a true ISSM (M, π) such that rank $M = n =$ the number of states of M?

(d-1). If it is, formulate an effective procedure for constructing the representing machine.

(d-2). If case (d-1) does not apply, then is p representable by a *true* ISSM (M, π) such that rank $M = n$ but the number of states of M exceeds n? If it is, then formulate an effective procedure for constructing (M, π).

(d-3). If neither (d-1) nor (d-2) apply, then is p representable by a *true* ISSM (M, π) such that rank $M > n$? [Note that rank $(M, \pi) =$ rank p may not equal rank M.] If it is, then formulate an effective procedure for constructing (M, π).

It is readily seen from examples that case (d-1) is not empty. It can also be shown that case (d-2) is not empty either [see Exercise 8 at the end of this section]. The author is not aware of any example proving that (d-3) is feasible, but there is no reason why it should not be.

EXERCISES

1. Prove that any relation of rank 1 is representable by a true ISSM.

2. Discuss the implications of Exercises 2–5 in Section 2 with regard to the decision whether a given relation is representable by a true ISSM.

3. Consider the relation given in the following table [X is a single-symbol alphabet and is omitted.] Assume that the relation is of rank 2 and find a *true* representation for it.

v	λ	0	1	00	01	10	11	000	001	010	011	$\cdots$
$p(v)$	1	$\frac{3}{10}$	$\frac{7}{10}$	$\frac{1}{4}$	$\frac{1}{20}$	$\frac{7}{20}$	$\frac{7}{20}$	$\frac{5}{24}$	$\frac{1}{24}$	$\frac{1}{40}$	$\frac{1}{40}$	$\cdots$

Compare with Example 11.

4. Consider the following initiated pseudomachine (M, π) [$X = \{0\}$ and is omitted. $Y = \{0, 1\}$]

$$A^M(0) = \begin{bmatrix} \frac{1}{2} & 0 & 0 \\ 0 & -\frac{1}{3} & 0 \\ 0 & 0 & -\frac{1}{4} \end{bmatrix}, \qquad A^M(1) = \begin{bmatrix} \frac{1}{2} & 0 & 0 \\ \frac{4}{3} & 0 & 0 \\ \frac{5}{4} & 0 & 0 \end{bmatrix}$$

$\pi = \left(\frac{4}{5} \ \frac{1}{10} \ \frac{1}{10}\right)$

a. Show that rank $(M, \pi) = 3$.

b. Show that $0 \le p_\pi^M(v) \le 1$ for all $v \in Y^*$

c. Show that there exists a three state true initiated machine (M^*, π^*) such that $p_\pi^M = p_{\pi^*}^{M^*}$.

5.a. Show that for every relation p of rank n there exists another relation p' such that $p \neq p'$ but $[p]_{2n-1} = [p']_{2n-1}$.

5.b. What can be said about rank p' apart from the problem of deciding representability?

6. Prove: A relation p is representable by a pseudo-ISSM if and only if p is of finite rank.

7. Find a relation p of rank n, representable by a true n-state ISSM (n chosen at convenience).

8. Consider the following ISSM: $X = \{0, 1\}$; $Y = \{0, 1\}$; $S = \{1, 2, 3, 4\}$; $\pi = $ (1 0 0 0), with the transitions from state to state deterministic as follows

Present state	Input	Output	Next state
1, 2	0	0	2
3, 4	0	1	3
1, 3	1	0	1
2, 4	1	1	4

Prove that the above ISSM represents a relation of rank 3, but no true ISSM with less than four states can represent it.

9. Let p be a relation known to be of finite rank. Let $r(k)$ denote the maximal rank of all compound sequence matrices $P(k)$ for p with $P(k) = [p(v_i v_j' | u_i u_j')]$ where $l(v_i, u_i), l(v_j', u_j') \leq k$.

Prove: If $r(k) = r(k + 1) = r(k + j) = m$, then either rank $p = m$ or rank $p \geq m + 2j$

10. Give the most efficient algorithm possible for finding rank $p \leq n$ for a given relation p.

OPEN PROBLEMS

1. Given a recursively computable relation p, formulate a decision procedure for ascertaining whether p is of finite rank, or prove that the problem is not decidable.

2. Given a pseudo-ISSM (M, π), does there exist a true ISSM (M^*, π^*) such that $(M^*, \pi^*) = (M, \pi)$, rank $M^* = $ rank M, and the number of states of M equals that of M^*?

Formulate a decision procedure for this problem, or prove that it is not decidable. If a decision procedure exists, give an algorithm for constructing (M^*, π^*) whenever possible

3. Same as 2, except the number of states of M^* is not required to equal that of M.

4. Same as 3, except that it is not required that rank M = rank M^*.

5. Formulate a decision procedure for the following problem, or prove that it is not decidable: Given any pseudo ISSM (M, π) are all the values $p_\pi^M(v|u)$ nonnegative?

4. Bibliographical Notes

Input–output relations and sequential functions were studied, in the deterministic case by Elgot and Mezei (1965), Gill (1966), Gray and Harrison (1966), Raney (1958), Tal (1966), and others. Derivates were introduced by Brzozowski (1964) for the deterministic case. The first subsection here is based on the work of Arbib (1967) with additions from Carlyle (1967), and the second and third subsections on the work of Carlyle (1963a, b, 1965, 1969). The above references also served as a source for some of the exercises. Additional references: Blackwell and Koopmans (1957), Booth (1965, 1966, 1967), Dharmadhikari (1963a, b, 1965, 1967), Fox (1959), Gilbert (1959) Page (1966). Recently, a connection between the theory of categories and that of input-output probabilistic relations was established by Heller (1965, 1967) and Depeyrot (1968). See also Depeyrot (1969a, b).

Chapter II
Markov
Chains

INTRODUCTION

This chapter is devoted to the theory of nonhomogeneous Markov chains and related topics. Nonhomogeneous Markov chains and systems are studied from a mathematical point of view, with regard to asymptotic behavior, compositon (direct sum and product), and decomposition. The last part of this chapter investigates "word functions" induced by Markov chains and valued Markov systems. These functions are studied with regard to characterization, equivalence, and representability by an underlying Markov chain or system. The reader is refered to the Preliminary Section in this book for an introduction and for the basic definitions used (see also the bibliographical remarks at the end of the chapter).

A. NONHOMOGENEOUS MARKOV CHAINS AND SYSTEMS

1. Functionals over Stochastic Matrices

The matrices to be considered in this subsection are countably infinite unless otherwise specified.

Definition 1.1: Given a stochastic matrix $P = [p_{ij}]$ and an arbitrary vector $\pi = (\pi_i)$ we define

$$d(P) = \sup_{j} \sup_{i_1, i_2} |p_{i_1 j} - p_{i_2 j}|, \quad d(\pi) = \sup_{i_1, i_2} |\pi_{i_1} - \pi_{i_2}|$$

$$\delta(P) = \sup_{i_1, i_2} \sup_{\{n'\}} \sum_{j \in \{n'\}} (p_{i_1 j} - p_{i_2 j})$$

where $\{n'\}$ denotes a subsequence of the sequence of natural numbers (to be denoted by $\{n\}$). If P is a finite matrix, then "sup" is to be replaced by "max" and "inf" by "min."

Notation: If a is a real number then $a^+ = \max(a, 0)$ and $a^- = \min(a, 0)$.

Proposition 1.1: $\delta(P) = \sup_{i_1, i_2} \sum (p_{i_1 j} - p_{i_2 j})^+$
The proof is left as an exercise.

Proposition 1.2: $0 \leq d(P) \leq \delta(P) \leq 1$.

Proof: It is a trivial consequence of the definition that $0 \leq d(P)$. For any fixed j, i_1, and i_2 it is clear that

$$(p_{i_1 j} - p_{i_2 j})^+ \leq \sup_{\{n'\}} \sum_{k \in \{n'\}} (p_{i_1 k} - p_{i_2 k}) = \sum (p_{i_1 k} - p_{i_2 k})^+$$

But $\sup_{i_1, i_2} |p_{i_1 j} - p_{i_2 j}| = \sup_{i_1, i_2}(p_{i_1 j} - p_{i_2 j})^+$ since the indexes i_1 and i_2 are interchangeable so that

$$\sup_{i_1, i_2} |p_{i_1 j} - p_{i_2 j}| = \sup_{i_1, i_2} (p_{i_1 j} - p_{i_2 j})^+ \leq \sup_{i_1, i_2} \sup_{\{n'\}} \sum_{k \in \{n'\}} (p_{i_1 k} - p_{i_2 j})$$

for any fixed j and therefore $d(P) = \sup_j \sup_{i_1, i_2} |p_{i_1 j} - p_{i_2 j}| \leq \delta(P)$. Finally, for fixed i_1 and i_2 we have that

$$\sum (p_{i_1 j} - p_{i_2 j})^+ \leq \sum p_{i_1 j} - \sum_{j \in \{n'\}} p_{i_2 j} \leq 1$$

and using Proposition 1.1 we get that $\delta(P) \leq 1$. $\blacksquare$

Proposition 1.3: If $P = [p_{ij}]$ and $Q = [q_{ij}]$ are stochastic matrices then $\delta(PQ) \leq \delta(P)\, \delta(Q)$.

Proof: Fix i_1 and i_2. We show first that

$$\sum_k (p_{i_1 k} - p_{i_2 k})^+ + \sum_k (p_{i_1 k} - p_{i_2 k})^- = \sum_k (p_{i_1 k} - p_{i_2 k}) = \sum_k p_{i_1 k} - p_{i_2 k} = 1 - 1 = 0$$

and, therefore

$$\sum_k (p_{i_1 k} - p_{i_2 k})^+ = -\sum_k (p_{i_1 k} - p_{i_2 k})^- \tag{1}$$

Denoting by $\sum'$ summation over a subset of the set of natural numbers we have

$$\sum_j (\sum (p_{i_1k} - p_{i_2k})q_{kj})^+ = \sum_j{}' \sum_k (p_{i_1k} - p_{i_2k})q_{kj} = \sum_k (p_{i_1k} - p_{i_2k}) \sum_j{}' q_{kj}$$

$$\leq \sum_k (p_{i_1k} - p_{i_2k})^+ \sup_k \sum_j{}' q_{kj}$$

$$+ \sum_k (p_{i_1k} - p_{i_2k})^- \inf_k \sum_j{}' q_{kj}$$

$$= \sum_k (p_{i_1k} - p_{i_2k})^+ (\sup_k \sum_j{}' q_{kj} - \inf_k \sum_j{}' q_{kj})$$

where the indices involved in the summation $\sum'$ may depend on i_1 and i_2. But

$$\sup_k \sum_j{}' q_{kj} - \inf_k \sum_j{}' q_{kj} = \sup_{k_1, k_2} \sum_j{}' (q_{k_1j} - q_{k_2j})$$

$$\leq \sup_{k_1, k_2} \sum_j (q_{k_1j} - q_{k_2j})^+ = \delta(Q)$$

which is independent on i_1 and i_2.

Thus, $\sum_j (\sum (p_{i_1k} - p_{i_2k})q_{kj})^+ \leq \sum_k (p_{i_1k} - p_{i_2k})^+ \delta(Q)$ so that

$$\delta(PQ) = \sup_{i_2, i_2} [\sum_j (\sum (p_{i_1k} - p_{i_2k})q_{kj})^+] \leq \sup_{i_1, i_2} [\sum (p_{i_1k} - p_{i_2k})^+ \delta(Q)]$$

$$\leq \delta(Q) \sup_{i_1, i_2} \sum_k (p_{i_1k} - p_{i_2k})^+ = \delta(P)\delta(Q) \ \blacksquare$$

Definition 1.2: If $\xi = (\xi_i)$ is an arbitrary vector and P an arbitrary matrix, then $|\xi| = \sup_i |\xi_i|$, $|P| = \sup_{i,j} |p_{ij}|$; $||\xi|| = \sum |\xi_i|$ provided that $\sum |\xi_i| < \infty$ and $||\xi|| = \infty$ otherwise; $||P|| = \sup_i \sum_j |p_{ij}|$ provided that $\sum_j |p_{ij}| < \infty$ for all i, and $||P|| = \infty$ otherwise.

Proposition 1.4: Let $P = (p_{ij})$ be a stochastic matrix and let ξ be a nonzero vector of the same dimension as P such that $||\xi|| < \infty$ and $\sum \xi_i = 0$ $[\xi = (\xi_i)]$ then $||\xi P|| \leq ||\xi|| \delta(P)$.

Proof: Define the vectors $\zeta^1 = (\zeta_i^1)$ and $\zeta^2 = (\zeta_i^2)$ as

$$\zeta_i^1 = 2 \frac{\xi_i^+}{||\xi||} \quad \text{and} \quad \zeta_i^2 = 2 \frac{|\xi_i^-|}{||\xi||}$$

Then using an argument similar to the one used in proving formula (1) we have that both ζ^1 and ζ^2 are stochastic vectors and $\zeta^1 - \zeta^2 = 2(\xi/||\xi||)$.

Let Q be a matrix such that its first row is ζ^1 all the other rows being equal to ζ^2. Then

$$2\delta(QP) = 2 \sum_j (\sum_k (\zeta_k^1 - \zeta_k^2)p_{kj})^+ = \sum_j |\sum_k (\zeta_k^1 - \zeta_k^2)p_{kj}|$$

again using the formula (1).

By the definition of ζ^1 and ζ^2 we have that

$$\sum_j |\sum_k (\zeta_k^1 - \zeta_k^2)p_{kj}| = 2\sum_j |\sum_k \frac{\xi_k}{||\xi||}p_{kj}|$$

$$= \frac{2}{||\xi||} \sum_j |\sum_k \xi_k p_{kj}| = 2 \frac{||\xi P||}{||\xi||}$$

Thus, $\|\xi P\|/\|\xi\| = \delta(QP) \leq \delta(Q)\,\delta(P) \leq \delta(P)$ by Propositions 1.2 and 1.3, so that $\|\xi P\| \leq \|\xi\|\delta(P)$. ∎

Corollary 1.5: If P is a matrix such that all its rows have the properties of the vector ξ in Proposition 1.4 and Q is a stochastic matrix then

$$\|PQ\| \leq \|P\|\,\delta(Q)$$

Corollary 1.6: If P and Q are stochastic matrices, then $\|PQ - Q\| \leq 2\delta(Q)$. In particular if π is a stochastic vector and ρ is row of Q, then $\|\pi Q - \rho\| \leq 2\delta(Q)$.

Proof: $\|PQ - Q\| = \|(P - I)Q\| \leq \|P - I\|\delta(Q) \leq (\|P\| + \|I\|)\delta(Q) = 2\delta(Q)$. [See Exercise 8 at the end of this section.] ∎

Definition 1.3: Given a stochasic matrix $P = [p_{ij}]$, $\gamma(P)$ is defined as

$$\gamma(P) = \inf_{i_1 i_2} \sum_{j=1}^{\infty} \min(p_{i_1 j},\, p_{i_2 j})$$

Proposition 1.7: Let P be a stochastic matrix, then $\delta(P) = 1 - \gamma(P)$.

Proof: Denote

$$\gamma_{i_1 i_2}(P) = \sum \min(p_{i_1 j},\, p_{i_2 j}) \qquad \text{and} \qquad \delta_{i_1 i_2}(P) = \sum_j (p_{i_1 j} - p_{i_2 j})^+$$

then

$$\delta_{i_1 i_2}(P) = \sum_j (p_{i_1 j} - p_{i_2 j})^+ = \sum_j (p_{i_1 j} - \min(p_{i_1 j},\, p_{i_2 j}))$$

$$= 1 - \sum_j \min(p_{i_1 j},\, p_{i_2 j}) = 1 - \gamma_{i_1 i_2}(P)$$

Therefore, $\delta(P) \geq \delta_{i_1 i_2}(P) = 1 - \gamma_{i_1 i_2}(P)$, which implies that $\delta(P) \geq 1 - \gamma(P)$. Similarly, $\delta_{i_1 i_2}(P) = 1 - \gamma_{i_1 i_2}(P) \leq 1 - \gamma(P)$ which implies that $\delta(P) \leq 1 - \gamma(P)$. Combining the two inequalities we have that $\delta(P) = 1 - \gamma(P)$. ∎

Proposition 1.8: If P and Q are stochastic matrices and η a column vector such that $|\eta_i| \leq 1$ for all i, then $d(PQ) \leq \delta(P)d(Q)$ and $d(P\eta) \leq \delta(P)d(\eta)$.

Proof: It suffices to prove the second inequality. Let i_1 and i_2 be two arbitrary rows in P. Since $\sum_j |p_{i_1 j} - p_{i_2 j}| \leq 2$, we can find for any given ϵ a number k_0 such that

$$\sum_{j=k_0+1}^{\infty} |p_{i_1 j} - p_{i_2 j}| < \epsilon$$

Let $\eta_{j_0} = \min_{j < k_0} \eta_j$ and assume that $\sum p_{i_1 j}\eta_j \geq \sum p_{i_2 j}\eta_j$; then

$$0 \leq \sum_j p_{i_1 j}\eta_j - \sum_j p_{i_2 j}\eta_j = |\sum_j p_{i_1 j}\eta_j - \sum_j p_{i_2 j}\eta_j|$$

and replacing $p_{i_1 j_0}$ by $1 - \sum_{j \neq j_0} p_{i_1 j}$ and $p_{i_2 j_0}$ by $1 - \sum_{j \neq j_0} p_{i_2 j}$ we get

$$\sum_j p_{i_1 j} \eta_j - \sum p_{i_2 j} \eta_j = \sum_{j \neq j_0} p_{i_1 j} (\eta_j - \eta_{j_0}) - \sum_{j \neq j_0} p_{i_2 j} (\eta_j - \eta_{j_0})$$

$$= \sum_{j \neq j_0} (p_{i_1 j} - p_{i_2 j})(\eta_j - \eta_{j_0})$$

$$\leq \sum_{j=1}^{k_0} (p_{i_1 j} - p_{i_2 j})(\eta_j - \eta_{j_0}) + 2\epsilon$$

By the definition of η_{j_0} all the terms of the form $\eta_j - \eta_{j_0}$ are nonnegative in the above sum so that by omitting the terms such that $p_{i_1 j} \leq p_{i_2 j}$ the sum is increased. Also $(\eta_j - \eta_{j_0}) \leq d(\eta)$ with the result that

$$|\sum_j p_{i_1 j} \eta_j - \sum_j p_{i_2 j} \eta_j| \leq \sum_j (p_{i_1 j} - p_{i_2 j})^+ d(\eta) + 2\epsilon \leq \delta(P)d(\eta) + 2\epsilon$$

Since $\epsilon > 0$ is arbitrarily small and i_1, i_2 are arbitrary, the proposition follows. ∎

Proposition 1.9: If P and Q are stochastic matrices and η is a vector as in Proposition 1.8, then $|P\eta - \eta| \leq d(\eta)$ and $|PQ - Q| \leq d(Q)$.

Proof: The same method used in the proof of the previous proposition can be used here beginning with the inequality $0 \leq \sum_j p_{i_1 j} \eta_j - \sum \epsilon_{i_1 j} \eta_j$ where ϵ_{ij} is equal to 0 except for a unique, but arbitrary, entry which is equal to 1, and continuing the same way as in the previous proof. The details are left to the reader. ∎

Example: Let P be the matrix

$$\begin{pmatrix} 0 & \frac{1}{3} & \frac{2}{3} \\ \frac{1}{4} & \frac{1}{2} & \frac{1}{4} \\ \frac{1}{2} & 0 & \frac{1}{2} \end{pmatrix}$$

then $\|P\| = 1$ [this is true for any stochastic matrix]; $|P| = \frac{2}{3}$; $d(P) =$ the maximal distance between two elements in the same column $= \frac{1}{2} [= |p_{11} - p_{13}|]$, $\delta(P) = \frac{1}{2} [= \sum_{i=1}^{3} (p_{1j} - p_{3j})^+]$ and $\gamma(P) = \frac{1}{2} (= \sum_{i=1}^{3} \min(p_{1i}, p_{3i}))$. The inequalities proved in this section are easily verified.

EXERCISES

1. Prove Proposition 1.1.

2. Prove Proposition 1.9.

3. Illustrate by examples all the inequalities proved in this section.

4. If P is a finite stochastic matrix of order n, then

   a. $d(P) \geq 1/n \, \delta(P)$.
   b. It is possible that $d(P) < 1$ and $\delta(P) = 1$.
   c. $d(P) = 0$ if and only if $\delta(P) = 0$.
If P is an infinite stochastic matrix, then

d. For any ϵ, there is P such that $d(P) < \epsilon$ but $\delta(P) = 1$.

e. $d(P) = 0$ if and only if $\delta(P) = 0$.

5. Prove: If $\gamma(P) \neq 0$ for a stochastic matrix P, then $\gamma(P)$ is not smaller than the minimal nonzero entry in P and is not smaller than the sum of the minimal elements in the columns of P.

6. Prove that every stochastic matrix P can be expressed in the form $P = E + Q$ where E is a stochastic constant matrix and $||Q|| \leq 2\delta(P)$

7. Prove: If P is a constant stochastic matrix, then $\delta(P) = d(P) = 0$ $[\gamma(P) = 1]$; if P is a degenerate nonconstant stochastic matrix, then $\delta(P) = d(P) = 1$ $[\gamma(P) = 0]$.

8. Prove that the functionals "$|| \ ||$" and "$| \ |$" have the following properties: For any matrices P, Q and real number α it is true that $||P|| \geq 0$, $||P + Q|| \leq ||P|| + ||Q||$, $||P|| = 0$ if and only if $P = 0$, $||\alpha P|| = |\alpha| \ ||P||$ [defining $0 \cdot \infty = \infty$], and similarly for "$| \ |$".

9. Let P be a Markov matrix representing a given Markov process. Let t_{ij} be the probability that the process will transite from both states i and j to some common consequent state in the first step. Prove that $t_{ij} > 0$, for any two states i and j, if and only if $\gamma(P) > 0$.

10. Prove that for arbitrary matrices A and B,

$$||AB|| \leq ||A|| \ ||B||$$

11. Let $A_1, \ldots, A_n$ and $\bar{A}_1, \ldots, \bar{A}_n$ be two sets of n matrices such that $||A_i - \bar{A}_i|| < \epsilon$, for $i = 1, 2, \ldots$, then $||\prod_{i=1}^{n} A_i - \prod_{i=1}^{n} \bar{A}_i|| \leq n\epsilon$.

12. Let P be a Markov matrix and let P_{i_0} be the Markov matrix such that all its rows are equal to the i_0 row of P. Prove that $\delta(P) \geq \frac{1}{2}||P - P_{i_0}||$ but for every ϵ there is an index i_0 such that $\delta(P) \leq \frac{1}{2}|| P - P_{i_0}|| + \frac{1}{2}\epsilon$.

13. A double stochastic matrix is a stochastic matrix $P = [p_{ij}]$ such that both $\sum_j p_{ij} = 1$, $i = 1, 2, \ldots$ and $\sum_i p_{ij} = 1$, $j = 1, 2 \ldots$, i.e., the sum of the entries in any column is also equal to 1. Prove:

a. If P is double stochastic and $\delta(P) = 0$, then P is of finite order, say n, and all the entries of P are equal to $1/n$.

b. The set of doubly stochastic matrices is closed under multiplication [since I is double stochastic this implies that the set of doubly stochastic matrices is a monoid.]

c. If P is a double stochastic matrix of finite order n such that $\delta(P) < 1$, and E is a matrix all the entries of which are equal to $1/n$, then

$$\lim_{m \to \infty} ||P^m - E|| = 0 \qquad [\lim_{m \to \infty} P^m = E]$$

d. If P is a countable double stochastic matrix, then $\delta(P) = 1$

14. Consider the following Markov matrix

$$P = \begin{bmatrix} 1-p & p \\ q & 1-q \end{bmatrix}, \qquad p+q>0, \quad p,q \geq 0$$

Prove that

$$\lim_{n \to \infty} P^n = \begin{bmatrix} \dfrac{q}{p+q} & \dfrac{p}{p+q} \\[2mm] \dfrac{q}{p+q} & \dfrac{p}{p+q} \end{bmatrix}$$

15. Prove that $\sup (\|\xi P\| / \|\xi\|) = \delta(P)$ where ξ ranges over vectors such that $\|\xi\| < \infty$ and $\sum \xi_i = 0$.

16. Prove that any vector ξ such that $\|\xi\| < \infty$ and $\sum \xi_i = 0$ can be expressed in the form $\xi = \sum_{i=1}^{\infty} \zeta_i$ where the $\zeta_i = (\zeta_{ij})$ vectors have only two nonzero entries, $\|\zeta_i\| < \infty$, $\sum_j \zeta_{ij} = 0$, and $\|\xi\| = \sum \|\zeta_i\|$.

2. Nonhomogeneous Markov Chains

The different functionals d, δ, γ introduced in the previous section provide, in a certain sense, a measure of the "distance" between two arbitrary rows of a given stochastic matrix. Thus if the matrix P is constant, then $\delta(P) = d(P) = 0$ and $\gamma(P) = 1$ [see Exercise 7 in the previous section]. These functionals will be used subsequently for studying the long-range behavior of Markov chains. As mentioned before, a nonhomogeneous Markov chain can be represented by an infinite sequence of Markov matrices $\{P_i\}_1^{\infty}$ such that the matrix P_i represents the transition probabilities of the system from state to state at time $t = i$. Let H_{mn} be defined as the matrix

$$H_{mn} = \prod_{i=m+1}^{n} P_i$$

then the ij entry in H_{mn} is the probability that the system will enter the state j at time $t = n$ if it was at state i at time $t = m$. We shall now distinguish between two cases for the long-range behavior of a given Markov chain.

Case 1: $\lim_{n \to \infty} \delta(H_{mn}) = 0$, $m = 0, 1, 2 \ldots$. In this case the chain is called *weakly ergodic*.

Case 2: For any given m there exists a constant stochastic matrix Q such that $\lim_{n \to \infty} \|H_{mn} - Q\| = 0$ in this case the chain is called *strongly ergodic*.

In addition to the two above distinctions, there may be other distinctions as well (e.g., the matrix Q in the second case may not be constant, or the limit—in both cases—may exist only for some m, but not for all m, etc.) but because of their restrictive nature those distinctions will not be considered here. We shall give now some characterizations of the above defined properties.

Theorem 2.1: A Markov chain is weakly ergodic if and only if there exists a subdivision of the chain into blocks of matrices $\{H_{i_j i_{j+1}}\}$ such that $\sum_{j=1}^{\infty} \gamma(H_{i_j i_{j+1}})$ diverges, $[i_1 = 0]$.

Proof: The condition is sufficient, since $\sum_{j=1}^{\infty} \gamma(H_{i_j i_{j+1}})$ diverges implies that for any j_0, $\lim_{n \to \infty} \prod_{j=j_0}^{n} (1 - \gamma(H_{i_j i_{j+1}})) = 0$ and using Propositions 1.3, 1.2, and 1.7, we have that

$$\delta(\prod_{i=m}^{m+n} P_i) \leq \delta(\prod_{i_j \geq m}^{m+n} H_{i_j i_{j+1}}) \leq \prod_{i_j \geq m}^{m+n} \delta(H_{i_j i_{j+1}}) = \prod_{i_j \geq m}^{n} (1 - \gamma(H_{i_j i_{j+1}}))$$

where $i_j \geq m$ means that the product begins with the first index $i_j \geq m$. Taking limits on both sides, we get that

$$\lim_{n \to \infty} \delta(\prod_{i=m}^{m+n} P_i) \leq \lim_{N \to \infty} \delta(\prod_{i_j > m}^{N} H_{i_j i_{j+1}}) = 0$$

with $N = m + n$. If $\lim_{n \to \infty} \delta(\prod_{i=m}^{n} P_i) = 0$, $m = 1, 2, \ldots$, then by Proposition 1.7,

$$\lim_{n \to \infty} \gamma(\prod_{i=m}^{n} P_i) = \lim_{n \to \infty} (1 - \delta \prod_{i=m}^{n} P_i)) = (1 - \lim_{n \to \infty} \delta(\prod_{i=m}^{n} P_i)) = 1$$

Let $0 < \epsilon < 1$ be a small constant, then if follows from the above inequalties that a sequence of blocks $H_{i_j i_{j+1}}$ can be found such that $\gamma(H_{i_j i_{j+1}}) > \epsilon$ so that $\sum_{j=1}^{\infty} \gamma(H_{i_j i_{j+1}})$ diverges. ∎

Theorem 2.2: A given Markov chain is weakly ergodic if and only if for each m there is a sequence of constant Markov matrices E_{mn} such that

$$\lim_{n \to \infty} \|H_{mn} - E_{mn}\| = 0$$

Proof of sufficiency: Let $\epsilon > 0$ be an arbitrary small number and let i_1, i_2 be two arbitrary indices. Let $H_{mn} = [a_{ij}]$, $E_{mn} = [e_{ij}]$ and suppose that n is so big that $\|H_{mn} - E_{mn}\| < \epsilon$. Then by (1)

$$\sum_j (a_{i_1 j} - a_{i_2 j})^+ = \tfrac{1}{2} \sum_j |a_{i_1 j} - a_{i_2 j}| \leq \tfrac{1}{2} \sum_j |a_{i_1 j} - e_{i_1 j} + e_{i_2 j} - a_{i_2 j}|$$

$$\leq \tfrac{1}{2}(\sum_j |a_{i_1 j} - e_{i_1 j}| + \sum_j |a_{i_2 j} - e_{i_2 j}|) < \tfrac{1}{2}(\epsilon + \epsilon) = \epsilon$$

[Cleary $e_{i_1 j} = e_{i_2 j}$ for E_{mn} is a constant matrix.] Since i_1 and i_2 are arbitrary, we have also that

$$\delta(H_{mn}) = \sup_{i_1 i_2} \sum_j (a_{i_1 j} - a_{i_2 j})^+ \leq \epsilon$$

Proof of necessity: Under the same notations as above, let n be so big that $\delta(H_{mn}) < \epsilon/2$. Let E_{mn} be a matrix such that all its rows are equal to some row, say the i_1th, of H_{mn}. Then

$$\sum_j |a_{i_2 j} - e_{i_1 j}| = \sum_j |a_{i_2 j} - a_{i_1 j}| = 2\sum (a_{i_2 j} - a_{i_1 j})^+ \leq 2\delta(H_{mn}) < 2(\epsilon/2) = \epsilon$$

Since i_1, i_2 and ϵ are arbitrary we have that

$$\|H_{mn} - E_{mn}\| = \sup_{i_1} \sum_j |a_{i_1 j} - e_{i_1 j}| < \epsilon \quad \blacksquare$$

Theorem 2.3: Let $\{P_i\}$ he a given Markov chain and let $P_i = E_i + R_i$ with E_i a constant stochastic matrix. Then the given Markov chain is weakly ergodic if and only if $\lim_{n \to \infty} \|\prod_{i=m}^{m+n} R_i\| = 0$.

Proof: It follows from Exercise 4 in the preliminary section that $P_i E_i = E_i$ and $E_i P_i$ is constant. Thus $(P_1 - E_1)(P_2 - E_2) = P_1 P_2 - E_1 P_2$ and by induction

$$\prod_{m=1}^{m+n} R_i = \prod_{m=1}^{m+n} (P_i - E_i) = \prod_{i=m}^{m+n} P_i - E_m \prod_{i=m+1}^{m+n} P_i$$

where the second term on the right-hand side is constant. It thus follows that the condition of Theorem 2.3 implies the condition of Theorem 2.2 which implies weak ergodicity. On the other hand

$$\left\| \prod_{i=m}^{m+n} P_i - E_m \prod_{i=m+1}^{m+n} P_i \right\| = \left\| (P_m - E_m) \prod_{i=m+1}^{m+n} P_i \right\| \leq \|P_m - E_m\| \delta(\prod_{i=m+1}^{m+n} P_i)$$

by Corollary 1.5 and, therefore, weak ergodicity implies the condition of Theorem 2.3. $\blacksquare$

Examples:

1. Let $\{P_i\}$ be a chain such there is $\epsilon > 0$ with $\gamma(P_i) \geq \epsilon > 0$ for all i [this condition will hold, for example, if all the entries in all the matrices P_i are $\geq \epsilon$, or even if in every matrix P_i there is a column such that all the entries in that column are $\geq \epsilon$], then the chain is weakly ergodic by Theorem 2.1.

2. Let P_i be a chain such that

$$P_{2n-1} = \begin{bmatrix} \frac{1}{4} & \frac{1}{2} & \frac{1}{4} \\ \frac{1}{2} & \frac{1}{2} & 0 \\ 0 & 0 & 1 \end{bmatrix}, \qquad P_{2n} = \begin{bmatrix} 0 & 0 & 1 \\ \frac{1}{2} & \frac{1}{2} & 0 \\ \frac{1}{4} & \frac{1}{2} & \frac{1}{4} \end{bmatrix}$$

one finds by straightforward computation that $\gamma(H_{2n-1,2n}) = \gamma(P_{2n-1} P_{2n}) = \frac{3}{4}$ [check the computation] the condition of the Theorem 2.1 holds true and the chain is weakly ergodic.

3. In the definition of weakly, ergodic chains it is required that $\lim_{n \to \infty} \delta(H_{mn}) = 0$ for $m = 0, 1, 2 \ldots$, that is, $\delta(H_{mn}) \to 0$ independently of m. This requirement is intended to exclude cases in which the ergodicity of the chain is induced by finitely many matrices in the chain. Consider, e.g., the chain $\{P_i\}_{i=0}^{\infty}$ with

$$P_0 = \begin{bmatrix} 1 & 0 & 0 \\ 1 & 0 & 0 \\ 1 & 0 & 0 \end{bmatrix}, \qquad P_i = \begin{bmatrix} 1 & 0 & 0 \\ 0 & 0 & 1 \\ 0 & 1 & 0 \end{bmatrix}$$

Clearly $H_{0n} = P_0$ for all n and $\gamma(H_{0n}) = 1$. But $\lim_{n\to\infty}\delta(H_{mn})$ does not exist for $m \geq 1$.

Theorems 2.1–2.3 characterize weak ergodicity of chains. The following theorem gives a characterization of strong ergodicity. It also confirms the intuitive feeling that strong ergodicity implies weak ergodicity.

Theorem 2.4: A Markov chain $\{P_i\}$ is strongly ergodic if and only if for every m there is a sequence of constant stochastic matrices $\{E_{mn}\}$ and a sequence of stochastic constant matrices $\{E_m\}$ such that (1) $\lim_{n\to\infty}||H_{mn} - E_{mn}|| = 0$ and (2) $\lim_{n\to\infty}||E_{mn} - E_m|| = 0$.

Proof: If (1) and (2) hold true, then

$$\lim_{n\to\infty} ||H_{mn} - E_m|| \leq \lim_{n\to\infty} (||H_{mn} - E_{mn}|| + ||E_{mn} - E_m||) = 0.$$

But if (1) and (2) hold true then E_m is independent on m. To prove this we note that $P_m H_{mn} = H_{m-1,n}$ and $P_m E_m = E_m$ [see Exercise 4 in the preliminary section] so that,

$$||E_{m-1} - E_m|| \leq ||E_{m-1} - H_{m-1,n}|| + ||P_m H_{mn} - P_m E_m|| + ||P_m E_m - E_m||$$
$$= ||E_{m-1} - H_{m-1,n}|| + ||P_m(H_{mn} - E_m)||$$
$$\leq ||E_{m-1} - H_{m-1,n}|| + ||H_{mn} - E_m||$$

by Exercise 1.10 [and $||P_m|| = 1$]. Taking limits in both sides we get

$$||E_{m-1} - E_m|| = \lim_{n\to\infty}||E_{m-1} - E_m||$$
$$= \lim_{n\to\infty}(||E_{m-1} - H_{m-1,n}|| + ||H_{mn} - E_m||) = 0.$$

Thus (1) and (2) imply that the chain is strongly ergodic. Conversely, if the chain is strongly ergodic, then setting $Q = E_{mn} = E_m$ for all m and n we have that (1) and (2) hold true. ∎

Corollary 2.5: A strongly ergodic chain is also weakly ergodic. A weakly ergodic chain which satisfies (2) is strongly ergodic.

Proof: Strong ergodicity implies the condition (1) in Theorem 2.4, which, by Theorem 2.2 implies weak ergodicity, Conversely, by Theorem 2.2 weak ergodicity implies (1) which together with (2) implies strong ergodicity by Theorem 2.4. ∎

Corollary 2.6: Conditions (1) and (2) in Theorem 2.4 and Corollary 2.5 can be replaced by the condition (2′) $\lim_{n\to\infty}||H_{mn} - E_m|| = 0$.

Proof: $||H_{mn} - E_m|| \leq ||H_{mn} - E_{mn}|| + ||E_{mn} - E_m|| \to 0$. Conversely (2′) implies (1) and (2) with $E_{mn} = E_m$ for all m and n. ∎

Corollary 2.7: Condition (2) in Theorem 2.4 and Corollary 2.5 can be replaced by the condition: there is a constant stochastic matrix E such that $(2'')$ $\lim_{n\to\infty}$ $||EH_{mn} - E|| = 0$.

Proof: $||EH_{mn} - E|| \leq ||EH_{mn} - H_{mn}|| + ||H_{mn} - E|| \leq 2\delta(H_{mn}) + ||H_{mn} - E||$ by Corollary 1.6. Condition (1) of Theorem 2.4 implies that $\delta(H_{mn}) \to 0$ and condition (2) in that theorem implies that $||H_{mn} - E_m|| = ||H_{mn} - E|| \to 0$ [E_m is independent on m as proved in the proof of that theorem]. Thus condition $(2'')$ holds with $E = E_m$. Conversely if (1) and $(2'')$ hold true, then let $E_m = E$. It follows that

$$||E_{mn} - E_m|| \leq ||E_{mn} - H_{mn}|| + ||H_{mn} - EH_{mn}|| + ||EH_{mn} - E|| \to 0$$

by (1), $(2'')$, and the fact that $\delta(H_{mn}) \to 0$. ∎

Theorem 2.8: Let $\{P_i\}$ and $\{\bar{P}_i\}$ be two Markov chains such that $\sum_i ||P_i - \bar{P}_i|| < \infty$ then, for any $\epsilon > 0$, there is an integer m_0 such that $||H_{mn} - \bar{H}_{mn}|| < \epsilon$, for all $m \geq m_0$ and all $n > m$, [$\bar{H}_{mn}$ is the product of $\bar{P}_i$s corresponding to H_{mn}].

Proof: Let $P_i - \bar{P}_i = E_i$ with $||E_i|| = e_i$, then $H_{mn} = \prod_i (\bar{P}_i + E_i) = \bar{H}_{mn} + R_{mn}$ where R_{mn} contains all possible products of $\bar{P}_i$ and E_i matrices. Using the facts that $||E_i|| = e_i$ is finite for all i, $||\bar{P}_i|| = 1$ for all i [$\bar{P}_i$ is stochastic] and $||AB|| \leq ||A|| \; ||B||$ for any two matrices A and B [see Exercise 1.10] we have that

$$||R_{mn}|| \leq \sum e_i + \sum_{i,j} e_i e_j + \sum_{i,j,k} e_i e_j e_k + \cdots + \prod_{i=m+1}^{n} e_i = \prod_{i=m+1}^{n} (1 + e_i) - 1$$

Note that the e_is are nonnegative. Now as $\sum e_i < \infty$, the product $\prod_{i=m+1}^{n} (1 + e_i)$ converges and, therefore, for any ϵ, there is m with $||R_{mn}|| < \epsilon$. The theorem is thus proved. ∎

Corollary 2.9: Let $\{P_i\}$ and $\{\bar{P}_i\}$ be two Markov chains satisfying the conditions of Theorem 2.8. If one of the chains is weakly ergodic, then so is the other.

Proof: Assume that $\lim_{n\to\infty} \delta(H_{mn}) = 0$, $m = 0, 1\ldots$. Let C_{mn} be a matrix all the rows of which are equal to some row say i_0 of H_{mn} and Let $\bar{C}_{mn}$ be a matrix all the rows of which are equal to the corresponding i_0 row of $\bar{H}_{mn}$.

$$||\bar{H}_{mn} - \bar{C}_{mn}|| < ||\bar{H}_{mn} - H_{mn}|| + ||H_{mn} - C_{mn}|| + ||C_{mn} - \bar{C}_{mn}||$$

and for any i_0, $||C_{mn} - \bar{C}_{mn}|| \leq ||\bar{H}_{mn} - H_{mn}||$, since the rows of C_{mn} are equal to the i_0 row of H_{mn} and the rows of $\bar{C}_{mn}$ are equal to the i_0 row of $\bar{H}_{mn}$ by definition. Moreover, by Exercise 1.12 $||H_{mn} - C_{mn}|| \leq 2\delta(H_{mn})$ and by Theorem 2.8 one can choose an m such that $||\bar{H}_{mn} - H_{mn}||$ is as small as wanted. Let us now combine the above arguments together. Given ϵ, choose i_0 to be an integer such that $\delta(\bar{H}_{mn}) \leq \frac{1}{2}||\bar{H}_{mn} - \bar{C}_{mn}|| + \epsilon/2$, this is possible by Exercise 1.12. Choose m_0 so that $||H_{m_0 n} - \bar{H}_{m_0 n}|| < \epsilon/3$. For any $m \geq m_0$ there is n such that $\delta(H_{mn}) < \epsilon/6$ thus, for the fixed i_0 and for any $m \geq m_0$, there is n such that

$$||\bar{H}_{mn} - \bar{C}_{mn}|| < \frac{\epsilon}{3} + \frac{2\epsilon}{6} + \frac{\epsilon}{3} = \epsilon$$

and

$$\delta(\bar{H}_{mn}) < \frac{1}{2}||\bar{H}_{mn} - \bar{C}_{mn}|| + \frac{\epsilon}{2} < \epsilon$$

Finally, for $i < m_0$, we have that $\delta(\bar{H}_{in}) \leq \delta(\bar{H}_{i,m_0-1})\ \delta(\bar{H}_{m_0n}) \leq \delta(\bar{H}_{m_0n})$ so that $\lim_{n\to\infty}\delta(\bar{H}_{mn}) = 0.$ ∎

EXERCISES

1. Prove that a Markov chain $\{P_i\}$ such that $\sum \gamma(P_i)$ diverges is weakly ergodic.

2. Prove that if a Markov chain $\{P_i\}$ is weakly ergodic then every convergent subsequence of the sequence H_{mn} (for fixed m) converges to a constant matrix. [A_i converges to A means that $||A_i - A|| \to 0$.]

3. Let $\{P_i\}$ be a Markov chain. Prove: If there exists a vector π such that $\lim_{n\to\infty}||\pi H_{mn} - \pi|| = 0$, then also $\lim_{n\to\infty}||\pi P_n - \pi|| = 0$.

4. Let $\{P_i\}$ be a Markov chain such that there is $\epsilon > 0$ with $\gamma(P_i) > \epsilon$ for all i, and let $\{\bar{P}_i\}$ be an arbitrary Markov chain. Prove that there is a constant stochastic matrix S such that

$$\lim_{n\to\infty}||\bar{P}_n P_n \bar{P}_{n-1} P_{n-1} \cdots \bar{P}_1 P_1 - S|| = 0$$

Generalize this result.

The following exercises (5–11) deal with the distinction between finite and countable Markov chains.

5. Prove by an example that for any ϵ there is a countable Markov matrix P_ϵ such that $d(P_\epsilon) < \epsilon$ but $\delta(P_\epsilon) = 1$.

6. Prove that a finite Markov chain is weakly ergodic if and only if $\lim_{n\to\infty} d(H_{mn}) = 0$. Is the above statement true for countable Markov chains? Explain.

7. Prove that a finite Markov chain is strongly ergodic if and only if there is a constant stochastic matrix Q such that $\lim_{n\to\infty}|H_{mn} - Q| = 0$. Is the above statement true for the countable case? Explain.

8. Prove that if the Markov chain in Theorem 2.2 is finite, then the condition of that theorem can replaced by the condition: $\lim_{n\to\infty}|H_{mn} - E_{mn}| = 0$. Discuss the countable case.

9. Same as Exercise 8 but for Theorem 2.3 with the condition replaced by the condition that $\lim_{n\to\infty}|\prod_{i=m}^{m+n} R_i| = 0$.

10. Same as Exercise 8 but for Theorem 2.4 with the conditions replaced by the conditions

(1) $\lim\limits_{n\to\infty} |H_{mn} - E_{mn}| = 0$

(2) $\lim\limits_{n\to\infty} |E_{mn} - E_m| = 0$

11. Prove that all the other theorems in this section can be replaced by similar theorems with the norm "$|\ |$" replacing the norm "$||\ ||$" whenever it occurs and discuss the countable case.

12. Markov chains in general can be classified according to the following four types:

Type	$\|H_{mn} - Q_m\| \to 0$	$\delta(H_{mn}) \to 0$
Strongly ergodic	Yes	Yes
Weakly ergodic	No	Yes
Convergent	Yes	No
Oscillating	No	No

where $\|H_{mn} - Q_m\| \to 0$ means that for any m, there is a matrix Q_m (not necessarily constant) such that $\lim_{n\to\infty}\|H_{mn} - Q_m\| = 0$. In Corollary 2.9 it is proved that if two chains satisfy the conditions of Theorem 2.8 and one of them is weakly ergodic then so is the other. Prove that the same is true for all the other three types of chains above.

13. Prove that if all the matrices in the Markov chain are equal one to the other (the chain is homogeneous), then weak ergodicity implies strong ergodicity.

14. Prove that if all the matrices in a Markov chain are doubly stochastic, then weak ergodicity implies that the matrices are of finite order and implies strong ergodicity.

3. Nonhomogeneous Markov Systems

The difference between Markov systems, to be introduced in this section, and Markov chains, discussed in the previous section, is that in the Markov system model one studies the set of all possible products of Markov matrices taken from a (finite) given set of such matrices, while in the Markov chain model one investigates a specific given infinite product of Markov matrices and its possible subproducts. The approach in this section is closer to the automaton concept where the set of all words over a given alphabet is studied with regard to the transitions induced on the states of the automaton by the different words.

The words correspond here to products of Morkov matrices which induce a probabilistic transition between the states of the automaton.

It is to be noted, however, that a homogeneous Markov chain is a particular case of both a nonhomogeneous Markov chain and a Markov system—the case where only one Markov matrix and its powers is considered.

Definition 3.1: A Markov system over a [finite] alphabet Σ is a pair $(S, \{A(\sigma)\})$ where S is a [at most countable] set of states and $\{A(\sigma)\}$ is a set of Markov matrices [representing the transitions between the states] such that the matrix $A(\sigma)$ is associated to the symbol $\sigma \in \Sigma$.

Notation: If x is a word in Σ^* (the set of all words over Σ including the empty word denoted by Λ) such that $x = \sigma_1 \cdots \sigma_k$ then $A(x) = A(\sigma_1)A(\sigma_2) \cdots A(\sigma_k)$; $A(x) = [a_{ij}(x)]$ and $a_{ij}(x)$ is the transition probability from state i to state j associated with the word x.

It will be assumed that the alphabet Σ is finite. We shall, however, mention later some of the implications induced by the assumption that Σ is infinite. When two systems are compared it is always assumed that they are over the same Σ.

Definition 3.2: A Markov system $(S, \{A(\sigma)\})$ is weakly ergodic if for any $\epsilon > 0$, there is an integer $n = n(\epsilon)$ such that $\delta(A(x)) \leq \epsilon$ for all words x such that $l(x) \geq n(\epsilon)$ where $l(x)$ denotes the length of the word x.

    Remark: If a Markov system is weakly ergodic, then $\delta(A(x)) \to 0$ uniformly, the magnitude of $\delta(A(x))$ depending only on the length of x and not on the specific symbols contained in x. Such a requirement of uniformity will be too restrictive for the strong ergodicity and therefore strong ergodicity will not be dealt with for Markov systems.

    Note that $A(xy) = A(x)A(y)$ so that $\delta(A(xy)) \leq \delta(A(x))\delta(A(y)) \leq \delta(A(x))$ and therefore if and only if $\delta(A(x)) \leq \epsilon$ for all x with $l(x) = n(\epsilon)$, then $\delta(A(x)) \leq \epsilon$ for all x with $l(x) \geq n(\epsilon)$.

Theorem 3.1: A Markov system is weakly ergodic if and only if there is an integer k such that $\delta(A(x)) < 1$ for all x with $l(x) = k$.

    Proof: Necessity follows directly from the definition. To prove sufficiency set $\delta = \max_{l(x)=k} \delta(A(x)) < 1$. [there are only finitely many words x with $l(x) = k$ because Σ is finite.] Let n_0 be an integer such that $\delta^{n_0} < \epsilon$ for a given $\epsilon > 0$. Let x be a word such that $l(x) \geq kn_0$, then $x = y_1 \cdots y_{n_0} y$ where $l(y_1) = \cdots = l(y_{n_0}) = k$ and $l(y) \geq 0$. Thus, $\delta(A(x)) \leq \delta(A(y_1)) \cdots \delta(A(y_{n_0})) \leq \delta^{n_0} < \epsilon$. It follows that the system is weakly ergodic. ∎

    Remark: The theorem will remain true even if the alphabet Σ is infinite provided the requirement that $\delta(A(x)) < 1$ is replaced by the requirement that there is a real number $\delta < 1$ such that $\delta(A(x)) < \delta$ for all x with $l(x) \geq k$.

Theorem 3.2: Let $(S, \{A(\sigma)\})$ and $(S, \{\bar{A}(\sigma)\})$ be two systems such that the first is weakly ergodic and the second is arbitrary. There is $\epsilon > 0$ such that if $||A(\sigma) - \bar{A}(\sigma)|| \leq \epsilon$ for all $\sigma \in \Sigma$, then the second system is also weakly ergodic.

Proof: Using Theorem 3.1, we must prove that there is ϵ such that if $||A(\sigma) - \bar{A}(\sigma)|| \leq \epsilon$ for all $\sigma \in \Sigma$, then there is n such that $\delta(A(x)) < 1$ for all x with $l(x) \geq n$. Let $A_{i_0}(x)$ be the matrix such that all its rows are equal to the i_0 row of $A(x)$, then $||A(x) - A_{i_0}(x)|| \leq 2\delta(A(x))$ by Exercise 1.12. As the first system is weakly ergodic, there is n_0 such that $\delta(A(x)) < \frac{1}{6}$ for all x with $l(x) \geq n_0$, i.e., $||A(x) - A_{i_0}(x)|| < \frac{1}{3}$ for all such x and any i_0. Let $\bar{x}$ be a fixed but arbitrary word with $l(\bar{x}) = n_0$ and choose i_0 so that $\delta(\bar{A}(\bar{x})) < \frac{1}{2}||\bar{A}(\bar{x}) - \bar{A}_{i_0}(\bar{x})|| + \frac{1}{2}$. Such an i_0 exists by Exercise 1.12. Finally, let ϵ be a number $0 < \epsilon < 1/(3n_0)$, and let $||A(\sigma) - \bar{A}(\sigma)|| < \epsilon$ for all $\sigma \in \Sigma$. Then, by Exercise 1.11, we have that $||A(\bar{x}) - \bar{A}(\bar{x})|| < \frac{1}{3}$ (for $l(\bar{x}) = n_0$). Thus,

$$\delta(\bar{A}(\bar{x})) < \tfrac{1}{2} + \tfrac{1}{2}||\bar{A}(\bar{x}) - \bar{A}_{i_0}(\bar{x})||$$

$$\leq \tfrac{1}{2} + \tfrac{1}{2}(||\bar{A}(\bar{x}) - A(\bar{x})|| + ||A(\bar{x}) - A_{i_0}(\bar{x})|| + ||A_{i_0}(\bar{x}) - \bar{A}_{i_0}(\bar{x})||)$$

$$\leq \tfrac{1}{2} + \tfrac{1}{2}(\tfrac{1}{3} + \tfrac{1}{3} + \tfrac{1}{3}) = 1$$

since $||A_{i_0}(\bar{x}) - \bar{A}_{i_0}(\bar{x})|| \leq ||A(x) - \bar{A}(\bar{x})|| < \frac{1}{3}$. But $\bar{x}$ is arbitrary and therefore we have that $\delta(\bar{A}(x)) < 1$ for all x with $l(x) = n_0$ provided that $||A(\sigma) - \bar{A}(\sigma)|| < 1/(3n_0)$ for all $\sigma \in \Sigma$, where n_0 is an integer such that $\delta(A(x)) < \frac{1}{6}$ for all x with $l(x) \geq n$. To complete the proof we note that if $\delta(\bar{A}(x)) < 1$ for all x with $l(x) = n_0$, then this is true also for all x with $l(x) \geq n_0$, as mentioned before. ∎

Theorem 3.3: Let $(S, \{A(\sigma)\})$ and $(S, \{\bar{A}(\sigma)\})$ be two systems such that the first system is weakly ergodic. For any $\delta > 0$, there is $\epsilon > 0$ such that if $||A(\sigma) - \bar{A}(\sigma)|| \leq \epsilon$ for all $\sigma \in \Sigma$ then $||A(x) - \bar{A}(x)|| \leq \delta$ for all $x \in \Sigma^*$.

Proof: By the previous theorem, there is ϵ_1 such that $||A(\sigma) - \bar{A}(\sigma)|| \leq \epsilon_1$, for all $\sigma \in \Sigma$, implies that both systems are weakly ergodic. Thus there is ϵ_1 such that there is n_0 with both $\delta(A(x)) \leq \delta/6$ and $\delta(\bar{A}(x)) \leq \delta/6$ for all x with $l(x) \geq n_0$ and the given δ provided that $||A(\sigma) - \bar{A}(\sigma)|| \leq \epsilon_1$. For the number n_0 above, there is ϵ_2 such that if $||A(\sigma) - \bar{A}(\sigma)|| \leq \epsilon_2$ then $||A(x) - \bar{A}(x)|| \leq \delta/3$ for all x with $l(x) < n_0$ [this follows from Exercise 1.11]. Let $\epsilon = \min(\epsilon_1, \epsilon_2)$. Then for all x with $l(x) < n_0$, $||A(x) - \bar{A}(x)|| \leq \delta/3 < \delta$. If $x = yz$ with $l(z) = n_0$ and $l(y) \geq 0$ i.e., if $l(x) \geq n_0$ then, using Corollary 1.6 we have that

$$||A(x) - \bar{A}(x)|| = ||A(yz) - \bar{A}(yz)||$$

$$\leq ||A(y)A(z) - A(z)|| + ||\bar{A}(y)\bar{A}(z) - \bar{A}(z)|| + ||A(z) - \bar{A}(z)||$$

$$\leq 2\delta(A(z)) + 2\delta(\bar{A}(z)) + ||A(z) - \bar{A}(z)||$$

$$\leq \frac{\delta}{3} + \frac{\delta}{3} + \frac{\delta}{3} = \delta \quad \blacksquare$$

Remarks: Theorem 3.3 provides an interesting application: Assume that a system $(S, \{A(\sigma)\})$ is given together with an initial distribution π over the states, and it is required to compute the values of the vector $\pi A(x)$ for some word $x = \sigma_1 \cdots \sigma_k$. If the number of states in countably infinite, then it will be impossible to compute the exact values of the entries of $\pi A(x)$. If the system is weakly ergodic, then using Theorem 3.3 one can change the vector π into a new vector $\bar{\pi}$ such that $\|\pi - \bar{\pi}\| < \epsilon$ and $\bar{\pi}$ has only finitely many nonzero entries. The rows of $A(\sigma_1)$ corresponding to zero values in $\bar{\pi}$ can be replaced by zero rows and one can choose finitely many columns in the remaining rows so that by replacing the other columns by zero columns one gets a matrix $\bar{A}(\sigma_1)$ such that $\|A(\sigma_1) - \bar{A}(\sigma_1)\| \le \epsilon$ and $\bar{A}(\sigma_1)$ has only finitely many nonzero entries. The process is repeated for $A(\sigma_2) \cdots A(\sigma_k)$. As $\|\pi - \bar{\pi}\| \le \epsilon$ and $\|A(\sigma_i) - \bar{A}(\sigma_i)\| \le \epsilon$, $\|\pi A(x) - \bar{\pi}\bar{A}(x)\| \le \delta$ with ϵ a function of δ. An infinite computation can thus be replaced by a finite computation and the resulting error can be kept under control. Theorem 3.3 may also be used for rounding off the entries in the individual matrices $A(\sigma)$ [in order to simplify the computation, or to make computation possible when the entries are irrational] and keeping the resulting error in long computations under control.

Because of the importance of Theorem 3.3, one is induced to ask whether the condition of that theorem is best [i.e., whether it is also a necessary condition for the theorem to hold true]. That this is not the case is shown by Exercise 3.4. On the other hand it is clear that the theorem is not true in general, e.g., let I be the unit matrix of order n and let P be any double stochastic matrix such that $\|P - I\| < \epsilon$ and such that $\delta(P) < 1$, then, independently on ϵ we have that $\lim_{m \to \infty} P^m = E$ where E is a matrix such that all its entries are equal to $1/n$ [see Exercise 1.13c]. Thus, for large enough m and $n > 2$,

$$\|I - P^m\| \ge \|I - E\| - \|E - P^m\| = 1 + \frac{n-2}{n} - \|E - P^m\| > 1$$

independently of ϵ.

One additional question with regard to Theorem 3.3 to be considered here is the following: Assume that we drop the requirement that the first system is ergodic and require instead that $\bar{A}(\sigma)$ has zero entries in the same places where $A(\sigma)$ has zero entries [i.e., no new transitions are added in the approximation]. Is this new condition necessary or sufficient, or both, for the theorem to hold true? It is clear that this new condition is not necessary, since a weakly ergodic system may have zero entries in its $A(\sigma)$ matrices and the theorem does not impose any restrictions on the corresponding entries in the matrices $\bar{A}(\sigma)$. The following example will show that the above condition is not sufficient either.

Example: Let

$$
A(\sigma_1) = \begin{bmatrix} p & 1-p & 0 & 0 \\ 0 & 1 & 0 & 0 \\ 0 & 0 & q & 1-q \\ 0 & 0 & 0 & 1 \end{bmatrix}; \qquad A(\sigma_2) = \begin{bmatrix} 1-p & 0 & p & 0 \\ 1 & 0 & 0 & 0 \\ q & 0 & 1-q & 0 \\ 0 & 0 & 1 & 0 \end{bmatrix}
$$

then, by straightforward computation one finds that

$$
A(\sigma_1^n) = \begin{bmatrix} p^n & 1-p^n & 0 & 0 \\ 0 & 1 & 0 & 0 \\ 0 & 0 & q^n & 1-q^n \\ 0 & 0 & 0 & 1 \end{bmatrix}
$$

$$
A(\sigma_1^n\sigma_2) = \begin{bmatrix} 1-p^{n+1} & 0 & p^{n+1} & 0 \\ 1 & 0 & 0 & 0 \\ q^{n+1} & 0 & 1-q^{n+1} & 0 \\ 0 & 0 & 1 & 0 \end{bmatrix}
$$

Denote $\sigma_1^n\sigma_2$ by x_n. It is easily seen that if words of the form x_n only are considered, then the subsystem consisting of the first and third states is independent of the other two states, i.e., if $A'(x_n)$ denotes the submatrix of $A(x_n)$ corresponding to the first and third state

$$
A'(x_n) = \begin{bmatrix} 1-p^{n+1} & p^{n+1} \\ q^{n+1} & 1-q^{n+1} \end{bmatrix}
$$

then $A'(x_n x_m) = A'(x_n)A'(x_m)$. Let now $p = q = \frac{1}{4}$. In this case

$$
A'(x_n) = \begin{bmatrix} 1 - \dfrac{1}{4^{n+1}} & \dfrac{1}{4^{n+1}} \\ \dfrac{1}{4^{n+1}} & 1 - \dfrac{1}{4^{n+1}} \end{bmatrix}
$$

$A'(x_n)$ being doubly stochastic, we have that [see Exercise 1.13c]

$$
\lim_{m\to\infty} A'(x_n^m) = \begin{bmatrix} \frac{1}{2} & \frac{1}{2} \\ \frac{1}{2} & \frac{1}{2} \end{bmatrix}
$$

But if $p = \frac{1}{4}$ and $q = \frac{1}{4} - \epsilon$ with $0 < \epsilon < \frac{1}{4}$, then the matrix $A'(x_n)$ will have the form

$$
\begin{bmatrix}
1 - \dfrac{1}{4^{n+1}} & \dfrac{1}{4^{n+1}} \\[2ex]
\left(\dfrac{1}{4} - \epsilon\right)^{n+1} & 1 - \left(\dfrac{1}{4} - \epsilon\right)^{n+1}
\end{bmatrix}
$$

So that [see Exercise 1.14]

$$
\lim A'(x_n{}^m) =
\begin{bmatrix}
\dfrac{\left(\dfrac{1}{4} - \epsilon\right)^{n+1}}{\left(\dfrac{1}{4} - \epsilon\right)^{n+1} + \dfrac{1}{4^{n+1}}} & \dfrac{\dfrac{1}{4^{n+1}}}{\left(\dfrac{1}{4} - \epsilon\right)^{n+1} + \dfrac{1}{4^{n+1}}} \\[5ex]
\dfrac{\left(\dfrac{1}{4} - \epsilon\right)^{n+1}}{\left(\dfrac{1}{4} - \epsilon\right)^{n+1} + \dfrac{1}{4^{n+1}}} & \dfrac{\dfrac{1}{4^{n+1}}}{\left(\dfrac{1}{4} - \epsilon\right)^{n+1} + \dfrac{1}{4^{n+1}}}
\end{bmatrix}
$$

And for any $\epsilon > 0$ and $\delta > 0$, there is n with

$$
\frac{\left(\dfrac{1}{4} - \epsilon\right)^{n+1}}{\left(\dfrac{1}{4} - \epsilon\right)^{n+1} + \dfrac{1}{4^{n+1}}} < \delta
$$

(let the reader prove this fact). Let $B(\sigma_i)$ be the matrix $A(\sigma_i)$ when $p = q = \frac{1}{4}$ and let $\bar{B}(\sigma_i)$ be the matrix $A(\sigma_i)$ when $p = \frac{1}{4}$ and $q = \frac{1}{4} - \epsilon$, $0 < \epsilon < \frac{1}{4}$. Then $\|B(\sigma_i) - \bar{B}(\sigma_i)\| < 2\epsilon$, but for any such ϵ, there is a word of the form $x_n{}^m$ such that the 1, 1 entry of $B(x_n{}^m)$ is bigger than $\frac{3}{8}$ and the corresponding entry in $\bar{B}(x_n{}^m)$ is smaller than $\frac{1}{8}$ so that $\|B(x_n{}^m) - \bar{B}(x_n{}^m)\| > \frac{1}{4}$ which shows that the consequence of Theorem 3.3 is not true for this example although $\bar{B}(\sigma_i)$ has nonzero entries in the same places as $B(\sigma_i)$.

EXERCISES

1. Discuss Theorems 3.2 and 3.3, in the case where Σ is infinite.

2. Show that if all the Markov systems considered are finite then all the theorems of this section are true with the norm "$\| \quad \|$" replaced by the norm "$| \quad |$" and δ replaced by d.

3. Prove that any system $(S, \{(\sigma)\})$ such that $|S| = 2$ is weakly ergodic if and only if the matrices $\begin{bmatrix} 1 & 0 \\ 0 & 1 \end{bmatrix}$ and $\begin{bmatrix} 0 & 1 \\ 1 & 0 \end{bmatrix}$ are not included in the set $\{A(\sigma)\}$.

4*. Prove the following proposition: Let $(S, \{A(\sigma)\})$ and $(S, \{\bar{A}(\sigma)\})$ be two systems such that $|S| = 2$. For any $\delta > 0$, there is $\epsilon > 0$ such that if

1. $\|A(\sigma) - \bar{A}(\sigma)\| \leq \epsilon$ for all $\sigma \in \Sigma$ with

$$
A(\sigma) \neq \begin{bmatrix} 1 & 0 \\ 0 & 1 \end{bmatrix} \quad \text{and} \quad A(\sigma) \neq \begin{bmatrix} 0 & 1 \\ 1 & 0 \end{bmatrix}
$$

2. If, $A(\sigma) = \begin{bmatrix} 1 & 0 \\ 0 & 1 \end{bmatrix}$ or $A(\sigma) = \begin{bmatrix} 0 & 1 \\ 1 & 0 \end{bmatrix}$, then $A(\sigma) = \bar{A}(\sigma)$.

Then $\|A(x) - \bar{A}(x)\| \leq \delta$.

5. Prove that a weakly ergodic system such that all its matrices are double stochastic, has only finitely many states, is strongly ergodic and the limiting matrix is such that all its entries are equal. [A system is strongly ergodic if $\lim_{l(x)\to\infty} \|A(x) - Q\| = 0$ for some constant stochastic matrix Q.]

4. Graph Properties and Decision Problems

Up to this section no restriction was assumed with regard to the finiteness or infiniteness of the Markov chains or systems considered. In this section, however, we shall assume that the chains or systems have only finitely many states. This restriction will enable us to simplify the classification of the states of a chain. In addition we shall be able to prove some decidability theorems under the finiteness restriction although it is not known whether these theorems are true in the infinite case. Some of the difficulties encountered in this case will be illustrated in the exercises following this section. For more information on infinite homogeneous Markov chains, the reader is referred to the books by Kemeny, Snell, and Knapp (1966), and Feller (1958).

Given a Markov matrix $P = [p_{ij}]$ with state set S, the graph associated with P is a pair (S, Γ) where Γ is a binary relation on S ($\Gamma \subseteq S \times S$) such that $(i, j) \in S$ if and only if $p_{ij} > 0$. If $i \in S$, then $i\Gamma$ denotes the set of states

$$i\Gamma = \{j : (i, j) \in \Gamma\}$$

A sequence of states $(i_0, i_1, \ldots, i_n)$ is a *path* of length n if every pair of adjacent states in the sequence is in Γ. Then state j is a *consequent* of length n of i if there is a path of length n beginning with i and ending with j. A pair of states have a *common consequent* (of order n) if there is an integer n such that $i\Gamma^n \cap j\Gamma^n \neq \varnothing$ where Γ^n means the composition of Γ with itself n times [$(i, j) \in \Gamma^2$ if and only if there is k such that $(i, k) \in \Gamma$ and $(k, j) \in \Gamma$.] The graph is *strongly connected* if there is a path connecting any pair of states.

We are now able to classify the states of a given graph (S, Γ). A state is called *transient* if it has a consequent of which it is not itself a consequent. A state which is not transient is *nontransient*.

Remarks

1. It is decidable whether a given state is transient or not [see Exercise 4.1].

2. There must be nontransient states in any graph. Otherwise, one can construct an infinite sequence of states $i_0, i_1, \ldots i_k, \ldots$ such that for $k > j$, i_k is a consequent of i_j and i_j is not a consequent of i_k (the relation of consequence is

transitive). All the states in the sequence must therefore differ one from the other, and, as the chain is finite, this is impossible.

3. If i is a nontransient state and j is a consequent of i, then j is also nontransient. For let k be any consequent of j, then k is a consequent of i which implies that i is a consequent of k [i is nontransient] which implies that j is a consequent of k [since j is a consequent of i].

The set of nontransient states is divided into *ergodic classes*, where an ergodic class is a maximal strongly connected set of states and two states belong to the same ergodic class if and only if they are consequents of each other. In order to be able to proceed with the classification we need now the following:

Lemma: A set of positive integers that is closed under addition contains all sufficiently large multiples of its greatest common divisor.

Proof: Let d be the gcd of the given set of numbers, then there is a finite set of these numbers, say $n_1, n_2, \ldots, n_k$, such that d is their gcd [Let n_1 be the first number in the set. If $n_1 = d$, we are done, if $n_1 > d$, then there is an n_2 such that the gcd of $(n_1, n_2) = d_2$ is $\geq d$. If $d_2 = d$, we are done. If $d_2 \neq d$, we continue the process getting a sequence of numbers $n_1, n_2, n_3, \ldots$ which must terminate as the d_i's are decreasing.] By a well-known theorem of arithmetic, there are integers [negative or positive] $a_1, a_2, \ldots, a_k$ such that $a_1 n_1 + \cdots + a_k n_k = d$. Let m be the positive part and let n be the absolute value of the negative part in the left-hand side of the above equation. Then m and n are numbers in the given set [for the set is closed under addition].

Let q be any number, then q can be written in the form $q = an + b$ with $b \leq n - 1$. Multiplying by d we get $dq = dan + db$. But $d = m - n$ so that $db = (m - n)b$ and $dq = dan + (m - n)b = (da - b)n + bm$. Thus for any q such that $a \geq (n - 1)/d$ the value $da - b$ will be nonnegative with the result that dq is in the set. The lemma is thus proved. ∎

Let E be an ergodic class of states, let i and j be two states in E and let N_{ij} be the set of integers n_{ij} such that there is a path of length n_{ij} connecting the two states i and j. The sets N_{ij} are not empty by the definition of E. Consider now the two sets of integers N_{ii} and N_{jj} and let d_i and d_j be their gcd respectively. By the previous lemma we have that for sufficiently large k, $kd_j \in N_{jj}$ [since the sets N_{jj} are clearly closed under addition]. Let $a \in N_{ij}$ and $c \in N_{ji}$ be two integers, then for sufficiently large k, $a + kd_j + c \in N_{ii}$. It follows that d_i divides $a + kd_j + c$, and, since d_i also divides $(a + c) \in N_{ii}$, we have that d_i also divides kd_j for all sufficiently large k. But this is possible only if d_i divides d_j. Similarly d_j divides d_i or $d_i = d_j$. The consequence is that all the sets N_{ii} have the same gcd to be denoted by d. Let a and b be integers in N_{ij} and let c be in N_{ji}. Then $a + c \in N_{ii}$ and $b + c \in N_{ii}$ so that $a + c \equiv 0 \pmod{d}$ and $b + c \equiv 0 \pmod{d}$ or $a \equiv b \pmod{d}$. It follows that all the integers in N_{ij} are congruent to each other (mod d) and in particular to the smallest integer in N_{ij}, to be denoted by t_{ij}. [If $i \neq j$, then $t_{ij} \neq 0$ and if $i = j$ we may define $t_{ii} = 0$, for any integer in N_{ii} is congruent to 0 (mod d).]

We are now able to divide any ergodic class E into periodic subclasses as follows: Two states i and j in E are in the same periodic class if and only if $j \in i\Gamma^n$ and $n \equiv 0 \pmod{d}$. It is easy to see that the relation of being in the same periodic class is an equivalence relation (see Exercise 4.3), and any ergodic class is thus subdivided into exactly d periodic subclasses [d is the gcd of the sets N_{ii}] $C_1, C_2, \ldots, C_d$ where any path connecting a state in C_i to a state in $C_j, i < j$ has length n with $n \equiv j - i \pmod{d}$ and $j - i = t_{ij}$.

Example: Consider the graph in Figure 12. The states 1, 2, 3 are transient. The set of states $\{6, 7, 10\}$ is an ergodic class and the sets $\{6\}, \{7\}, \{10\}$ are its periodic subclasses with $d = 3$. The set of states $\{4, 5, 8, 9\}$ is another ergodic

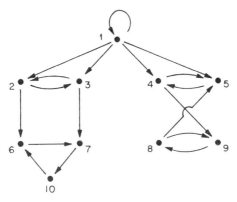

Figure 12. *Schematic representation of a transition graph.*

class and the sets $\{4, 8\}$ and $\{5, 9\}$ are its periodic subclasses with $d = 2$. Note that, by a proper rearrangement of the states, the matrix whose graph is as above can be written in the form shown in Figure 13 (nonzero entries are represented by a $\times$ sign). Thus every ergodic (E_1, E_2) class is represented in a square main diagonal submatrix with all the entries in the remaining parts of the corresponding rows being zero. The periodic subclasses are represented in [not necessarily] square submatrices filling the intersection of a set of rows corresponding to one periodic class with a set of columns corresponding to another periodic class in the same ergodic class. All the other entries in the corresponding rows are zero.

The rearrangement of states, illustrated above, is possible in general and any stochastic matrix can be rearranged so as to have the above form.

Definition 4.1: A matrix is SIA (stochastic, indecomposable, and aperiodic) if it is stochastic and its graph has only one ergodic class with period $d = 1$ [i.e., there are no periodic subclasses].

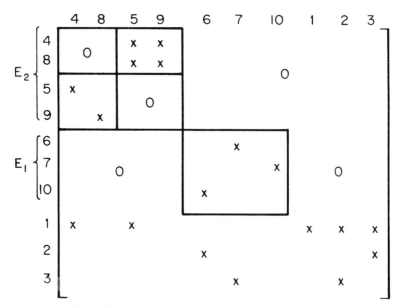

Figure 13. *Canonical representation of stochastic matrix.*

Definition 4.2: A stochastic matrix satisfies the condition H_1 if every pair of states in the associated graph has a common consequent.

Lemma 4.1: A stochastic matrix is SIA if and only if it satisfies the condition H_1.

Proof: Let P be an SIA matrix of order n, and let i and j be two of its states. There is m ($\leq n - 1$) such that both i and j have consequent states i' and j' of order m and i', j' are nontransient. Since there is only one ergodic set which is not periodic, there is an m_1 such that $m_1 \in N_{i'i'}$ and $m_1 \in N_{j'i'}$ so that i' is a common consequent of order $m + m_1$ of both i and j.

Assume now that P satisfies H_1 and that there are several ergodic classes in the graph $G_1, G_2, \ldots, G_r$. Let $i_1 \in G_1$ and $i_j \in G_j$ be a pair of vertices in different classes, then i_1 and i_j have a common consequent k which is nontransient (k is a consequent of nontransient states). Hence i_1 and i_j are consequents of k which implies that $k \in G_1$ and $k \in G_j$ or $G_1 = G_j$. It follows that there is a single ergodic class in the graph. Assume that the ergodic class is divisible into several periodic subclasses $C_1, \ldots, C_d$ and let i_1 and i_j be a pair of vertices in different classes C_1 and C_j respectively. Then i_1 and i_j have a common consequent k which is nontransient and belongs, therefore, to a periodic class C_k. Then k is a consequent of order $k - 1 \pmod{d}$ of i_1 and a consequent of order $k - j \pmod{d}$ of i_j and [since k is a common consequent of both i_1 and i_j] $k - 1 \equiv k - j \pmod{d}$ or $1 \equiv j \pmod{d}$ or $C_1 \equiv C_j$. Thus there is no periodic subdivision of the ergodic class and the proof is complete. ∎

Lemma 4.2: Let (S, Γ) be a graph with n states. If a pair of states i and $j, i, j \in S$, has a common consequent, then it has a common consequent of order ν where $\nu \le n(n-1)/2$.

Proof: If states i and j have a common consequent, then there exists a sequence of (unordered) pairs of states [with $i = i_0, j = j_0$]

$$(i_0 i_0), (i_1 i_1), \ldots, (i_\mu i_\mu)$$

such that (1) $i_k = j_k, k = 0, 1, 2, \ldots, \mu - 1$; (2) $i_k \in i\Gamma^k, j_k \in j\Gamma^k$; (3) $i_\mu = j_\mu$.
If the sequence contains two equal pairs, then omit the part of the sequence between these pairs, including the second of the equal pairs. Repeat this procedure until a reduced sequence is obtained

$$(i_0 i_0), (i_1' j_1'), \ldots, (i_k' j_k'), \ldots, (i_\nu' j_\nu')$$

such that (1) $i_k' \ne j_k', k = 0, 1, \ldots, \nu - 1$; (2) $i_k' \in i\Gamma^k, j_k' \in j\Gamma^k$; (3') $(i_k' j_k') \ne (i_j' j_j'), k \ne j, k, j = 0, 1, 2, \ldots, \nu$: (4') $i_\nu' = j_\nu'$.
Now by (2') and (4'), $i_\nu' = j_\nu'$ is a common consequent of order ν of the states i and j, while by (1') and (3'), ν is at most $n(n-1)/2$. ∎

Remark: It is not known whether the bound given in Lemma 4.2 is sharp. It can be shown however that the difference between the above bound and any sharper bound is of the order of magnitude $n/2$ where $n = |S|$ [see Exercise 4.4].

Definition 4.3: A stochastic matrix is called *scrambling* if every pair of states in the associated graph has a common consequent of order 1.

Lemma 4.3: Let P be a finite stochastic matrix, $\gamma(P) > 0$ if and only if P is scrambling.

Proof: $\min_{i_1, i_2} \sum_j \min (p_{i_1 j}, p_{i_2 j}) > 0$ if and only if for any i_1 and i_2, there is a j with both $p_{i_1 j}$ and $p_{i_2 j} > 0$.

Theorem 4.4: Let P be a finite stochastic matrix. P satisfies H_1 if and only if there is an integer $k \le n(n-1)/2$ such that $\gamma(P^k) > 0$.

Proof: If P satisfies H_1 then, by Lemma 4.2 there is a $k \le n(n-1)/2$ such that P^k is scrambling [the common consequent property is hereditary, i.e., if two states have a common consequent of order n then they have a common consequent of order $\ge n$] so that by Lemma 4.3 $\gamma(P^k) > 0$. If there is k with $\gamma(P^k) > 0$, then P^k is scrambling, i.e., P satisfies H_1. ∎

Corollary 4.5: It is decidable whether a finite homogeneous Markov chain is ergodic or not.

Definition 4.4: A stochastic system $(S, \{A(\sigma)\})$ satisfies condition H_2 (of order k) if there is an integer k such that all the matrices $A(x)$ with $l(x) \ge k$ are scrambling.

Corollary 4.6: A stochastic system is weakly ergodic if and only if it satisfies condition H_2.

Proof: By Lemma 4.3, Proposition 1.7, Theorem 3.1, and Definition 4.4. ∎

Remarks:

a. If all the matrices $A(\sigma)$ are equal one to the other (the homogeneous case) then the condition H_2 reduces to the condition H_1.

b. It suffices that the matrices $A(x)$ with $l(x) = k$ be scrambling for the condition H_2 to be satisfied [see Exercise 4.6].

Theorem 4.7: If a stochastic system $(S, \{A(\sigma)\})$ satisfies the H_2 condition, then it satisfies this condition of order k with

$$k \leq \tfrac{1}{2}(3^n - 2^{n+1} + 1)$$

where $n = |S|$.

Proof: Assume that there is a matrix $A(x)$ with $l(x) > \tfrac{1}{2}(3^n - 2^{n+1} + 1)$ and $A(x)$ is not scrambling. Then there are two states i_1 and i_2 which do not have a common consequent by $A(x)$. Let $x = \sigma_1 \cdots \sigma_v$ and consider the following sequence of unordered pairs of sets of states

$$(\alpha_0^{\,1}, \alpha_0^{\,2}), (\alpha_1^{\,1}, \alpha_1^{\,2}), \ldots, (\alpha_v^{\,1}, \alpha_v^{\,2})$$

where $\alpha_0^{\,1} = i_1, \alpha_0^{\,2} = i_2$ and

$$\alpha_{i+1}^1, \alpha_{i+1}^2$$

are the consequents of the states in $\alpha_i^{\,1}, \alpha_i^{\,2}$ respectively by the matrix $A(\sigma_i)$.

By the definition of the matrix $A(x)$ and of the αs, we have that all αs are nonvoid sets and every pair of αs is a disjoint pair of sets. Let $\alpha_i^{\,3}$ denote the set of states in S which are not in $\alpha_i^{\,1} \cup \alpha_i^{\,2}$. There are 3^n different partitions of S into 3 disjoint subsets $\alpha_i^{\,1}, \alpha_i^{\,2}, \alpha_i^{\,3}$, but $2^{n+1} - 1$ of these have $\alpha_i^{\,1}$ or $\alpha_i^{\,2}$ or both empty. [There are 2^n partitions of S into two sets $\alpha_i^{\,1}$ and $\alpha_i^{\,3}$ or $\alpha_i^{\,2}$ and $\alpha_i^{\,3}$, but the partition with $S = \alpha_i^{\,3}$ is counted in both cases.] Thus there are $3^n - 2^{n+1} + 1$ ordered partitions $(\alpha_i^{\,1}, \alpha_i^{\,2}, \alpha_i^{\,3})$ of S such that both $\alpha_i^{\,1}$ and $\alpha_i^{\,2}$ are not empty. If the order between $\alpha_i^{\,1}$ and $\alpha_i^{\,2}$ is not taken into account then the number of such partitions reduces to $\tfrac{1}{2}(3^n - 2^{n+1} + 1)$. This argument implies that there are two equal pairs in the above sequence say $(\alpha_j^{\,1}, \alpha_j^{\,2}) = (\alpha_k^{\,1}, \alpha_k^{\,2})$, $j < k < n$. It follows that any matrix of the form

$$A(\sigma_1 \cdots \sigma_{j-1}) A^r(\sigma_j \cdots \sigma_{k-1}), \qquad r = 1, 2, \ldots$$

is not scrambling and the condition H_2 is not satisfied. ∎

Corollary 4.8: It is decidable whether a given stochastic system satisfies the H_2 condition.

Proof: By Lemma 4.3, Theorem 4.7, and Definition 4.4. ∎

Remark: To decide that a given system does not satisfy H_2 one must check all matrices $A(x)$ with $l(x) \leq \frac{1}{2}(3^n - 2^{n+1} + 1)$ which will make the procedure difficult and for large n, even impracticable. One may facilitate the computation by disregarding any matrix $A(x)$ which has a scrambling matrix as a factor, for any such matrix is a priori scrambling [see Exercise 4.6]. On the other hand it is shown in the following example that the bound of Theorem 4.7 is sharp and cannot be improved in general.

Theorem 4.9: The bound in Theorem 4.7 is sharp.

Proof: Fix n, let K be a set of n states and let the following sequence by any enumeration of *all different unordered* pairs, of *nonvoid disjoint* sets of states from K:

$$(\alpha_0^1, \alpha_0^2), (\alpha_1^1, \alpha_1^2), \ldots, (\alpha_k^1, \alpha_k^2) \tag{2}$$

such that the number of states in any set of the form $\alpha_i = \alpha_i^1 \cup \alpha_i^2$ is not smaller than in the set α_{i-1} for $i = 1, 2, \ldots, k$. As stated before $k + 1 = \frac{1}{2}(3^n - 2^{n+1} + 1)$.

If φ is a set of states and $A(x)$ is a matrix in a system, denote by $A(x, \varphi)$ the set of states which are consequents of those in φ by $A(x)$. Let $(K, \{A(\sigma)\})$ be a system such that $|\Sigma| = k$ and the matrices $A(\sigma_1), \ldots, A(\sigma_k)$ satisfy the following property:

$$A(\sigma_i, \varphi) = \begin{cases} K & \text{if } \varphi \cap [K - \alpha_{i-1}] \neq \varnothing \\ \alpha_i^1 & \text{if } \varphi \subseteq \alpha_{i-1}^1 \\ \alpha_i^2 & \text{if } \varphi \subseteq \alpha_{i-1}^2 \\ \alpha_i & \text{otherwise} \end{cases} \tag{3}$$

Note that the number of states in $A(\sigma_i, \varphi)$ can be smaller than in φ only in the second or third case in (3). This follows from the definition of sequence (2), and we shall refer to this property as the *conditional monotone* property. Note also that if (3) is satisfied for one-element sets, it is satisfied for any sets.

We will show now that the stochastic system as defined above satisfies the H_2 condition, but there is a word $x \in \Sigma^*$ with $l(x) = k$ such that $A(x)$ is not scrambling.

The second assertion follows from the fact that the matrix $A(x) = A(\sigma_1, \sigma_2, \ldots, \sigma_k)$ is not scrambling by the definition of the sequence (2) and by (3).

To prove the first assertion, assume that there is a matrix $A(x) = A(\sigma_{i_1} \cdots \sigma_{i_t})$ which is not scrambling and such that $l(x) = t > k$. Thus there are two states i_1 and i_2 not having a common consequent by $A(x)$. Set $i_1 = \beta_0^1$, $i_2 = \beta_0^2$, $\beta_j^1 = A(\sigma_{i_j}, \beta_{j-1}^1)$ and $\beta_j^2 = A(\sigma_{i_j}, \beta_{j-1}^2)$ and consider the following sequence

$$(\beta_0^1, \beta_0^2), \ldots, (\beta_t^1, \beta_t^2) \tag{4}$$

This is a sequence of unordered pairs of nonvoid disjoint [by assumption] sets of states, and as $t \geq k + 1$, the sequence contains at least two equal pairs, say

$$(\beta_p{}^1, \beta_p{}^2) = (\beta_q{}^1, \beta_q{}^2), \qquad p < q \tag{5}$$

Consider the following subsequence of (4)

$$(\beta_p{}^1, \beta_p{}^2), \ldots, (\beta_{r-1}^1, \beta_{r-1}^2), (\beta_r{}^1, \beta_r{}^2), \ldots, (\beta_q{}^1, \beta_q{}^2) \tag{6}$$

As before, we shall denote by β_i the set $\beta_i = \beta_i{}^1 \cup \beta_i{}^2$.

The matrix $A(\sigma_{i_r})$ transforms the sets $(\beta_{r-1}^1, \beta_{r-1}^2)$ into the sets $(\beta_r{}^1, \beta_r{}^2)$, but $A(\sigma_{i_r})$ is one of the $A(\sigma_i)$s say $A(\sigma_{i_r}) = A(\sigma_h)$. The following cases must be considered:

(a) $\qquad \beta_{r-1}^1 \cap (K - \alpha_{h-1}) \neq \varnothing \qquad$ or $\qquad \beta_{r-1}^2 \cap (K - \alpha_{h-1}) = \varnothing$

This is impossible, for this would imply that $\beta_r{}^1 \cap \beta_r{}^2 \neq \varnothing$ by (3), contrary to the assumption that these sets are disjoint.

(b) $\qquad\qquad\qquad \beta_{r-1} \subset \alpha_{h-1}^1 \qquad$ or $\qquad \beta_{r-1} \subset \alpha_{h-1}^2$

which is also impossible, as in this case we get that

$$\beta_r{}^1 = A(\sigma_{i_r}, \beta_{r-1}^1) = \alpha_h{}^1 \,(\text{or } \alpha_h{}^2) = A(\sigma_{i_r}, \beta_{r-1}^2) = \beta_r{}^2$$

contrary, by (3), to our assumption that $\beta_r{}^1 \cap \beta_r{}^2 \neq \varnothing$.

(c) $\quad\begin{aligned} &\beta_{r-1}^1 \cap \alpha_{h-1}^1 \neq \varnothing, \qquad \text{together with} \quad \beta_{r-1}^1 \cap \alpha_{h-1}^2 \neq \varnothing, \text{ or} \\ &\beta_{r-1}^2 \cap \alpha_{h-1}^1 \neq \varnothing, \qquad \text{together with} \quad \beta_{h-1}^2 \cap \alpha_{h-1}^2 \neq \varnothing \end{aligned}$

which is also impossible, as in this case we get, by (3), that $\beta_r{}^1 \cap \beta_r{}^2 \neq \varnothing$.

(d) $\quad\begin{aligned} &\beta_{r-1}^1 \subseteq \alpha_{h-1}^1, \qquad \text{together with} \quad \beta_{r-1}^2 \subseteq \alpha_{h-1}^2, \quad \text{or} \\ &\beta_{r-1}^1 \subseteq \alpha_{h-1}^2, \qquad \text{together with} \quad \beta_{r-1} \subseteq \alpha_{h-1}^1 \end{aligned}$

and the inclusion is proper in at least one part of the conditions, which is also impossible, since by the conditional monotone property and by the impossibility of case (b) [applying the same argument to all pairs in sequence (6)], we get that the number of states in β_q is larger than that in β_p, contrary to (5).

(e) $\quad\begin{aligned} &\beta_{r-1}^1 = \alpha_{h-1}^1, \qquad \text{together with} \quad \beta_{r-1}^2 = \alpha_{h-1}^2, \quad \text{or} \\ &\beta_{r-1}^1 = \alpha_{h-1}^2, \qquad \text{together with} \quad \beta_{r-1}^2 = \alpha_{h-1}^1 \end{aligned}$

In this case we get that sequence (6) is a middle part of sequence (3), which is impossible since all the sets in (2) are different, contrary to (5).

All possible cases are covered by (a)–(e), and the proof is complete. Note that the bound in Theorem 4.7, although sharp, is independent of the number of letters in the alphabet Σ. On the other hand the number of letters in the counterexamples of Theorem 4.9 grows with n. It would be therefore interesting to find out whether the bound in Theorem 4.7 can be improved under the condition that the number of letters in Σ is kept fixed or small [say 2 letters]. No answer to this question is presently available. ∎

Definition 4.5: A stochastic system $(S, \{A(\sigma)\})$ is *definite* [of order k] if there is an integer k such that all the matrices $A(x)$ with $l(x) \geq k$ are constant and this property does not hold true for all words x with $l(x) < k$.

Corollary 4.10: If $(S, \{A(\sigma)\})$ is a definite stochastic system of order k and $y = ux$ is a word such that $l(x) = k$, $l(u) \geq 0$ $[l(y) \geq k]$ then $A(y) = A(x)$.

Proof: $A(y) = A(u)A(x) = A(x)$, by Exercise 1.4 in the preliminary section since $A(x)$ is constant.

A final problem to be discussed in this section is the decision problem for definite stochastic systems. This problem is solved by the following.

Theorem 4.11: If a stochastic system $(S, \{A(\sigma)\})$ such that $|S| = n$ is definite of order k, then $k \leq n - 1$.

Proof: Denote by V the set of all n-dimensional vectors $\bar{v} = (v_1, \ldots, v_2)$ such that $\sum v_i = 0$; denote by H^i the set of matrices $H^i = \{A(x) : l(x) = i\}$ and denote by VH^i the linear closure of the set of vectors of the form $\bar{v}A(x)$, $v \in V$, $A(x) \in H^i$, i.e.,

$$VH^i = \{\sum_{i=1}^{r} \bar{v}_i A(x); \bar{v}_i \in V, A(x) \in H^i, r = 0, 1, \ldots\}$$

Then (a) V is a linear space, (b) VH^i is a linear space $VH^i \subseteq V$.

To prove (b) we note that any vector of the form $\bar{v}A(x)$ is in V, which is closed under addition; the set VH^i is closed under vector addition by definition, and is closed under multiplication by a constant because the set V is closed under such multiplication [i.e., $c \sum \bar{v}_i A(x) = \sum (c\bar{v}_i)A(x) = \sum \bar{v}_i' A(x)$].

(c) $VH^{i+1} \subseteq VH^i$. This follows from the fact that $VH \subseteq V$ and $VH^{i+1} = (VH)H^i \subseteq VH^i$.

(d) If for some i, $VH^i = VH^{i+1}$, then $VH^i = VH^{i+j}$, $j = 1, 2, \ldots$. This follows from the fact that $VH^{i+2} = (VH^{i+1})H$.

(e) If the system is definite of order k then VH^k is the space containing the zero vector as its single element [i.e., dim $VH^k = 0$], but this is not true for VH^i, $i < k$.

This follows from the fact that if and only if $A(x)$ is constant then $\bar{v}A(x) = \mathbf{0}$ for all $\bar{v} \in V$.

Consider now the sequence of linear spaces

$$V(=VH^0) \supseteq VH \supseteq VH^1 \supseteq \cdots \supseteq VH^i \cdots$$

Because of property (d) this sequence must have the form

$$VH^0 \supset VH \supset VH^1 \supset \cdots \supset VH^p = VH^{p+1} = VH^{p+2} = \cdots$$

[the sequence cannot descrease indefinitely because dim $V = n - 1$]. Thus, if the system is definite of order k, then necessarily $VH^p = VH^k = \{0\}$ by property (e) so that $n - 1 = \dim VH^0 > \dim VH^1 > \cdots > \dim VH^k = 0$. Hence, $k \leq n - 1$. ∎

Corollary 4.12: If P is a stochastic matrix of order n such that P^k is constant but P^{k-1} is not, then $k \leq n - 1$.

Corollary 4.13: It is decidable whether a given stochastic system is definite.

Example: Consider the following set of 3×3 matrices

$$A(\sigma_1) = \begin{pmatrix} \frac{1}{4} & \frac{1}{2} & \frac{1}{4} \\ \frac{1}{8} & \frac{1}{2} & \frac{3}{8} \\ \frac{1}{4} & \frac{1}{2} & \frac{1}{4} \end{pmatrix}, \qquad A(\sigma_2) = \begin{pmatrix} \frac{1}{4} & \frac{1}{2} & \frac{1}{4} \\ \frac{1}{6} & \frac{1}{2} & \frac{1}{3} \\ \frac{1}{4} & \frac{1}{2} & \frac{1}{4} \end{pmatrix}$$

Straightforward computation shows that

$$A(\sigma_1\sigma_1) = A(\sigma_2\sigma_1) = \begin{pmatrix} \frac{5}{24} & \frac{1}{2} & \frac{7}{24} \\ \frac{5}{24} & \frac{1}{2} & \frac{7}{24} \\ \frac{5}{24} & \frac{1}{2} & \frac{7}{24} \end{pmatrix}$$

and

$$A(\sigma_2\sigma_2) = A(\sigma_1\sigma_2) = \begin{pmatrix} \frac{3}{16} & \frac{1}{2} & \frac{5}{16} \\ \frac{3}{16} & \frac{1}{2} & \frac{5}{16} \\ \frac{3}{16} & \frac{1}{2} & \frac{5}{16} \end{pmatrix}$$

This system is therefore definite of order 2.

EXERCISES

1. Prove that the property of being a nontransient state is decidable and find an optimal algorithm for deciding it. [A property is decidable if there is an algorithm with the aid of which one can decide, after finitely many steps, whether an element of a certain class has or has not the property.]

2. Prove that the relation of being in the same ergodic class is an equivalence relation.

3. Prove that the relation of being in the same periodic class is an equivalence relation.

4. Find a graph (S, Γ) such that $|S| = n$, it satisfies the H_1 property, but there is a pair of states $i, j \in S$ which do not have a common consequent of order m [m is a function of n] where m is as close as possible to the bound of Lemma 4.2.

5. Provide a full proof for Corollary 4.5.

6. Let P and Q be stochastic finite matrices. Prove that the product PQ is scrambling if one of the matrices P or Q [or both] is scrambling.

7. On the basis of Theorem 4.7 and Exercise 4.6 above, give an algorithm for deciding whether a given stochastic system satisfies H_2.

8. Consider the following condition: A stochastic matrix P satisfies *condition* H_3 of order k if there is an integer k and a state j such that j is a consequent of order k of all the states (including j). Prove: If P has finite order, then the conditions H_1 and H_3 are equivalent.

9. Let f be a 1–1 function from the set of all disjoint unordered pairs of integers into the set of intergers. Let $P = [p_{ij}]$ be an infinite stochastic matrix such that $p_{ij} \neq 0$ if and only if there is a k with $f(i, k) = j$. Show that P has the H_1 property, but it does not have the H_3 property.

10. Find an infinite stochastic matrix P which satisfies the H_3 property of order 1 but $\gamma(P) = 0$. [Compare with Lemma 4.3.]

11. Find an infinite stochastic matrix P such that $\lim_{n \to \infty} d(P^n) = 0$ but $\lim_{n \to \infty} \delta(P^n) = 1$.

In the following exercises it is assumed that the matrices are of finite order.

12. Let P be a stochastic matrix, Prove that there is a stochastic matrix Q such that

$$\lim_{n \to \infty} \frac{1}{n} \sum_{m=1}^{n} P^m = Q$$

13. The matrix Q in Exercise 12 is constant if and only if there is a single ergodic class in the graph associated with the given matrix.

14. If, and only if, there are no periodic subclasses in any ergodic class of P, then

$$\lim_{n \to \infty} \frac{1}{n} \sum_{m=1}^{n} P^m = \lim_{n \to \infty} P^n = Q$$

and Q is constant.

15. Show that in any of the Exercises 12–14 the matrix Q satisfies the equation $QP = PQ = Q$ or $Q[I - P] = 0$, providing a means for computing it.

16. Prove that if the graph associated with a matrix P contains a single ergodic class, then there is a unique solution to the system of $n + 1$ equations

$$(x_1, \ldots, x_n)[I - P] = 0$$
$$x_1 + \cdots + x_n = 1$$

17. Let $\bar{P}_r$ be the $(n - 1)$-dimensional matrix obtained from P by substracting the rth row from all its rows and then deleting the rth row and column. Let $\bar{x}_r$ be the vector obtained from the vector x by deleting its rth entry. Prove:

a. If, and only if, there is a single ergodic class in the graph of P, then

$$\det(I - \bar{P}_r) \neq 0 \qquad \text{for any} \quad r$$

b. Let ξ_r be the rth row of P, then the solution to the system of equations in Exercise 16 [given that there is a single ergodic set in the graph of P] is

$$(x_1, \ldots, x_{r-1}, x_{r+1}, \ldots, x_n) = \bar{\xi}_{rr}(I - \bar{P}_r)^{-1}$$

$$x_r = 1 - \sum_{i \neq r} x_i$$

18. If

$$P = \begin{bmatrix} \frac{1}{2} & \frac{1}{4} & \frac{1}{4} \\ \frac{1}{2} & 0 & \frac{1}{2} \\ \frac{1}{4} & \frac{1}{4} & \frac{1}{2} \end{bmatrix}$$

compute $\lim_{n \to \infty} P^n$.

19. Let $P(\sigma)$ be a set of stochastic matrices, let $\bar{P}_r(\sigma)$ be defined as in Exercise 17 and let $\bar{\xi}_{rr}(\sigma)$ be the rth row of $P(\sigma)$ with the rth entry deleted. Let $x = \sigma_1 \cdots \sigma_k$. a. Prove by induction that

$$\bar{\xi}_{rr}(x) = \bar{\xi}_{rr}(\sigma_1)\bar{P}_r(\sigma_2 \cdots \sigma_k) + \bar{\xi}_{rr}(\sigma_2)\bar{P}_2(\sigma_3 \cdots \sigma_k) + \cdots$$
$$+ \bar{\xi}_{rr}(\sigma_{k-1})\bar{P}_r(\sigma_k) + \bar{\xi}_{rr}(\sigma_k)$$

b. Show that with the aid of the above formula one can compute the entries of a 2-dimensional matrix $P(x)$ directly from the values of the 2-dimensional matrices $P(\sigma)$ as follows:

$$P_{21}(x) = P_{21}(\sigma_k) + \sum_{i=1}^{k-1} P_{21}(\sigma_i) \prod_{j=i+1}^{k} (P_{11}(\sigma_j) - P_{21}(\sigma_j))$$

$$P_{12}(x) = P_{12}(\sigma_k) + \sum_{i=1}^{k-1} P_{12}(\sigma_i) \prod_{j=i+1}^{k} (P_{11}(\sigma_j) - P_{21}(\sigma_j))$$

$$P_{11}(x) = 1 - P_{21}(x); \qquad P_{22}(x) = 1 - P_{21}(x)$$

20. Show that if $P = [P_{ij}]$ is a 2-dimensional matrix, then $\det P = P_{11} - P_{21}$.

21. Let P be an SIA matrix of order n and let η_r^k denote the rth column of P^k. Show that the set of vectors $\{\eta_r^k\}$ are all contained in an $(n-1)$-dimensional subspace of the n-dimensional Euclidean space.

22. Show by examples that it is possible to have two finite stochastic matrices A and B such that

a. $\gamma(A^k) = 0 = \gamma(B^k)$ for all integers k, but there is an integer k such that $\gamma((AB)^k) > 0$.

b. There is an integer k such that $\gamma(A^k) > 0 < \gamma(B^k)$ but for all integers k $\gamma((AB)^k) = 0$.

23. Two stochastic matrices P and Q are called similar ($P \sim Q$) if they have the same associated graph. Prove that if Q is an SIA matrix and $PQ \sim P$, then P is scrambling.

24. Let $(S, \{A(\sigma)\})$ be a stochastic system. Prove that all the matrices $A(x)$ are SIA if and only if the system is weakly ergodic. Let t be the number of all the different graphs associated with $|S|$-dimensional SIA matrices. Prove that if the given system has the property that all the matrices of the form $A(x)$ are SIA, then all the matrices $A(x)$ with $l(x) \geq t + 1$ are scrambling [use Exercise 23].

25. Let $(S, \{A(\sigma)\})$ be a weakly ergodic Markov system. Prove that

$$\lim_{l(x) \to \infty} \|A(yx) - \lim_{n \to \infty} A(x^n)\| = 0$$

for any word y.

26. Let $(S, \{A(\sigma)\})$ be a stochastic system such that $|S| = n$ and having the following property: For any $\sigma \in \Sigma$, if α and β are two disjoint subsets of S and also $A(\sigma, \beta)$ and $A(\sigma, \alpha)$ are disjoint then $|A(\sigma, \alpha) \cup A(\sigma, \beta)| > |\alpha \cup \beta|$. Prove that any such system satisfies the condition H_2 of order $n - 1$ and prove that the bound $n - 1$ above is sharp for such systems.

27. Let $(S, \{A(\sigma)\})$ be a system such that all the matrices $A(\sigma)$ have the same graph which satisfies H_1. Then the system is weakly ergodic.

28. Find a sequence of infinite stochastic matrices P_k such that for every integer k, $P_k{}^k$ is scrambling but P_k^{k-1} is not.

29. Find a sequence of infinite state systems of stochastic matrices $S_k = \{A_{kj}(x)\}$ such that S_k satisfies H_2 of order k but S_k does not satisfy H_2 of smaller order.

30. Find a sequence of stochastic infinite matrices P_k such that $P_k{}^k$ satisfies H_3 but P_k^{k-1} does not satisfy H_3.

31. Show that there exists an infinite stochastic matrix P such that P satisfies H_3 but $\gamma(P^k) = 0$ for $k = 1, 2, \ldots$.

OPEN PROBLEMS

1. Let P be an infinite stochastic matrix and assume that there is an integer k such that $\gamma(P^k) > 0$. Does this imply that P satisfies H_3?

2. Is the condition "$\gamma(P^k) > \epsilon > 0$ for some ϵ and some integer k" decidable for infinite stochastic matrices P?

3. Is the condition that $\lim_{n \to \infty} d(P^n) \to 0$ implied by H_1 or H_3 for infinite stochastic matrices?

4. Find a sharp bound for Lemma 4.2 or show that the given bound is sharp.

5. Improve the bound of Theorem 4.7 under the assumption that the alphabet is bounded [e.g., 2 letters] or show that it is impossible to improve the bound.

5. Eigenvalues of Stochastic Matrices and Particular Cases

We shall list here for future reference the properties of the eigenvalues of stochastic matrices without going into details. A detailed account on these properties, as well as their proofs, can be found in the book of Frechet (1938). See also Feller (1957), Frazer, Duncan, and Collar (1938), Turnbull and Aitken (1932), Turakainen (1968) and Yasui and Yajima (1969).

Let A be a stochastic matrix $A = [a_{ij}]$ and let $\lambda_1, \ldots, \lambda_r$ be the distinct eigenvalues of A [$r \leq n =$ the order of A]. Then

1. $|\lambda_i| \leq 1$ for $i = 1, 2, \ldots, r$.
2. There is an index i such that $\lambda_i = 1$.
3. If and only if the eigenvalue $\lambda_i = 1$ is simple, there is a single ergodic class in the graph of A.
4. Let $A^m = [a_{ij}^{(m)}]$, then for $m > n$ the following identity holds

$$a_{ij}^{(m)} = \sum_{k=1}^{r} \lambda_k^{m} \omega_{ijk}(m)$$

where $\omega_{ijk}(m)$ is a polynomial in m of smaller order than the multiplicity of λ_k.

5. There are periodic classes in the graph of A if and only if there are eigenvalues λ_i such that $\lambda_i \neq 1$ but $|\lambda_i| = 1$, in which case all these λ_i are roots of unity, and the subsum corresponding to these eigenvalues in the formula in 4 above is not identically equal to zero.

6. If the eigenvalues of A are all simple then the formula in 4 reduces to

$$a_{ij}^{(m)} = \sum_{k=1}^{n} \left[\sum_{\nu=1}^{n} x_{\nu}^{(k)} y_{\nu}^{(k)}\right]^{-1} x_i^{(k)} y_j^{(k)} \lambda_k^{m}$$

where $x_i^{(k)}$ and $y_i^{(k)}$ are the ith entries in the column or row eigenvector, correspondingly, of the eigenvalue λ_k.

7. If the eigenvalues of A are all simple, then A can be written in the form $A = \sum_{i=1}^{n} \lambda_i A_i$, where $\lambda_1 = 1$, and the As are square matrices such that $A_i A_j = 0$ if $i \neq j$, $A_i^2 = A_i$ and $A_1 = \lim_{m \to \infty} A^m$, if the limit exists.

8. If A and B are two stochastic matrices which commute and have simple eigenvalues, then they both have the same A_1 [i.e., they both have the same limiting matrix, if it exists] and the same A_is, $i > 1$, will appear in the expansion in 7.

9. Let the formula in (4) be written in the form

$$\sum_{k=1}^{r} \lambda_k^{m} \omega_{ijk}(m) = \omega_{ij}(m) + \epsilon_{ij}(m)$$

where $\omega_{ij}(m)$ is the subsum corresponding to the eigenvalues λ_k such that $|\lambda_k| = 1$ and $\epsilon_{ij}(m)$ is the remaining subsum. Then $\omega_{ij}(m)$ is a periodic function of m [over the integers] having finitely many values and $\epsilon_{ij}(m)$ is a function of m such that $\lim_{m \to \infty} |\epsilon_{ij}(m)| = 0$.

Some of the properties listed above will be used in subsequent sections. Some others should be used in the proofs of the following exercises; the rest of them are given for the sake of completeness. Unfortunately the properties of the eigenvalues of individual matrices A_i have very little to do, in general, with the properties of the eigenvalues of their products of the form $\prod A_i$. Therefore the main use of the properties of eigenvalues is for the homogeneous case [see, however, the above-cited works of Turakainen (1968) and Yasui and Yajima (1969)]. In that case (the homogeneous) there is a strong connection between the properties of the eigenvalues and the classification of states given in the previous section. This is shown by properties 3, 5, and 9.

EXERCISES

1. Let $(s, \{A(\sigma)\})$ be a finite state system such that all the eigenvalues of the matrices $A(\sigma)$ are simple, $A(\sigma_i)A(\sigma_j) = A(\sigma_j)A(\sigma_i)$ for all i and j, and the products of "corresponding" eigenvalues other than $+1$ tend to zero. Then the system is strongly ergodic. [By corresponding eigenvalues we mean eigenvalues corresponding to the same matrix A_i in the expansion of $A(\sigma)$, property 7. Because of property 8 all the matrices $A(\sigma)$ have the same matrices A_i in their expansion.]

2. Show by an example that there are stochastic matrices having the same limit but which do not commute [$AB \neq BA$ but $\lim A^n = \lim B^n = Q$].

3. Prove that 2-state stochastic matrices which have the same limit commute.

In the following exercises the matrices are assumed to be of order 2 and the eigenvalue which differs from $+1$ (if there is such an eigenvalue) of a matrix A will be denoted by λ^A.

4. Prove that if $A = [a_{ij}]$ is a two state stochastic matrix then $\lambda^A = \det A = a_{11} - a_{21}$.

5. If $A = [a_{ij}]$ and $B = [b_{ij}]$ and $AB = C = [c_{ij}]$ then

$$c_{12} = a_{12}\lambda^B + b_{12}; \qquad c_{21} = a_{21}\lambda^B + b_{21}$$

extend this formula by induction to longer products of 2-state stochastic matrices.

6. Let $\Sigma = \{0, 1, \ldots, d-1\}$ and define

$$A(i) = \begin{bmatrix} 1 - \dfrac{i}{d} & \dfrac{i}{d} \\ 1 - \dfrac{i+1}{d} & \dfrac{i+1}{d} \end{bmatrix}, \qquad i = 0, 1, \ldots, d-1$$

Prove that

$$a_{12}(x) = .\sigma_k \sigma_{k-1} \cdots \sigma_1$$

where $x = \sigma_1, \ldots, \sigma_k \in \sum^*$ and $.\sigma_k \sigma_{k-1} \cdots \sigma_1$ is an ordinary d-ary fraction.

7. Let $(S, \{A(\sigma)\})$ be a system such that the ratio $a_{12}(\sigma)/a_{21}(\sigma)$ is independent of σ and $\lambda^{A(\sigma)} < 1$ for all σ then the system is strongly ergodic [find the limiting matrix].

8. Let $(S, (P_i))$ be a two state Markov chain. If $\prod_{i=m} \lambda^{P_i}$ tends to some limit which can be calculated and the ratio between the $1, 2$ element and the $2, 1$ element of P_i is independent on i then the limit H_{mn} can be calculated [find the formula].

9. Find H_{1n} where

$$P_i = \begin{bmatrix} 1 - \dfrac{2n_2}{i^3 + 1} & \dfrac{2n_2}{i^3 + 1} \\ \dfrac{2n_1}{i^3 + 1} & 1 - \dfrac{2n_1}{i^3 + 1} \end{bmatrix}$$

where $n_1, n_2 > 0$ and $n_1 + n_2 = 1$. *Hint:* $\prod_{n=2}^{\infty} [(n^3 - 1)/(n^3 + 1)] = \frac{2}{3}$.

10. Let $(S, \{A(\sigma)\})$ be an n-state stochastic system such that all the eigenvalues of $A(\sigma)$ are simple for all σ all the eigenvalues of $A(\sigma)$ different from $+1$ have modulus <1 and such that $\lim_{n\to\infty} A(\sigma_i^n) = \lim_{n\to\infty} A(\sigma_j^n)$ for all i and j [the limit exists necessarily by the above required properties] then the system is strongly ergodic.

11. Formulate and prove a theorem which parallels the theorem in Exercise 10 for n-state Markov·chains.

12.* Prove: For any integer n, there exist a finite set of stochastic matrices such that any probabilistic vector of order n having finite binary expansion, can be realized as a row in a finite product of these matrices [compare with Exercise 6 above].

6. Bibliographical Notes

Most of the material and exercises of Sections 1 and 2 are based on the work of Dobrushin (1956), Hajnal (1958), Kozniewska (1962), Paz and Reichaw (1967) and Paz (1968b). While Section 3 is based mostly on Paz (1968b, 1970d), a particular case of Theorem 3.3 was first proved by Rabin (1963) and the example in that section is due to Kesten (private communication).

Section 4 and some of its exercises are based on the work of Paz (1965) and Wolfowitz (1963). A (very) particular case of Corollary 4.12 was proved by Blogovescensky (1960) but the method of proof of that corollary here is due to Youval [see Perles *et al.* (1963)]. Exercise 25 at the end of Section 4 is from

Larisse and Schützenberger (1966) and Exercise 26 from Sarymsakov (1958) References for Section 5 are given at the beginning of that section. Additional references for the whole part A: Sirazdinov (1950), Sarymsakov (1952, 1956, 1958), Sarymsakov and Mustafin (1957), Sapogov (1949, 1950, 1967), Rosenblatt (1957), Bernstein (1936, 1944, 1946), Dynkin (1954), Doob (1953), Frechet (1938), Kalman (1968), Kalman *et al.* (1969), Kemeny and Snell (1960), Kemeny *et al.* (1966), Kolmogorov (1958), Linnik (1948, 1969a, b), Lovell (1969), Marik and Ptak (1960), Markov (1913, 1951), Mott (1957), Mott and Schneider (1957), and Paz (1963).

B. OPERATION ON MARKOV SYSTEMS

1. The Direct Sum and Product

Definition 1.1: Let A and B be two square matrices, A or order r and B of order s. The matrix

$$A \dotplus B = \begin{bmatrix} A & 0 \\ 0 & B \end{bmatrix}$$

of order $r + s$ is called their direct sum. It is easily verified that

$$(A_1 \dotplus B_1)(A_2 \dotplus B_2) = A_1 A_2 \dotplus B_1 B_2 \tag{7}$$

provided that the right-hand side of the equation is defined. Trivially, the direct sum of two stochastic matrices is stochastic.

Definition 1.2: Let $A = [a_{ij}]$ and $B = [b_{kl}]$ be two matrices [not necessarily stochastic] of order $m \times n$ and $p \times q$ respectively [thus the matrices are not necessarily square]. Then $A \otimes B$ denotes the Kronecker [or direct] product of A and B where

$$A \otimes B = C = [c_{ik, jl}] = [a_{ij} b_{kl}]$$

The double indices ik, jl of the elements of C are ordered lexicographically

$$ik = 11, 12, \ldots, 1p, \ldots, m1, \ldots, mp;$$
$$jl = 11, \ldots, 1q, \ldots, n1, \ldots, nq$$

Note that the elements in the ikth row of C are products of elements in the kth row of B, and similarly for the jlth column of C. C can thus be written in the form

$$C = \begin{bmatrix} a_{11}B & \cdots & a_{1n}B \\ \vdots & & \\ a_{m1}B & \cdots & a_{mn}B \end{bmatrix}$$

Lemma 1.1: Let $A = [a_{ij}]$, $B = [b_{ij}]$, $A' = [a'_{ij}]$ and $B' = [b'_{ij}]$ be matrices such that the [ordinary] products AB and $A'B'$ are defined. Then

$$(AB) \otimes (A'B') = (A \otimes A')(B \otimes B') \tag{8}$$

Proof: The ij entry in AB is $\sum_t a_{it}b_{tj}$. The kl entry in $A'B'$ is $\sum_r a'_{kr}b'_{rl}$. Therefore the ik, jl entry in $(AB) \otimes (A'B')$ is $\sum_t a_{it}b_{tj} \sum_r a'_{kr}b'_{rl}$. The ik, mn entry in $A \otimes A'$ is $a_{im}a'_{kn}$. The mn, jl entry in $B \otimes B'$ is $b_{mj}b'_{nl}$. Therefore the ik, jl entry in $(A \otimes A')(B \otimes B')$ is

$$\sum_{m,n} a_{im}a'_{kn}b_{mj}b'_{nl} = \sum_m a_{im}b_{mj} \sum_n a'_{kn}b'_{nl}$$

as required.

Lemma 1.2: If A and B are stochastic matrices, then so is $A \otimes B$.

The proof is straightforward and is left to the reader.

Definition 1.3: If $(S, \{A(\sigma)\})$ and $(S', \{A'(\sigma)\})$ are two stochastic systems over the same alphabet Σ, then their direct sum is defined as $(S \cup S', \{A(\sigma) \dotplus A'(\sigma)\})$ and their direct product as $(S \times S', \{A(\sigma) \otimes A'(\sigma)\})$. It follows from (7) and (8) that the matrix related to a word $x \in \Sigma^*$ is $A(x) \dotplus A'(x)$ in the sum system and $A(x) \otimes A'(x)$ in the product system.

Lemma 1.3: Let $A = [a_{ij}]$ and $B = [b_{ij}]$ be two scrambling [see Definition A.4.3] matrices, then $C = [c_{ij}] = A \otimes B$ is also a scrambling matrix.

Proof: Let i_1k_1 and i_2k_2 be any two rows in C. A being scrambling, there is j_1 such that $a_{i_1j_1}, a_{i_2j_2} > 0$, similarly there is l, such that $b_{k_1l_1}, b_{k_2l_2} > 0$; this implies that $c_{i_1k_1j_1l_1} > 0$ and $c_{i_2k_2j_1l_1} > 0$ and therefore the states labeled i_1k_1 and i_2k_2 have a common consequent in the graph of C.

Corollary 1.4: Let $(S, \{A(\sigma)\})$ and $(S', \{A'(\sigma)\})$ be two quasidefinite stochastic systems, then $(S \times S', \{A(\sigma) \otimes A'(\sigma)\})$ is a quasidefinite system.

Proof: The proof is straightforward and is left to the reader.

Definition 1.4: Let $A = [a_{ij}]$ be a Markov matrix and let $\{B(q)\} = \{[b_{ij}(q)]\}$ be a set of Markov matrices, one matrix for every state q of A. The *cascade product* of A and $\{B(q)\}$ is the matrix $C = [c_{ik,jl}] = [a_{ij}b_{kl}(i)]$.

Definition 1.4 above can easily be extended to Markov systems but property (8) in Lemma 1.1 does not apply here, and there is no simple relation between an entry in a matrix corresponding to a word in a cascade product and the entries in the components of the system corresponding to the same word. Once a cascade product is formed it can be further combined in cascade product with another set of matrices, and so forth.

The reader who is familiar with deterministic automata theory will recognize that Definition 1.4 above is an extension of the parallel definition in the deterministic case. The graphical representation of a cascade product is given below in Figure 14. The two systems A and B are assumed to be Markovian. The next state of A depends on the present state of A and on the present input (line represented by X). The next state of B depends on the present state of both A (line represented by Y), and B and on the present input. The state of the system C is represented by a pair of states, one state from A and one from B (lines Y and Z). The system may further be generalized by introducing a combinatorial gate between line Y and box B, and another combinatorial gate between the lines Y and Z, and the actual output of the system.

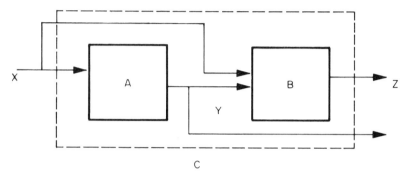

Figure 14. *Graphical representation of a cascade product of Markov matrices.*

Note that if the system B is independent on the input line Y, then the cascade product reduces to the previously defined Kronecker product and the connection between the two systems is a parallel connection.

In addition to the direct sum, Kronecker product, and cascade product defined above, one can define other forms of connections or combinations of connections. The basic problem is, however, to find conditions under which a given Markovian system can be decomposed into simpler parts, using these interconnections. This topic will be dealt with in the next section.

EXERCISES

1. Prove the relation (7).

2. Prove Lemma 1.2.

3. Prove Corollary 1.4.

4. Prove Corollary 1.4 for definite systems [see Definition A.4.5].

5. Prove that Corollary 1.4 holds true when one of the systems is quasidefinite and the other is definite.

6. Prove that the box C in Figure 14 represents a Markovian system [i.e., its next state depends on its present state and present input only] provided that the systems A and B are such.

2. Decomposition

Definition 2.1: A set S' of states of a Markov system A is a persistent subsystem of A if and only if the set of states which are accessible from S' are in S'.

Note that it follows from Definition 2.1 above that the submatrices of the matrices of A corresponding to states in S' are Markov matrices.

Definition 2.2: A Markov system $(S, C(\sigma))$ is *decomposable* if and only if it is isomorphic to a persistent subsystem of a cascade product of two (or more) Markov systems such that the number of states of every component in the product is smaller than the number of states of A.

Let $C = (S, \{C(\sigma)\})$ be a Markov system and assume that it is decomposable. Then $C(\sigma)$ is a submatrix of the matrix $[c_{ik,jl}(\sigma)]$ [the row and column indices have been written as double indices to facilitate the exposition], and [see Definition 1.4] after a proper assignment of indices,

$$[c_{ik,jl}(\sigma)] = [a_{ij}(\sigma) \cdot b_{kl}(i, \sigma)] \tag{9}$$

where $A = (S', \{A(\sigma)\})$ and $B = (S'', \{B(i, \sigma)\})$ are Markov systems with $|S'| < |S|$ and $|S''| < |S|$. There may be entries $c_{ik,jl}(\sigma)$ in (9) which do not belong to $C(\sigma)$, since it is required only that $S \subset S' \times S''$ [C is a persistent submachine of the cascade product], in which case the Eq. (9) contains "don't care" conditions.

Summing up both sides of Eq. (9) over l and noting that $B(i, \sigma)$ are stochastic for every i and σ, we have that for fixed $i, k,$ and j

$$\sum_l c_{ik,jl}(\sigma) = a_{ij}(\sigma) \tag{10}$$

The right-hand side of (10) does not depend on k and therefore also the left-hand side must have this property.

Summing up now both sides of Eq. (9) for j and noting that $A(\sigma)$ is stochastic we have that for fixed $i, k,$ and l

$$\sum_j c_{ik,jl}(\sigma) = b_{kl}(i, \sigma) \tag{11}$$

Combining (9), (10), and (11) we have that for every i, j, k, l the following equation must hold true

$$\sum_l c_{ik,jl}(\sigma) \sum_j c_{ik,jl}(\sigma) = c_{ik,jl}(\sigma) \tag{12}$$

We are now able to formulate two necessary conditions for decomposability.

Definition 2.3: A partition on the state set S of a system is a collection of subsets of S such that each state in S belongs to one and only one such subset. Each subset as above will be called a block of the partition. If the number of blocks is bigger than one and smaller than the number of states, then the partition is nontrivial.

Let $C = (S, \{C(\sigma)\})$ be a Markovian system which is decomposable. It follows from Eq. (10) above and the remark after that the system must satisfy the following:

Lumpability condition: There exists a nontrivial partition on the state set S such that for any σ, the sum of the columns of the matrix $C(\sigma)$ corresponding to any block of the partition, is a column having equal values in entries corresponding to the same block of the partition.

Remark: One sees easily that the partition in the lumpability condition above is represented in Eq. (10) by the first part of the row [or column] double index, i.e., two states are in the same block if they have the same i in their row-ik index (or the same j in their column-jl index). Thus, summing up all $c_{ik,jl}(\sigma)$ for fixed j [i.e., in a given block] results in a value which depends on i [i.e., on the corresponding block] but not on k.

It follows now from (12) that if the system $(S, \{C(\sigma)\})$ is decomposable, one must also have the following:

Condition of Separability: There exist two nontrivial partitions on the state set, π with blocks π_j and τ with blocks τ_l such that: (1) $|\pi_j \cap \tau_l| \leq 1$ for all j and l; (2) if $\pi_j \cap \tau_l = jl$, then for all ik and all σ

$$\sum_l c_{ik,jl}(\sigma) \sum_j c_{ik,jl}(\sigma) = c_{ik,jl}(\sigma)$$

Remark: The partitions π and τ in the separability condition are represented in Eq. (12) by the first and second part of the column [or row] index correspondingly. Thus two states are in the same block of π if they have the same j and they are in the same block of τ if they have the same l in their jl-column index.

The previous considerations suggest the following:

Theorem 2.1: A Markov system $(S, \{C(\sigma)\})$ is decomposable if and only if it satisfies the conditions of lumpability and separability with the same π partition in both conditions.

Proof: Necessity has been proved already. It is easy to show that the conditions are also sufficient, for if a system $(S, \{C(\sigma)\})$ satisfies the two conditions, then, by a proper reindexing of the entries of the matrices $C(\sigma)$ into double indices: $C(\sigma) = [c_{ik,jl}(\sigma)]$ with i, j ranging over the blocks of π and k, l ranging over the blocks of τ, one can define the matrices $A(\sigma)$ and $B(i, \sigma)$ by way of the Eqs. (10) and (11). [If for some l and k, $\pi_l \cap \tau_k = \varnothing$ then this represents a "dno't care" condition and the corresponding entries in the $B(i, \sigma)$ matrices can be chosen at will.] ∎

The decomposition procedure will be illustrated in the following example.

Example 13: Let $C = (S, \{C(\sigma)\})$ be a Markov system such that $S = \{1, 2, 3, 4, 5\}$ [for the sake of simplicity the states are identified with their index if no ambiguity results], $\Sigma = \{a, b\}$, and

$$C(a) = \begin{bmatrix} \frac{1}{4} & 0 & \frac{1}{4} & 0 & \frac{1}{2} \\ \frac{1}{4} & 0 & \frac{1}{4} & 0 & \frac{1}{2} \\ \frac{1}{2} & \frac{1}{4} & \frac{1}{6} & \frac{1}{12} & 0 \\ 0 & \frac{3}{4} & 0 & \frac{1}{4} & 0 \\ 0 & 0 & \frac{1}{2} & \frac{1}{2} & 0 \end{bmatrix}, \qquad C(b) = \begin{bmatrix} 1 & 0 & 0 & 0 & 0 \\ \frac{1}{2} & \frac{1}{2} & 0 & 0 & 0 \\ 0 & \frac{1}{2} & 0 & \frac{1}{2} & 0 \\ \frac{1}{3} & \frac{1}{6} & \frac{1}{3} & \frac{1}{6} & 0 \\ \frac{1}{3} & 0 & \frac{1}{3} & 0 & \frac{1}{3} \end{bmatrix}$$

Consider the partitions $\pi = (\pi_1, \pi_2, \pi_3) = (\{1, 2\}, \{3, 4\}, \{5\})$ and $\tau = (\tau_1, \tau_2) = (\{1, 3, 5\}, \{2, 4\})$. It is easy to verify that π satisfies the lumpability condition and π and τ satisfy the separability condition. Using Eq. (10) we have $\sum_{j \in \pi_l} c_{ij}(\sigma) = a_{kl}(\sigma)$, $i \in \pi_k$; $k, l = 1, 2, 3$, or

$$A(a) = \begin{bmatrix} \frac{1}{4} & \frac{1}{4} & \frac{1}{2} \\ \frac{3}{4} & \frac{1}{4} & 0 \\ 0 & 1 & 0 \end{bmatrix}, \qquad A(b) = \begin{bmatrix} 1 & 0 & 0 \\ \frac{1}{2} & \frac{1}{2} & 0 \\ \frac{1}{3} & \frac{1}{3} & \frac{1}{3} \end{bmatrix}$$

Using Eq. (11) now we have $\sum_{j \in \tau_l} c_{kj}(\sigma) = b_{il}(m, \sigma)$, if $k \in \tau_i \cap \pi_m \neq \varnothing$; $m = 1, 2, 3$; $i, l = 1, 2$. If $m = 3$ and $i = 2$, then $\tau_i \cap \tau_m = \varnothing$, and the values $b_{il}(m, \sigma)$ can be chosen for this case in an arbitrary way subject to the condition that the $B(i, \sigma)$ matrices are stochastic. Choosing $b_{21}(3, \sigma) = b_{22}(3, \sigma) = \frac{1}{2}$ for $\sigma = a, b$ we have

$$B(1, a) = \begin{bmatrix} 1 & 0 \\ 1 & 0 \end{bmatrix}, \qquad B(2, a) = \begin{bmatrix} \frac{2}{3} & \frac{1}{3} \\ 0 & 1 \end{bmatrix}, \qquad B(3, a) = \begin{bmatrix} \frac{1}{2} & \frac{1}{2} \\ \frac{1}{2} & \frac{1}{2} \end{bmatrix}$$

$$B(1, b) = \begin{bmatrix} 1 & 0 \\ \frac{1}{2} & \frac{1}{2} \end{bmatrix}, \qquad B(2, b) = \begin{bmatrix} 0 & 1 \\ \frac{2}{3} & \frac{1}{3} \end{bmatrix}, \qquad B(3, b) = \begin{bmatrix} 1 & 0 \\ \frac{1}{2} & \frac{1}{2} \end{bmatrix}$$

and the decomposition is completely defined.

Corollary 2.2: Let $(S, \{C(\sigma)\})$ be a Markov system such that there are two nontrivial partitions π and τ on its state set satisfying the following properties:

1. Both π and τ satisfy the lumpability condition.
2. π and τ satisfy the separability condition.

Then the system is decomposable into a Kronecker product of two systems.

Proof: Consider again Eq. (11) and let $b_{kl}(i, \sigma)$, $b_{kl}(j, \sigma)$ be two different elements in its right-hand side with fixed k, l, σ. $b_{kl}(i, \sigma)$ is the sum of the elements corresponding to the block τ_l of τ in a row corresponding to the block π_i of π in the matrix $C(\sigma)$ [to be more specific, the index of the row is $\pi_i \cap \tau_k$]. Similarly, $b_{kl}(j, \sigma)$ is the sum of the elements in the row with index $\pi_j \cap \tau_k$ corresponding to the block τ_l of τ in $c(\sigma)$. It follows from the fact that τ satisfies the lumpability condition that $b_{kl}(j, \sigma) = b_{kl}(i, \sigma)$, the summation being over entries in the same block of $\tau(\tau_l)$ and the rows belonging to the same block of $\tau(\tau_k)$. Thus $B(i, \sigma) = B(j, \sigma)$ for all pairs i, j so that the B

system can be represented in the form $(S'', \{B(\sigma)\})$ and is independent on the state of the system A, which proves the corollary. ∎

Remarks:

a. Given a Markov system $(S, \{C(\sigma)\})$ which satisfies the lumpability condition above one can still use Eq. (10) to define a new system $(S', \{A(\sigma)\})$ with $|S'| < |S|$ and such that the original system is homomorphic to the new one [i.e., there is a mapping ϕ from S to S' such that $a_{ij}(x) = \sum_{l \in \phi^{-1}(j)} c_{kl}(x)$, $k \in \phi^{-1}(i)$ for all $x \in \Sigma^*$; the states in S' will be the blocks of π and if $m \in \pi_n$ then $\phi(m) = n$]. The new system is, however, not isomorphic to the original one which cannot be recovered back from it. Some of the information on the transition probabilities from a particular state to another is lost in the lumping process and only the information about the transition probabilities from a *block* of states to another block is retained. [see Exercises 1, 2 at the end of this section.]

b. The set of all partitions over a set of states, including the trivial partitions have a lattice structure. One can define a partial order $\leq$ over partitions, where $\pi \leq \tau$ means that each block of τ is the union of one or more blocks of π. Thus if $S = \{1, 2, 3, 4\}$, $\pi = (\{1, 2\}, \{3\}, \{4\})$ $\tau = (\{1, 2, 3\}, \{4\})$, then $\pi \leq \tau$.

Let 1 be the partition with all the states in a single block and 0 the partition with each state in a separate block and, using the partial order defined above, define $\pi + \tau$ to be $\text{lub}(\pi, \tau)$ and $\pi \cdot \tau$ to be $\text{glb}(\pi, \tau)$. Clearly $0 \leq \pi \leq 1$ for any partition π and, as the lattice of partitions over a finite set in finite, $\pi + \tau$ and $\pi \cdot \tau$ always exist. Thus $(\{1, 2\}, \{3\}, \{4, 5, 6\}) + (\{1\}, \{2, 3\} \{4, 5\}, \{6\}), = (\{1, 2, 3\}\{4, 5, 6\})$ and $(\{1\}, \{2\}, \{3\}, \{4, 5\}, \{6\})$ is the product of the above two partitions. In addition to the above properties, one can also prove the following:

Theorem 2.3: If π and τ are two partitions over the set of states S of a Markov system $(S, \{C(\sigma)\})$ such that both partitions satisfy the lumpability condition and in addition

$$\sum_{j \in \pi_k \cap \tau_l} c_{ij}(\sigma) = [\sum_{j \in \pi_k} c_{ij}(\sigma)][\sum_{j \in \tau_l} c_{ij}(\sigma)] \tag{13}$$

then $\pi \cdot \tau$ is a partition satisfying the lumpability condition.

Proof: Because of the lumpability condition for both π and τ the sum $\sum_{j \in \pi_k} c_{ij}(\sigma)$ has the same value for all $i \in \pi_f$ and the sum $\sum_{j \in \tau_g} c_{ij}(\sigma)$ has the same value for all $i \in \tau_g$ where π_f and τ_g are arbitrary blocks in π and τ respectively. It follows that the sum $\sum_{j \in \pi_k \cap \tau_l} c_{ij}(\sigma)$ has the same value for all $i \in \pi_f \cap \tau_g$. But $\pi_f \cap \tau_g$ and $\pi_k \cap \tau_l$ are arbitrary blocks of $\pi \cdot \tau$ and all the blocks of $\pi \cdot \tau$ have this form, which proves the theorem. ∎

Using the algebra of partitions and the theorem above one can find all possible pairs of partitions satisfying the necessary conditions for decomposition. It is to be mentioned, however, that, in contrast to the deterministic case, there exist no clear-cut theory of decomposition for Markov systems. The conditions of lumpability and separability are restrictive and cannot be both satisfied in general.

c. Generalizations of the results in this section can be achieved through introducing combinatorial gates between the various parts in an interconnection of systems or through combinations of various types of decomposition. In addition a decomposition can be carried through several steps leading to more than two component subsystems. Those possibilities have been mentioned before. There may be also decompositions based on interconnections more general than the cascade type as will be shown later. [See exercises 9–12 at the end of this section.] Still another possibility is the possibility of state splitting. This will be illustrated now by the following:

Example 14: Let $(S, \{C(\sigma)\})$ be the 3-state system over $\Sigma = \{a, b\}$ with

$$C(a) = \begin{bmatrix} 0 & \frac{1}{3} & \frac{2}{3} \\ \frac{2}{9} & \frac{5}{9} & \frac{2}{9} \\ \frac{2}{3} & \frac{1}{3} & 0 \end{bmatrix}, \qquad C(b) = \begin{bmatrix} \frac{1}{3} & \frac{1}{2} & \frac{1}{6} \\ \frac{2}{9} & \frac{5}{9} & \frac{2}{9} \\ \frac{1}{6} & \frac{1}{2} & \frac{1}{3} \end{bmatrix}$$

An easy check will show that the above system is not decomposable. One can try, however, to split some state into two, to get another 4-state system which will be decomposable into two 2-state components. Suppose some state say s_i is split into two (or more) states s_{i_1} and s_{i_2}, i.e., the ith row in each matrix is duplicated and then the ith column is divided into two columns whose sum is equal to the original one. Trivially, the new system satisfies the lumpability condition for the partition which will merge the states s_{i_1} and s_{i_2} into a single block and leaving all the other states alone. The new system is therefore equivalent to the old one provided that the states s_{i_1} and s_{i_2} are merged at its output, and a decomposition of the new system provides us, therefore, with a decomposition of a system which is externally equivalent to the original one. In our example one may try to split the second state so as to have a 4-state system with matrices

$$C'(a) = \begin{bmatrix} 0 & a_{12} & a_{13} & \frac{2}{3} \\ \frac{2}{9} & a_{22} & a_{23} & \frac{2}{9} \\ \frac{2}{9} & a_{32} & a_{33} & \frac{2}{9} \\ \frac{2}{3} & a_{42} & a_{43} & 0 \end{bmatrix}, \qquad C'(b) = \begin{bmatrix} \frac{1}{3} & b_{12} & b_{13} & \frac{1}{6} \\ \frac{2}{9} & b_{22} & b_{23} & \frac{2}{9} \\ \frac{2}{9} & b_{32} & b_{33} & \frac{2}{9} \\ \frac{1}{6} & b_{42} & b_{43} & \frac{1}{3} \end{bmatrix}$$

and the a_{ij} and b_{ij} will be determined by a series of equations requiring that:

(1) The sum of the two a columns and the two b columns equal to the corresponding columns in the original matrices $C(a)$ and $C(b)$; (2) there is a partition π say $\pi = \{\{s_1 s_2\}, \{s_3 s_4\}\}$ which satisfies the lumpability condition; and (3) there is a partition τ say $\tau = \{\{s_1 s_3\}, \{s_2 s_4\}\}$, such that π and τ satisfy the

separability condition. Formulation of these equations is an easy matter to do and is left as an exercise. The resulting matrices are

$$C'(a) = \begin{bmatrix} 0 & \frac{1}{3} & 0 & \frac{2}{3} \\ \frac{2}{9} & \frac{1}{9} & \frac{4}{9} & \frac{2}{9} \\ \frac{2}{9} & \frac{4}{9} & \frac{1}{9} & \frac{2}{9} \\ \frac{2}{3} & 0 & \frac{1}{3} & 0 \end{bmatrix}, \qquad C'(b) = \begin{bmatrix} \frac{1}{3} & \frac{1}{3} & \frac{1}{6} & \frac{1}{6} \\ \frac{2}{9} & \frac{4}{9} & \frac{1}{9} & \frac{2}{9} \\ \frac{2}{9} & \frac{1}{9} & \frac{4}{9} & \frac{2}{9} \\ \frac{1}{6} & \frac{1}{6} & \frac{1}{3} & \frac{1}{3} \end{bmatrix}$$

A decomposition of the system is now obtained in the same way as in Example 13. The resulting decomposition (for π and τ as specified above) is

$$A(a) = \begin{bmatrix} \frac{1}{3} & \frac{2}{3} \\ \frac{2}{3} & \frac{1}{3} \end{bmatrix}, \qquad A(b) = \begin{bmatrix} \frac{2}{3} & \frac{1}{3} \\ \frac{1}{3} & \frac{2}{3} \end{bmatrix}$$

$$B(a, 1) = \begin{bmatrix} 0 & 1 \\ \frac{2}{3} & \frac{1}{3} \end{bmatrix}, \qquad B(b, 1) = \begin{bmatrix} \frac{1}{2} & \frac{1}{2} \\ \frac{1}{3} & \frac{2}{3} \end{bmatrix}$$

$$B(a, 2) = \begin{bmatrix} \frac{1}{3} & \frac{2}{3} \\ 1 & 0 \end{bmatrix}, \qquad B(b, 2) = \begin{bmatrix} \frac{2}{3} & \frac{1}{3} \\ \frac{1}{2} & \frac{1}{2} \end{bmatrix}$$

d. In deterministic machine theory, it has been proved that, by properly splitting the states of an n-state machine one can always decompose an externally equivalent machine, in a cascade form, into two component machines, one of them having a set of transition matrices which are either permutation or reset matrices and the other having only n-1 states. This fact has served as a basis for the classical theorem of Krohn and Rhodes (1963) showing that every deterministic machine can be "embedded" into a cascade interconnection of a sequence of machines of a certain simple and cannonical form. Unfortunately, it seems reasonable to assume that the Krohn–Rhodes theorem does not carry over, in its original form, to the stochastic case. One of the reasons for this is that even if state splitting is allowed the conditions for cascade decomposability seem to be restrictive for stochastic systems and cannot always be met. Note, however, that a cascade interconnection of a sequence of systems $A_1, A_2, \ldots, A_k$ has the property that the next state of a system A_i in the interconnection depends on the present input, on its present state and on the present state of all other systems A_j with $j < i$, but does not depend on the present state of any system A_j with $j > i$. This means that the interconnectivity in the decomposition is not maximal a fact which has some advantage from the realization point of view. We will show now that if the interconnectivity is allowed to be maximal, then any n-state Markov system can be decomposed into a sequence of 2-state Markov systems.

Definition 2.6: Let

$$A = (S, \{A(\sigma, t)\}_{\substack{\sigma \in \Sigma \\ t \in T}}) \qquad \text{and} \qquad B = (T, \{B(\sigma, s)\}_{\substack{\sigma \in \Sigma \\ s \in S}})$$

be two Markov systems. The system $(S \times T, \{C(\sigma)\}_{\sigma \in \Sigma})$ is the maximal interconnection of A and B if

$$C(\sigma) = [C_{st, s't'}(\sigma)] \quad \text{and} \quad c_{st, s't'}(\sigma) = a_{ss'}(\sigma, t)b_{tt'}(\sigma, s) \qquad (14)$$

$([a_{ss'}(\sigma, t)] = A(\sigma, t); [b_{tt'}(\sigma, s)] = B(\sigma, s)).$

Thus, in a maximal interconnection, the next state of each system depends on the present state of both systems and on the present input.

It is easily proved that a maximal interconnection of two Markov systems is a Markov system. A maximal interconnection reduces to a cascade interconnection if all the matrices of one of the two component systems corresponding to the same input, σ, are equal. Once the maximal interconnection of two systems is formed the resulting system can be further maximally interconnected with a third system and so on. The resulting system will be called a maximal interconnection of the sequence of systems involved. Definition 2.6 is illustrated in Figure 15.

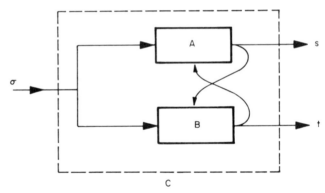

Figure 15. *Graphical representation of a maximal interconnection of Markov systems.*

We are now able to state the following:

Theorem 2.4: For each n-state Markov system $A = (S, \{A(\sigma)\})$ there exist two systems B_1 with state set T_1 containing two states and B_2 with state set T_2 containing n-1 states and a partition ρ on the state set $T_1 \times T_2 = T$ of their maximal interconnection $C = (T, \{C(\sigma)\})$ such that if states of C belonging to the same block of ρ are merged, then the resulting system is equivalent to the original given system A.

Proof: Given the system A with state set $S = \{s_1 \cdots s_n\}$, split the state s_n into $n - 1$ states $s_n^1 \cdots s_n^{n-1}$, i.e., let A' be a new system having state set $S' = \{s_1 \cdots s_{n-1}, s_n^1 \cdots s_n^{n-1}\}$ and matrices $A'(\sigma) = \{a'_{ij}(\sigma)\}$.

Define the following two partitions over S'

$$\pi = (\{s_1 \cdots s_{n-1}\}, \{s_n^1 \cdots s_n^{n-1}\}), \qquad \tau = (\{s_1 s_n^1\}, \{s_2 s_n^2\}, \cdots, \{s_{n-1} s_n^{n-1}\})$$

We shall define the matrices $A'(\sigma)$ in a way such that the above two partitions will enable us to express the system A' as a maximal interconnection of two systems, a two state system $B = (\pi, \{B(\sigma, \tau_j)\})$ whose states are the blocks of π, and an $(n-1)$-state system $B' = (\tau, \{B'(\sigma, \pi_i)\})$ whose states are the blocks of τ, In addition we will require that the partition $\{\{s_1\}, \ldots, \{s_{n-1}\}, \{s_n^1 \cdots s_n^{n-1}\}\}$ satisfy the lumpability condition for A' so that after the states $s_n^1 \cdots s_n^{n-1}$ are merged, the resulting system is equivalent to the original system A. In order to satisfy all the above conditions one must have that, for any fixed row in $A'(\sigma)$, say the ith, the following equations hold

(a) $$\sum_{s_j \in \pi_k} a'_{ij}(\sigma) \sum_{s_j \in \tau_l} a'_{ij}(\sigma) = a'_{it}(\sigma) \qquad \text{with} \qquad s_t = \pi_k \cap \tau_l$$

(b) $$\sum_{j \geq n} a'_{ij}(\sigma) = \begin{cases} a_{in}(\sigma) & \text{if } i \leq n \\ a_{nn}(\sigma) & \text{if } i > n \end{cases}$$

(c) $$a'_{ij}(\sigma) = \begin{cases} a_{ij}(\sigma) & \text{if } i,j \leq n-1 \\ a_{nj}(\sigma) & \text{if } i \geq n \quad j \leq n-1 \end{cases}$$

Equations (b) and (c) are necessary and sufficient for the lumpability requirement while Eq. (a) is equivalent to property (14). This follows from the fact that $\sum_{t'} c_{st,s't'}(\sigma) = a_{ss'}(\sigma, t)$ in (14) is equivalent to $\sum_{s_j \in \pi_k} a'_{ij}$ here and $\sum_{s'} c_{st,s't'}(\sigma) = b_{tt'}(\sigma, s)$ in (14) is equivalent to $\sum_{s_j \in \tau_l} a'_{ij}(\sigma)$ here. Combining these two equations one gets from (14) that

$$\sum_s c_{st,s't'}(\sigma) \sum_{t'} c_{st,s't'}(\sigma) = c_{st,s't'}(\sigma)$$

which is equivalent to the Eq. (a) here. Now Eq. (a), (b), and (c) above uniquely determine the matrix $A'(\sigma)$ given the matrix $A(\sigma)$. Indeed for $i < n$, $k \leq n-1$ we have by (a) that

$$\left(\sum_{j \in \pi_2} a'_{ij}(\sigma) \right)(a'_{ik}(\sigma) + a'_{i,k+n-1}(\sigma)) = a'_{i,k+n-1}(\sigma) \qquad (15)$$

Using (b) and (c) we change this equation into the following equation, where $a'_{i,k+n-1}(\sigma)$ is unknown and all the other values are known,

$$a_{in}(\sigma)(a_{ik}(\sigma) + a'_{i,k+n-1}(\sigma)) = a'_{i,k+n-1}(\sigma) \qquad (16)$$

or, by transposing the second left summand to the right-hand side we have

$$a_{in}(\sigma)a_{ik}(\sigma) = a'_{i,k+n-1}(\sigma) \, [1 - a_{in}(\sigma)] \qquad (17)$$

thus

$$a'_{i,k+n-1}(\sigma) = a_{in}(\sigma) \frac{a_{ik}(\sigma)}{1 - a_{in}(\sigma)} \qquad (18)$$

Since $1 - a_{in}(\sigma) = \sum_{j<n} a_{ij}(\sigma) \geq a_{ik}(\sigma)$, both sides of the equation are nonnegative. If $a_{in}(\sigma) = 0$, then $a'_{i,k+n-1}(\sigma) = 0$ and if $a_{in}(\sigma) = 1$, then $a'_{i,k+n-1}(\sigma)$ can be arbitrarily chosen provided that $\sum_{k=1}^{n-1} a'_{i,k+n-1}(\sigma) = 1$ and all the summands are nonnegative. It follows if the values $a'_{i,k+n-1}(\sigma)$, $i \leq n$, $k \leq n-$

1 are chosen according to (18) then the requirements (a), (b), and (c) are satisfied, since the derivation of (18) is reversible and (15) implies also the following

$$(\sum_{s_j \in \pi_1} a'_{ij}(\sigma))(a'_{ik}(\sigma) + a'_{i,k+n-1}(\sigma)) = (1 - \sum_{s_j \in \pi_2} a'_{ij}(\sigma))(a'_{ik}(\sigma) + a'_{i,k+n-1}(\sigma))$$

$$= a'_{ik}(\sigma) + a'_{i,k+n-1}(\sigma)$$

$$- (\sum_{s_j \in \pi_2} a'_{ij}(\sigma))(a'_{ik}(\sigma) + a'_{i,k+n-1}(\sigma))$$

$$= a'_{ik}(\sigma) + a'_{i,k+n-1}(\sigma) - a'_{i,k+n-1}(\sigma) = a'_{ik}(\sigma)$$

as required. As for the case $i > n$, it follows from (c) that the first $n - 1$ entries in each such row must be equal to the corresponding entry in the nth row and therefore by (18) this must be true for the full rows, i.e., the nth row in $A'(\sigma)$ as determined by (c) and (18) must be duplicated $n - 1$ times. It thus follows from the construction that the system $A = (S, \{A'(\sigma)\})$ can be represented as a maximal interconnection of the two systems $B = (T_1, B(\sigma, \tau_i)\})$ and $B' = (T_2, \{B'(\sigma, \pi_j)\})$ where the elements of T_1 and T_2 are the blocks of π and τ respectively and the matrices $B(\sigma, \tau_i) = [b_{kl}(\sigma, \tau_i)]$ and $B'(\sigma, \pi_j) = [b'_{kl}(\sigma, \pi_j)]$ are defined by

$$b_{kl}(\sigma, \tau_i) = \sum_{p \in \pi_l} a'_{mp}(\sigma), \quad s_k = \tau_i \cap \pi_k, \quad k, l = 1, 2; \ i = 1, 2 \cdots n - 1$$

and

$$b'_{kl}(\sigma, \pi_j) = \sum_{p \in \tau_l} a'_{mp}(\sigma) \quad s_k = \pi_j \cap \tau_k; \quad k, l = 1, 2, \ldots, n - 1; j = 1, 2$$

One sees easily from the construction that if ρ is the partition $\rho = (\{s_1\}, \cdots \{s_{n-1}\}, \{s_n^1 s_n^2 \cdots s_n^{n-1}\})$ then the system A' is equivalent to A when all states in a block of A' are merged into a single state. ∎

Corollary 2.5: For each n-state Markov system $A = (S, \{A(\sigma)\})$ there exist $n - 1$, 2-state systems B_i with state sets T_i respectively and a partition ρ on the state set $T = T_1 \times T_2 \times \cdots \times T_{n-1}$ of their maximal interconnection $C = (T, \{C(\sigma)\})$ such that if states of C belonging to the same block of ρ are merged, then the resulting system is equivalent to the original given system A.

Proof: By Theorem 2.4 and induction. ∎

Example 15: Let $A = (S, \{A(\sigma)\})$ be the 3-state system over $\Sigma = \{a, b\}$ with

$$A(a) = \begin{bmatrix} \frac{1}{2} & \frac{1}{4} & \frac{1}{4} \\ \frac{1}{3} & \frac{1}{3} & \frac{1}{3} \\ 0 & 1 & 0 \end{bmatrix}, \quad A(b) = \begin{bmatrix} 0 & 0 & 1 \\ \frac{1}{2} & 0 & \frac{1}{2} \\ 0 & \frac{1}{4} & \frac{3}{4} \end{bmatrix}$$

Using (b), (c), and (18) we construct the system $A' = (S', \{A'(\sigma)\})$ with

$$A'(a) = \begin{bmatrix} \frac{1}{2} & \frac{1}{4} & \frac{1}{6} & \frac{1}{12} \\ \frac{1}{3} & \frac{1}{3} & \frac{1}{6} & \frac{1}{6} \\ 0 & 1 & 0 & 0 \\ 0 & 1 & 0 & 0 \end{bmatrix}, \qquad A'(b) = \begin{bmatrix} 0 & 0 & 1 & 0 \\ \frac{1}{2} & 0 & \frac{1}{2} & 0 \\ 0 & \frac{1}{4} & 0 & \frac{3}{4} \\ 0 & \frac{1}{4} & 0 & \frac{3}{4} \end{bmatrix}$$

so that $\rho = (\{s_1'\}, \{s_2'\{\{s_3'^1 s_3'^2\}\})$, and A' is equivalent to A if states $s_3{}^1$ and $s_3{}^2$ are merged. Let $\pi = (\pi_1, \pi_2) = (\{s_1 s_2\}, \{s_3{}^1 s_3{}^2\})$ and $\tau = (\tau_1 \tau_2) = (\{s_1 s_3{}^1\}, \{s_2 s_3{}^2\})$. Using these partitions and the method outlined in the proof of Theorem 2.4, the systems $B = (T_1\{B(\sigma, \pi_j)\})$ and $B' = (T_2\{B'(\sigma, \tau_i)\})$ are derived where

$$B(a, \tau_1) = \begin{bmatrix} \frac{3}{4} & \frac{1}{4} \\ 1 & 0 \end{bmatrix}, \qquad B(a, \tau_2) = \begin{bmatrix} \frac{2}{3} & \frac{1}{3} \\ 1 & 0 \end{bmatrix}$$

$$B(b, \tau_1) = \begin{bmatrix} 0 & 1 \\ \frac{1}{4} & \frac{3}{4} \end{bmatrix}, \qquad B(b_1 \tau_2) = \begin{bmatrix} \frac{1}{2} & \frac{1}{2} \\ \frac{1}{4} & \frac{3}{4} \end{bmatrix}$$

and

$$B'(a, \pi_1) = \begin{bmatrix} \frac{2}{3} & \frac{1}{3} \\ \frac{1}{2} & \frac{1}{2} \end{bmatrix}, \qquad B'(a, \pi_2) = \begin{bmatrix} 0 & 1 \\ 0 & 1 \end{bmatrix}$$

$$B'(b, \pi_1) = \begin{bmatrix} 1 & 0 \\ 1 & 0 \end{bmatrix}, \qquad B'(b, \pi_2) = \begin{bmatrix} 0 & 1 \\ 0 & 1 \end{bmatrix}$$

EXERCISES

1. Let $A = (S, \{A(\sigma)\})$ be an n-state Markov system and let $\pi = (\pi_1 \pi_2 \cdots \pi_k)$ be a partition over S satisfying the lumpability condition. Let U be a stochastic $k \times n$ matrix such that $U = [u_{ij}]$ and $u_{ij} \neq 0$ only if $s_j \in \pi_i$ [note that U is not unique]. Finally, let V be an $n \times k$ stochastic matrix such that $V = [v_{ij}]$ and $v_{ij} = 1$ if and only if $s_i \in \pi_j$.

   a. Prove that the system $\hat{A} = (\pi, \{UA(\sigma)V\})$ is k-state *Markov system* where the matrices $UA(\sigma)V$ represent the transition probabilities between the blocks of π, i.e., $\hat{A}$ is the system derived from A if the states belonging to the same block of π are merged into a single state.

   b. Prove that for exery $\sigma \in \Sigma$, $VUA(\sigma)V = A(\sigma)V$.

   c. Prove that for all $x \in \Sigma^* \, UA(x)V = \hat{A}(x)$ where by definition $\hat{A}(\sigma) = UA(\sigma)V$ and $\hat{A}(x) = \hat{A}(\sigma_1) \cdots \hat{A}(\sigma_k)$ if $x = \sigma_1 \cdots \sigma_k$.

   d. Let $\tau = (\tau_1 \cdots \tau_k)$ be any partition on S. Let U be a Markov matrix $U = [u_{ij}]$, $u_{ij} \neq 0$ if and only if $s_j \in \tau_i$ and all nonzero entries in a row of U are equal. Let V be a matrix defined as above for τ. If for every $\sigma \in \Sigma$, $VUA(\sigma)V = A(\sigma)V$, then τ satisfies the lumpability condition.

   e. Let $\rho = (\rho_1 \cdots \rho_k)$ any partition on S such that there exists a Markov matrix $U = [u_{ij}]$ with $u_{ij} \neq 0$ only if $s_j \in p_i$ satisfying $UA(\sigma)VU = UA(\sigma)$ for all $\sigma \in \Sigma$ (V is defined as before, for the partition ρ). Then for all $x \in \Sigma^*$, $UA(x)V = \hat{A}(x)$ where $\hat{A}(\sigma) = UA(\sigma)V$ and $\hat{A}(x) = \hat{A}(\sigma_1) \cdots \hat{A}(\sigma_k)$, if $x = \sigma_1 \cdots \sigma_k$.

2. Let $(S, \{A(\sigma)\})$ be the following 4-state system over $\Sigma = \{a, b\}$

$$A(a) = \begin{bmatrix} 0.2 & 0.3 & 0.3 & 0.2 \\ 0.4 & 0.1 & 0 & 0.5 \\ 0.1 & 0.2 & 0.4 & 0.3 \\ 0.3 & 0 & 0.2 & 0.5 \end{bmatrix}, \quad A(b) = \begin{bmatrix} 0.25 & 0.15 & 0.4 & 0.2 \\ 0.2 & 0.2 & 0.1 & 0.5 \\ 0.3 & 0.45 & 0.1 & 0.15 \\ 0.45 & 0.3 & 0.15 & 0.1 \end{bmatrix}$$

and let π be the partition $\pi = (\{s_1 s_2\}, \{s_3 s_4\})$. Prove that π satisfies the lumpability condition; find corresponding U and V matrices and define the system $(\pi, \{UA(\sigma)V\})$.

3. Let $A = (S, \{A(\sigma)\})$ be the following 4-state Markov system over $\Sigma = \{a, b\}$

$$A(a) = \begin{bmatrix} 0.2 & 0.2 & 0.3 & 0.3 \\ 0 & 0.4 & 0 & 0.6 \\ 0.4 & 0.1 & 0.4 & 0.1 \\ 0.25 & 0.25 & 0.25 & 0.25 \end{bmatrix}, \quad A(b) = \begin{bmatrix} 0.3 & 0 & 0.7 & 0 \\ 0 & 0.3 & 0 & 0.7 \\ 0.08 & 0.12 & 0.32 & 0.48 \\ 0.06 & 0.14 & 0.24 & 0.56 \end{bmatrix}$$

and let $\pi = (\{s_1 s_2\}, \{s_3 s_4\})$, $\tau = (\{s_1 s_3\}, \{s_2 s_4\})$ be two partitions on S. Prove that π satisfies the lumpability condition and that π and ρ satisfy the separability condition. Decompose the A system accordingly in a cascade form.

4. Let $A = (S, \{A(\sigma)\})$ be the following three-state system over $\Sigma = \{a, b\}$)

$$A(a) = \begin{bmatrix} 0.2 & 0.5 & 0.3 \\ 0^{\cdot}3 & 0.55 & 0.15 \\ 0.45 & 0.45 & 0.1 \end{bmatrix}, \quad A(b) = \begin{bmatrix} 0.3 & 0.7 & 0 \\ 0.06 & 0.38 & 0.56 \\ 0.14 & 0.62 & 0.24 \end{bmatrix}$$

Split the second state into two states so as to get a new system A' which can be decomposed into a cascade product of two 2-state Markov systems.

5. Prove that the maximal interconnection of two Markov systems is a Markov system, i.e., the next state of the interconnection depends on its present state but not on its previous history.

6. Let $A = (S, \{A(\sigma)\})$ be the following 4-state Markov system over $\Sigma = \{a, b\}$

$$A(a) = \begin{bmatrix} \frac{1}{2} & \frac{1}{3} & \frac{1}{6} & 0 \\ \frac{1}{3} & 0 & \frac{1}{3} & \frac{1}{3} \\ 0 & \frac{1}{2} & \frac{1}{2} & 0 \\ \frac{1}{4} & \frac{1}{4} & \frac{1}{4} & \frac{1}{4} \end{bmatrix}, \quad A(b) = \begin{bmatrix} 1 & 0 & 0 & 0 \\ 0 & \frac{1}{2} & \frac{1}{4} & \frac{1}{4} \\ \frac{1}{3} & \frac{1}{6} & \frac{1}{6} & \frac{1}{3} \\ \frac{1}{6} & \frac{1}{3} & \frac{1}{4} & \frac{1}{4} \end{bmatrix}$$

Apply Corollary 2.5 to this system find the three corresponding 2-state systems and find the three corresponding 2-state systems B_1, B_2, and B_3.

7. Let T_i in Corollary 2.5 be $T_i = \{t_{i1}, t_{i2}\}$. Prove that the partition p in that corollary can be written in the following form: $p = (p_1 \cdots p_n)$ with $p_j = \{(t_{11}, t_{21} \ldots t_{j2} t^{j+1}, \ldots, t^{n-1}): t^{j+1} \in T_{j+1}, \ldots, t^{n-1} \in T_{n-1}\}$ if $j < n - 1$ and $p_{n-1} = \{(t_{11}, t_{21}, \ldots, t_{n-1,2})\}$, $p_n = \{(t_{11}, \ldots, t_{n-1,1})\}$.

8. Consider the following:

Definition: Two partitions π and τ for a system $A = (S, \{A(\sigma)\})$ are a *partition pair* if for each pair of blocks π_f and τ_g, $\sum_{j \in \tau_g} a_{ij}(\sigma) = \sum_{j \in \tau_g} a_{kj}(\sigma)$ for all $i, k \in \pi_f \cap \tau_l$, for each l such that $\pi_f \cap \tau_l \neq \varnothing$ and for each $\sigma \in \Sigma$.

    a. Prove that if and only if τ satisfies the lumpability condition then (τ, τ) is a partition pair.

    b. Prove that for any partition τ, $(0, \tau)$ is a partition pair.

9. Prove that if a Markov system A is deterministic [its matrices are degenerate] and π and τ are two partitions over S such that $\pi \cdot \tau = 0$, then these partitions satisfy the separability condition.

10. Prove the following:

Theorem: A Markov system with state set S is decomposable in a cascade form if there exist partitions π, 0^π, and τ on S such that

    a. π satisfies the lumpability condition and $0^\pi \geq \pi$;

    b. π and τ satisfy the separability condition;

    c. $(0^\pi \cdot \tau, \tau)$ is a partition pair [see Exercise 8 for the definition of a partition pair].

Remark: The above theorem is a generalization of the "if" part of Theorem 2.1 taking care of the possibility of having a combinatorial gate [represented by the partition 0^π] between the output [i.e., the state] of the first component in the decomposition and the second component. Note that if $0^\pi = \pi$ then $0^\pi \cdot \tau = 0$ and $(0, \pi)$ is a partition pair [see Exercise 8] so that the third condition of the theorem is superfluous.

11. Prove that if condition (c) in the theorem of Exercise 10 is deleted and the requirement that also the partition τ satisfy the lumpability condition is added then the system satisfying the changed conditions can be decomposed into a Kronecker product of two systems.

12. Formulate and prove a theorem generalizing the theorem in Exercise 10 so as to include the possibility of decomposing a given system into a cascade product of more than two smaller [i.e., with fewer states] systems.

OPEN PROBLEM

Can every n-state Markov system be "embedded" in a nontrivial way into a cascade type interconnection of systems which have a specific simple form?

In other words, is there any theorem which can be proved for Markov systems and which parallels in some way the Krohn–Rhodes theorem for the deterministic case?

3. Bibliographical Notes

Operations such as "Kronecker product" or direct sum for matrices can be found in any standard textbook, e.g., Mac Dufee (1964). Section 1 here is based on Paz (1966) and Bacon (1964). Decomposition of deterministic machines has been dealt with by many authors. An exposition of that theory (including the Krohn and Rhodes (1963) theory) can be found in Hartmanis and Stearns and Ginzburg (1968). Lumpability for homogeneous Markov chains has been dealt with in the book of Kemeny and Snell (1960). Decomposition of stochastic automata was first studied by Bacon (1964). The possibility of state splitting for stochastic machines was considered first by Fujimoto and Fukao (1966).

Theorem 2.4 and Corollary 2.5 here are based on Paz (1970b). Finally, Heller (1967) considered some aspects of decomposition theory for stochastic automata from the point of view of the theory of categories and a similar approach was undertaken by Depeyrot (1968) who studied various types of decompositions, including some interesting particular cases. Additional references: Gelenbe (1969a), Kuich and Walk (1966a), Kuich (1966).

C. WORD-FUNCTIONS

Let f be a function

$$f : \Sigma^* \to R \qquad (19)$$

where Σ is a given alphabet and R is the set of real numbers. Functions of the form (19) will be called word functions. There are at least three ways to relate word functions to Markov chains. First, [see Definition 1.1 in Section I, C] if an input–output relation [induced by an SSM] is restricted in a way such that the input alphabet X contains a single letter and $Y = \Sigma$, then the resulting function is a word function.

If f is induced by the SSM $A = (S, \pi, \{A(y)\}_{y \in Y}, \eta)$, then $f(v) = \pi(A(v)\eta$ with $v \in Y^* = \Sigma^*$, and the matrices $A(y)$ have the property that $\sum_y A(y)$ is stochastic. This case has been dealt with in Section I, C, 1. In the next two sections we shall consider two additional ways of relating word functions to Markov chains.

1. Functions of Markov Chains

a. *Preliminaries*

Let (π, S, A) be a [homogeneous] Markov chain with [finite] state set S initial distribution π and transition matrix A. Let Σ be a partition on S. We shall use the following notations: the elements of S [states] are denoted by s, indexed if necessary; sequences of states are denoted by u, indexed if necessary; elements of Σ [blocks of the partition] are denoted by σ, indexed if necessary; finally, sequences of blocks of Σ are denoted by v, indexed if necessary.

The chain being discrete, $s(t)$ and $\sigma(t)$ denote the state of the chain and its corresponding block at time t and, for $u = s_1 \cdots s_j$ and $v = \sigma_1 \cdots \sigma_k$, $p(u)$ and $p(v)$ denote the probability that $s(1) = s_1, \ldots, s(j) = s_j$ and $s(1) \in \sigma_1, \ldots, s(k) \in \sigma_k$ respectively. Let $u_1 u_2, v_1 v_2$ be sequences of states and symbols in S and Σ respectively, $u_1 = s_1 \cdots s_i, u_2 = s_1' \cdots s_j', v_1 = \sigma_1 \cdots \sigma_k, v_2 = \sigma_1' \cdots \sigma_t'$. Then $p(u_1 S^r u_2)$ and $p(v_1 \Sigma^q v_2)$ denote the probabilities that $s(1) = s_1$, $\ldots, s(i) = s_i, s(i + r + 1) = s_1', \ldots, s(i + r + j) = s_j'$ and $s(1) \in \sigma_1, \ldots$, $s(k) \in \sigma_k, s(k + q + 1) \in \sigma_1', \ldots, s(k + q + t) \in \sigma_t'$ respectively. A Markov chain and a function $p(v)$ as above are *stationary* if $p(S^r u) = p(uS^r) = p(u)$ and $p(\Sigma^r v) = p(v\Sigma^r) = p(v)$ respectively, i.e., if the probability of being in a specific state at time t is independent of time. Any function $p(v)$ as above with domain Σ^* $[p(\lambda) = 1$, by definition] and range in the interval $[0, 1]$ is called a *function of a Markov chain* and the elements of Σ are its states. Trivially, a Markov chain is stationary if and only if $\pi A = \pi$ [if this is the case, then π is called a stationary distribution for A] and a function of a stationary Markov chain is stationary. [The converse is, however, not necessarily true.] If B is any square matrix of the same order as A, then $B_{\sigma_i \sigma_j}$ denotes the submatrix of B with rows in σ_i and columns in σ_j. If ξ and η are $|S|$-dimensional row and column vectors respectively, then ξ_{σ_i} and η_{σ_j} denote the subvectors corresponding to the elements in σ_i and σ_j respectively. The symbol η will denote as before an $|s|$-dimensional column vector all the entries of which are equal to one.

We shall prove now some simple properties of functions of Markov chains. If (π, S, A) is a Markov chain and p is a function of it with state set Σ, then

1. $p(v_1 \Sigma^k v_2) = \sum_{v = \sigma_1 \cdots \sigma_k} p(v_1 v v_2)$.

2. If in particular v_2 is λ, then

$$p(v_1 \Sigma^k) = \sum_{v = \sigma_1 \cdots \sigma_k} p(v_1 v) = p(v_1)$$

3. If $v = \sigma_1 \cdots \sigma_i$, then

$$p(v) = \pi_{\sigma_1} A_{\sigma_1 \sigma_2} \cdots A_{\sigma_{i-1} \sigma_i} \eta_{\sigma_i} \qquad (20)$$

4. Denote $A_{\sigma_1\sigma_2} A_{\sigma_2\sigma_3} \cdots A_{\sigma_{k-1}\sigma_k} = A_{\sigma_1\cdots\sigma_k}$ [thus $A_{v_1\sigma v_2} = A_{v_1\sigma} A_{\sigma v_2}$) and $\pi_{\sigma_1} A_{\sigma_1 v\sigma}$ $= \pi_{\sigma_1 v\sigma}; A_{\sigma v\sigma_2}\eta_{\sigma_2} = \eta_{\sigma v\sigma_2}$. Then,

$$p(\sigma_1 v_1 \sigma v_2 \sigma_2) = \pi_{\sigma_1} A_{\sigma_1 v_1\sigma} A_{\sigma v_2\sigma_2}\eta_{\sigma_2} = \pi_{\sigma_1 v_1\sigma}\eta_{\sigma v_2\sigma_2} \qquad (21)$$

5. If for some $v, p(v) = 0$, then for any $v', p(vv') = 0$.

Proofs are trivial and left to the reader

Remark: It follows from formula (20) above that there is a time lag between a function $p(v)$ when considered as an input–output relation with single input letter [Section I,C] and same function when considered as a function of a Markov chain, e.g., $p(\sigma_1\sigma_2) = \pi A(\sigma_1)A(\sigma_2)\eta$ in the first case and $p(\sigma_1\sigma_2) = \pi_{\sigma_1} A_{\sigma_1\sigma_2}\eta_{\sigma_2}$ in the second case. This difference is made clear when single symbols are considered, for $p(\sigma_1) = \pi A(\sigma_1)\eta$ in the first case is the probability of having output σ_1 *after* the process was started and moved into a next state while $p(\sigma_1) = \pi_{\sigma_1}\eta_{\sigma_1}$ in the second case is the probability of having output σ_1 to begin with, even before the process moved into a new state. This time lag is responsible for the differences between the results in the next section and the parallel results in Section I,C,1.

b. The Rank of a Function of a Markov Chain

Definition 1.1: Let p be a function of a Markov chain with state set [of p] Σ. Let $\sigma \in \Sigma, v_1 \cdots v_k, v_1' \cdots v_l' \in \Sigma^*$. Then $P_\sigma(v_1 \cdots v_k; v_1' \cdots v_l')$ is the $k \times l$ matrix [to be called a compound sequence matrix for f] whose ij element is $p(v_i\sigma v_j')$ and $r(P_\sigma(v_1 \cdots v_k; v_1' \cdots v_l'))$ is its rank.

Definition 1.2: Let p and Σ be as in Definition 1.1. Then, for $\sigma \in \Sigma$, the rank of σ [to be denoted by $r(\sigma)$] is defined as

$$r(\sigma) = \sup_k \{k = r(P_\sigma(v_1 \cdots v_j; v_1' \cdots v_j'); j = 1, 2, \ldots; v_1, \ldots, v_j, v_1', \ldots, v_j' \in \Sigma^*\}$$

Thus $r(\sigma)$ is the maximal rank of a matrix of the form $P_\sigma(v_1 \cdots v_j; v_1' \cdots v_j')$ if such a maximal rank exists; the rank of p [to be denoted by $r(p)$] is defined as the sum of the ranks of its states.

In the following theorems we shall use some arguments very similar to the arguments used in Section I, C. Some results, parallel to results proved in that section, will be taken as granted here. The reader is refered to that section for details.

Theorem 1.1: Let p and Σ be as in Definition 1.1. For $\sigma \in \Sigma, r(\sigma) \leq |\sigma|$ with the consequence that $r(p) \leq |S|$; where $|\sigma|$ is the number of states in S belonging to the block σ when Σ is considered as a partition on the state set S of the underlying Markov chain.

Proof: Any compound sequence matrix $P_\sigma(v_1 \cdots v_k; v_1' \cdots v_k')$ is the product of two matrices: a left factor matrix G_σ whose rows are the vectors $\pi_{v_i\sigma}$ and a right factor matrix H_σ whose columns are the vectors $\eta_{\sigma}v_j{}'$ [see (21)]. But the $\pi_{v_i\sigma}$ are $|\sigma|$-dimensional vectors for any v_i and similarly the $\eta_{\sigma v_j{}'}$ are $|\sigma|$-dimensional vectors. Thus

$$r(P_\sigma(v_1 \cdots v_k; v_1{}' \cdots v_k{}')) = r(G_\sigma H_\sigma) \leq \min(r(G_\sigma), r(H_\sigma)) \leq |\sigma|$$

and $r(p) = \sum_{\sigma \in \Sigma} r(\sigma) \leq |S|$.

Corollary 1.2: If $\sigma \in \Sigma$ is a state of p such that $|\sigma| = 1$ and $r(\sigma) \neq 0$ [$r(\sigma) = 0$ implies that $p(v\sigma v') = 0$ for any v and v' which means that the state can be discarded], then $r(\sigma) = 1$.

We shall need also the following:

Proposition 1.3: If σ is a state of p such that $r(\sigma) = 1$, then for any $v, v' \in \Sigma^*$

$$p(v\sigma v')p(\sigma) = p(v\sigma)p(\sigma v') \tag{22}$$

Proof: Since $r(\sigma) = 1$, we have that $r(P_\sigma(\lambda, v; \lambda, v')) \leq 1$ or

$$\det \begin{vmatrix} p(\sigma) & p(\sigma v') \\ p(v\sigma) & p(v\sigma v') \end{vmatrix} = 0$$

from which (22) follows immediately. ∎

Remark: A function p of a Markov chain is called *regular* if $r(p) = |S|$. It follows from Proposition 1.3 above that in the degenerate case where $S = \Sigma$ [the partition on S is trivial], i.e., if a Markov chain itself is considered as a function of a Markov chain, this function is regular provided that all its states are accessible [$r(s) \neq 0$ for all $s \in S$].

c. Probabilistic Sequential Functions over Σ^*

In this section we shall consider probabilistic word functions over Σ^* given in some arbitrary way [i.e., not necessarily induced by Markov chains]. By "probabilistic sequential functions" we mean word functions f with domain Σ^* satisfying the following conditions:

$$f(\lambda) = 1 \tag{23}$$

$$\sum_{\sigma \in \Sigma} f(v\sigma) = f(v), \qquad v \in \Sigma^* \tag{24}$$

$$0 \leq f(v) \leq 1, \qquad v \in \Sigma^* \tag{25}$$

If property (25) is not satisfied but properties (23) and (24) are, then the function is called sequential. By "given" functions we mean functions such that the values $f(v)$ can be computed effectively [there exists an algorithm for computing them] for every $v \in \Sigma^*$.

The rank of a (probabilistic) sequential function is defined as in Definition

1.2 in Section b above, that definition being independent on the existence of an underlying Markov chain for the given function. The following lemma parallels Lemma 2.2 in Section I, C. The proof which is similar to the proof of that lemma is omitted.

Lemma 1.4. Let f be a sequential function of finite rank and let $P_\sigma(v_1 \cdots v_k; v_1' \cdots v_k')$ be a given compound sequence matrix of maximal rank for f and $\sigma \in \Sigma$. Another compound sequence matrix of the same rank can be derived from the given one having the form $P_\sigma(\lambda, \bar{v}_2 \cdots \bar{v}_k; \lambda, \bar{v}_2' \cdots \bar{v}_k')$.

Definition 1.3. A [finite] *pseudo Markov chain* is a system $(\pi, S, A, \bar{\eta})$ where π, S, and A are as in a Markov chain but π and A are not necessarily stochastic and $\bar{\eta}$ is an $|S|$-dimensional arbitrary column vector satisfyiug the equation $\pi\bar{\eta} = 1$.

For $u = s_1 \cdots s_k \in S^*$ the values $p(u)$ induced by a pseudo Markov chain are defined as $p(\lambda) = \pi\bar{\eta} = 1$ and $p(s_1 \cdots s_k) = \pi_{s_1} A_{s_1 s_2} \cdots A_{s_{k-1} s_k} \bar{\eta}_{s_k}$ where $\pi_{s_i}, \bar{\eta}_{s_j}$ are the s_i and s_j entries in π and η respectively and $A_{s_i s_j}$ is the $s_i s_j$ entry in A [$p(u)$ will be sometimes called a pseudoprobability.]

If Σ is a partition on the state set of a pseudo Markov chain, then a function f over Σ^* with state set Σ defined by $f(\lambda) = 1$ and $f(\sigma_1 \cdots \sigma_k) = \pi_{\sigma_1} A_{\sigma_1 \sigma_2} \cdots A_{\sigma_{k-1} \sigma_k} \bar{\eta}_{\sigma_k}$ is called a function of a pseudo Markov chain.

We are now able to prove the following:

Theorem 1.5: Any [probabilistic] sequential function of finite rank is a function of a pseudo Markov chain.

Proof: By the finite rank assumption and by Lemma 1.4, there exist, for each $\sigma \in \Sigma$, regular matrices $P_\sigma(\lambda, v_{\sigma_2} \cdots v_{\sigma k(\sigma)}; \lambda, v_{\sigma_2}' \cdots v_{\sigma k(\sigma)}')$ with $k(\sigma) = r(\sigma)$. We shall denote those fixed matrices by P_σ, and use also the following additional notations for $\sigma, \delta \in \Sigma$ and $v \in \Sigma^*$

$$P_{\sigma\delta}(v) = P_\sigma(\lambda, v_{\sigma 2}, \ldots, v_{\sigma k(\sigma)}; v, vv_{\delta 2}', \ldots, vv_{\delta k(\delta)}'); \qquad P_{\sigma\delta}(\lambda) = P_{\sigma\delta} \quad (26)$$

$$P_{\sigma\sigma}(v) = P_\sigma(v) \quad (27)$$

[Note that $P_\sigma(\lambda) = P_\sigma$ as defined above.]

$$P_{\sigma\lambda}(v) = P_\sigma(\lambda, v_{\sigma 2}, \ldots, v_{\sigma k(\sigma)}; v); \qquad P_{\sigma\lambda}(\lambda) = P_{\sigma\lambda} \quad (28)$$

$$P_{\lambda\sigma\delta}(v) = P_\sigma(\lambda; v, vv_{\delta 2}', \ldots, vv_{\delta k(\delta)}'); \qquad P_{\lambda\sigma\delta}(\lambda) = P_{\lambda\sigma\delta} \quad (29)$$

Thus $P_{\sigma\lambda}(v)$ and $P_{\lambda\sigma\delta}(v)$ are the first column and row of $P_{\sigma\delta}(v)$ respectively.

Using a procedure similar to the one used in Section I,C,3, one can prove the following relations

$$P_{\delta\delta'}(v\sigma v'\sigma') = A_{\delta v\sigma} P_{\sigma\delta'}(v'\sigma') \quad (30)$$

To prove this we consider an arbitrary column, the jth one, in the relation (30) which, by (28), has the form

$$P_{\delta\lambda}(v\sigma v'\sigma' v_{\delta' j}') = A_{\delta v\sigma} P_{\sigma\lambda}(v'\sigma' v_{\delta' j}') \quad (31)$$

the ith element in (31) has the form

$$f(v_{\delta i}\delta v \sigma v' \sigma' v'_{\delta' j}) = \sum a_{ij}(\delta v \sigma) f(v_{\sigma j}\sigma v' \sigma' v'_{\delta' j}) \qquad (32)$$

and (32) follows from the fact that

$$\left| P_\sigma \begin{array}{c} f(\sigma v' \sigma' v'_{\delta' j}) \\ f(v_{\sigma 2}\sigma v' \sigma' v'_{\delta' j}) \\ \\ f(v_{\sigma k(\sigma)}\sigma v' \sigma' v'_{\delta' j}) \\ f(v_{\delta i}\delta v \sigma) \; f(v_{\delta i}\delta v \sigma v'_{\sigma 2}) \; \cdots \; f(v_{\delta i}\delta v \sigma v' \sigma' v'_{\delta' j}) \end{array} \right| = 0 \qquad (33)$$

Since $|P_\sigma| \neq 0$, and one can develop the above determinant (33) according to its last column and represent the last element in the column as a combination of the others. Note that the coefficients of the combination depend on the three variables δ, v, and σ only [for fixed i and j] so that they can be denoted by $a_{ij}(\delta v \sigma)$. Equation 30 is therefore proved with $A_{\delta v \sigma} = [a_{ij}(\delta v \sigma)]$.

Consider again Eq. (30) with $v = v', \sigma' = \lambda$, and $\delta' = \sigma$. The resulting equation will be

$$P_{\delta \sigma}(\sigma) = A_{\delta \sigma}P_{\sigma \sigma} = A_{\delta \sigma}P_\sigma \qquad \text{or} \qquad A_{\delta \sigma} = P_{\delta \sigma}(\sigma)P_\sigma^{-1} \qquad (34)$$

Equation (34) can now be used for computing the matrices $A_{\delta \sigma}$. If we set in (30) $\delta' = \sigma$, $v'\sigma' = \lambda$, we get the equation

$$P_{\delta \sigma}(v \sigma) = A_{\delta v \sigma}P_\sigma \qquad (35)$$

Replacing $\delta' = \sigma'$ in (30) results in

$$P_{\delta \sigma'}(v \sigma v' \sigma') = A_{\delta v \sigma}P_{\sigma \sigma'}(v' \sigma') \qquad (36)$$

Using (35) in both sides of (36) gives

$$A_{\delta v \sigma v' \sigma'}P_{\sigma'} = A_{\delta v \sigma}A_{\sigma v' \sigma'}P_{\sigma'} \qquad \text{or} \qquad A_{\delta v \sigma v' \sigma'} = A_{\delta v \sigma}A_{\sigma v' \sigma'} \qquad (37)$$

Equation (37) can now be used for computing the matrices A_v, $|v| > 2$ from the matrices $A_{\sigma \delta}$.

Finally, the first column in (35) has the form

$$P_{\delta \lambda}(v \sigma) = A_{\delta v \sigma}P_{\sigma \lambda} \qquad (38)$$

Note that the first entry in $P_{\delta \lambda}(v \sigma)$ is $f(\delta v \sigma)$.

Let π_σ be a $k(\sigma)$-dimensional row vector of the form $\pi_\sigma = (10\ldots)$. Let π be the $r(f)$-dimensional row vector $\pi = (\pi_{\sigma_1}\pi_{\sigma_2}\ldots\pi_{\sigma_k})$ where $\sigma_1 \ldots \sigma_k$ is the sequence of elements of Σ ordered in some arbitrary but fixed order. Let A be the $r(f) \times r(f)$ matrix formed from the matrices $A_{\sigma \delta}$

$$A = \begin{bmatrix} A_{\sigma_1 \sigma_1} & \cdots & A_{\sigma_1 \sigma_k} \\ \vdots & & \\ A_{\sigma_k \sigma_1} & \cdots & A_{\sigma_k \sigma_k} \end{bmatrix}$$

Let $\bar{\eta}$ be the $r(f)$-dimensional column vector $\bar{\eta} = (P^{\mathrm{T}}_{\sigma_1\lambda}, \ldots, P^{\mathrm{T}}_{\sigma_k\lambda})^{\mathrm{T}}$, then, by (38)

$$\pi_\delta A_{\delta v\sigma}\bar{\eta}_\sigma = (10 \cdots 0)\, A_{\delta v\sigma}P_{\sigma\lambda} = (10 \cdots 0)P_{\delta\lambda}(v\sigma) = f(\delta v\sigma)$$

and $\pi\bar{\eta} = \sum_\sigma f(\sigma) = 1$, so that f is a function of the pseudo Markov chain $(\pi, S, A, \bar{\eta})$ above with $|S| = r(f)$. ∎

Corollary 1.6: Let $(\pi, S, A, \bar{\eta})$ be a psuedo Markov chain as derived in Theorem 1.5 for a given function f of finite rank. Then $A\bar{\eta} = \bar{\eta}$ and if f is stationary [i.e., $\sum_\sigma f(\sigma v) = f(v)$] then $\pi A = \pi$. Let G_σ and H_σ be the matrices whose rows and columns, respectively, are $\pi_{v_{\sigma i}\sigma}$ and $\bar{\eta}_{\sigma v'_{\sigma j}}$. Then G_σ and H_σ are nonsingular having the same rank as P_σ ($P_\sigma = G_\sigma H_\sigma$).

Proof: By (34), $A_{\delta\sigma} = P_{\delta\sigma}(\sigma)\, P_\sigma^{-1}$, so that by (29) $\pi_\delta A_{\delta\sigma} = P_{\lambda\delta\sigma}(\sigma)P_\sigma^{-1}$ and $\sum_\delta \pi_\delta A_{\delta\sigma} = (\sum_\delta P_{\lambda\delta\sigma}(\sigma))P_\sigma^{-1}$. But if f is stationary then

$$\sum_\delta P_{\lambda\delta\sigma}(\sigma) = \sum_\delta (f(\delta\sigma), f(\delta\sigma v'_{\sigma 2}), \ldots, f(\delta\sigma v'_{\sigma k(\sigma)}))$$
$$= (f(\sigma), f(\sigma v'_{\sigma 2}), \ldots, f(\sigma v'_{\sigma k(\sigma)})) = P_{\lambda\sigma\sigma}$$

Thus $\sum_\delta \pi_\delta A_{\delta\sigma} = P_{\lambda\sigma\sigma}P_\sigma^{-1} = \pi_\sigma$ and this implies that $\pi A = \pi$ proving the second part of the corollary. For the first part we have by (38) that $P_{\delta\lambda}(\sigma) = A_{\delta\sigma}P_{\sigma\lambda} = A_{\delta\sigma}\bar{\eta}_\sigma$. Therefore,

$$\sum_\sigma A_{\delta\sigma}\bar{\eta}_\sigma = \sum_\sigma P_{\delta\lambda}(\sigma) = \sum_\sigma (f(\delta\sigma), f(v_{\delta 2}\delta\sigma), \ldots, f(v_{\delta k(\delta)}\delta\sigma))^{\mathrm{T}}$$
$$= (f(\delta), f(v_{\delta 2}\delta), \ldots, f(v_{\delta k(\delta)}))^{\mathrm{T}} = \bar{\eta}_\delta$$

This implies that $A\bar{\eta} = \bar{\eta}$. To prove the last part of the corollary, we remark that the rows of G_σ and the columns of H_σ are $r(\sigma)$-dimensional and, since $P_\sigma = G_\sigma H_\sigma$ and P_σ is a nonsingular $r(\sigma) \times r(\sigma)$ matrix, G_σ cannot have more than $r(\sigma)$ rows and H_σ cannot have more than $r(\sigma)$ columns and both matrices must be nonsingular. This completes the proof. ∎

Consider again Theorem 1.1. It is clear that the theorem remains true if f is a function of a pseudo Markov chain. Combining Theorem 1.1 with Theorem 1.5 results in the following:

Theorem 1.7: A sequential function f over Σ^* is a function of a pseudo Markov chain if and only if it is of finite rank.

d. Construction of the Underlying Pseudo Markov Chain

In order to be 'able to construct the underlying pseudo Markov chain for a given function of finite rank f, one can use Theorem 1.5 provided that that the matrices P_σ can be found for each $\sigma \in \Sigma$ and provided that the values of the function f can be computed effectively for the arguments contained in the matrices P_σ and $P_{\delta\sigma}(\sigma)$ (see (34)). In fact the function f is *uniquely determined* by its values contained in the matrices P_δ and $P_{\delta\sigma}(\sigma)$ *only*. We shall show in this section that the matrices P_σ [and therefore also $P_{\delta\sigma}(\sigma)$] can be determined effectively if a bound is given on the rank of f. If it is only known that f is of finite rank but no bound is given for its rank, then the actual rank of f cannot be determined and the matrices P_σ cannot be found in general. [See the remarks at the end of Section I,C,3.] The matrices P_σ for the bounded case can be found by using the following:

Theorem 1.8: Let f be a sequential function of rank k and let $\sigma \in \Sigma$ be one of its states whose rank is $k(\sigma)$. A nonsingular matrix $P_\sigma = [f(v_i \sigma v_j')]$ can be found such that $l(v_i \sigma v_j') \leq 2(k - |\Sigma|) + 1$.

Proof: By Theorem 1.5, f can be represented as a function of a pseudo Markov chain $(\pi, S, A, \bar\eta)$ with $|S| = k$. Consider the set of all vectors of the form π_{v_σ} [see (21)]. Those vectors are $r(\sigma)$-dimensional row vectors and therefore, using a procedure similar to the one used in Section I,B,1 [see Exercise 5 at the end of that section], one can find a basis for those vectors, $\pi_{v_{1\sigma}}, \ldots,$ $\pi_{v_{k(\sigma)}\sigma}$ such that $l(v_i \sigma) \leq r(\sigma)$, $i = 1, 2, \ldots, k(\sigma)$. Let the matrix whose rows are denoted by $\pi_{v_{i\sigma}}$ be denoted by G_σ and $r(G_\sigma) = r(\sigma)$. Using the same argument for vectors of the form $\eta_{\sigma v'}$ which are $r(\sigma)$-dimensional column vectors one can find a matrix H_σ such that $r(H_\sigma) = r(\sigma)$, its columns are a basis for all the vectors of the form $\eta_{\sigma v}$ [thus there are $r(\sigma)$ columns in H_σ] and any of its columns $\eta_{\sigma v'}$ has the property that $l(\sigma v') \leq r(\sigma)$. Consider the matrix $G_\sigma H_\sigma$. It is an $r(\sigma) \times r(\sigma)$ square matrix of rank $r(\sigma)$ [since $r(G_\sigma) = r(H_\sigma) = r(\sigma)$] and therefore nonsingular. Its entries are of the form $\pi_{v_{i\sigma}} \eta_{\sigma v_j'} = p(v_i \sigma v_j')$. Thus, $G_\sigma H_\sigma$ is a matrix satisfying the requirements of a P_σ matrix and its elements $p(v_i \sigma v_j')$ have the property that $l(v_i \sigma v_j') = l(v_i) + l(v_j') + l(\sigma) \leq 2r(\sigma) - 1$. But $r(\sigma) \leq r(f) - |\Sigma| + 1$ [since $r(f) = \sum_{\sigma \in \Sigma} r(\sigma) \geq r(\sigma) + |\Sigma| - 1$] and therefore $l(v\sigma v_j') \leq 2(r(f) - |\Sigma| + 1) - 1 = 2(r(f) - |\Sigma|) + 1$. ∎

Corollary 1.9: If f is a sequential function of rank k and state set Σ, then the values $f(v)$ with $l(v) = 2(k - |\Sigma| + 1)$ uniquely determine the function.

Proof: The matrices P_σ can be found using only values $f(v)$ with $l(v) \leq 2(k - |\Sigma|) + 1$ and the matrices $P_{\delta\sigma}(\sigma)$ have entries of the form $p(v_{\delta i} \delta\sigma v_{\sigma j}')$ with $l(v_{\delta i})$ and $l(v_{\sigma j}')$ smaller or equal to $r(\delta)$ and $r(\sigma)$ respectively. Thus $l(v_{\delta i} \delta\sigma v_{\sigma j}') \leq r(\sigma) + r(\delta) + 2 \leq 2(k - |\Sigma| + 1)$. But the matrices P_σ and $P_{\delta\sigma}(\sigma)$ uniquely determine the function f [see Theorem 1.5] and this completes the proof. ∎

e. *Equivalent Functions*

Definition 1.4: Let $\mathcal{M} = (\pi, S, A, \bar\eta)$ and $\mathcal{M}' = (\pi', S', A', \bar\eta')$ be two pseudo Markov chains and let Σ and Σ' be two partitions on S and S' respectively such that $|\Sigma| = |\Sigma'|$. $\mathscr{M}$ and $\mathscr{M}'$ are *equivalent* with respect to Σ and Σ' if there is a one-to-one mapping $\phi : \Sigma \to \Sigma'$ such that $f(v) = f'(v')$ for all $v \in \Sigma^*$, $v' \in \Sigma'^*$. Where f and f' are the functions with state sets Σ and Σ' respectively induced by $\mathscr{M}$ and $\mathscr{M}'$; if $v = \sigma_1 \cdots \sigma_k$, then $v' = \sigma_1' \cdots \sigma_k'$ and $\phi(\sigma_i) = \sigma_i'$; if $v = \lambda$, then $v' = \lambda$.

Theorem 1.10: Let $\mathscr{M}, \mathscr{M}', \Sigma, \Sigma'$ be as in Definition 1.4. Let H be a matrix the columns of which are a basis for the set of all vectors of the form $\eta_{\sigma v}$ and let H be the matrix $[\Sigma = \{\sigma_1 \ldots \sigma_k\}]$

$$H = \begin{bmatrix} H_{\sigma_1} & & & \\ & H_{\sigma_2} & & 0 \\ & & \cdot & \\ & & & \cdot \\ 0 & & & H_{\sigma_k} \end{bmatrix}$$

then $\mathscr{M}$ and $\mathscr{M}'$ are equivalent with respect to Σ and Σ' if there exists an $|S'| \times |S|$ matrix X and a one to one mapping $\phi \colon \Sigma \to \Sigma'$ such that:

(1) $X_{\sigma'\sigma} \neq 0$ only if $\sigma' = \phi(\sigma)$ where $X_{\sigma'\sigma}$ is the submatrix of X with rows corresponding to the block $\sigma' \in \Sigma'$ and columns corresponding to the block $\sigma \in \Sigma$; (2) $\pi' XH = \pi H$; (3) $XAH = A'XH$; (4) $\bar{\eta}' = X\bar{\eta}$.

Proof: (1) and (2) imply that

(5) $$\pi'_{\sigma'} X_{\sigma'\sigma} H_\sigma = \pi_\sigma H_\sigma$$

(1) and (3) imply that

(6) $$X_{\sigma\sigma} A_{\sigma\delta} H_\delta = A'_{\sigma'\delta'} X_{\delta'\delta} H_\delta$$

(1) and (4) imply that

(7) $$\bar{\eta}_{\delta'} = X_{\delta'\delta} \bar{\eta}_\delta$$

Now $f(\sigma_1 \ldots \sigma_k) = \pi_{\sigma_1} \bar{\eta}_{\sigma_1 \cdots \sigma_k} = \pi_{\sigma_1} A_{\sigma_1 \sigma_2} \cdots A_{\sigma_{k-1}\sigma_k} \bar{\eta}_{\sigma_k}$. Using (5) and observing that $\bar{\eta}_{\sigma_1 \cdots \sigma_k}$ is a linear combination of the columns of H_{σ_1} we have

$$\pi_{\sigma_1} \bar{\eta}_{\sigma_1 \cdots \sigma_k} = \pi'_{\sigma_1'} X_{\sigma_1'\sigma_1} \bar{\eta}_{\sigma_1 \cdots \sigma_k} = \pi'_{\sigma_1'} X_{\sigma_1'\sigma_1} A_{\sigma_1 \sigma_2} \bar{\eta}_{\sigma_2 \cdots \sigma_k}$$

Using (6) and observing that $\bar{\eta}_{\sigma_2 \cdots \sigma_k}$ is a linear combination of the columns of H_{σ_2} and repeating as many times as necessary we have

$$f(\sigma_1 \ldots \sigma_k) = \pi'_{\sigma_1'} A'_{\sigma_1'\sigma_2'} \ldots A'_{\sigma'_{k-1}\sigma_k'} X_{\sigma_k'\sigma_k} \bar{\eta}_{\sigma_k}$$
$$= \pi'_{\sigma_1'} \cdots {}_{\sigma_k'} \eta'_{\sigma_k} = f'(\sigma_1' \cdots \sigma_k')$$

by (7). The proof is complete.

Remark: Theorem 1.10 provides us with a sufficient condition for equivalence of two functions of different pseudo Markov chains. In fact, one can prove [see Theorem 1.12 below] that the conditions of the above theorem are also necessary if the chain $\mathscr{M}$ with partition Σ over its state set resulted from a construction as in the proof of Theorem 1.5. If the matrix H in the conditions (2) and (3) of Theorem 1.10 is ignored, then a weaker set of sufficient conditions for equivalence results. These weaker conditions are summarized in the following:

Corollary 1.11: Let $\mathscr{M}, \mathscr{M}', \Sigma, \Sigma'$ be as in Definition 1.4. $\mathscr{M}$ and $\mathscr{M}'$ are equivalent with respect to Σ and Σ' if there exists an $|S'| \times |S|$ matrix and a one-to-one mapping $\varphi: \Sigma \to \Sigma'$ such that: (1) $X_{\sigma'\sigma} \neq 0$ only if $\sigma' = \varphi(\sigma)$; (2) $\pi'X = \pi$; (3) $XA = A'X$; (4) $\bar{\eta}' = X\bar{\eta}$.

Consider the following problem: Given a probabilistic sequential function f of finite rank k, is this function representable as a function of a [true] Markov chain? If yes, then find an underlying Markov chain.

Using Theorem 1.5 we can find an underlying pseudo Markov chain such that f is a function of it over some state set. We can try now to use Theorem 1.10 or Corollary 1.11 replacing $\mathscr{M}$ or $\mathscr{M}'$ by the psuedo Markov chain above and trying to find another *true* Markov chain which will satisfy the requirements of the theorem or its corollary.

Let conditions (1)–(4) of Theorem 1.10 be considered as equations, with $\mathscr{M}'$ replaced by the pseudo Markov chain found by using Theorem 1.5, and $\mathscr{M}$, X, and φ variables. If the given function is a function of a true Markov chain, then a solution to those equations must exists with A, π stochastic and $\bar{\eta}$ having all its entries equal to one. This follows from the following:

Theorem 1.12: Let $\mathscr{M}, \mathscr{M}', \Sigma, \Sigma'$ be as in Definition 1.4. If $\mathscr{M}$ and $\mathscr{M}'$ are equivalent with respect to Σ and Σ' and $\mathscr{M}'$ is a pseudo Markov chain derived as in Theorem 1.5, then $\mathscr{M}$ and $\mathscr{M}'$ satisfy the conditions (1)–(4) of Theorem 1.10 for some matrix X.

Proof: By (34) [see proof of Theorem 1.5] $P_{\delta\sigma}(\sigma) = A'_{\delta\sigma} P_\sigma$ where $A_{\delta\sigma}{}'$ are submatrices of the matrix A'. As $\mathscr{M}$ and $\mathscr{M}'$ are equivalent we have also that $P_\sigma = [f(v_{\sigma i}\sigma v'_{\sigma j})] = [f'(v_{\sigma i}\sigma v'_{\sigma j})] = P_\sigma'$ [f and f' denote the functions corresponding to $\mathscr{M}$ and $\mathscr{M}'$ respectively] so that $P_\sigma = G_\sigma H_\sigma$ where G_σ and H_σ are as in Corollary 1.6 and $P_{\delta\sigma}(\sigma) = G_\delta A_{\delta\sigma} H_\sigma$. Thus $G_\delta A_{\delta\sigma} H_\sigma = P_{\delta\sigma}(\sigma) = A'_{\delta\sigma} P_\sigma = A'_{\delta\sigma} G_\sigma H_\sigma$. Let H be a matrix as in the formulation of Theorem 1.10 and let G be a matrix constructed in the same way from the matrices G_σ. Then the above equation implies that $GAH = A'GH$ and this is condition (3) in Theorem 1.10 with G replacing X and satisfying (1) in that theorem.

Now

$$\pi_\sigma H_\sigma = \pi_\sigma(\eta_{\sigma v'_{\sigma 1}} \cdots \eta_{\sigma v'_{\sigma k(\sigma)}}) = (f(\sigma v'_{\sigma 1}) \cdots f(\sigma v'_{\sigma k(\sigma)}))$$

By the construction of π' in Theorem 1.5, π_σ' is a vector with first entry equal to one, all the other entries being equal to zero. Therefore, $\pi_\sigma' G_\sigma' H_\sigma' = \pi_\sigma' P_\sigma' = (f'(\sigma v'_{\sigma 1}) \ldots f'(\sigma v'_{\sigma k(\sigma)}))$. Since $f = f'$, $\pi H = \pi'GH$ verifying (2) of Theorem 1.10.

Finally, $\eta_\sigma{}' = (f'(\sigma) \ldots f'(v_{\sigma k(\sigma)}\sigma))^T$ by the definition of $\eta_\sigma{}'$ and

$$G_\sigma \eta_\sigma = \begin{bmatrix} \pi_\sigma \\ \vdots \\ \pi_{v_{\sigma k(\sigma)}\sigma} \end{bmatrix} \eta_\sigma = (f(\sigma) \cdots f(v_{\sigma k(\sigma)}\sigma))^T$$

and this completes the proof for $f = f'$. ∎

It follows from Theorem 1.12 that if no solution exists to the conditions of Theorem 1.10 considered as equations, with $\mathscr{M}'$ the pseudo Markov chain derived as in Theorem 1.5 for the given function and $\mathscr{M}$ a variable true Markov chain, then the given function is not a function of a true Markov chain. Conversely, any solution to the above four equations with the given restrictions provides an underlying Markov chain for the given function. Unfortunately the use of Theorem 1.10 with its conditions considered as equations, as above, is not practical in general for there are too many free parameters involved [the rank of $\mathscr{M}'$, the matrix X, the partition Σ, the matrix H, etc.]. On the other hand if the roles of $\mathscr{M}$ and $\mathscr{M}'$ are interchanged, i.e., the conditions of Theorem 1.10 are considered as equations; with $\mathscr{M}$ known and derived as in Theorem 1.5 and $\mathscr{M}'$ an unknown Markov chain then Theorem 1.10 is equivalent to its Corollary 1.11. This follows from the fact that in this case H is a nonsingular matrix for every $\sigma \in \Sigma$ [see Corollary 1.6] so that H is nonsingular and can therefore be deleted from both sides of conditions (2) and (3) in that theorem. These considerations together with Corollary 1.11 and Theorem 1.12 lead also to the following:

Theorem 1.13: Let f be a probabilistic sequential function *of rank k*. Let $\bar{\mathscr{M}}$ be the pseudo Markov chain with partition Σ over its states such that f is its function as found in Theorem 1.5. f is a function of a true Markov chain *with k states* if and only if the conditions of Corollary 1.11, when considered as equations with $\mathscr{M} = \bar{\mathscr{M}}$ or $\mathscr{M}' = \bar{\mathscr{M}}$ the other chain involved being variable, admit a solution such that the matrix X is nonsingular.

Proof is left to the reader.

f. Examples

We conclude this subsection with some examples in which we shall make use of Corollary 1.11 to solve some particular cases.

Example 16: Let f be a probabilistic sequantial function of rank k and let $\mathscr{M} = (\pi, S, A, \bar{\eta})$ be some underlying pseudo Markov chain with partition Σ over S, as derived in Theorem 1.5. If all entries in A are nonnegative, then f is a function of a true Markov chain with k states.

Proof: We remark first that all the entries in $\bar{\eta}$ are positive, for they have the form $f(v_{\sigma i}\sigma)$ and if for some i and σ, $f(v_{\sigma i}\sigma) = 0$ then P_σ has its ith row equal to zero [the entries in the ith row of P are of the form $f(v_{\sigma i}\sigma v'_{\sigma j})$] which is impossible since P_σ is nonsingular. Let now X_σ be a square diagonal matrix with ith diagonal entry equal to $(f(v_{\sigma i}\sigma))^{-1}$ and let X be the [nonsingular] matrix

$$X = \begin{bmatrix} X_{\sigma_1} & & 0 \\ & \ddots & \\ 0 & & X_{\sigma_k} \end{bmatrix}$$

Then $X\bar{\eta} = \eta'$, η' is a vector all the entries of which are equal to one. Let A' be the matrix $A' = XAX^{-1}$ and let $\pi' = \pi X^{-1}$. Then all the entries in π' and A' are nonnegative; since, by construction, X and X^{-1} are diagonal and nonnegative, π is nonnegative and so is A by assumption. Furthermore, $\pi'\eta' = \pi'X\bar{\eta} = \pi\bar{\eta} = 1$ [$\pi\eta = 1$ by the definition in Theorem 1.5] and $A'\eta' = A'X\bar{\eta} = XA\bar{\eta} = X\bar{\eta} = \eta'$ [$A\bar{\eta} = \bar{\eta}$ by Corollary 1.6] and therefore π' and A' are Markov matrices [since η' is a vector all the entries of which are equal to one]. It follows from Corollary 1.11 that the pseudo Markov chain $\mathscr{M}$ with partition Σ is equivalent to the true Markov chain $\mathscr{M}' = (\pi', S, A', \eta')$ with same partition Σ. ∎

Example 17: Let f, $\mathscr{M}$, and Σ be as in Example 16. Let $\mathscr{H}_\sigma$ be the set of all vectors of the form $\bar{\eta}_{\sigma v'}$ and let $\mathscr{H}_\sigma^+$ be the set of all $r(\sigma)$-dimensional row vectors π^σ such that $\pi^\sigma\bar{\eta}_{\sigma v'} \geq 0$ for any $\bar{\eta}_{\sigma v'} \in \mathscr{H}_\sigma$. If, for every $\sigma \in \Sigma_1$ $\mathscr{H}_\sigma^+$ contains a finite set of vectors $\pi_1^\sigma \cdots \pi_{t(\sigma)}^\sigma$ such that every very vector in $\mathscr{H}_\sigma^+$ can be expressed as a *nonnegative* combination of them, then f is a function of a true Markov chain.

Proof: We remark first that if $\pi_1^\sigma, \ldots, \pi_{t(\sigma)}^\sigma$ is a set of vectors satisfying the condition stated above then also the set $k_1\pi_1^\sigma, \ldots, k_{t(\sigma)}\pi_{t(\sigma)}^\sigma$ satisfies that condition with $k_1, \ldots, k_{t(\sigma)}$ an arbitrary sequence of positive constants. Let X_σ be the $t(\sigma) \times r(\sigma)$ matrix with ith row equal to $k_{\sigma i}\pi_i^\sigma$ where the $k_{\sigma i}$s are positive constants chosen so as to have $k_{\sigma i}\pi_i^\sigma\eta_\sigma = 1$. To prove that such a choice is possible, we must prove that $\pi_i^\sigma\eta_\sigma > 0$. Indeed, $\pi_i^\sigma\eta_\sigma \geq 0$ by assumption and if $\pi_i^\sigma\eta_\sigma = 0$, then $0 = \pi_i^\sigma\eta_\sigma = \pi_i^\sigma \sum_\delta \eta_{\sigma\delta}$ which would imply that $\pi_i^\sigma\eta_{\sigma\delta} = 0$ [for $\pi_i^\sigma\eta_{\delta\sigma} \geq 0$] and by induction $\pi_i^\sigma\eta_{\sigma v} = 0$ for any element $\eta_{\sigma v}$. We would have in particular that $\pi_i^\sigma H_\sigma = 0$ where H_σ is the nonsingular matrix as defined in Corollary 1.6 this implying that $\pi_i^\sigma = 0$. It follows that a matrix X_σ as above can be constructed and $X_\sigma\eta_\sigma = \eta_\sigma'$ where η_σ' is a column vector with all its entries equal to one. Consider now a vector of the form $k_{\sigma i}\pi_i^\sigma A_{\sigma\delta}$. This vector belongs to $\mathscr{H}_\delta^+$, for $k_{\sigma i}\pi_i^\sigma A_{\sigma\delta}\eta_{\delta v} = k_{\sigma i}\pi_i^\sigma\eta_{\sigma\delta v} \geq 0$, and can therefore be expressed as a nonnegative combination of the vectors

$k_{\delta i}\pi_i^{\delta}$. One can thus construct a matrix $A'_{\sigma\delta}$, such that $X_\sigma A_{\sigma\delta} = A'_{\sigma\delta}X_\delta$ where the ith row of $A'_{\sigma\delta}$ is the vector of the coefficients of the nonnegative combination of the rows of X_δ corresponding to the row $k_{\sigma i}\pi_i^{\sigma}A_{\sigma\delta}$ in the left-hand side of the equation. Finally, π_σ is in $\mathscr{H}_\sigma^+$ [for $\pi_\sigma\eta_{\sigma v} \geq 0$] and therefore can be expressed as a nonnegative combination of the rows of X_σ in the form $\pi_\sigma = \pi_\sigma' X_\sigma$ with π_σ' nonnegative.

Let X be the matrix with diagonal blocks X_σ, the other entries being zero; let A' be the matrix whose $\sigma\delta$ blocks are $A'_{\sigma\delta}$; let $\pi' = (\pi'_{\sigma_1}\ldots\pi'_{\sigma_k})$ and $\eta'^{\mathrm{T}} = (\eta'^{\mathrm{T}}_{\sigma_1}\cdots\eta'^{\mathrm{T}}_{\sigma_k})^{\mathrm{T}}$ with $\Sigma = \{\sigma_1\ldots\sigma_k\}$. It follows from Corollary 1.11 that the resulting chain is equivalent to the given one with respect to Σ. But the resulting chain is Markovian since η' has alread the required properties (all its entries are equal to one), π', and A' are nonnegative with $\pi'\eta' = \pi'X\eta = \pi\eta$ and $A'\eta' = A'X\eta = XA\eta = X\eta = \pi'$ so that π and A' are stochastic. ∎

Example 18: Let $\mathscr{M} = (\pi, S, A, \eta)$ be the pseudo Markov chain with

$$A = \begin{bmatrix} 0.5 & 0 & 0 & 0 & 0.5 \\ 0 & -0.4 & 0 & 0 & 1.4 \\ 0 & 0 & 0.5 & 0 & 0.5 \\ 0 & 0 & 0 & -0.3 & 1.3 \\ 0.25 & 0.084 & 0.25 & -0.078 & 0.494 \end{bmatrix}$$

$S = \{s_1, s_2, \ldots, s_5\}$, $\pi = (0.25\ 0.03\ 0.25\ -0.03\ 0.5)$ and $\eta = (1\ 1\ 1\ 1\ 1)^{\mathrm{T}}$. Let Σ be the partition $\Sigma = \{\{s_1 s_2\}, \{s_3 s_4\}, \{s_5\}\} = \{\alpha, \beta, \gamma\}$ over S. We show first that the resulting function f is a function of a true Markov chain. To prove this fact we use Corollary 1.11 and the argument used in the previous example. Let X be the (regular) matrix

$$X = \begin{bmatrix} 0.7 & 0.3 & 0 & 0 & 0 \\ 1.55 & -0.55 & 0 & 0 & 0 \\ 0 & 0 & 0.7 & 0.3 & 0 \\ 0 & 0 & 1.5 & -0.5 & 1 \\ 0 & 0 & 0 & 0 & 1 \end{bmatrix}$$

Then $X\eta = \eta$ and one verifies easily that the equations $\pi = \pi'X$ and $XA = A'X$ can be solved for π' and A' with nonnegative entries [the reader is urged to complete the computations]. It follows that the chain $\mathscr{M}' = (\pi', S, A', \eta)$ is Markovian [the same argument used in the previous example will prove this]. If the partition Σ is as before [for the given $\mathscr{M}$ chain], then the resulting function f' [identical to the given one] is a function of a true Markov chain.

Consider now the partition $\overline{\Sigma} = \{\{s_1 s_2 s_3 s_4\}, \{s_5\}\} = \{\delta, \gamma\}$ over S. The induced function $\bar{f}$ is again a function of a *true* Markov chain the $\mathscr{M}'$ chain: for the blocks of $\overline{\Sigma}$ can be constructed by merging blocks of Σ. [This implies that

Corollary 1.11 can be used for the partition Σ with same matrix X and the resulting underlying chain $\mathcal{M}'$ will be the same as before.] To compute the actual values of $\bar{f}$ one can use a 4-state pseudo Markov chain $\bar{\mathcal{M}} = (\bar{\pi}, \bar{S}, \bar{A}, \bar{\eta})$ instead of the given one $\mathcal{M}$ with $\bar{\mathcal{M}}$ derived from $\mathcal{M}$ by merging the state s_1 and s_3, i.e., $\bar{\pi} = (0.5 \ 0.03 \ -0.03 \ 0.5)$,

$$\bar{A} = \begin{bmatrix} 0.5 & 0 & 0 & 0.5 \\ 0 & -0.4 & 0 & 1.4 \\ 0 & 0 & -0.3 & 1.3 \\ 0.5 & 0.084 & -0.078 & 0.494 \end{bmatrix}$$

$\bar{S} = \{\bar{s}_1 \bar{s}_2 \bar{s}_3 \bar{s}_4\}, \bar{\eta} = (1 \ 1 \ 1 \ 1)^{\mathrm{T}}$ and the partition Σ' will be $\bar{\Sigma}' = \{\{\bar{s}_1 \bar{s}_2 \bar{s}_3\}, \{\bar{s}_4\}\}$ $= \{\delta, \gamma\}$. The function $\bar{f}$ induced by M with partition $\bar{\Sigma}$ is equal to the function induced by $\bar{\mathcal{M}}$ with partition $\bar{\Sigma}'$ because the states s_1 and s_3 have the same distribution in $\mathcal{M}$ [the pseudo probability of a sequence of states is not changed if the state s_1 is replaced by state s_3 or vice versa in the sequence], and they are both in the same block of $\bar{\Sigma}$.

We find now $r(\bar{f})$. Clearly, $r(f) = r(\delta) + r(\gamma) = r(\delta) + 1$ for γ is a single state block [see Corollary 1.2], and by Theorem 1.1, $r(\delta) \leq |\delta| = 3$. To find the actual value of $r(\delta)$ we compute the values $\bar{f}(\delta^n)$ for $n = 1, 2, \ldots 5$:

$$f(\delta^i) = (0.5 \ 0.03 \ -0.03) \begin{bmatrix} (0.5)^{i-1} & 0 & 0 \\ 0 & (-0.4)^{i-1} & 0 \\ 0 & 0 & (-0.3)^{i-1} \end{bmatrix} \begin{bmatrix} 1 \\ 1 \\ 1 \end{bmatrix}$$

$$= 0.5(0.5)^{i-1} + 0.03(-0.4)^{i-1} - 0.03(-0.3)^{i-1}$$

$$= 0.5(0.5)^{i-1} + 0.3((-0.4)^{i-1} - (-0.3)^{i-1})$$

resulting in

$$f(\delta^i) = 0.5, \ 0.247, \ 0.1271, \ 0.6139 \text{ and } 0.031775$$

respectively for $i = 1, 2 \ldots 5$. Let P_δ be the compound sequence matrix based on the sequences $v_1 = v_1' = \lambda, v_2 = v_2' = \delta \ v_3 = v_3' = \delta^2$, then

$$P_\delta = \begin{bmatrix} 0.5 & 0.247 & 0.1271 \\ 0.247 & 0.1271 & 0.06139 \\ 0.1271 & 0.06139 & 0.031775 \end{bmatrix}$$

which can easily shown to be nonsingular. Thus, $r(\delta) = 3$ and $r(\bar{f}) = 4$.

We shall complete this example by showing that $\bar{f}$, although a function of a 5-state true Markov chain is not a function of a true 4-state markov chain. To prove this, we use Theorem 1.13. If $\bar{f}$ is a function of a true 4-state Markov chain, then by Theorem 1.13 $[r(\bar{f}) = 4$ as proved above and $\mathcal{M}$ is a four state pseudo Markov chain] we would have that $X\bar{A} = A'X$ for some stochastic A' and X nonsingular of the form

$$X = \begin{bmatrix} x_\delta & 0 \\ 0 & X_\gamma \end{bmatrix}$$

Thus, $X_\delta \bar{A}_{\delta\delta} = A'_{\delta\delta} X_\delta$ or $X_\delta \bar{A}_{\delta\delta} X_\delta^{-1} = A'_{\delta\delta}$. $\bar{A}_{\delta\delta}$ and $A'_{\delta\delta}$ being similar matrices, their traces must be equal. But the trace of $\bar{A}_{\delta\delta}$ is negative by the definition of $\bar{A}$ and the trace of $A'_{\delta\delta}$ cannot be negative for A' is assumed to be stochastic. Thus $\bar{f}$ cannot be a function of a 4-state Markov chain and the proof is complete.

Remark: Example 18 shows that functions of true Markov chains may exist such that the number of states of the underlying Markov chain is strictly bigger than the rank of the corresponding function. One may ask now whether there exist functions of finite rank which are *not* representable as a function of a true Markov chain. Fox (1967) and Dharmadhikari (1967) [see also Heller (1965)] showed, by examples, that the answer to the above question is positive. The examples of Fox and Dharmardhikari are too involved to be reproduced here, moreover, their proofs seem to be incomplete. For additional aspects of functions of Markov chains, the reader is referred to the following exercises and the bibliographical notes which follow.

EXERCISES

1. Prove the properties (1)–(5) of a function of a Markov chain given in Subsection 1, a.

2. Prove Lemma 1.4.

3. Let $0 < a_1 < a_2 \cdots < a_{n-k+1} < 1$ be a sequence of numbers and define the $n \times n$ matrix $M = [m_{ij}]$ as follows

$$m_{ij} \begin{cases} = 0 & \text{if } 1 \le i,j \le n-k+1 \text{ and } i \ne j \\ = a_i & \text{if } 1 \le i,j \le n-k+1 \text{ and } i = j \\ = (1-a_j)/(k-1) & \text{if } 1 \le j \le n-k+1 < i \le n \\ = (1-a_i)/(k-1) & \text{if } 1 \le i \le n-k+1 < j \le n \\ = (2(k-1)-n+\sum_{i=1}^{n-k+1} a_i)/(k-1)^2 & \text{if } n-k+1 < i,j \le n \end{cases}$$

Let $\mathscr{M} = (S, \pi, M)$ be a Markov chain with $|S| = n$, π an n-dimensional vector all the entries of which are equal to $\frac{1}{2}$ and M is as above. Finally, let Σ be the partition $\Sigma = \{\{s_1 \ldots s_{n-k+1}\}, \{s_{n-k}\}, \ldots, \{s_n\}\}$. Prove that the function f of the Markov chain $\mathscr{M}$ with partition Σ over S is such that $r(f) = n$ and compute the value of the determinant of $P_\sigma(v_1 \ldots v_{n-k+1}; v_1' \ldots v'_{n-k+1})$, where $v_1 = v_1' = \lambda$, $v_i = v_i' = \sigma^{i-1}$ for $i > 1$ and σ is the first block in Σ, for f.

4. Let f be a function of a Markov chain with state set $\Sigma = \{\sigma_i\}$. Let $\bar{f}$ be the function $\bar{f}(v) = f(\tilde{v})$ where for any $v = \sigma_{i_1}\sigma_{i_2} \cdots \sigma_{i_k}$; $\tilde{v} = \sigma_{i_k} \cdots \sigma_{i_1}$. Prove

that if the underlying Markov chain for f is stationary and its initial distribution has only positive values, then $\tilde{f}$ is a function of a Markov chain.

5. Let f be a function of a pseudo Markov chain of finite rank, with state set $\Sigma = \{\sigma, \delta\}$ such that $r(\delta) = 1$. Then a compound sequence matrix P_σ [see (27)] of maximal rank for f can be chosen such that all the entries in P_σ have one of the forms, $f(\delta\sigma^k\delta)$, $f(\delta\sigma^k)$, $f(\sigma^k\delta)$, or $f(\sigma^k)$.

6. Let f be a function of a true Markov chain of finite rank with state set $\Sigma = \{\sigma_i\}$. Prove that any matrix P_{σ_i} [see (27)] of maximal rank for f can be expressed as a finite sum of nonnegative matrices of rank 1.

7. Let f be a sequential function of finite rank and let $\mathscr{M} = (\pi, S, A, \bar{\eta})$ be a pseudo Markov chain as derived in Theorem 1.5 for f. Prove that another pseudo Markov chain $\mathscr{M}'$ for f can be found such that $\mathscr{M}' = (\pi', S, A', \bar{\eta}')$ with $\bar{\eta}' = (1, 1, \ldots, 1)^{\mathrm{T}}$, $A'\bar{\eta}' = \bar{\eta}'$ and $\pi'\bar{\eta}' = 1$ [i.e., the vector π' and the matrix A' are "pseudo stochastic" with row sums equal to one].

8. Let $\mathscr{M}, \mathscr{M}', \Sigma, \Sigma'$ be as in Definition 1.4 and assume that $\mathscr{M}$ and $\mathscr{M}'$ are equivalent with respect to Σ and Σ'. In addition assume that $|S| = \mathrm{rank}\, f$ where f is the function induced by $\mathscr{M}$ (or $\mathscr{M}'$) with partition Σ. Prove that there exist two matrices B, C such that B is $|S| \times |S'|$ C is $|S'| \times |S|$, $B \cdot C = I$ where I is the $|S| \times |S|$ unit matrix and $A = BA'C$.

9. Let f be a probabilistic sequential function over the state set $\Sigma = \{\sigma_i\}$ such that $r(\sigma_i) \leq 2$ for every $\sigma_i \in \Sigma$. Then f is a function of a true Markov chain.

10*. Let f be a function of the Markov chain $\mathscr{M} = (\pi, S, A, \eta)$ with state set $\Sigma = \{\sigma_i\}$.

Prove the following relations:

a. $P_{\sigma_i\lambda}(\Sigma^{k_0-1}\sigma_{i_1}\Sigma^{k_1-1}\cdots\sigma_{i_n}\Sigma^{k_n-1}\sigma_{i_{n+1}}) = (A^{k_0})_{\sigma_i\sigma_{i_1}}(A^{k_1})_{\sigma_{i_1}\sigma_{i_2}}\cdots(A^{k_n-1})_{\sigma_{i_n}\sigma_{i_{n+1}}}P_{\sigma_{i_{n+1}}}$

[See (28) and other definitions in Section 1,a]

b. $f(\sigma\Sigma^{k_0-1}\sigma_{i_1}\Sigma^{k_1-1}\cdots\sigma_{i_j}\Sigma^{k_j-1}\delta) = \pi_\sigma(A^{k_0})_{\sigma\sigma_{i_1}}\cdots(A^{k_j})_{\sigma_{i_j}\delta}\eta_\delta$

c. $f(v\Sigma^n v')$ converges as $n \to \infty$ for every v and v' if and only if $f(v_{\sigma i}\sigma\Sigma^n\delta v'_{\delta j})$ converges as $n \to \infty$ for every $\sigma, \delta \in \Sigma$, and every i and j.

d. $f(v\Sigma^n v') \to f(v)f(v')$ as $n \to \infty$ for every v and v' if and only if $f(v_{\sigma i}\sigma\Sigma^n\delta v'_{\delta j})$ $\to f(v_{\sigma i}\sigma)f(\delta v'_{\delta j})$ for every σ, δ, i, and j.

e. A^n converges as $n \to \infty$ if and only if $f(v\Sigma^n v')$ converges as $n \to \infty$ for every v and v'

11*. A sequential probabilistic function f, $f: \Sigma^* \to [0, 1]$, is termed "mixing" if $f(v\Sigma^n v') \to f(v)f(v')$ as $n \to \infty$ for every v and v'. Prove the following:

Theorem: Let f be a sequential probabilistic function of finite rank and mixing. Let g_m be the function derived from f by the definition

$$g_m(\sigma_{i_1}\cdots\sigma_{i_k}) = f(\sigma_{i_1}\Sigma^m\sigma_{i_2}\Sigma^m\cdots\sigma_{i_k}\Sigma^m)$$

Then there exists an integer m^* such that g_m is a function of a true Markov chain for any $m \geq m^*$. ∎

11. Let f, $\mathcal{M}$, and Σ be as in Example 16. Prove that f is a function of a true Markov chain if the following condition holds true. For any $\sigma \in \Sigma$, a finite set of $r(\sigma)$-dimensional row vectors $\pi_1^\sigma \cdots \pi_{k(\sigma)}^\sigma$ can be found such that

1. $\pi_i^\sigma \eta_\sigma > 0$, $i = 1, 2, \ldots, k(\sigma), \sigma \in \Sigma$.
2. $\pi_i^\sigma A_{\sigma\delta}$ can be expressed as a nonnegative combination of the vectors π_i^δ for every σ and $\delta \in \Sigma$.
3. π_σ can be expressed as a nonnegative combination of the vectors π_i^σ for every $\sigma \in \Sigma$.

12. Find the true Markov chain equivalent to the pseudo Markov chain in Example 18 with the partition Σ and the matrix X as given in that example.

OPEN PROBLEMS

1. Find an algorithm for ascertaining whether a given probabilistic sequential function of rank k is a function of a true Markov chain.

2. Find an algorithm for ascertaining whether a given function of a true Markov chain of rank k has an underlying true Markov chain with only k states.

3. Provided that the conditions given in Example 17 or in Exercise 11 above are known to hold true for a given function f [e.g., this would be the case if $r(\sigma) \leq 2$ for any state σ of f—see Exercise 9 above] give an algorithm for finding the actual underlying true Markov chain.

Bibliographical Notes

Functions of Markov chains where first studied by Blackwell and Koopmans (1957). [See also the work of Harris (1955) who considered a related problem.] Gilbert (1959) proved some of their basic properties The subject has been investigated afterwards by several authors: Fox (1959); Fox and Rubin (1965, 1967), who were able to use the theory for estimating the temporal behavior of cloud cover (based on statistical data taken in the Boston area they proved that the stochastic process involved can be represented as a function of a Markov chain but not as a Markov chain); Dharmadhikari (1963a, b, 1965, 1967) considered various aspects of the problem and gave some sufficient conditions for a sequential function to be a function of a Markov chain; Carlyle (1967) considered a special case. Finally some new additions to the theory have been achieved by Heller (1965) and Depeyrot (1968). The section presented here is based mainly on the work of Gilbert (1959) with additions and some of the exercises based on the subsequent work. Thus Gilbert is to be credited for the basic ideas underlying the theorems and corollaries 1.1-to 1.9, with some clarifications by Dharmadhikari who is to be credited also with the Examples 17,18 and Exercises 9 and 10. Theorem 1.10 and its corollary 1.11 is new. Theorems 1.12 and 1.13 are a generalization of a theorem of Gilbert who is to be credited also with Exercise 3. Exercises 5 and 6 are due to Fox. Finally Exercise 11 is similar to a theorem of Heller. Additional reference: Burke and Rosenblatt (1958).

2. Function Induced by Valued Markov Systems

A theory of input–output relations was developed in Section I, C. In the light of that theory, functions of Markov chains can be considered as output relations, since, if $f(v)$ is such a function, then the value $f(v)$ can be interpreted as the probability that the word v is the *output* of a given Markov chain. In this section we shall develop a theory of word functions which can be considered as input relations derived from nonhomogeneous Markov chains.

a. Valued Markov Systems

Definition 2.1: A valued Markov system is a 4-tuple $(\pi, S, \{A(\sigma)\}, \{\eta_i\}_{i \in Z})$ where $(S, \{A(\sigma)\})$ is a Markov system, π is a probabilistic vector of dimension $|S|$ and $\{\eta_i\}$ is a finite set of $|S|$-dimensional arbitrary column vectors [the entries in η_i are arbitrary real numbers]. With every $i \in Z$ the function f_i over Σ^*, induced by the valued Markov system is defined as $f_i(u) = \pi A(u)\eta_i$ with $u = \sigma_i \cdots \sigma_k$ $\in \Sigma^*$ and $A(u) = A(\sigma_1) \cdots A(\sigma_k)$. $f_i(\lambda) = \pi\eta_i$ by definition. The functions $f_i(u)$ will be called *input* (*word*) functions.

The values of the input functions $f_i(u)$ can be interpreted as expectations or costs, since, denoting by η_{ij} the jth entry in η_i we have that $f_i(u) = \Sigma\pi_j(u)\eta_{ij}$ and $\pi_j(u)$ is a probability [the probability that the Markov system when started with distribution π will end scanning the word u in state j]. If the values η_{ij} are either 0 or 1 the $f_i(u)$ can be interpreted as a probability [the probability that the system when started with distribution π will end scanning the word u in one of the states s_j such that $\eta_{ij} = 1$].

Input functions $f_i(u)$ induced by valued Markov system differ from the functions considered in the previous section in that they do not satisfy necessarily the relations (23) and (24). In addition, although input functions can be induced by input–output relations, the correspondence is not always one to one. Thus, let A be an SSM, given in the Moore form, $A = (S, X, Y, \{A(X)\}, \Lambda)$ [see Definition 2.1 in Chapter I] with initial distribution π. Define the valued Markov system $(S, \pi, \{A(x)\}, \{\eta_y\}_{y \in Y})$ with $X = \Sigma$, $Z = Y$ and $\eta_{yi} = 1$ if and only if $\Lambda(s_i) = y$. It is easily seen that the input functions f_y induced by the valued Markov system can be defined in terms of the input–output relation induced by the SSM with

$$f_y(u) = \sum_{l(v)=l(u)-1} P_\pi(vy|u), \; l(u) \geq 1.$$

On the other hand, it may happen that two nonequivalent input output relations induce the same input function. This is shown by the following.

Example 19: Let $A = (S, X, Y, \{A(x)\}, \Lambda)$ and $A' = (S, X, Y, \{A'(x)\}, \Lambda)$ be two SSM [with common S, X, Y, and Λ] such that $X = \{0, 1\}$, $Y = \{a, b\}$, $S = \{s_1, s_2, s_3, s_4\}$, $\Lambda(s_1) = \Lambda(s_2) = a$, $\Lambda(s_3) = \Lambda(s_4) = b$,

$$A(0) = A'(0) = \begin{bmatrix} \frac{1}{2} & 0 & 0 & \frac{1}{2} \\ \frac{1}{2} & 0 & 0 & \frac{1}{2} \\ \frac{1}{2} & 0 & 0 & \frac{1}{2} \\ \frac{1}{2} & 0 & 0 & \frac{1}{2} \end{bmatrix}$$

$$A(1) = \begin{bmatrix} \frac{1}{2} & 0 & 0 & \frac{1}{2} \\ 0 & \frac{1}{2} & \frac{1}{2} & 0 \\ \frac{1}{2} & 0 & 0 & \frac{1}{2} \\ 0 & \frac{1}{2} & \frac{1}{2} & 0 \end{bmatrix}, \quad A'(1) = \begin{bmatrix} 1 & 0 & 0 & 0 \\ 0 & 0 & 0 & 1 \\ 1 & 0 & 0 & 0 \\ 0 & 0 & 0 & 1 \end{bmatrix}$$

and some initial distribution $\pi = (\frac{1}{2} \, 0 \, 0 \, \frac{1}{2})$. The two resulting input–output relations are not equivalent, e.g., $p^A(ab|11) = \frac{1}{4}$, but $p^{A'}(ab|11) = 0$. On the other hand, for any v, y, and u one finds easily that

$$\sum_v p_\pi(vy|u) = \pi A(u)\eta_y = \tfrac{1}{2} = \pi A'(u)\eta_y = \sum_v p_\pi'(vy|u)$$

so that the resulting input function is the same.

The above considerations show that input-word functions cannot generally be reduced, in a unique way, to other type of word functions discussed before and therefore a specific theory will be developed for them. On the other hand many of the properties of input functions are similar to properties of the other types of functions, and so are many proofs to related theorems. In all such cases we shall omit those proofs, leaving them to the reader.

b. Generalized Events and Their Rank

In deterministic automata theory an event E is understood to be a subset of the set of all words over a given alphabet. Such an event can be represented by its characteristic function $f_E[f_E(u) = 1$ if $u \in E$ and $f_E(u) = 0$ otherwise]. We shall agree to term such an event as a 0-1-event the term being a name for both the event and its characteristic function with values either zero or one.

Extending this terminology, any word function will be called an event and a set of word functions will be called a *generalized event*.

Definition 2.2: Let $E_g = \{f_n\}_{n \in Z}$ be a generalized event, and let $u_1, \ldots, u_k$, $u_1', \ldots, u_l' \in \Sigma^*$; $n_1, \ldots, n_l \in Z$. Then $P(u_1, \ldots, u_k; (u_1', n_1), \ldots, (u_l' n_l))$ is the $k \times l$ matrix [to be called a compound sequence matrix] whose ij element is $(f_{n_j}(u_i u_j'))$ and its rank is denoted by $r(P(u_1, \ldots, u_k; (u_1' n_1), \ldots, (u_l' n_l)))$.

Definition 2.3: Let E_g be as in Definition 2.2, then $r(E_g)$ (the rank of the generalized event E_g) is defined as

$$r(E_g) = \sup_k \{k = r(P(u_1, \ldots, u_j; (u_1' n_1), \ldots, (u_j' n_j)))\};$$

$$j = 1, 2, \ldots; u_1, \ldots, u_j, u_1', \ldots, u_j' \in \Sigma^*; n_1, \ldots, n_j \in \Sigma\}$$

[Thus $r(E_g)$ is the maximal rank of matrix of the form $P(u_1, \ldots, u_j; (u'_1 n_1), \ldots, (u_j' n_j))$ if such a maximal rank exists.]

Theorem 2.1: Let E_g be a generalized event induced by a valued (pseudo) Markov system with $|S|$ states. Then $r(E_g) \leq |S|$. [As before the prefix "pseudo" means that the vector π and the matrices $A(\sigma)$ are not required to be stochastic.]

Proof: Under the conditions of the theorem, every matrix of the form $P(u_1, \ldots, u_j; (u_1' n_1), \ldots, (u_j' n_j))$ can be expressed as a product of two matrices: a left factor matrix G whose rows are $|S|$ dimensional vectors of the form $\pi(u_i)$ and a right factor H whose columns are $|S|$-dimensional vectors of the form $\eta_{n_j}(u_j')$.

Lemma 2.2: Let E_g be a generalized event of finite rank and let $P(u_1, \ldots, u_j; (u_1' n_1'), \ldots, (u_j' n_j))$ be a given compound sequence matrix of maximal rank for it. Another compound sequence matrix of the same rank can be derived from the given one and having the form

$$P(\lambda, \bar{u}_2, \ldots, \bar{u}_j; (u_1' n_1), \ldots, (u_j' n_j))$$

Proof: Same as the proof of Lemma 2.2 in Section I, C and left to the reader.

Theorem 2.3: Let E_g be a generalized event of finite rank. Then there exists a valued pseudo Markov system A such that E_g is identical with the set of input functions induced by A.

Proof: [Some of the details in the proof, being similar to the corresponding parts in the proof of Theorem 1.5, will be omitted.] Let $P(\lambda, u_2, \ldots, u_k; (u_1' n_1), \ldots, (u_k' n_k))$ be a compound sequence matrix of maximal rank for E_g [such a matrix exists by the finite rank assumption and by Lemma 2.2]. We shall denote this matrix by P. Consider the following determinant

$$\begin{vmatrix} & & \vdots & f_n(u') \\ & P & \vdots & \vdots \\ & & \vdots & f_n(u_k u') \\ \hline f_{n_1}(uu_1') & \cdots & f_{n_k}(uu_k') & f_n(uu') \end{vmatrix} = 0 \tag{39}$$

The determinant being of order $k + 1$ is equal to zero for any variables u, u' $\in \Sigma^*$ and $n \in \Sigma$ [all the other factors appearing in the determinant i.e., $u_1, \ldots, u_k, u_1', \ldots, u_k', n_1, \ldots, n_k$ being constant and $u_1 = \lambda$.]

Developing the determinant according to its last column and dividing by $|P|$ we have

$$f_n(uu') = \sum_{l=1}^{k} a_l(u) f_n(u_l u') \tag{40}$$

where the values $a_l(u)$ are the resulting coefficients depending on u only. Replacing u by $u_i u$, u' by $u' u_j'$ and n by n_j [u, u', and n are variables in (40)] we have

$$f_{n_j}(u_i u u' u_j') = \sum_{l=1}^{k} a_l(u_i u) f_{n_j}(u_l u' u_j') \tag{41}$$

or in matrix form

$$P(uu') = A(u)P(u') \tag{42}$$

where we have used the definitions

$$P(\lambda) = P \qquad \text{and} \qquad P(u) = P(\lambda, \ldots, u_k; (uu_1' n_1), \ldots, (uu_k', n_k))$$

and $A(u)$ being the matrix of corresponding coefficients. Thus,

$$P(\sigma) = A(\sigma)P \qquad \text{or} \qquad A(\sigma) = P(\sigma)P^{-1} \tag{43}$$

and combining (42) and (43) we have

$$A(\sigma\sigma') = A(\sigma)A(\sigma'), \qquad A(\lambda) = I \tag{44}$$

Consider again (40) and replace u by $u_i u$ and n by j. We have

$$f_j(u_i uu') = \sum_l a_l(u_i u) f_j(u_l u') \tag{45}$$

Let $\eta_j(u)$ be the column vector defined by $\eta_j(u) = (f_j(u_1 u), \ldots, f_j(u_k u))^T$, then comparing (45) with (41), we can write (45) in the following matrix form

$$\eta_j(uu') = A(u)\eta_j(u'), \qquad u, u' \in \Sigma^*, \quad i \in Z \tag{46}$$

But $u_1 = \lambda$ so that $\eta_j(\lambda) = (f_j(\lambda), \ldots, f_j(u_k))^T$ and by (46), we have that

$$\eta_j(u) = A(u)\eta_j(\lambda) = (f_j(u), \ldots, f_j(u_k u))^T \tag{47}$$

Define now the valued pseudo Markov system $A = (\pi, S, \{A(\sigma)\}, \{\eta_i\})$ where $|S| = k$; $A(\sigma)$ are the matrices as defined in (43); π is the k-dimensional vector

$\pi = (1\ 0\ \cdots\ 0)$ and η_i are the k-dimensional column vectors defined by (47) with $u = \lambda$.

We have, for $u = \sigma_1 \cdots \sigma_m$ (using (44) and (47)) that

$$\pi A(\sigma_1), \ldots, A(\sigma_m)\eta_i = (1\ 0\ 0\ \cdots\ 0)A(\sigma_1)\cdots A(\sigma_m)\eta_i = (1\ 0\ \cdots\ 0)A(u)\eta_i$$
$$= (1\ 0\ \cdots\ 0)\eta_i(u) = f_i(u) \quad \blacksquare$$

Combining Theorems 2.1 and 2.3 we have the following:

Theorem 2.4: An event E_g can be represented as the set of input functions induced by a valued pseudo Markov system A if and only if E_g has finite rank.

The proofs of the following corollaries and theorems are similar to corresponding proofs in the previous Section 1 and are left to the reader.

Corollary 2.5: Let A be a valued pseudo Markov system as constructed in the proof of Theorem 2.3 for a given generalized event E_g of finite rank. Let G be the matrix whose rows are $\pi(u_i)$ and let H be the matrix whose columns are the vectors $\eta_{n_j}(u_j')$ with $P = GH$. Then G and H are nonsingular. [The words u_i, u_j' and the η_j are the fixed words in the proof with $P(u_1, \ldots, u_k; (u_1'n_1), \ldots, (u_k'n_k))$ nonsingular.]

Theorem 2.6: Let E_g be a generalized event of rank k. Then a nonsingular P matrix as in the proof of Theorem 2.3 can be found such that $P = [f_{n_j}(u_iu_j')]$ and $l(u_iu_j') \leq 2k - 2, i, j = 1, 2, \ldots, k$

Corollary 2.7: Let E_g be a generalized event of rank k, then the values $f_i(u)$ with $l(u) \leq 2k - 1$ uniquely determine the whole event.

It follows from Theorem 2.6 and its Corollary 2.7 that if, and only if, a given generalized event is known to be of finite rank and a bound is *given* for its rank, then an underlying valued pseudo Markov system can be constructed effectively.

c. A Necessary Condition for Representability

The following theorem provides a useful necessary condition for a given generalized event to be representable as a set of output functions of a valued (pseudo) Markov system.

Theorem 2.8. Let $E_g = \{f_i\}_{i \in Z}$ be a generalized event such that it can be represented as a set of input functions of a valued pseudo Markov system. Then for every $i \in Z$ and $u \in \Sigma^*$, there exists a set of numbers $c_0, \ldots, c_{k-1}$ such that for every $u', u'' \in \Sigma^*$ the following equality holds

$$f_i(u'u^ku'') = c_{k-1}f_i(u'u^{k-1}u'') + \cdots + c_0f_i(u'u'') \tag{48}$$

If an underlying valued system can be found such that it is *true* Markov then

$$c_0 + c_1 + \cdots + c_{k-1} = 1 \tag{49}$$

Proof: Let $A = (\pi, S, \{A(\sigma)\}, \{\eta_i\})$ be an underlying system for E_g. The matrix $A(u)$ satisfies its minimal polynomial so that there exists numbers $b_0, \ldots, b_k$ such that $b_0 I + \cdots + b_k [A(u)]^k = 0$. But $[A(u)]^k = A(u^k)$ so that the equation above can be put in the following form [after dividing by b_k and transferring the last term to the right-hand side].

$$c_0 I + \cdots + c_{k-1} A(u^{k-1}) = A(u^k)$$

Multiplying each term in the equation by $\pi A(u')$ to the left and by $A(u'')\eta_i$ to the right we have

$$c_0 f_i(u' u'') + \cdots + c_{k-1} f_i(u' u^{k-1} u'') = f_i(u^k)$$

If the system A is true Markov, then $A(u)$ is a Markov matrix so that one of its eigenvalues is equal to one. Inserting this eigenvalue into the minimal polynomial we have

$$b_0 + \cdots + b_{k-1} = -b_k \quad\text{or}\quad c_0 + \cdots + c_{k-1} = 1 \quad\blacksquare$$

d. Equivalent Valued Markov Systems

Definition 2.4: Let $A = (\pi, S, \{A(\sigma)\}, \{\eta_i\}_{i \in Z})$ and $A' = (\pi', S', \{A'(\sigma)\}, \{\eta_i'\}_{i \in Z'})$ be two valued (pseudo) Markov systems over the same alphabet Σ. A is equivalent to A' if there is a one to one mapping $\phi: Z \to Z'$ such that $f_i^A(u) = f_{i(i)}^{A'}(u)$ for every $u \in \Sigma^*$.

Given a valued [pseudo] Markov system A one can construct effectively [using a procedure similar to the one used in Section [I, B, 1], two matrices G and H such that G has linearly independent rows of the form $\pi(u) = \pi A(u)$, and any row vector of the form $\pi(u)$ is a linear combination of the rows of G; H has linearly independent columns of form $\eta_i(u) = A(u)\eta_i$, and any column vector of the form $\eta_i(u)$ is a linear combination of the columns of H.

Using the above notations we can prove now the following:

Theorem 2.9: Two valued pseudo Markov systems A and A' as in Definition 2.4 are equivalent if there exists a matrix X of due dimensions and a mapping $\phi: Z \to Z'$ such that (1) $\pi' XH = \pi H$; (2) $XA(\sigma)H = A'(\sigma)XH$ for every $\sigma \in \Sigma$; (3) $\eta'_{\phi(i)} = X\eta_i$ for every $i \in Z$.

Proof: The proof is left to the reader. [The method used in the proof of Theorem 1.10, with due changes to meet the different definitions, will do.] $\blacksquare$

Corollary 2.10: Two valued pseudo Markov systems A and A' as in Definition 2.4 are equivalent if there exist a matrix X of due dimensions and a mapping $\phi: Z \to Z'$ such that (1) $\pi' X = \pi$; (2) $XA(\sigma) = A'(\sigma)X$ for every $\sigma \in \Sigma$; (3) $\eta'_{\phi(i)} = X\eta_i$ for every $i \in Z$.

Definition 2.5: A valued pseudo Markov system A is *minimal* if the rank of its induced generalized event equals the number of its states.

Lemma 2.11: Let A be a minimal valued pseudo Markov system. Then any G^A and H^A matrix for A are nonsingular.

Proof: $G^A H^A$ is a compound sequence matrix for A of maximal rank because any other compound sequence matrix for A can be written in the form $G' H'$ where the rows of G' and the columns of H' are linear combinations of the rows of G^A and the columns of H^A correspondingly. If follows that $\min(r(G^A), r(H^A)) \geq r(G^A H^A) = |S|$. But G^A has $|S|$ columns and H^A has $|S|$ rows and therefore $r(G^A) \leq |S|$, $r(H^A) \leq |S|$. Thus, $r(G^A) = r(H^A) = |S|$ and both matrices are nonsingular. ∎

Theorem 2.12: Let A be a valued pseudo Markov system with $E_g{}^A$ the corresponding generalized event. Let A' be the minimal valued pseudo Markov system as constructed in Theorem 2.3 for the given $E_g{}^A$ [by definition A and A' are equivalent]. Then a matrix X exists such that (1) $\pi H^A = \pi' X H^A$; (2) $XA(\sigma)H^A = A'(\sigma)XH^A$; (3) $\eta_i{}' = X\eta_i$.

The proof which is similar to the proof of Theorem 1.12 [with due changes to meet the different definitions] is left to the reader.

Corollary 2.13: If the system A in Theorem 2.12 is minimal, then there exist a nonsingular matrix X such that the necessary conditions of Theorem 2.12 can be replaced by the following; (1) $\pi = \pi' X$; (2) $XA(\sigma) = A'(\sigma)X$; (3) $\eta_i{}' = X\eta_i$.

Proof: If A is minimal, then H^A is nonsingular [see Lemma 2.11] and can be reduced in the conditions of Theorem 2.12. Furthermore, one can assume that the matrix X in the proof of Theorem 2.12 is a G matrix for A [see the proof of Theorem 1.12] which by Lemma 2.11 is nonsingular in this case. ∎

Corollary 2.14: Let A and A'' be two equivalent valued pseudo Markov systems such that A'' is minimal, then there exist a matrix X and a one to one mapping $\phi: Z \rightarrow Z''$ such that: (1) $\pi H^A = \pi'' X H^A$; (2) $XA(\sigma)H^A = A''(\sigma)XH^A$; (3) $\eta''_{\phi(i)} = X\eta_i$.

Proof: Let A and A' be as in Theorem 2.12, and let A'' and A' be as in Corollary 2.13 [with A replaced by A'']. Then $\pi H^A = \pi' X' H^A$ for some matrix X' and $\pi' = \pi'' X^{-1}$ [X is Corollary 2.13 is nonsingular] so that $\pi H^A = \pi'' X^{-1} X' H^A$. Similarly, $X'A(\sigma)H^A = A'(\sigma)X' H^A$ and $A'(\sigma) = XA''(\sigma)X^{-1}$ so that $X'A(\sigma)H^A = XA''(\sigma)X^{-1}X' H^A$ or $X^{-1}X'A(\sigma)H^A = A'' X^{-1} X' H^A$. Finally, $\eta_i{}' = X'\eta_i$ and $X^{-1}\eta_i{}' = \eta_i{}''$ so that $\eta_i{}'' = X^{-1}X'\eta_i$. Where the elements of Z' and Z'' are rearranged if necessary so that the $\eta_{n'}'$ and $\eta_{n''}''$ vectors corresponding to the same η_n vector have the same index ($n' = n'' = n$). ∎

As in the previous section Theorem 2.9 and its Corollary 2.10 can be used for finding a valued true Markov system equivalent to a given valued pseudo Markov system. For this purpose, the conditions of that theorem [or corollary] will be considered as equations with one of the systems known the other being required to satisfy the Markovian properties.

The possibility of transforming valued pseudo Markov systems into valued true Markov systems has practical significance, since the later systems can be constructed in practice using relays, transistors, or other electrical devices [see Chapter I, Section 3].

If the A' system in Theorem 2.9 is assumed to be known, then one can assume that A' is also *minimal*, this additional assumption being justified by the fact that the construction in the proof of Theorem 2.3 provides a minimal equivalent system to any given system. In this case we have that the conditions of Theorem 2.9 are not only sufficient but also necessary [see Corollary 2.14 above]. On the other hand the unknown system A has too many free parameters making the use of the theorem impracticable.

If the A system in Theorem 2.9 is assumed to be known, then the additional assumption that A is minimal [bearing on Theorem 2.3 as before] will make the conditions of Theorem 2.9 equivalent to the conditions of its Corollary 2.10, for in this case H^A is a nonsingular matrix. On the other hand, the conditions of Corollary 2.10 are only sufficient conditions a fact which must be remembered when one proves that they cannot be satisfied in some cases.

We shall give now a useful geometrical interpretation to the conditions of Corollary 2.10 when considered as equations. Assume that the A system in Corollary 2.10 is given and consider the conditions in the corollary as equations to be solved for an unknown system A' subject to the restriction that A' is true Markovian. As there is no restriction on the vectors η_i' in the definition of a valued Markov system the third equation can be taken as a definition of the vectors η_i' once the other two equations are solved. If A is a matrix, denote by $C(A)$ the convex set of vectors generated by the rows of A. Then the equation $XA(\sigma) = A'(\sigma)X$ can be solved for a Markovian matrix $A'(\sigma)$ and given X if and only if $C(XA(\sigma)) \subseteq C(X)$ for in this and only in this case each row of $XA(\sigma)$ can be expressed as a convex combination of the rows of X and the probabilistic vector whose entries are the combination coefficients will be the corresponding row of $A'(\sigma)$. Similarly the first equation is equivalent to the condition that $\pi \in C(X)$. We have thus proved the following:

Theorem 2.15: The conditions of the Corollary 2.10 when considered as equations with the system A given can be solved by a valued *true* Markov system if and only if there exist a matrix X such that (1) $\pi \in C(X)$; (2) $C(XA(\sigma)) \subseteq C(X)$ for every $\sigma \in \Sigma$.

We shall use now Theorem 2.15 to prove two additional theorems.

Theorem 2. 16: Let $A = (\pi, S, \{A(\sigma)\}, \{\eta_i\})$ be a valued pseudo Markov system such that $\sum |\pi_i| \leq 1$ where $\pi = (\pi_i)$ and if $\xi_i^A(\sigma) = (\xi_{ij}^A(\sigma))$ is the ith row in $A(\sigma)$ then $\sum_j |\xi_{ij}(\sigma)| \leq 1$ for $i = 1, 2, \ldots, |S|$. Then A is equivalent to a valued *true* Markov system A' with state set S' and $|S'| = 2|S|$.

Proof: Let X be the $|S| \times 2|S|$ matrix

$$X = \begin{bmatrix} 1 & 0 & \cdots & 0 \\ 0 & 1 & \cdots & 0 \\ & & \vdots & \\ 0 & 0 & \cdots & 1 \\ -1 & 0 & \cdots & 0 \\ 0 & -1 & \cdots & 0 \\ & & \vdots & \\ 0 & 0 & \cdots & -1 \end{bmatrix}$$

Let $XA(\sigma) = B(\sigma)$ with rows $\xi_i{}^B(\sigma) = (\xi_{ij}^B(\sigma))$. Then $\xi_i{}^B(\sigma) = \pm \xi_j{}^A(\sigma)$ for some j so that $\sum_j |\xi_{ij}^B(\sigma)| \leq 1$. This implies that $C(B(\sigma)) \subseteq C(X)$ and $\sum |\pi_i| \leq 1$ implies that also $\pi \in C(X)$ and the conditions of Theorem 2.15 are satisfied. The number of states of the resulting valued Markov system will be equal to the number of rows of X which is equal to $2|S|$. ∎

Theorem 2.17: Let $E_g = \{f_i\}_{i \in Z}$ be a generalized event of rank k. There exist another generalized event $E_g' = \{f_i'\}_{i \in Z}$ over the same alphabet Σ and a constant c such that E_g' is induced by a valued *true* Markov system with $2k$ states and for any $u \in \Sigma^*$ and any $i \in Z$, $c^{l(u)} f_i(u) = f_i'(u)$.

Proof: Let $A = (\pi, S, \{A(\sigma)\}, \{\eta_i\})$ be the valued pseudo Markov system constructed as in the proof of Theorem 2.3, for E_g. Note that $|S| = k$ and π is the k-dimensional vector $\pi = (1\ 0\ \cdots\ 0)$. Let $\bar{A}_c$ be a valued pseudo Markov chain derived from A and defined as $\bar{A}_c = (\pi, S, \{\bar{A}(\sigma)\}, \{\eta_i\})$ with $\bar{A}(\sigma) = cA(\sigma)$. If $\{\bar{f}_i\}$ are the functions induced by $\bar{A}_c$, then clearly $\bar{f}_i(u) = c^{l(u)} f_i(u)$ for any $i \in Z$ and any $u \in \Sigma^*$. Now choose the constant c so that $\bar{A}_c$ will satisfy the conditions of Theorem 2.16 [the vector $\pi = (1\ 0\ \cdots\ 0)$ already satisfies these conditions] which is of course possible. By Theorem 2.16, there exists a valued true Markov system A' with $2|S|$ states and functions $\{f_i'\}$ such that $f_i'(u) = \bar{f}_i(u) = c^{l(u)} f(u)$ for every $i \in Z$ and $u \in \Sigma^*$. ∎

Remark: Note that the scaling factor $c^{l(u)}$ depends on the length of the word u but not on the word itself. On the other hand it is easy to see that the Theorem 2.17 would not be true in general if the scaling factor is removed because the values $f_i(u)$, being induced by a valued *pseudo* Markov chain, may grow, in some particular cases, beyond any bound when $l(u)$ increases while the corresponding values $f_i'(u)$ being induced by a valued *true* Markov system, are bounded.

EXERCISES

1. Prove that any function of a finite (pseudo) Markov chain can be represented also as an input function of a valued pseudo Markov system.

2. Prove Lemma 2.2.

3. Prove Corollary 2.5.

4. Prove Theorem 2.6.

5. Prove Corollary 2.7.

6. Let A, A', A'' be valued pseudo Markov systems such that A and A' satisfy the conditions of Theorem 2.9 while A' and A'' satisfy the conditions of Corollary 2.10 [with A and A' in the corollary replaced by A' and A'']. Then A and A'' satisfy the conditions of Theorem 2.9 [with A' in that theorem replaced by A''].

7. Let A and A' be two equivalent valued pseudo Markov systems. Prove the following properties:

   a. If A' is minimal then the number of states of A is greater than or equal to the number of states of A'.

   b. If both A and A' are minimal, then they both have the same number of states.

   c. If both A and A' are minimal, then the corresponding matrices $A(\sigma)$ and $A'(\sigma)$ of A and A' have the same set of distinct eigenvalues.

8. Let E_g be a generalized event and let $r([E_g]_k)$ be the maximal rank of any compound sequence matrix for E_g such that the values $f_i(u)$ making the entries of these matrices have the property that $l(u) \leq k$. Assume that for a given E_g we have that for some integer k, $r([E_g]_k) = r([E_g]_{k+1}) = \cdots = r([E_g]_{k+j}) = t$. Then either $r(E_g) = t$ or $r(E_g) \geq t + 2j$.

9. Based upon Exercise 8 give an algorithm for finding $r(E_g)$ when a given generalized event is known to be of finite rank and a bound is given on its rank.

10. Let $A = (\pi, S, \{A(\sigma)\}, \{\eta_i\})$ be a valued pseudo Markov system such that $\pi = (\pi_i)$, $\pi_i \geq 0$, $\sum \pi_i \leq 1$ and for any row $\xi_i(\sigma) = (\xi_{ij}(\sigma))$ in any matrix $A(\sigma)$, $\xi_{ij}(\sigma) \geq 0$ and $\sum_j \xi_{ij}(\sigma) \leq 1$. Then there exists a valued true Markov system A' with $|S| + 1$ states and equivalent to A.

11. Let $A = (\pi, S, \{A(\sigma)\}, \{\eta_i\})$ be a valued pseudo Markov system such that $\pi = (\pi_i)$, $0 \leq \pi_i \leq 1$ and all matrices $A(\sigma) = [a_{ij}(\sigma)]$ have nonnegative entries and $\sum_{i=1}^{|S|} a_{ij}(\sigma) \leq 1$. Then there exists a valued *true* Markov system A' with $2^{|S|}$ states and equivalent to A.

12. If A and A' are two valued pseudo Markov system satisfying the conditions of Corollary 2.10, with $X \neq 0$, then corresponding matrices $A(\sigma)$ and $A'(\sigma)$ have at least one common eigenvalue.

13. Let $A = (\pi, S, \{A(\sigma)\}, \{\eta_i\})$ be a valued pseudo Markov system such that $\pi = (\pi_i)$, $0 \leq \pi_i \leq 1$ and the maximal eigenvalue, in absolute value, of any

matrix $A(\sigma)A^{\mathrm{T}}(\sigma)$ is less or equal than $1/|S|$. Then there exists a valued true Markov system A' with $2^{|S|}$ states which is equivalent to A.

14. Prove that in Theorem 2.17 the valued true Markov system A' underlying the generalized event E_g' may be assumed to have the additional property that all the entries η_{ij}' in all the vectors η_i' of A' have the property: $0 \leq \eta_{ij}' \leq 1$ but in this case the relation between the functions will be

$$f_i'(u) = ac^{l(u)}f_i(u) + b$$

for any $u \in \Sigma^*$ and $i \in Z$ where a, b, c are constants.

15. Consider the following:

Definition: A word vector function is a function ϕ with domain Σ^* and values in the set of all n-dimensional real valued vectors, where Σ^* is the set of all words over a given alphabet Σ. A word vector function ϕ is realizable by a PA [probabilistic automaton] if there exists a PA $A = (\pi, S, \{A(\sigma)\}, \pi^F)$ such that for every $x \in \Sigma^*$, $\phi(x) = \pi(x)$ [η^F is a single vector having only 0-1 entries]. Prove the following:

Theorem: A word vector function ϕ is realizable by a PA if and only if the following two conditions hold true.

1. For any $x \in \Sigma^*$ and $\sigma \in \Sigma$ if $\phi(x) = \sum \alpha_i\phi(x_i)$, then $\phi(x\sigma) = \sum \alpha_i\phi(x_i\sigma)$ where $x_1 \cdots x_i \in \Sigma^*$ and α_i are constants.

2. Let $\phi(x_1) \cdots \phi(x_i)$ be any set of linearly independent vectors and let $\sigma \in \Sigma$. There exist a stochastic matrix $A(\sigma)$ such that $\phi(x_i)A(\sigma) = \phi(x_i\sigma)$.

OPEN PROBLEMS

1. Find an algorithm for ascertaining whether a given generalized event E_g of rank k can be represented as a set of input functions of a valued true Markov system.

2. Find an algorithm for ascertaining whether a given generalized event E_g of rank k can be represented as a set of input functions of a valued true Markov system with k states.

3. Define, in a meaningful way, and study "output functions" induced by non-homogeneous Markov systems with more than one letter in the alphabet Σ.

Bibliographical Notes

The exposition of Section 2 above is based mainly on the work of Carlyle and Paz (1970), except for Theorem 2.8 which is a straightforward generalization of a Theorem of Nasu and Honda (1968). It is to be mentioned also that a particular case of valued Markov system was introduced first by Page (1966) and a restricted variant of Theorem 2.17 (see also Exercise 14 above) was proved first by Turakainen (1968). Word vector functions (exercise 15 above) were considered by Bukharaev (1965) Salomaa (1966) and Turakainen (1968).

Chapter III

Events, Languages, and Acceptors

INTRODUCTION

This chapter is devoted to probabilistic languages and events. The closure properties of those languages and events and their relation to regular events are studied. Some particular cases such as definite, quasidefinite, and exclusive events are investigated and the problem of approximating probabilistic events by nonprobabilistic ones is considered.

A. EVENTS

Although the abstract models to be considered in this chapter are particular cases of models discussed in the previous chapter, the problems to be investigated are different and motivated by the approach of the mathematical logic discipline to parallel problems encountered in the deterministic case. The following notations will be used: An *event* is a single word function f over an alphabet Σ [$f: \Sigma^* \to$ real numbers] with the following subcases: an event f is *pseudo probabilistic* if it can be represented as the function induced by a valued pseudo Markov system with a single vector in the set $\{\eta_i\}$; A pseudo probabilistic event is an *expectation event* if the underlying system is a valued *true* Markov system; an expectation event is a *probabilistic event* if the underlying system has the additional property that all the entries of the (single) column vector are equal to 1 or 0. We shall write η^F instead of η with $F \subset S$ and the ith entry of η^F equal to 1 if and only if $s_i \in F$. Such a system will be called a *probabilistic automaton*.

A probabilistic event f is a *regular event* if the underlying probabilistic automaton is deterministic and the function f can assume only the values 0 or 1. The term regular event will be used both for the function f as above and for the set of words u such that $f(u) = 1$. [This abuse of language is made in order to simplify the notations and no confusion will arise as long as context is clear.]

An event f is called *constant* if $f(u) = c$ for all $u \in \Sigma^*$ and c is a constant [real number]. The following operations on events are defined [any two events, when combined, are assumed to be defined over the same alphabet Σ]:

1. $(f \pm g)(u) = f(u) \pm g(u)$ for any $u \in \Sigma^*$.
2. $(fg)(u) = f(u)g(u)$ for any $u \in \Sigma^*$.
3. $(\alpha f)(u) = \alpha(f(u))$ for any $u \in \Sigma^*$ and α a real number.
4. $(f \vee g)(u) = \max(f(u), g(u))$ for any $u \in \Sigma^*$.
5. $(f \wedge g)(u) = \min(f(u), g(u))$ for any $u \in \Sigma^*$.
6. $\bar{f}(u) = 1 - f(u)$ for any $u \in \Sigma^*$.
7. $\tilde{f}(u) = f(\tilde{u})$ where $u = \sigma_k \cdots \sigma_1$ if $u = \sigma_1 \cdots \sigma_k \in \Sigma^*$.

Some additional operations will be considered later and defined in due place.

1. Probabilistic Events

By definition, the class of PEs [probabilistic events] contains, as a proper subclass, the class of regular events. In addition it also contains the constant events as proved in the following:

Proposition 1.1. The constant functions $f(u) = c$ with $0 \le c \le 1$ are PEs.

Proof: Let f be the function $f(u) = c$ for all $u \in \Sigma^*$ and $0 \le c \le 1$. Let $A = (\pi, S, \{A(\sigma)\}, \eta^F)$ be an automaton over any alphabet Σ such that $S = \{1, 2\}$; $x = (c \quad 1 - c)$; $\eta^F = \binom{1}{0}$ and

$$A(\sigma) = \begin{bmatrix} c & 1 - c \\ c & 1 - c \end{bmatrix} \quad \text{for all} \quad \sigma \in \Sigma$$

Then

$$p(u) = \pi A(u)\eta^F = (c \quad 1 - c) \begin{bmatrix} c & 1 - c \\ c & 1 - c \end{bmatrix} \begin{bmatrix} 1 \\ 0 \end{bmatrix} = c$$

since $A(\sigma)$ are constant matrices and, therefore, $A(u) = A(\sigma)$, for any $u \in \Sigma^*$. [For the definition of constant matrices see the Preliminary Section.] ∎

Proposition 1.2: If f is a PE, then so is $\bar{f}$.

Proof: Let $A = (\pi, S, \{A(\sigma)\}, \eta^F)$ be the underlying probabilistic automaton (PA) for f. Let η be a column vector all the entries of which are equal to 1. Let $\eta^{\bar{F}}$ be the vector such that $\eta^{\bar{F}} + \eta^F = \eta$. For any $u \in \Sigma^*$, we have that $\pi A(u)(\eta^F + \eta^{\bar{F}}) = \pi(u)\eta = 1$, since $\pi(u)$ is a probabilistic vector. Therefore, $f(u) = \pi(u)\eta^F = 1 - \pi(u)\eta^{\bar{F}}$. Thus, $\bar{A} = (\pi, S, \{A(\sigma)\}, \eta^{\bar{F}})$ defines the function $\bar{f}$. ∎

Proposition 1.3: If f and g are PEs, then also fg is a PE.

Proof: Let $A = (\pi, S, \{A(\sigma)\}, \eta^F)$ and $A' = (\pi', S\{A'(\sigma)\}, \eta^{F'})$ be the respective underlying PAs for f and g. Define $A \otimes A' = (\pi \otimes \pi', S \times S', \{A(\sigma) \otimes A'(\sigma)\}, \eta^F \otimes \eta^{F'})$ where $\otimes$ denotes the Kronecker product [see Definition 1.2 and Lemma 1.1 in Section II, B, 1]. Then

$$f^{A \otimes A'}(u) = (\pi \otimes \pi')(A(\sigma_1) \otimes A'(\sigma_1)) \cdots (A(\sigma_k) \otimes A'(\sigma_k))(\eta^F \otimes \eta^{F'})$$

$$= (\pi A(\sigma_1) \cdots A(\sigma_k)\eta^F)(\pi' A'(\sigma_1) \cdots A'(\sigma_k)\eta^{F'})$$

$$= f(u)g(u) \qquad \text{where} \quad u = \sigma_1 \cdots \sigma_k$$

Since $A \otimes A'$ is a PA, the proposition is proved. ∎

Corollary 1.4: If f is a PE and c is a number $0 \leq c \leq 1$, then cf is a PE.

Proof: Let g in Proposition 1.3 be $g \colon g(u) = c$ and use Proposition 1.1. ∎

Proposition 1.5: Let f, g, h be PEs. Then the function $fh + g\bar{h}$ is a PE.

Proof: Let $A' = (\pi', s', \{A'(\sigma)\}, \eta^{F'})$ and $A'' = (\pi'', S'', \{A''(\sigma)\}, \eta^{F''})$ be the underlying PAs. Define the PA B as

$$B = (S \times S' \times S'', \pi \otimes \pi' \otimes \pi'', \{A(\sigma) \otimes A'(\sigma) \otimes A''(\sigma)\},$$

$$\eta^F \otimes \eta^{S'} \otimes \eta^{F''} + \eta^S \otimes \eta^{F'} \otimes \eta^{\bar{F}''})$$

Note that if an entry in one of the two products of η vectors is equal to 1, then the corresponding entry in the second vector is equal to 0 [since $\eta^{F''}$ has a zero entry if and only if the corresponding entry in $\eta^{F''}$ is equal to one] and therefore the sum of the two vectors has only zero or one entries.

Now, [η^S is an $|S|$-dimensional vector with all its entries equal to 1]

$$f^B(u) = (\pi \otimes \pi' \otimes \pi'')(A(u) \otimes A'(u) \otimes A''(u))(\eta^F \otimes \eta^{S'} \otimes \eta^{F''})$$

$$+ (\pi \otimes \pi' \otimes \pi'')(A(u) \otimes A'(u) \otimes A''(u))(\eta^S \otimes \eta^{F'} \otimes \eta^{\bar{F}''})$$

$$= (\pi A(u)\eta^F) \otimes (\pi' A'(u)\eta^{S'}) \otimes (\pi'' A''(u)\eta^{F''})$$

$$+ (\pi A(u)\eta^S) \otimes (\pi' A'(u)\eta^{F'}) \otimes (\pi'' A''(u)\eta^{\bar{F}''})$$

$$= f(u)h(u) + g(u)\bar{h}(u)$$

as required. ∎

Corollary 1.6: Let $f_1 \ldots f_k$, $h_1 \ldots h_k$ be two sets of PEs such that $\sum_{i=1}^{k} h_i = 1_f$ where 1_f denotes the constant function with all its values equal to 1. Then $\sum f_i h_i$ is a PE.

Proof: The proof is a trivial extension of the proof of Proposition 1.5 and is left to the reader.

Corollary 1.7: Let $f_1 \ldots f_k$ be a set of PEs and let $a_1 \ldots a_k$ be a set of numbers $0 \le a_i$ and $\sum a_i = 1$. Then $\sum a_i f_i$ is a PE.

Proof: Replace the functions h_i in Corollary 1.6 by the constant functions $h_i = a_i$. ∎

Theorem 1.8. Let f be a PE, then $\tilde{f}$ is also a PE.

Proof: Let f be defined by the PA $A = (\pi, S, \{A(\sigma)\}, \eta^F)$, then $\tilde{f}$ is defined by the pseudo probabilistic automaton (SPA) $A^T = ((\eta^F)^T, S, \{A^T(\sigma)\}, \pi^T)$. To prove this let $u = \sigma_1 \ldots \sigma_k$, then

$$f^{A^T}(u) = (\eta^F)^T A^T(\sigma_1) \cdots A^T(\sigma_k)\pi^T$$
$$= (\pi A(\sigma_k) \cdots A(\sigma_1)\eta^F)^T$$
$$= \pi A(\sigma_k) \cdots A(\sigma_1)\eta^F = f(\tilde{u})$$

We must prove that A^T has an equivalent PA. To this end, let X be a $2^{|S|} \times |S|$ matrix whose rows are all $|S|$-dimensional vectors with entries zero or one. Then $(\eta^F)^T$ is a row of X. In addition $C(XA^T(\sigma)) \subset C(X)$ [$C(A)$ denotes the convex set of vectors generated by the rows of A]. This follows from the fact that multiplying a row of X by $A^T(\sigma)$ amounts to the summing up of some of the rows of $A^T(\sigma)$ [the rows of X have only zero and one entries]. But the rows of $A^T(\sigma)$ are columns of $A(\sigma)$ which is stochastic so that the resulting vector has all its entries between zero and one and therefore belongs to $C(X)$. The conditions of Theorem 2.15 in Section II, C are thus satisfied and therefore there exists an SPA $A' = (\pi', S', \{A'(\sigma)\}\eta')$ such that A^T is equivalent to A', $|S'| = 2^{|S|}$, π', and the matrices $A'(\sigma)$ are stochastic, and $\eta' = X\pi^T$ [by the construction in Corollary 2.10 of Section II, C]. Let $X^{(i)}$ be the ith column of X, let $\pi = (\pi_i)$ and define the following PAs derived from A': $A_i = (\pi', S', \{A'(\sigma)\}, X^{(i)})$ Each A_i is a PA because the vectors $X^{(i)}$ have only zero and one entries. Let f^i be the PE induced by A_i. Then,

$$\sum \pi_i f^i(u) = \sum \pi_i(\pi' A'(u) X^{(i)})$$
$$= \pi' A'(u) \sum \pi_i X^{(i)} = \pi' A'(u) X\pi^T$$
$$= \pi' A'(u)\eta' = f^{A'}(u) = f^{A^T}(u) = \tilde{f}(u)$$

But the f^i's are PEs and therefore, by Corollary 1.7 also $\tilde{f}$ is a PE. ∎

Proposition 1.9: Let f and g be PEs and let h be the function defined as

$h(u) = 1$ if $f(u) \geq g(u)$ and $h(u) = 0$ if $f(u) < g(u)$. If h is a regular event, then $f \vee g$ and $f \wedge g$ are PEs.

Proof: One verifies easily that $\max(f, g) = fh + g\bar{h}$ and $\min(f, g) = f\bar{h} + gh$ so that this proposition is a particular case of Proposition 1.5. ∎

Theorem 1.10: The class of PEs is not closed in general under the operations $\vee$ and $\wedge$.

Proof: Let $A = (\pi, S, \{A(\sigma)\}, \pi^F)$ be the automaton such that: $\pi = \{a, b\}$, $S = (1, 2, 3, 4,)$ $F = \{1, 4\}$, $\pi = (\frac{1}{2} \ 0 \ \frac{1}{2} \ 0)$ and,

$$A(a) = \begin{bmatrix} \frac{1}{2} & \frac{1}{2} & 0 & 0 \\ 0 & 1 & 0 & 0 \\ 0 & 0 & 1 & 0 \\ 0 & 0 & 0 & 1 \end{bmatrix}, \quad A(b) = \begin{bmatrix} 1 & 0 & 0 & 0 \\ 0 & 1 & 0 & 0 \\ 0 & 0 & \frac{1}{2} & \frac{1}{2} \\ 0 & 0 & 0 & 1 \end{bmatrix}$$

Let $n_a(u)$ and $n_b(u)$ be the number of occurences of a and b respectively in the word u. It is easily verified that

$$f^A = \tfrac{1}{2} + \tfrac{1}{2}(2^{-n_a(x)} - 2^{-n_b(x)})$$

Thus

$$f^A(u) = \begin{cases} = \tfrac{1}{2} & \text{if } n_a(x) = n_b(x) \\ > \tfrac{1}{2} & \text{if } n_a(x) < n_b(x) \\ < \tfrac{1}{2} & \text{if } n_a(x) > n_b(x) \end{cases}$$

Let $g(u)$ be the constant event $g(u) = \tfrac{1}{2}$ for all $u \in \Sigma^*$. Then $f^A(u) \vee g(u)$ and $f^A(u) \wedge g(u)$ *are not* probabilistic events. In fact we shall prove that the above events are not even pseudo probabilistic [a class which includes the class of PEs]. Assume the contrary, then there exists a pseudo Markov system B whose input function is $f^A \vee g$ so that for any integer k we have that

$$f^B(a^k b^{k+1}) = \max(f^A(a^k b^{k+1}), \tfrac{1}{2}) = f^A(a^k b^{k+1}) > \tfrac{1}{2}$$

and for $i \leq k$

$$f^B(a^k b^i) = \max(f^A(a^k b^i), \tfrac{1}{2}) = \tfrac{1}{2}$$

By Theorem 2.8 in Section II, C with $u' = a^k$, $u = b$ and $u'' = \lambda$, there are constants $c_0, \ldots, c_k$ such that

$$f^B(a^k b^{k+1}) = c_k f^B(a^k b^k) + \cdots + c_1 f^B(a^k b) + c_0 f^B(a^k)$$

implying that $\tfrac{1}{2} < \tfrac{1}{2} \sum_{i=0}^{k} c_i$, while if $u' = a^{k+1} u = b$ and $u'' = \lambda$ we have, for the same set of constants depending on u only, that

$$f^B(a^{k+1} b^{k+1}) = c_k f^B(a^{k+1} b^k) + \cdots + c_0 f^B(a^{k+1})$$

or $\tfrac{1}{2} = \tfrac{1}{2} \sum_{i=1}^{k} c_i$, which is impossible. $f^A \vee g$ is thus proved not to be a *pseudo probabilistic event* and the proof for $f^A \wedge g$ is similar. ∎

Corollary 1.11: The class of pseudo probabilistic events (and therefore also the class of probabilistic events) is a proper subclass of the class of events.

2. Pseudo Probabilistic Events

The class of SPEs [pseudo probabilistic events] includes, as a proper subclass, the class of PEs since the values of a PE f are bounded while the values of an SPE may increase beyond and bound. On the other hand, not every event is an SPE, this has been proved by Corollary 1.11. One can prove now in the same way as in the previous section that:

1. The SPEs include all constant functions $f = c$ where c is any real number.
2. If f is an SPE, then so are $\bar{f}, \tilde{f}$, and αf where α is any real number.
3. If f and g are SPEs, then so is $f \cdot g$.

The SPEs have also the following properties:

Proposition 2.1: If f and g are SPEs then so is $f + g$.

Proof: Let f be defined by $A = (\pi, S, \{A(\sigma)\}, \eta)$ and g by $A' = (\pi', S', \{A'(\sigma)\}, \eta')$. Let A'' be the system $A'' = (\pi'', S'', \{A''(\sigma)\}, \eta'')$ with $S'' = S \cup S'$, $\pi'' = (\pi \, \pi') \, \eta'' = (\eta^{\mathrm{T}} \, \eta'^{\mathrm{T}})^{\mathrm{T}}$
and

$$A''(\sigma) = \begin{bmatrix} A(\sigma) & 0 \\ 0 & A'(\sigma) \end{bmatrix}$$

one verifies easily that $f^{A''} = f^A + f^{A'}$. ∎

Proposition 2.2: Let f and g be SPEs and let h be the event

$$h(u) = \begin{cases} 1 & \text{if } f(u) \le g(u) \\ 0 & \text{if } f(u) < g(u) \end{cases}$$

If h is regular, then the events $f \vee g$ and $f \wedge g$ are SPEs.

Proof: Similar to the proof of Proposition 1.9.

Proposition 2.3: The class SPE is not closed in general under the operations $\vee$ and $\wedge$.

Proof: The proof is included in the proof of Theorem 1.10 for the functions f and g used in the proof are PEs and therefore also SPEs while $f \vee g$ and $f \wedge g$ where proved not to be SPEs. ∎

Theorem 2.4: Let f be an SPE, there exists a PE g and constant numbers b, c, d with $d \ge 0$ and $0 \le c \le 1$ such that $dg(u) - b = c^{l(u)} f(u)$ for any $u \in \Sigma^*$.

Proof: Let $A = (\pi, S, \{A(\sigma)\}, \eta)$ be the underlying system for f. We have proved already [Theorem 2.17 in Section II, C] that there exists a system $A' = (\pi', S', \{A'(\sigma)\}, \eta')$ such that the vector π and the matrices $A(\sigma)$ are stochastic, and $f'(u) = c^{l(u)} f(u)$ for some constant c and any $u \in \Sigma^*$. Two additional transformations are needed in order to change η' so as to fit the definitions of a PA. Let A'' be the system derived from A' defined as $A'' = (\pi', S', \{A'(\sigma)\}, a(\eta' + \bar{b}))$ where $\bar{b}$ is a column vector all the entries of which are equal to b, a and b being two numbers chosen in a way such that all the entries of the vector $a(\eta' + \bar{b})$ are between zero and one. As $a(\eta' + \bar{b})$ has entries between zero and one, it can be expressed as a convex combination of a set of vectors $\{\eta_i\}$ such that the entries in any vector η_i are either zero or one. Thus, $a(\eta' + \bar{b}) = \sum \alpha_i \eta_i$ with $\alpha_i \geq 0$, $\sum \alpha_i = 1$, $\eta_i = (\eta_{ij})$ and either $\eta_{ij} = 1$ or $\eta_{ij} = 0$ for all i. Let A_i be the PA $A_i = (\pi', S', \{A'(\sigma)\}, \eta_i)$, then for any $u \in \Sigma^*$ we have that

$$\sum \alpha_i f^{A_i}(u) = \sum \alpha_i (\pi' A'(u) \eta_i) = \pi' A'(u) \sum \alpha_i \eta_i$$
$$= \pi' A'(u)[a(\eta' + \bar{b})] = a(\pi' A'(u) \eta' + \pi' A'(u) \bar{b})$$
$$= af'(u) + ab$$

[since $\pi' A'(u)$ is a stochastic vector and all the entries in $\bar{b}$ are equal to b]. Let g be the event defined as $g(u) = \sum \alpha_i f^{A_i}(u)$. It follows from Corollary 1.7 [the f^{A_i} are PEs] that g is a PE. But $g(u) = af'(u) + ab = ac^{l(u)} f(u) + ab$. Thus $a^{-1} g(u) - b = c^{l(u)} f(u)$ for any $u \in \Sigma^*$. Setting $a^{-1} = d$ will complete the proof. It follows from the proof that $a \geq 0$ and therefore also $d \geq 0$, while the constant c is $0 \leq c \leq 1$. ∎

EXERCISES

1. Let f and g be PEs. Find a PE h such that $h(u) > \frac{1}{2}$ if $f(u) > g(u)$ and $h(u) \leq \frac{1}{2}$ if $f(u) \leq g(u)$.

2. Let f be a PE. Prove that the sets $\{u: f(u) = 0\}$, $\{u: f(u) > 0\}$, $\{u: f(u) = 1\}$ are regular events.

3. Let $A = (\pi, S, \{A(\sigma)\}, \eta^F)$ and $A' = (\pi', S', \{A'(\sigma)\}, \eta^{F'})$ be PAs with $S \cap S' = \phi$, and let $A'' = (\pi'', S'', \{A''(\sigma)\}, \eta^{F''})$ be the PA defined by $\pi'' = (\alpha\pi \ \beta\pi')$, $\alpha, \beta \geq 0$ and $\alpha + \beta = 1$; $S'' = S \cup S'$, $\eta^{F''} = ((\eta^F)^T (\eta^{F'})^T)^T$ and

$$A''(\sigma) = \begin{bmatrix} A(\sigma) & 0 \\ 0 & A'(\sigma) \end{bmatrix}$$

Show that $f^{A''}(u) = f^A(u) + f^{A'}(u)$ for all $u \in \Sigma^*$.

4. Prove Corollary 1.7 using the construction in Exercise 3 above, and show that the resulting automaton is more economical [as to the number of its states] when the construction in Exercise 3 is used.

5. Let $A = (\pi, S, \{A(\sigma)\}, \eta^r)$ be a PA. Find an equivalent system $A' = (\pi', S', \{A'(\sigma)\}, \eta')$ such that π' has the form $\pi' = (1\ 0\ \cdots\ 0)$, $|S'| = |S| + 1$, the matrices $A'(\sigma)$ are stochastic, the vector $\eta' = (\eta_i')$ has the property that $0 \le \eta_i' \le 1$ for all i.

6. Use the construction in Exercise 5 above in the proof of Theorem 1.8 to replace the use of Corollary 1.7 and show that the resulting PA for f is more economical [as to the number of its states] if the construction in Exercise 5 is used [even if the construction in Exercise 3 is used for proving Corollary 1.7].

7. Prove that any finite dimensional vector $\xi = (\xi_i)_{i=1}^n$ such that $0 \le \xi_i \le 1$ can be expressed in the form $\xi = \sum_{i=1}^m a_i \xi^i$ where ξ^i are vectors all the entries of which are 0 or 1 and $a_i \ge 0$, $\sum a_i = 1$. Provide an explicit construction for the above decomposition.

8. Prove: If f is a PE, then the functions $g_{u'}(u) = f(u'u)$ and $h^{u'}(u) = f(uu')$ for a fixed $u' \in \Sigma^*$ and all $u \in \Sigma^*$ are PEs.

9. Prove that there are SPE f and g such that $|f - g|$ is not an SPE.

10. Prove that if f is an SPE such that the matrices in the underlying system are doubly stochastic then a corresponding system defining $\tilde{f}$ can be found with doubly stochastic matrices.

OPEN PROBLEM

Find a class of events, properly including the regular events and included [properly] in the class of PEs which is closed under union intersection and complementation.

3. Bibliographical Notes

Most of the material presented in this section appeared in the literature under various names and with variations. Thus Proposition 1.1 and Exercise 2 are due to Starke (1966b, c), Propositions 1.2 and 1.3 are due to Paz (1966), Proposition 1.4 and Exercise 8 should be credited to Bukharaev (1967), Propositions 1.5–1.9 and Exercises 1 and 5 are from Nasu and Honda (1968), while Theorems 1.10 and 1.11 were given in a restricted form in Nasu and Honda (1968).

Pseudo probabilistic events were studied by Turakainen (1968) who is to be credited for Propositions 2.1, 2.4, and Exercise 3. Many of the proofs are however new and some propositions are given here in a stronger version than the original. Zadeh (1965) introduced the concept of fuzzy sets generalizing the classical set concept. The events as introduced here are in fact fuzzy sets with the "universal" set being the set of all words over a given alphabet.

Other related papers: Paz (1967c), Carlyle and Paz (1970).

B. CUT-POINT EVENTS

1. Closure Properties

Definition 1.1: Let f be an SPE and λ a real number. The set of words $T(f, \lambda)$ is defined as

$$T(f, \lambda) = \{u : f(u) > \lambda\}$$

and is called a general cut-point event (GCE). If f is a PE defined by the automaton A and $0 \leq \lambda < 1$, then $T(f, \lambda)$ to be denoted also by $T(A, \lambda)$ is called a probabilistic cut-point event [PCE].

Using the theorems of the previous section, we shall now study the closure properties of PCEs and their relation to GCEs. In fact the first proposition shows that the two classes of events are identical.

Proposition 1.1: The class of PCEs is identical to the class of GCEs

Proof: The class of PCEs is clearly a subclass of GCEs. To prove the converse, let $E = \{u : f(u) > \lambda\}$ be an event such that f is SPE. By Proposition A, 2.1 the function $f' = f - \lambda$ is also an SPE and has the property that $f'(u) > 0$ if and only if $f(u) > \lambda$. By Theorem A, 2.4 there is a PE g and numbers $0 \leq c \leq 1$, $0 \leq d$ and arbitrary b such that $c^{l(u)} f'(u) = dg(u) - b$ for all $u \in \Sigma^*$. If $b = 0$, then clearly the set $\{u : f'(u) > 0\}$ is equal to Σ^* or to ϕ and these events are PCEs as will be shown subsequently. If $f \neq 0$, then $E = \{u : f(u) > \lambda\} = \{u : f'(u) > 0\} = \{u : g(u) > b/d\}$ where $g(u)$ is a PE. Thus E is a PCE and the proposition is proved. ∎

Proposition 1.2: The class of regular events is a subset of the class of PCEs.

Proof: If E is a regular event, then its characteristic function can be represented in a degenerate PA [see Section A, 1]. Thus there is a PE f such that $E = T(f, 0)$. ∎

Proposition 1.3: The class of PCEs is not changed if the defining pseudo probabilistic automata are restricted to have only degenerate initial distributions.

Proof: By Exercise 5, Section A, 2. ∎

Proposition 1.4: Let $T(f, \lambda)$ be a PCE and let μ be a number $0 < \mu < 1$. There is a PE g such that $T(f, \lambda) = T(g, \mu)$.

Proof: If $\mu < \lambda$, then $\mu = a\lambda$ with $0 < a < 1$ and, using Corollary A, 1.4, we may use the PE $g = af$. Clearly $f(u) > \lambda$ if and only if $g(u) > \mu$. If $\lambda < \mu$, then let g be defined as

$$g = \frac{1 - \mu}{1 - \lambda} f + \frac{\mu - \lambda}{1 - \lambda}$$

By Corollary A, 1.7 g is a PE and $f(u) > \lambda$ if and only if

$$g(u) > \frac{(1 - \mu)\lambda}{1 - \lambda} + \frac{\mu - \lambda}{1 - \lambda} = \mu$$

as required. ∎

Remark: The requirement that $0 < \mu$ is necessary since any PCE of the form $T(f, 0)$ defines a regular event [see Exercise 2, Section A, 2] and the class of PCEs properly contains the regular events. This fact will be proved later.

Proposition 1.5: If E is a PCE and R is a regular event then $E \cup R$, $E \cap R$ and $E - R$ (meaning the set of words in E but not in R) are PCEs.

Proof: Let $E = T(f, \lambda)$ and $R = T(g, 0)$ where $g(u)$ is either 0 or 1 for all $u \in \Sigma^*$. Then fg is a PE by Proposition A, 1.3. It is easily verified that $E \cap R = T(fg, \lambda)$ for $fg(u) > \lambda$ if and only if $f(u) > \lambda$ and $g(u) = 1$. Consider now the function $f\bar{g} + g$. By Proposition A, 1.5 this function is a PE [the function h in that proposition is the function $\bar{g}$ here and the function g is the constant function with value 1 here]. If $g(u) > 0$, then $(f\bar{g} + g)(u) = 1 > \lambda$. If $g(u) = 0$, then $(f\bar{g} + g)(u) > \lambda$, if and only if $f(u) > \lambda$. It follows that $T(f\bar{g} + g, \lambda) = E \cup R$. To complete the proof we note that $E - R = E \cap \bar{R}$ and $\bar{R}$ is a regular event. ∎

The *reverse* of an event E, to be denoted by $\tilde{E}$, is defined in the usual way, i.e, $\tilde{E}$ contains all the words $\sigma_1 \cdots \sigma_k$ such that $\sigma_k \cdots \sigma_1$ are in E. We are now able to prove the following:

Proposition 1.6: The class of PCEs is closed under the reverse operation.

Proof: Let E be the PCE $E = T(f, \lambda)$. Then $\tilde{E} = T(\tilde{f}, \lambda)$ because $\tilde{E} = \{u : u = \sigma_1 \cdots \sigma_k, \sigma_k \cdots \sigma_1 \in E\} = \{u : u = \sigma_1 \cdots \sigma_k, f(\sigma_k \cdots \sigma_1) > \lambda\} = \{u : u = \sigma_1 \cdots \sigma_k, \tilde{f}(\sigma_1 \cdots \sigma_k) > \lambda\}$ and by Theorem A, 1.8 $\tilde{f}$ is a PE. ∎

Proposition 1.7: Let $E = T(f, \lambda)$ be a PCE such that the set $\{u : f(u) = \lambda\}$ is regular, then $\bar{E} = \Sigma^* - E$ is a PCE.

Proof: $E = T(f, \lambda) = \{u : f(u) > \lambda\}$; therefore, $\bar{E} = \{u : f(u) \leq \lambda\} = \{u : \bar{f}(u) \geq 1 - \lambda\} = \{u : \bar{f}(u) > 1 - \lambda\} \cup \{u : \bar{f}(u) = 1 - \lambda\} = \{u : \bar{f}(u) > 1 - \lambda\} \cup \{u : f(u) = \lambda\}$. ∎

To complete the proof we use Propositions A, 1.2 and B, 1.5.

Remark: In the proof of Theorem A,1.10 a PE f is given such that all three sets $\{x : f(x) > \lambda\}, \{x : f(x) < \lambda\}$ and $\{x : f(x) = \lambda\}$ are nonregular for $\lambda = \frac{1}{2}$. Thus the condition of Proposition 1.7 does not hold true in all cases.

Proposition 1.8: The class of PCEs is closed under the operation of finite derivation. [The derivate of an event E with respect to the word u is the event $D(E) = \{u' : uu' \in E\}$].

Proof: Let E be the PE induced by the PA $A = (S, \pi, \{A(\sigma)\}, \eta^F)$. Let A_u be the PA $A_u = (S, \pi(u), \{A(\sigma)\}, \eta^F)$ where $\pi(u) = \pi A(u)$, then $T(f^{A_u}, \lambda) = \{w : \pi(u)A(w)\eta^F > \lambda\} = \{w : \pi A(uw)\eta^F > \lambda\} = \{w : uw \in E\}$. It follows that $D_u(E)$ is a PCE. ∎

Proposition 1.9: Let E be an event and assume that all the events of the from $D_u(E)$ for $l(u) = k$, k an arbitrary fixed integer, are PCEs. Then E is a PCE.

Proof: We shall prove the proposition for $k = 1$; the proof in the general case is similar. We remark first that $E = (\cup_{\sigma \in \Sigma} D_\sigma(E)) \cup F$ where F is empty or contains the word e only,† and is therefore a regular event. Since PCEs are closed under union with regular events it suffices to prove that $E' = \cup_{\sigma \in \Sigma} D_\sigma(E)$ is a PCE. Our second remark is concerned with the possibility of inducing a "delay" into a PA. Let $A = (S, \pi, \{A(\sigma)\}, \eta^F)$ be a PA defining the event $T(A, \lambda)$. Define the PA $A' = (S', \pi', \{A(\sigma)\}, \eta^{F'})$ as follows: $S' = S \cup s^*$, $s^* \notin S$; π' is the degenerate probabilistic vector having a 1 in its first entry only, the other entries being 0; $F' = F$ and, finally, $A'(\sigma)$ is the matrix

$$A'(\sigma) \begin{bmatrix} 0 & \pi \\ 0 & A(\sigma) \end{bmatrix}$$

It is easily verified that for any word $u = \sigma_1 \cdots \sigma_k \in \Sigma^*$, $l(u) \geq 1$,

$$p^{A'}(\sigma_1\sigma_2 \cdots \sigma_k) = p^A(\sigma_2 \cdots \sigma_k), \qquad P^{A'}(\sigma_i) = p^A(e), p^{A'}(e) = 0$$

Let f_{σ_i} be the characteristic function of the event $\sigma_i\Sigma^*$; as the $\sigma_i\Sigma^*$ are regular events f_{σ_i} are PEs by Proposition 1.2. and $\sum_{\sigma_i \in \Sigma} f_{\sigma_i} = f_1 = $ the constant function $f_1(u) = 1$ if $l(u) \geq 1$. Assume that $D_{\sigma_i}(E) = T(A_i, \lambda)$; one may assume the same λ for all σ_i because of Proposition 1.4. Finally, let A_i' be the PA derived from the A_i as above, i.e., $p^{A_i'}(\sigma_1 \cdots \sigma_k) = p^{A_i}(\sigma_2 \cdots \sigma_k)$. We claim that $E' = T(A, \lambda)$, where $f^A = \sum_{\sigma_i \in \Sigma} f_{\sigma_i} f^{A_i'}$ [which is a PE by the Corollary A, 1.6]. To prove our claim we remark that for any word u with $l(u) \geq 1$ if $u = \sigma_i w$, then $f_{\sigma_i}(u) = 1, f_{\sigma_j}(u) = 0$ for $j \neq i$, and $f^{A_i'}(u) = f^{A_i}(w)$. Thus, for $u = \sigma_i w$, $f^A(u) = f^{A_i}(w)$ with the result that $u \in T(A, \lambda)$ if and only if $w \in D_{\sigma_i}(E)$ or $T(A, \lambda) = \cup_{\sigma_i \in \Sigma} \sigma_i D_i(E)$. This completes the proof. ∎

Theorem 1.10: There are events which are not CPE.

Proof: We define an event E over a single letter alphabet $\Sigma = \{\sigma\}$ which is not a PE. Let $u_1, u_2, \ldots$ be a lexicographical enumeration of all nonempty words over a two letter alphabet $\Delta = \{a, b\}$. Let x be the infinite sequence of

†The empty word will be denoted by e instead of λ whenever necessary in order to avoid confusion with the cut-point λ.

letters from Δ resulting from the concatenation of the words $u_1, u_2, \ldots$ in their proper order [e.g., $u_1 = a, u_2 = b, u_3 = aa, u_4 = ab$, etc., and $x = abaaab \cdots$]. Let $x(n)$ denote the nth letter in the sequence x and define the event over Σ

$$E = \{\sigma^n : x(n) = a\}$$

then E is not a CPE. To prove this, assume the contrary. Thus $E = T(f, \lambda)$ for some PE f and some cut point λ. This means that $f(\sigma^n) > \lambda$ for $x(n) = a$ and $f(\sigma^n) \leq \lambda$ for $x(n) = b$. By Theorem 2.8 in Section II, C, there exists a set of constants $c_0, \ldots, c_{n-1}$ such that for any integer k

$$f(\sigma^{k+n}) = c_0 f(\sigma^k) + c_1 f(\sigma^{k+1}) + \cdots + c_{n-1} f(\sigma^{k+n+1}) \qquad (*)$$

Let $\epsilon_0 \cdots \epsilon_n, \delta_0 \cdots \delta_n$ be two words in Δ^* defined as follows: if $c_i > 0$, then $\epsilon_i = b$ and $\delta_i = a$; if $c_i \leq 0$, then $\epsilon_i = a$ and $\delta_i = b$; $\epsilon_n = a, \delta_n = b$. By the construction of the sequence x, there are integers k_1 and k_2 such that $x(k_1)x(k_1 + 1) \cdots x(k_1 + n) = \epsilon_0 \cdots \epsilon_n$ and $x(k_2)x(k_2 + 1) \cdots x(k_2 + n) = \delta_0 \cdots \delta_n$. It follows from that if $c_i > 0$, then $x(k_1 + i) = b$ and $f(\sigma^{k_1+i}) \leq \lambda$, and also $x(k_2 + i) = a$ and $f(\sigma^{k_2+i}) > \lambda$. If $c_i \leq 0$, then $x(k_1 + i) = a$ and $f(\sigma^{k_1+i}) > \lambda$ and also $x(k_2 + i) = b$ and $f(\sigma^{k_2+i}) \leq \lambda$. $x(k_1 + n) = a$ so that $f(\sigma^{k_1+n}) > \lambda$, and $x(k_2 + n) = b$ so that $f(\sigma^{k_2+n}) \leq \lambda$. We evaluate now the formula (*) first for $k = k_1$. We have

$$\lambda < f(\sigma^{k_1+n}) = \sum_{i=0}^{n-1} c_i f(\sigma^{k_1+i}) \leq \lambda \sum_{i=0}^{n-1} c_i \qquad \text{or} \qquad \sum_{i=0}^{n-1} c_i > 1$$

The inequality on the right follows from the fact that the values $f(\sigma^{k_1+i})$ corresponding to positive coefficients c_i are not decreased while the values $f(\sigma^{k_1+i})$ corresponding to negative coefficients c_i [if there exist such coefficients] are decreased. On the other hand, evaluating the formula (*) for $k = k_2$ we have

$$\lambda \geq f(\sigma^{k_2+n}) = \sum_{i=0}^{n-1} c_i f(\sigma^{k_2+n}) \geq \lambda \sum_{i=0}^{n-1} c_i \qquad \text{or} \qquad \sum_{i=0}^{n-1} c_i \leq 1$$

since in this case the values $f(\sigma^{k_2+n})$ corresponding to positive coefficients [if there are such] are decreased and values $f(\sigma^{k_2+n})$ corresponding to negative coefficients are not decreased. Thus, $1 < \sum_{i=1}^{n-1} c_i \leq 1$ which is impossible, and therefore the event E is not a CPE. ∎

Remark: The reader familiar with the theory of abstract languages will find it easy to show that the event E defined above is context sensitive. It could not be context free, for any context free event over a single letter is also regular [this is a well-known fact] and regular events are CPEs. On the other hand, the only property of the sequence used in the proof of Theorem 1.10 is that any word of Δ^* be a subsequence of x. Thus, by defining the sequence x in a more complicated way, but still having that property, it would be possible to find an event which is recursive, not context sensitive and not a CPE.

EXERCISES

1. Let A be a given PA. Prove that the sets of words $\{u : p^A(u) = 0\}, \{u : p^A(u) > 0\}, \{u : p^A(u) = 1\}$ and $\{u : p^A(u) < 1\}$ are all regular sets.

2. Let A be a PA such that S contains two elements only and Σ contains one element only. Prove that $T(A, \lambda)$ is a regular set for any $\lambda, 0 \leq \lambda < 1$.

3. Consider the following PA: $A = (S, \pi, \{A(\sigma)\}, \eta^F)$ over $\Sigma = \{\sigma_1, \sigma_2\}$, where $S = \{s_1, s_2, \ldots, s_8\}$; $\pi = (1\ 0 \cdots 0)$; $\eta^F = (\eta_i^F)$ is defined by the requirement that

$$\eta_i^F = \begin{cases} 1 & \text{if } i = 4 \\ 0 & \text{otherwise} \end{cases}$$

and $A(\sigma_k) = [a_{ij}(\sigma_k)]$ is defined by the relations:

$$a_{12}(\sigma_1) = a_{33}(\sigma_1) = a_{48}(\sigma_1) = a_{55}(\sigma_1) = a_{67}(\sigma_1)$$
$$= a_{88}(\sigma_1) = a_{18}(\sigma_2) = a_{48}(\sigma_2) = a_{68}(\sigma_2) = a_{78}(\sigma_2) = a_{88}(\sigma_2) = 1$$
$$a_{22}(\sigma_1) = a_{77}(\sigma_1) = \epsilon, \qquad a_{25}(\sigma_1) = a_{73}(\sigma_1) = 1 - \epsilon,$$
$$a_{23}(\sigma_2) = a_{26}(\sigma_2) = a_{56}(\sigma_2) = a_{58}(\sigma_2) = \tfrac{1}{2},$$
$$a_{34}(\sigma_2) = \delta, \qquad a_{38}(\sigma_2) = 1 - \delta, \qquad \text{and} \qquad a_{ij}(\sigma_k) = 0$$

in all other cases with $0 < \epsilon < 1, 0 < \delta < 1$. Let λ be the number defined as $\lambda = \delta/2$. Describe explicitly the sets of words $\{u : f^A(u) > \lambda\}, \{u : f^A(u) = \lambda\}$ $\{u : f^A(u) > \lambda\}$ and show that these sets are not regular.

4. Same as previous exercise with $\lambda = \tfrac{1}{2}$ and the PA $A = (S, \pi, \{A(\sigma)\}, \eta^F)$ defined es follows: $\Sigma\{\sigma_1, \sigma_2\}, S = \{s_1, \ldots, s_6\}, \pi = (1\ 0 \cdots 0), \eta_i^F = 1$ if $i = 5$, and $\eta_i^F = 0$ otherwise,

$$a_{12}(\sigma_1) = a_{33}(\sigma_1) = a_{55}(\sigma_1) = a_{66}(\sigma_1)$$
$$= a_{16}(\sigma_2) = a_{46}(\sigma_2) = a_{56}(\sigma_2) = a_{66}(\sigma_2) = 1$$
$$a_{22}(\sigma_1) = a_{23}(\sigma_1) = a_{44}(\sigma_1) = a_{45}(\sigma_1)$$
$$= a_{24}(\sigma_2) = a_{25}(\sigma_2) = a_{34}(\sigma_2) = a_{36}(\sigma_2) = \tfrac{1}{2}$$

$a_{ij}(\sigma_k) = 0$ in all other cases.

5. Let A and B be two PAs prove that the set of words $\{u : f^A(u) > f^B(u)\}$ is a PCE.

6*. Consider the following PA: $A = (S, \pi, \{A(\sigma)\}, \eta^F)$ over the alphabet $\Sigma = \{\sigma_1 \cdots \sigma_k\}$ where $S = \{s_1, s_2\}$ π and η^F are arbitrary and the matrices $A(\sigma_i)$ are defined as

$$A(\sigma_i) = \begin{bmatrix} 1 - a_i & a_i \\ b_i & 1 - b_i \end{bmatrix}$$

and are such that for all i and j, $a_i + b_i \neq 0$, $a_i b_i \neq 1$ and $a_i b_j = a_j b_i$. Prove that $T(A, \lambda)$ is a regular set, for any cut-point λ.

7. Let M be an SSM [see Definition 1.1, Section I, A]. Let (u, v) be a pair of words of same length over the input and output alphabets X and Y respectively of M. Let y be a symbol in the output alphabet Y and let $0 \leq \lambda < 1$ be a real number. Let $A(u)$ be the matrix $A(u) = \sum_v A(v|u)$ [summation is over all v with $l(u) = l(v)$] and let $p^M(y|u)$ denote the probability that the machine M will have y as its *last* output when the word u is fed into it. a. Prove that if the set of different matrices $A(u), u \in X^*$ is finite then the set of words

$$T(M, \lambda, y) = \{u : p^M(y|u) > \lambda\}$$

is a regular set for any λ and y as above.

b. Assuming that the set $\{A(u) : u \in X^*\}$ contains at most m different elements, find the number of states of a minimal automaton defining $T(M, \lambda, y)$.

8. Prove that if in Exercise 7 the matrices $A(x), x \in X$ are degenerate stochastic [i.e., deterministic], then the set of words $\{u : p^M(y|u) > \lambda\}$ is regular for any y and λ as in that exercise.

OPEN PROBLEMS

1. Are PCEs closed under union, intersection, and complementation?

2. Give a decision precedure for ascertaining whether a set of matrices $\{A(\sigma)\}$ generates only finitely many different matrices in the set $A(u), u \in \Sigma^*$.

2. Regular Events and Probabilistic Cut-Point Events

The following theorem, due to Nerode, is very useful and we shall have the occasion to use it many times. It serves as a characterization of regular events. [In order to comply with the common notation, we shall denote, from here and on, by $x, y, z, \ldots$, words over an alphabet Σ.]

Theorem 2.1: Let U be a set of words the following three conditions are equivalent:

1. U is a regular set.
2. U is the union of some of the equivalence classes of a right invariant equivalence relation over Σ^* of finite index.
3. The explicit right invariant equivalence relation E defined by the condition that for all x, y in Σ^*, xEy if and only if for all $z \in \Sigma^*$, whenever xz is in U, yz is in U and conversely, is a relation of finite index. The index of the relation is the least number of internal states of any automaton defining U.

The reader is referred to Rabin and Scott (1959) for the proof of this well-know theorem.

We shall need also the following combinatorial lemma due to Rabin [Rabin (1963)].

Lemma 2.2: Let $\mathscr{P}_n$ be the set of all n-dimensional probabilistic vectors [i.e., $\mathscr{P}_n = \{\bar{\xi} = (\xi_i), \xi_i \geq 0 \sum_{i=1}^n \xi_i = 1\}$] and let U_ϵ be a subset of $\mathscr{P}_n$ such that for any pair of vectors $\bar{\xi}$ and $\bar{\eta}$ in U_ϵ the inequality $\sum_{i=1}^n |\xi_i - \eta_i| \geq \epsilon$ [ϵ is a given positive real number] holds true. Then U_ϵ is a finite set containing at most $k(\epsilon)$ elements where $k(\epsilon) = (1 + 2/\epsilon)^{n-1}$.

Proof: Let $\bar{\xi} = (\xi_i)$ be a point in U_ϵ and define the set of points v_ξ in n-dimensional space as $v_\xi = \{\bar{\zeta} = (\zeta_i) : \xi_i \leq \zeta_i, \sum (\zeta_i - \xi_i) = \epsilon/2\}$. It is easy to see that each v_ξ is a translate of the set $v = \{\bar{\zeta} = (\zeta_i) : \zeta_i \geq 0, \sum \zeta_i = \epsilon/2\}$.

Since $\bar{\xi}$ is a probabilistic vector and $\xi_i \leq \zeta_i$ for all i we have also that v_ξ is a subset of the set of points $V_\epsilon = \{\bar{\zeta} = (\zeta_i) : \zeta_i \geq 0, \sum \zeta_i = 1 + \epsilon/2\}$. A point $\bar{\zeta}$ is an interior point in a set v_ξ [relative to the V_ϵ set] if and only if $\zeta_i > \xi_i$ for all i. Figure 16 exhibits the different sets defined above for $n = 3$. $\bar{\xi}$ and $\bar{\eta}$ are two points in U_ϵ. It follows from the definitions that two different sets v_ξ and v_η cannot have a common interior point. Assuming the contrary, if $\bar{\zeta}$ is an interior point of both v_ξ and v_η, then $\zeta_i > \xi_i$ and $\zeta_i > \eta_i$ for all i and, therefore, $|\xi_i - \eta_i| < |\zeta_i - \eta_i| + |\zeta_i - \xi_i|$ for all i. This would imply that

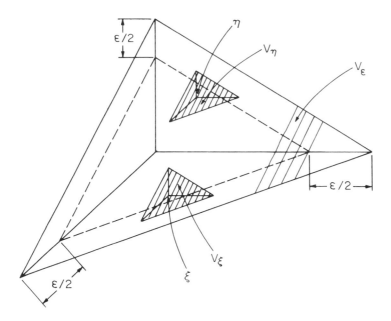

Figure 16. *Geometrical representation of the sets v_ξ for $n = 3$.*

$$\sum |\xi_i - \eta_i| < \sum |\zeta_i - \eta_i| + \sum |\zeta_i - \xi_i| = \frac{\epsilon}{2} + \frac{\epsilon}{2} = \epsilon$$

which is impossible by the definition of the set U_ϵ.

It is thus seen that the number of points in U_ϵ cannot be larger that the number of simplices v_ξ which can be packed into the symplex V_ϵ. To get an estimate of this number let $S(v_\xi)$ be the volume of the symplex v_ξ, then $S(v_\xi) = c(\epsilon/2)^{n-1}$ where c is a constant not depending on ϵ. Similarly, $s(V_\epsilon) = c(1 + \epsilon/2)^{n-1}$. Therefore, if k simplices v_ξ can be packed into V_ϵ then $kc(\epsilon/2)^{n-1} \leq c(1 + (\epsilon/2))^{n-1}$. Thus $k \leq (1 + (2/\epsilon))^{n-1}$ and this completes the proof. ∎

Remarks: One may prove that the set U_ϵ is finite in a much easier way by using the Bolzano–Weierstrass theorem, since the set U_ϵ can be shown to be bounded with no accumulation point under the measure $\sum |\xi_i|$. On the other hand, the proof given here provides also a bound on the number of elements in U_ϵ. This brings up an open problem. The bound of the lemma is clearly not sharp and a sharper bound can be proved provided one can get an estimate for the "covering ratio" of the packing problem involved in the proof. In a more explicit way, consider the following problem: Let V be a simplex of side length a and let v_i be simplices of side length $b \ll a$ and having the same linear dimension. Let k be the maximal number of simplices v_i which can be packed into V and such that all the $v_i s$ are in a relative translated position one to the other [no rotation is allowed]. Provide an estimate to the ratio $kS(v_i)/S(V)$, where S denotes the volume of the respective simplices. A solution to this problem will lower the bound of the lemma by the above ratio [which may depend on the dimension n of the involved simplices]. The next definition and theorem will provide a sufficient condition for a PCE to be a regular event.

Definition 2.1: Let A be a PA. The cutpoint λ is ϵ-isolated with respect to A if $|P^A(x) - \lambda| \geq \epsilon$ for all $x \in \Sigma^*$, for some $\epsilon > 0$.

Theorem 2.3: If λ is an ϵ-isolated cutpoint for a PA A, then there exists a deterministic automaton B such that $T(A, \lambda) = T(B)$. If A has n states, then B can be chosen to have m states where

$$m \leq \left(1 + \frac{1}{2\epsilon}\right)^{n-1}$$

Proof: Translating the equivalence E in Nerode's theorem [third condition] into probabilistic terms we have that $x, y \in \Sigma^*$ are nonequivalent words if there is a word z such that $p(xz) > \lambda$ and $p(yz) \leq \lambda$ or vice versa. This means that $\pi(x)\eta^F(z) > \lambda$ and $\pi(y)\eta^F(z) \leq \lambda$ or vice versa. It follows that $[\pi(x) - \pi(y)]\eta^F(z) \geq 2\epsilon$, since λ is isolated. Writing this inequality explicitly we have

$$\sum (\pi_i(x) - \pi_i(y))\eta_i^F \geq 2\epsilon \qquad (*)$$

but

$$\sum (\pi_i(x) - \pi_i(y))\eta_i^F \leq \sum (\pi_i(x) - \pi_i(y))^+ \max \eta_i^F(z)$$
$$+ \sum (\pi_i(x)) - \pi_i(y))^- \min \eta_i^F(z)$$
$$= \sum_i (\pi_i(x) - \pi_i(y))^+ (\max \eta_i^F(z) - \min \eta_i^F(z))$$
$$\leq \sum_i (\pi_i(x) - \pi_i(y))^+ = \tfrac{1}{2} \sum_i |\pi_i(x) - \pi_i(y)|$$

by using repeatedly an argument similar to that used in the proof of Proposition A, 1.3 in Chapter II and by the fact that $0 \leq \eta_i^F(z) \leq 1$ for all i.

Combining this with the previous inequality $(*)$ we have that, for non-equivalent words x and y, the following inequality holds

$$2\epsilon \leq \tfrac{1}{2} \sum_i |\pi_i(x) - \pi_i(y)| \qquad \text{or} \qquad \sum_i |\pi_i(x) - \pi_i(y)| \geq 4\epsilon$$

Thus the set of all vectors of the form $\pi(x)$ such that every two vectors in the set are nonequivalent is a set of the form $U_{4\epsilon}$ in Lemma 2.2 and this implies that this set is finite with

$$k \leq \left(1 + \frac{1}{2\epsilon}\right)^{n-1}$$

elements. Nerode's equivalence is thus shown to be of index $\leq k$, which exceeds the minimal number of states of a deterministic automaton defining the given PCE. ∎

Remark: The above theorem, due to Rabin (1963), is clearly one of the most interesting theorems in the theory of PCEs. The following is a quotation from Rabin's original paper and it shows its motivation for introducing the concept of an isolated cutpoint.

"Let A be a PA and $0 \leq \lambda < 1$. Given a tape $x \in \Sigma^*$, we devise the following probabilistic experiment E to test whether $x \in T(A, \lambda)$. We run x through A a large number N of times, and count the number $m(E)$ of times that A ended in a state in F. If $\lambda < m(E)/N$, we accept x; otherwise we reject it. Because of the probabilistic nature of the experiment, it is of course possible that we sometimes accept x even though $x \notin T(A, \lambda)$, or reject it even though $x \in T(A, \lambda)$. By the law of large numbers, however, there exist for each x such that $p(x) \neq \lambda$ and each $0 < \epsilon$ a number $N(x, \epsilon)$ such that

$$\Pr \left(E | \lambda < \frac{m(E)}{N(x, \epsilon)} \leftrightarrow x \in T(A, \lambda) \right) \geq 1 - \epsilon$$

In other words, the probability of obtaining the correct answer by the experiment E (consisting of running x through A $N(x, \epsilon)$ times and counting successes) is greater than $1 - \epsilon$.

To perform the above stochastic experiment we must know $N(x, \epsilon)$, which depends on $|p(x) - \lambda|$. Thus we actually have to know $p(x)$ in advance if we want to ascertain whether $x \in T(A, \lambda)$ with probability greater than $1 - \epsilon$ of being correct. Once we know $p(x)$, however, the whole experiment E is superfluous.

The way out is to consider values λ such that $|p(x) - \lambda|$ is bounded from below for all $x \in \Sigma^*$.

It is readily seen that there exists an integral valued function $N(\delta, \epsilon)$ such that for an isolated λ and any $x \in \Sigma^*$,

$$\Pr\left(E|\lambda < \frac{m(E)}{N(\delta, \epsilon)} \leftrightarrow x \in T(A, \lambda)\right) \geq 1 - \epsilon$$

Thus the proposed stochastic experiment for determining whether $x \in T(A, \lambda)$ can be performed without any a priori knowledge of $p(x)$. This fact makes it natural to consider isolated cut-points."

It is to be noticed here that in Rabin's argument above the testing procedure requires that the number $N(x, \epsilon)$ be determined before the experiment begins. If this requirement is removed, then we do *not* have to know $P(x)$ in advance for ascertaining whether $x \in T(A, \lambda)$ with given probability. This fact follows from the following theorem due to Darling and Robins (1968).

Theorem: Let $x_1, x_2, \ldots$ be a sequence of independent variables with $P_\delta(x_i = 1) = (1 + \delta)/2$, $P_\delta(x_i = -1) = (1 - \delta)/2$, $-1 \leq \delta \leq 1$, so that $E_\delta(x_i) = \delta$ [E denotes here expectation]. Let H^+ be the hypothesis that $\delta > 0$, and H^- the hypothesis that $\delta < 0$. For an arbitrary given $0 < \epsilon < 1$, there is a test of H^+ versus H^- such that if T denotes the sample size of the test, then

1. $P_\delta(T < \infty) = 1$, all $\delta \neq 0$.
2. $P_\delta(\text{accept } H^-) \leq \epsilon$, all $\delta > 0$; $P_\delta(\text{accept } H^+) \leq \epsilon$, all $\delta < 0$.
3. $E_\delta(T) < \infty$, all $\delta \neq 0$.

Since one may always assume that $\lambda = \frac{1}{2}$ [see Proposition 1.4], the above theorem shows that there is a testing procedure for a word x to ascertain whether $p(x) > \frac{1}{2}$ [H^+: $x_i = 1$ if x is accepted at the ith trial and $x_i = -1$ if x is rejected at the ith trial]. The testing procedure is finite with probability 1 [(1) in Darling and Robins theorem] and does not depend on $\delta(=|p(x) - \lambda|)$ but only on the required degree of reliability ϵ. The only assumption still necessary is that $P(x) \neq \lambda$.

It is also worth mentioning that to decide whether a given cut-points λ is isolated or not is an *open problem* which seems to be as difficult as the problem of deciding whether a given PCE is regular. Moreover the condition of Theorem 2.3 is only a sufficient condition for the PCE to be regular. This last fact will be proved latter [see Corollary 3.4].

EXERCISES

1. A cut-point λ is weakly isolated for a PA A if $|p(x) - \lambda| \geq \epsilon$ or $p(x) = \lambda$ for all $x \in \Sigma^*$. Prove that if λ is a weakly isolated point for A, then the event $T(A, \lambda)$ is regular.

2. Two PAs A and B are mutually isolated if $|p^A(x) - p^B(x)| > \lambda$ for all $x \in \Sigma^*$. Prove that if A and B are mutually isolated, then the event $E = \{x : p^A(x) > p^B(x)\}$ is a regular event.

3. Let $E = (E_i)$ be a partition of Σ^*. E is called regular if there are only finitely many blocks E_i in E and all E_is are regular events. Prove: Any regular partition $E = (E_i)$ of Σ^* can be represented in the form $E_i = T(A, \lambda_i)$ where A is a PA. Conversely, if A is a PA such that the set of values $\{p^A(x) : x \in \Sigma^*\}$ is finite, then the set of events $\{x : p^A(x) = k_i\}$ form a regular partition of Σ^*, where $k_1 \ldots, k_n$ is the set of all different possible values $p^A(x)$.

4. Prove that the bound of Lemma 2.2 can be improved for $n = 2$ so that

$$k(\epsilon) \leq \frac{2}{3} + \frac{1}{3\epsilon}$$

in this case.

4. Prove Theorem 2.3 for the following case: The automata A are allowed to have nonrestricted final vectors $\eta^F = (\eta_i^F)$ [i.e., η_i^F may assume any real value and is no longer restricted to the values 0 and 1], and in addition, the cut-point λ is also allowed to assume any real value, all the rest of the components of A remaining as in the original definition. Prove that for this case the bound of Theorem 2.3 is $k(\epsilon) = (1 + (d/2\epsilon))^{n-1}$ where $d = \max_i \eta_i^F - \min_i \eta_i^F$.

5. A cut-point λ is semiisolated for a PA A if $p^A(x) - \lambda \geq \epsilon$ for all x such that $p^A(x) > \lambda$ or else $\lambda - p^A(x) \geq \epsilon$ for all x such that $p^A(x) \leq \lambda$. Prove Theorem 2.3 with the term "isolated" replaced by the term "semiisolated" and give a new bound for this case.

OPEN PROBLEMS

1. Give a decision procedure for ascertaining whether a cut-point λ is isolated for a given PA.

2. Give an algorithm for finding all isolated cut-points of a given PA.

3. Give a sharp bound for Theorem 2.3.

3. The Cardinality of PCEs and Saving of States

Theorem 3.1: The class of PCEs is nondenumerable.

Proof: Let $\Sigma = \{0, 1\}$ and define A to be the PA $A = (\{s_0, s_1\}, \pi, \{A(\sigma)\}, \eta^F)$ where $\pi = (1\ 0)$; $\eta^F = \binom{0}{1}$;

$$A(0) = \begin{bmatrix} 1 & 0 \\ \frac{1}{2} & \frac{1}{2} \end{bmatrix}; \qquad A(1) = \begin{bmatrix} \frac{1}{2} & \frac{1}{2} \\ 0 & 1 \end{bmatrix}$$

It is easy to prove that for $x = \sigma_1 \cdots \sigma_k$, $p^A(x) = .\sigma_k \cdots \sigma_1$ where $.\sigma_k \cdots \sigma_1$ is an ordinary binary fraction [see Exercise A, 5.6 in Chapter II] and p^A is the function induced by A. Thus the set of numbers $\{p(x) : x \in \Sigma^*\}$ is dense in the open interval $(0, 1)$ for the given PA A. Let λ_1 and λ_2 be two cut-points $0 < \lambda_1 < \lambda_2 < 1$, then $T(A, \lambda_1) \neq T(A, \lambda_2)$ for there is a word x such that $p^A(x) > \lambda_1$ and $p^A(x) \leq \lambda_2$. This follows from the density of the values $p^A(x)$. Thus the set of different $T(A, \lambda)$s coincides with the set of different λs which is not countable [the λs are real numbers in the interval $(0, 1)$]. This completes the proof, since the class of PCE contains the events of the form $T(A, \lambda)$ above. ∎

Remark: It follows from the above theorem that there must be nonregular events representable in finite state machines [context free, context sensitive, etc.] which are representable in PAs. On the other hand, the proof of Theorem 3.1 is existential. We shall however exhibit in the following examples explicit nonregular events, some of them context free, which are represented in a PA.

Theorem 3.2: Let A be the PA defined in the proof of Theorem 3.1. The event $T(A, \lambda)$ is regular if and onlf if λ is a rational number.

Proof: The class of PCEs is closed under the reverse operation [Proposition 1.6] and so is the class of regular events. It suffices therefore to prove that an event of the form $\widetilde{T(A, \lambda)}$ is regular if and only λ is a rational number, where $\widetilde{T(A, \lambda)}$ is the reverse of $T(A, \lambda) = \{x = \sigma_1 \cdots \sigma_k : .\sigma_k \cdots \sigma_1 > \lambda\}$ or $T(A, \lambda) = \{x = \sigma_1 \cdots \sigma_k : .\sigma_1 \cdots \sigma_k > \lambda\}$. Assume first λ to be a rational number, i.e., $\lambda = \lambda_1 \lambda_2 \cdots \lambda_k \overline{\lambda_{k+1} \cdots \lambda_{k+m}}$ where $\overline{\lambda_{k+1} \cdots \lambda_{k+m}}$ is the recurring period in the expansion of λ. [One may always assume that the expansion of a rational number has a recurring period: for one can add the recurring period $\bar{I}$ to a finite binary expansion.] A finite automaton B defining $T(A, \lambda)$ in this case can be defined as $B = (S, s_0, M, F)$ where $S = \{s_0 \ldots s_{k+m+1}\}$, $\Sigma = \{0, 1\}$, $F = \{s_{k+m+1}\}$ and the function M is the function

$$M(\sigma_i, j) = \begin{cases} \left.\begin{matrix} \sigma_{i+1} \\ \sigma_{k-1} \end{matrix}\right\} & \text{if } j = \lambda_i \text{ for } \begin{cases} i \leq k + m - 2 \\ i = k + m - 1 \end{cases} \\ \sigma_{k+m} & \text{if } j = 0 \neq \lambda_i \\ \sigma_{k+m+1} & \text{if } j = 1 \neq \lambda_i \end{cases} \text{ for } i \leq k + m - 1 \\ \sigma_i & \text{if } j = 1, 2 \quad \text{for } i \geq k + m \end{cases}$$

$$j = 0, 1$$

It is easily verified that the above automaton defines the event $T(A, \lambda)$ as required [the reader is urged to draw a state graph for the automaton B], proving that $T(A, \lambda)$ is a regular event for rational λ. Assume now that λ is an irrational number $\lambda = .\lambda_1 \lambda_2 \cdots \lambda_k \lambda_{k+1} \cdots$. Consider the infinte sequence of symbols $\lambda_1 \lambda_2 \cdots \lambda_i \cdots \lambda_j \cdots$ where the λ_is are the consecutive digits appearing in the expansion of λ. No two different suffixes of the above sequence of the form $\lambda_i \lambda_{i+1} \cdots, \lambda_j \lambda_{j+1} \cdots i < j$ can be equal, since otherwise the sequence of digits $\lambda_i \lambda_{i+1} \cdots \lambda_{j-1}$ would recur periodically in the expansion of λ, a contradiction to the fact that λ is not a rational number. Let then k be the smallest integer such that $\lambda_{i+k} \neq \lambda_{j+k}$ for given $i < j$. Let z_{ij} be the word defined as

$$z_{ij} = \begin{cases} \lambda_{i+1} \cdots \lambda_{i+k} & \text{if } \lambda_{i+k} > \lambda_{j+k} \\ \lambda_{j+1} \cdots \lambda_{j+k} & \text{if } \lambda_{j+k} > \lambda_{i+k} \end{cases}$$

Then either $.\lambda_1 \cdots \lambda_j \lambda_{i+1} \cdots \lambda_{i+k} > \lambda$ and $.\lambda_1 \cdots \lambda_j \lambda_{j+1} \cdots \lambda_{j+k}' < \lambda$ in the first case ($\lambda_{i+k} > \lambda_{j+k}$) or $.\lambda_1 \cdots \lambda_i \lambda_{j+1} \cdots \lambda_{j+k} > \lambda$ and $.\lambda_1 \cdots \lambda_i \lambda_{i+1} \cdots \lambda_k < \lambda$ in the second case. Thus the word z_{ij} distinguishes between the words $x_i = \lambda_1 \cdots \lambda_i$ and $x_j = \lambda_1 \cdots \lambda_j$ for any i and $j \neq i$. It follows that Nerode's equivalence is of infinite index for the event $T(A, \lambda)$ and the event is therefore not a regular event. This completes the proof. ∎

Corollary 3.3: For any integer n there are regular events requiring at least an n-state deterministic machine for their realization but can be represented in a two-state PA.

Proof: The set of deterministic automata with n-states or less is finite but the set of events $T(A, \lambda)$ as defined in Theorem 3.2 with λ a rational number is infinite and any two such events are different [this fact is included in the proof of Theorem 3.1]. Thus, there must be events of the form $T(A, \lambda)$, λ rational requiring more than n-states for their deterministic realization. ∎

Corollary 3.4: There are regular events representable in PAs with a nonisolated cut-point λ.

Proof: As mentioned before the set of values $p^A(x)$ for the automaton A defined in Theorem 3.1 is dense in the interval $(0, 1)$. The events $T(A, \lambda)$, λ rational, are therefore regular although the cut-point λ is not isolated. ∎

Remark: Theorem 3.2 provides a class of explicit nonregular events representable in PAs Corollary 3.3 shows that it is sometime possible to save states [in exchange for precision] by representing a regular event in a PA. Corollary 3.4 shows that the condition of Theorem 2.3 is a sufficient but not necessary condition for regularity. In connection with Corollary 3.3 it will be interesting to find out what is the exact price [in time and/or precision] one has to pay in exchange for the saving of states.

Remarks on Equivalence and Reduction of States:† It is easy to see that most of the state theory developed in part 1 of the book for SSMs goes over to PAs after some small changes are introduced in the basic definitions and

---

†This section assumes knowledge of Chapter I of the book.

statements [e.g, the first column in H^A will be η^F and not η, etc.] Thus one can define reduced and minimal PAs, covering of PAs' accessible states, connected PAs, equivalent distribution for PAs etc, and prove practically all of the theorems proved for SSMs with regard to these notions. In addition a new notion of equivalence can be introduced for PAs. Consider the following two definitions:

Definition 3.1: Two distributions π and ρ are equivalent for a PA A if $\pi\eta^F(x) = \rho\eta^F(x)$ for all $x \in \Sigma^*$.

Definition 3.2: Two distributions π and ρ are λ-equivalent of order k for a PA A if $\pi\eta^F(x) > \lambda \leftrightarrow \rho\eta^F(x) > \lambda$ for all $x \in \Sigma^*$ with $l(x) \leq k$. π and ρ are λ-equivalent if the relation above is true for all $x \in \Sigma^*$.

Two distributions which are equivalent are ipso facto λ-equivalent [of order k] in other words equivalence is a [proper] refinement of λ-equivalence. It follows therefore from Theorem 3.2 that both types of equivalence may be of infinite index.

There are gedanken experiments for deciding whether two distributions π and ρ are equivalent [see Theorem B, 2.1 Chapter I for SSMs]. This is however not true for PAs as the following theorem shows.

Theorem 3.5: There is a PA and a number λ such that for any integer k there are at least two λ-equivalent distributions of order k which are not λ-equivalent.

Proof: Let E be the event over $\Sigma = \{0, 1\}$, $E = \{x = \sigma_1 \cdots \sigma_k : .\sigma_1 \cdots \sigma_k > \lambda, \lambda = .10100100001 \cdots \}$, i.e., the binary expansion of λ consists of all the terms of the form $0^k 1$, $k = 0, 1, \ldots$, ordered according to the magnitude of k. Then E is representable in a PA as in Theorem 3.2 and therefore E is also a [nonregular, since λ is irrational] PCE. Consider the two words

$$x_k = 101 \cdots \underbrace{100 \cdots 01}_{k} \quad \text{and} \quad y_k = 101 \cdots \underbrace{10 \cdots 010}_{k}$$

As proved in Theorem 3.2, these two words are not equivalent, but one sees easily that the shortest z such that either $x_k z \in E$ and $y_k z \notin E$ [or vice versa] is

$$z = \underbrace{0 \cdots 01}_{k}$$

Thus x_k and y_k are λ-equivalent of order k and this proves our theorems. ∎

We come now to the problem of merging of states. If two degenerate distributions [or states] are equivalent for a PA A, then the two states can be merged to get a new equivalent PA with fewer states [see Theorem B, 2.4 in Chapter I]. Is there any parallel procedure for λ-equivalence? In other words, if by some means we would be able to find out that two degenerate distributions are λ-equivalent [as mentioned before this question is not decidable by gedanken experiments], would this enable us to get another PA with fewer states which is λ-equivalent to the original one [meaning that for any initial distribution of the original PA there is a λ-equivalent distribution for the second PA and vice versa]? The answer to this problem is negative in general and is explained in the following argument.

Consider again the set of vectors $\mathscr{P}^A = \{\pi(x): x \in \Sigma^*\}$ considered now as points in n-dimensional space. These points are included in the n-dimensional simplex $\mathscr{P}(n) = \{\pi : \pi$ is an n-dimensional probabilistic vector.$\}$ The hyperplane containing all the points $\pi(x)\eta^F = \lambda$ divides $\mathscr{P}^A$ into two subsets $\mathscr{P}_+^A = \{\pi(x): \pi(x)\eta^F > \lambda\}$, $\mathscr{P}_-^A = \{\pi(x) : \pi(x)\eta^F \leq \lambda\}$ so that $\pi(x) \in \mathscr{P}_+^A$ if and only if $x \in T(A, \lambda)$. The merging of two extremal points in $\mathscr{P}(n)$ means geometrically a projection, along the line connecting those two points, of the n-dimensional simplex $\mathscr{P}(n)$ into the $(n - 1)$-dimensional simplex $\mathscr{P}(n - 1)$. Unless the line connecting the two merging points is parallel to the hyperplane $\{\pi : \pi\ \eta^F = \lambda\}$ it may happen that a point in $\mathscr{P}_+^A$ will have its projection in the set $\mathscr{P}_-^A$ of the $(n - 1)$-dimensional space. A situation like that in Figure 17 may occur where both words x_1 and x_2 are accepted, but if the states $\bar{s}_1$ and $\bar{s}_2$ are merged then the resulting automaton A' will accept x_1 and reject x_2.

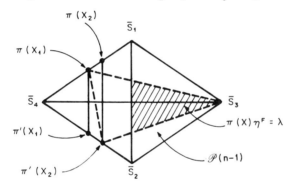

Figure 17. *Geometricol interpretation of merging of states for PAs with cutpoint.*

We conclude this section by an example showing that PAs over an alphabet Σ containing a single letter may still induce a nonregular PCE.

Theorem 3.6: There exists a 3-state PA A over an alphabet $\Sigma = \{\sigma\}$ containing a single letter and a cut-point λ such that $T(A, \lambda)$ is a nonregular event.

Proof: Consider the PA defined as follows: $S = \{s_1 s_2 s_3\}$, $\pi = (0\ 0\ 1)$, $\eta^F = (0\ 0\ 1)^{\mathrm{T}}$

$$A(\sigma) = \begin{bmatrix} \frac{2}{3} & 0 & \frac{1}{3} \\ \frac{5}{9} & \frac{1}{3} & \frac{1}{9} \\ \frac{1}{4} & \frac{1}{4} & \frac{1}{2} \end{bmatrix} \quad \text{with} \quad \lambda = \tfrac{4}{11}$$

The eigenvalues of $A(\sigma)$ are 1, $(\frac{1}{4} + i\frac{1}{12}\sqrt{7})$, $(\frac{1}{4} - i\frac{1}{12}\sqrt{7})$, each having multiplicity 1. [The reader is urged to verify the computations.] Determining the corresponding row and column eigenvectors and using formula (4) in Section II, A, 5, we find that

$$a_{33}^{(m)}(\sigma) = \frac{4}{11} + uv^m + \bar{u}\bar{v}^m \tag{1}$$

where†

$$u = \frac{7}{22} + i\frac{3\sqrt{7}}{154}, \qquad v = \frac{1}{4} + i\frac{1}{12}\sqrt{7}$$

and $\bar{u}$, $\bar{v}$ are the conjugates of u and v respectively. Writing formula (1) in a trigonometric form we get

$$a_{33}^{(m)}(\sigma) - \frac{4}{11} = c\rho^m \sin(n\theta + \gamma) \tag{2}$$

where $c = |u|$, $\rho = |v|$, $\gamma = \arg(u)$, and $\theta = \arg(v)$. Thus, if and only if $-\pi/2 < m\theta + \alpha < \pi/2$, then $a_{33}^{(m)}(\sigma) > 4/11$ or $\sigma^m \in T(A, \lambda)$. We shall need here

Lemma 3.7: If θ is rational in degrees [i.e., $\theta = 2\pi r$ where r is a rational number], then the only rational values of $\cos\theta$ are 0, $\pm\frac{1}{2}$, ± 1. If θ is irrational in degrees, then any subinterval of $(0, 2\pi)$ contains values of the form $m\theta$ (mod 2π).

The proof of this lemma, involving algebraic number theory, is omitted here and can be found in Niven (1956).

Checking our θ for the condition of the above lemma we find that $\cos\theta = \operatorname{Re}\lambda/|\lambda| = \frac{3}{4}$ which implies that θ is irrational in degrees. Let σ^{m_1} and σ^{m_2} be two words in $T(A, \lambda)$ such that $m_1\theta + \gamma = \alpha$, $m_2\theta + \gamma = \beta$, $-\pi/2 < \alpha$, $\beta < \pi/2$ and assume that $\alpha < \beta$. Then there is m_3 such that $\pi/2 < \gamma + (m_2 + m_3)\theta < \pi/2 + (\beta - \alpha)/2$ by the second statement of Lemma 3.7. It follows that $\gamma + (m_1 + m_3)\theta < \pi/2 - (\beta - \alpha)/2$. Thus $\sigma^{m_2+m_3} \notin T(A, \lambda)$ while $\sigma^{m_1+m_3} \in T(A, \lambda)$. We have proved that any two words in $T(A, \lambda)$ [this set is infinite by the second statement in Lemma 3.7] are nonequivalent according to Nerode's equivalence [Theorem 2.1] and Nerode's equivalence is therefore of infinite index. This completes the proof.

Remarks

1. Note that the cut-point λ used in Theorem 3.6 is a rational number. Thus the regularity or irregularity of events of the form $T(A, \lambda)$ is not connected to the rationality or irrationality of λ as one may guess from Theorem 3.2.

---

†We use here the notation v for eigenvalues in order to avoid confusion with the cut-point notation λ.

2. Theorem 3.6 provides an example of a PA over a single letter alphabet inducing a nonregular event. This is, however, not true in general; in other words there are many cases where such a PA defines a regular event. See Exercises 10–13 after this section for more details on PA over a single letter alphabet.

3. The example in Theorem 3.6 also provides an explicit case of a non-context-free event representable in a PA. This follows from the fact that all context-free events over a one letter alphabet are regular and the event in Theorem 3.6 is not regular and therefore not context free.

EXERCISES

1. An "*m*-adic two state PA" is a 2-state PA $A = (S, \pi, \{A(\sigma)\}, \eta^F)$ over the alphabet $\Sigma = \{0, 1, \ldots, m - 1\}$ where

$$A(i) = \begin{bmatrix} \dfrac{m - i}{m} & \dfrac{i}{m} \\ \dfrac{m - i - 1}{m} & \dfrac{i + 1}{m} \end{bmatrix}; \quad i = 0, 1, \ldots, m - 1$$

$$\pi = (1\ 0); \quad \eta^F = \begin{bmatrix} 0 \\ 1 \end{bmatrix}$$

Prove that if $x = \sigma_1 \cdots \sigma_k \in \Sigma^*$, then $p^A(x) = .\sigma_k \cdots \sigma_1$, this being an ordinary *m*-adic fraction.

2. Prove that if the symbol 1 is removed from the alphabet of the 3-adic PA, then the set of values $\{p^A(x) : x \in \Sigma^*, \Sigma = \{0, 2\}\}$ is a nowhere dense set [Cantor's discotinuum].

3. Prove that Theorem 3.2 is true for *m*-adic automata.

4. A number u is called accessible by a PA A if there is a word $x \in \Sigma^*$ such that $p^A(x) = u$. Prove that if λ is a rational number which is not accessible for the PA A in Exercise 2, then $T(A, \lambda)$ is a nonregular set for that A.

5. Let A be the 3-state PA over $\Sigma = \{0, 1, \ldots, m - 1\}$ such that $\pi = (1\ 0\ 0)$

$$\eta^F = \begin{bmatrix} 0 \\ 0 \\ 1 \end{bmatrix} \quad \text{and} \quad A(i) = \begin{bmatrix} \dfrac{1}{m} & \dfrac{m - i - 1}{m} & \dfrac{i}{m} \\ 0 & 1 & 0 \\ 0 & 0 & 1 \end{bmatrix}$$

Prove that $T(A, \lambda)$ is the event $\{x = \sigma_1 \cdots \sigma_k : .\sigma_1 \cdots \sigma_k > \lambda\}$.

6. Let ϕ be a real valued function over Σ^* such that $\phi(e) = 0$ [e is the empty word] and for all $x, \sigma \in \Sigma^*$,

$$\phi(\sigma x) = a(\sigma)\phi(x) + b(\sigma)$$

where $a(\sigma) + b(\sigma) \le 1$. Prove that any event of the form $\{x : \phi(x) > \lambda\}$ can be represented by a 3-state PA with cut-point λ.

7. Same as Exercise 6, but $\phi(x\sigma) = a(\sigma)\phi(x) + b(\sigma)$ and the PA has 2 states.

8. Let ψ be a a mapping from symbols in Σ to words in Σ^* and extend ψ to Σ^* by the requirements

$$\psi(e) = e, \qquad \psi(x\sigma) = \psi(x)\psi(\sigma)$$

Let $\Sigma = \{0, 1, \ldots, m - 1\}$ and denote by $.\psi(x)$ the m-adic expansion where the symbols in $\psi(x)$ are considered as digits $[.\psi(e) = 0]$. Prove that the event $\{x : .\psi(x) > \lambda\}$ can be represented in a 3-state automata with cut-point λ.

9. Prove that if in Exercise 8 the function ψ has the property that $\psi(i) = x_i$ with $l(x_i) = k$ for a fixed number $k \ge 1$ and all $i \in \Sigma$, then the event $\{x : .\psi(x) > \lambda\}$ is not regular if and only if λ is an irrational number of the form $\eta = .\psi(\sigma_1) \cdots \psi(\sigma_k) \cdots$.

10. Prove that a 3-state PA $A = (S, \pi, A(\sigma), \eta^F)$ over a single letter alphabet defines an irregular event if and only if (1) $\pi A(\sigma) \ne \pi$, (2) $A(\sigma)$ has an imaginary eigenvalue with argument irrational in degrees, and (3) the cut-point λ is equal to $\lim_{n\to\infty} a_{ij}^{(n)}$ [which "lim" always exists if (2) is satisfied and is independent on i] if $F = \{s_j\}$, and is equal to $\lim_{n\to\infty} a_{ij}^{(n)} + \lim_{n\to\infty} a_{ik}^{(n)}$ if $F = \{s_j, s_k\}$.

11. Prove that the number of nonregular events of the form $T(A, \lambda)$ where A is a given n-state PA over a single letter alphabet is $\le n$.

12. Prove the following theorem:

Theorem: Let A be a PA over a single letter alphabet. Let $v_1, \ldots, v_t$ be the eigenvalues of $A(\sigma)$ such that $|v_1| = \cdots = |v_t| = 1$ and let $v_p, \cdots, v_{p+q}$ be the eigenvalues of A with maximum absolute value such that $|v_p| = \cdots = |v_{p+q}| < 1$ and such that $\sum_{k=p}^{p+q} v_k^m \omega_{ijk}(m) \ne 0$ for all $m \ge m_0$, where m_0 is some integer and ω_{ijk} is as in formula (4) in Section II, A, 5 [λ_k in that formula is replaced by v_k here]. If $\arg v_p, \arg v_{p+1}, \cdots, \arg v_{p+q}$ are all rational in degree then $T(A, \lambda)$ is a regular event for any λ.

13. Prove the following corollary to the theorem in Exercise 12: If a PA A as in Exercise 12 has all its eigenvalues with rational arguments then $T(A, \lambda)$ is regular for any λ.

14. Prove that if a PA A over a one letter alphabet has only real eigenvalues, then $T(A, \lambda)$ is regular for any λ.

15. Prove that any 2-states PA A over a one letter alphabet defines a regular event $T(A, \lambda)$.

OPEN PROBLEMS

1. Find a decision procedure for checking whether any two given distributions for a PA are λ-equivalent for a given λ or prove that the problem is not decidable.

2. Provide a procedure with the aid of which one will be able to find a PA B with a minimal number of states such that the event $T(B, \lambda)$ for some λ equals a given event $T(A, \mu)$.

4. Particular Cases

a. Exclusive PCEs

The class of events to be dealt with in this section is properly included in the class of PCEs and properly includes regular events. In addition they have most of the closure properties regular events have.

Definition 4.1: An event of the form $\{x : x \in \Sigma^*, p^A(x) \neq \lambda\}$ where A is a PA and λ is a real number $0 \leq \lambda < 1$ is an exclusive PCE and is denoted by the notation $T_{\neq}(A, \lambda)$.

Proposition 4.1: The regular events are properly included in the class of exclusive PCEs.

Proof: It is clear that any regular event can be represented in the form $T_{\neq}(A, 0)$ where A is a deterministic automaton [see the proof of Proposition 1.2]. On the other hand, for the PA given in Exercise 1.4, we have that $T_{\neq}(A, \frac{1}{2})$ is the complement of the event $E = \{x : x \in \Sigma^*, x = \sigma_1^{m+1}\sigma_2\sigma_1^m, m \geq 0\}$ which is not a regular event. Regular events being closed under complimentation we have that $T_{\neq}(A, \frac{1}{2})$ is not regular and this completes the proof.

Proposition 4.2: The class of exclusive PCEs is properly included in the class of PCEs.

Proof: Let $T_{\neq}(A, \lambda)$ be an exclusive PCE. By Proposition A, 2.1 there is an SPE p^B such that for all words $x \in \Sigma^*$, $p^B(x) = p^A(x) - \lambda$ so that $T_{\neq}(A, \lambda) = T_{\neq}(B, 0)$. Let C be the pseudo probabilistic automaton $C = B \otimes B$ (see definition in the proof of Proposition A,1.3). As in the proof of Proposition A,1.3, $p^C(x) = p^B(x)p^B(x)$ for all $x \in \Sigma^*$. Thus $T_{\neq}(B, 0) = T(C, 0)$. Now using Proposition 1.1 we have that there is a PA D and a cut-point μ such that $T(C, 0) = T(D, \mu)$. This proves that any exclusive PCE is a PCE, since $T(D, \mu) = T_{\neq}(A, \lambda)$. To prove that inclusion is proper, let A be the PA defined in in Exercise 1.4. Then $T(A, \frac{1}{2}) = \{\sigma_1^m\sigma_2\sigma_1^n : m \leq n\}$ so that the event $E =$

$\{\sigma_1{}^m \sigma_2 \sigma_1{}^n : \leq n\}$ is a PCE. We will show that this event is, however, not an exclusive PCE. Assume the contrary, then there is a PA B such that $E = T_{\neq}(B, \frac{1}{2})$ [by Proposition 1.4 λ may always be assumed to be equal to $\frac{1}{2}$]. Using Theorem 2.8 in Section II, C with $u = \sigma_1$ we have that there is a sequence of numbers $c_0, c_1, \ldots, c_{n-1}$ such that $\sum_{i=0}^{n-1} c_i = 1$ and for the words $u' = \sigma_1{}^n \sigma_2$ and $u'' = e$ [the empty word] the following equality holds true:

$$p^B(\sigma_1{}^n \sigma_2 \sigma_1{}^n) = c_{n-1} p^B(\sigma_1{}^n \sigma_2 \sigma_1{}^{n-1}) + \cdots + c_1 p^B(\sigma_1{}^n \sigma_2 \sigma_1) + c_0 p^B(\sigma_1{}^n \sigma_2)$$

But the words $\sigma_1{}^n \sigma_2 \sigma_1{}^{n-1}, \ldots, \sigma_1{}^n \sigma_2$ are not in E and therefore their probability by B is $\frac{1}{2}$. This implies that $p^B(\sigma_1{}^n \sigma_2 \sigma_1{}^n) = \frac{1}{2} \sum_{i=0}^{n-1} c_i = \frac{1}{2}$ which contradicts the fact that $p^B(\sigma_1{}^n \sigma_2 \sigma_1{}^n) \neq \frac{1}{2}$ since $\sigma_1{}^n \sigma_2 \sigma_1{}^n \in E$. The proof is complete. ∎

Theorem 4.3: The class of exclusive PCEs is closed under union.

Proof: Let $T_{\neq}(A, \lambda)$ and $T_{\neq}(B, \mu)$ be two exclusive PCEs. As in the proof of Proposition 4.2, there are pseudo probabilistic automata C and D such that $T_{\neq}(A, \lambda) = T(C, 0)$ and $T_{\neq}(B, \mu) = T(D, 0)$ with $p^C(x) \geq 0$, $p^D(x) \geq 0$ for all $x \in \Sigma^*$. Then $T(C + D, 0) = T(C, 0) \cup T(D, 0)$ where $C + D$ is the automaton defining the function $p^{C+D}(x) = p^C(x) + p^D(x)$ [see Proposition A,2.1]. By Proposition 1.1 there is a PA A' such that $T(A', v) = T(C + D, 0) = T_{\neq}(A, \lambda) \cup T_{\neq}(B, \mu)$ for some cut-point v and, as follows from the proof of that theorem, $P^{A'}(x) \geq v$ for all $x \in \Sigma^*$ so that $T(A', v) = T_{\neq}(A', v)$ as required. ∎

Theorem 4.4: The class of PCEs is closed under intersection with exclusive PCEs.

Proof: Let $T(A, \lambda)$ and $T_{\neq}(B, \mu)$ be a PCE and an exclusive PCE respectively. Then there are automata A' and B' such that $T(A, \lambda) = T(A', 0)$ and $T_{\neq}(B, \mu) = T_{\neq}(B', 0)$. It follows that $T(A' \otimes B' \otimes B', 0) = T(A, \lambda) \cap T_{\neq}(B, \mu)$. By Proposition 1.1 there is a PA C and a cut-point v such that $T(A \otimes B' \otimes B', 0) = T(C, v)$ and this completes the proof. ∎

Proposition 4.5: The class of exclusive PCEs is closed under intersection.

Proof: One can assume that $T_{\neq}(A, \lambda) = T_{\neq}(A', 0)$, and similarly $T_{\neq}(B, \mu) = T_{\neq}(B', 0)$ so that $T_{\neq}(A' \otimes B', 0) = T_{\neq}(A, \lambda) \cap T_{\neq}(B, \mu)$. ∎

EXERCISES

1. Let A be the PA in Proposition A,1.10. Prove that the event $T(A, \frac{1}{2})$ is not an exclusive PCE.

2. Prove that the event $\{0^n 1^n : n = 1, 2 \ldots\}$ is not an exclusive PCE.

3. Define the event $T_=(A, \lambda) = \{x : x \in \Sigma^*, p^A(x) = \lambda\}$ for a given PA and a cut-point λ. Prove that the class of events of the form $T_=(A, \lambda)$ is closed under union and intersection and includes the regular events.

4. Prove that the event $\{0^n 1^n : n \geq 1\}$ can be written in the form $T_=(A, \lambda)$ where A is a PA with cut-point λ.

OPEN PROBLEM

Are the events $T_=(A, \lambda)$ included in the class of PCE and, if yes, is the inclusion proper?

b. Definite PCEs

Definition 4.2: A PA A is weakly k-definite if and only if for any $x \in \Sigma^*$ with $l(x) \geq k$ and any initial distributions π and ρ† we have that $p_\pi{}^A(x) = p_\rho{}^A(x)$.

Proposition 4.6: If A is a weakly k-definite PA and $z = yx$ is a word in Σ^* with $l(x) \geq k$, then $p^A(z) = p^A(x)$.

Proof: $p_\pi{}^A(z) = \pi A(y)A(x)\eta^F = \pi(y)A(x)\eta^F = p_{\pi(y)}(x) = p_\pi(x)$ [$p^A(x)$ is independent on the initial distribution since $l(x) \geq k$]. ∎

Corollary 4.7: If A is a weakly definite PA, then $T(A, \lambda)$ is a definite PCE for any cut-point.

Proof: It follows from Proposition 4.2 that the set of values $p^A(x)$ is finite [it is smaller than or equal to the different values in the set $\{p^A(x) : l(x) \leq k\}$] and for any $z = yx$, $l(x) \geq k$ and any λ, $p^A(z) = p^A(x)$ so that $p^A(z) > \lambda$ if and only if $p^A(x) > \lambda$. ∎

Proposition 4.8: A PA A is weakly k-definite if and only if for any word $x \in \Sigma^*$ with $l(x) \geq k$ the vectors $\pi(x)$ and $\rho(x)$ are equivalent for any initial distribution π and ρ.

Proof: If $\pi(x)$ is equivalent to $\rho(x)$, then $p_\pi(x) = \pi(x)\eta^F = \rho(x)\eta^F = p_\rho(x)$ by Definition 3.1. Conversely, if $p_\pi(x) = p_\rho(x)$ for all $x \in \Sigma^*$ with $l(x) \geq k$ then, for any $y \in \Sigma^*$ and $x \in \Sigma^*$ with $l(x) \geq k$ we have that $p_\pi(xy) = p_\rho(xy)$. But $p_\pi(xy) = \pi(x)\eta^F(y)$ and $p_\rho(xy) = \rho(x)\eta^F(y)$. Thus for all $y \in \Sigma^*$, $\pi(x)\eta^F(y) = \rho(x)\eta^F(y)$ which implies that $\pi(x)$ and $\rho(x)$ are equivalent vectors. ∎

Corollary 4.9: If A is a weakly k-definite PA, then for any $x \in \Sigma^*$ with $l(x) \geq k$ the rows of the matrix $A(x)$ considered as distributions are equivalent one to the other.

Proof: Any row in a matrix $A(x)$ can be written in the form $\pi(x)$ where π is a degenerate stochastic vector. ∎

Remark: The converse of Corollary 4.9 is also true and is left as an exercise.

†For the purpose of this definition it is assumed that A does not have an a priori fixed initial distribution.

Definition 4.2: A PA is k-definite if it is weakly k-definite, but is not weakly $(k-1)$ definite. It is definite if it is k-definite for some $k > 0$.

It follows from the above definition and from Proposition 4.8 that if and only if a PA is k-definite, then any two vectors $\pi(x)$ and $\rho(x)$ with $l(x) \geq k$ are equivalent, but there are two nonequivalent vectors $\pi(x)$ and $\rho(x)$ with $l(x) = k - 1$.

As in the case of SSMs one can define, for a given PA A, a matrix H^A such that its columns are a basis for all column vectors of the form $\eta^F(x)$, $x \in \Sigma^*$ [see Section I,B,1]. The first two columns of H^A will be η^F and $\eta^{\bar{F}}$ [$\bar{F} = S - F$]. The procedure for constructing H^A will be exactly the same as that used for constructing H and the rank of a PA A will be defined as rank A = rank H^A. [This rank is always less or equal than the number of states of A.] As the columns of H^A are a basis for the set of vectors $\eta^F(x)$ we have that two vectors π and ρ are equivalent initial distributions for A if and only if $(\pi - \rho)H^A = 0$. We are now able to prove the following:

Theorem 4.10: Let A be a PA. If A is k-definite, then $k \leq$ rank $A - 1$.

Proof: The proof is almost the same as the proof of Theorem 4.11 in Section II,A. As in that proof, we define the set of matrices $K^i = \{A(x) : l(x) = i\}$ [to avoid ambiguity we use here the notation K^i instead of H^i there] and the linear spaces $V = \{\bar{v} = (v_i) : \sum v_i = 0\}$,

$$VK^i = \{\sum_{i=1}^{r} \bar{v}_i A(x); \quad \bar{v}_i \in V, \quad A(x) \in K^i, \quad r = 1, 2, \ldots\}$$

so that all the statements (a)–(d) in the proof of Theorem 4.11 in Section II,A are still true. As for statement (e), we change it to the following statement (e'): If the PA is k-definite, then the space VH^k is the nullspace of H^A [i.e., dim $VH^k = n -$ dim A, where n is the number of states of A].

To prove this statement, assume it is not true. Then there is a vector of the form $\bar{v} = \sum \bar{v}_i A(x_i)$ such that $\bar{v}_i \in V$, $x_i \in \Sigma^*$, $l(x_i) = k$ and $\bar{v}H^A \neq \bar{0}$. This implies that at least one of the summands $\bar{v}_i A(x_i)$ has this property, i.e., there is a $\bar{v}_i \in V$ and a matrix $A(x_i)$ such that $l(x_i) = k$ and $\bar{v}_i A(x_i)H^A \neq 0$. Let $\bar{v}_i = (v_{ij})$ with $\sum_{j=1}^{n} v_{ij} = 0$, then setting $\sum_{i=1}^{n} v_{ij}^+ = -\sum_{i=1}^{n} v_{ij}^- = c$ [$c \neq 0$ necessarily] we define the two distributions $\pi = (\pi_j)$ with $\pi_j = v_{ij}^+/c$ and $\rho = (\rho_j)$ with $\rho_j = |v_{ij}^-|/c$. It follows that $(1/c)(\pi - \rho)A(x)H^A = \bar{v}_i A(x)H^A \neq 0$ or $(\pi(x) - \rho(x))H^A \neq 0$ this implying that $\pi(x)$ is not equivalent to $\rho(x)$ although $l(x) = k$, and this is a contradiction.

Continuing the same way as in the end of the proof of Theorem 4.11 in Section II,A we have a sequence of decreasing numbers

$$n - 1 = \text{dim } VK^0 > \text{dim } VK^1 > \cdots \text{dim } VK^k = n - \text{dim } H^A$$

Hence, $k \leq$ dim $H^A - 1$. ∎

Corollary 4.11: If the rank of a k-definite PA A equals the number of its states, then $k \leq n - 1$ and the matrices $A(x)$ corresponding to words x with $l(x) \geq k$ are all constant matrices.

Proof: The first statement of the corollary is evident. As for the second statement, any two rows in a matrix $A(x)$ with $l(x) \geq k$ considered as distributions are equivalent, but no two different distributions π and ρ can satisfy the equation $(\pi - \rho)H^A = 0$ if rank $H^A = n$ [i.e., H^A is a nonsingular matrix].

EXERCISES

1. Prove that if the rows in any matrix $A(x)$, $l(x) \geq k$ of a given PA A are equivalent one to the other, then A is a weakly k-definite PA.

2. Let A be a k-definite PA. Prove that there are two distinct distributions for A which are j-equivalent [two distributions π and ρ are j equivalent for a PA A if $p_\pi{}^A(x) = p_\rho{}^A(x)$ for all x with $l(x) \leq j$] where $j = 1, 2, \ldots, k - 1$.

3. Let A be a definite PA, then the matrices $A(\sigma)$ are all singular.

4. Prove that if the set of matrices $\{A(u) : u \in X^*\}$ in Exercise 1.7 is a k-definite set, then the event $T(M, \lambda, y)$ is definite. Find the order of definiteness of $T(M, \lambda, y)$ in this case.

c. Quasidefinite PCEs

Definition 4.3: A PA A is quasidefinite if and only if for any $\epsilon > 0$ there is a number $k(\epsilon)$ such that for all $x \in \Sigma^*$ with $l(x) \geq k(\epsilon)$ and any two initial distributions for $A, \pi,$ and ρ†, $|p_\pi(x) - p_\rho(x)| \leq \epsilon$.

Proposition 4.12: If A is a quasidefinite PA, then for any $\epsilon > 0$ there is a number $k(\epsilon)$ such that for all $x \in \Sigma^*$ with $l(x) \geq k(\epsilon)$ and any $y \in \Sigma^*$ we have that $|p_\pi{}^A(yx) - p_\pi{}^A(x)| \leq \epsilon$.

Proof: $p_\pi{}^A(yx) = p_{\pi(y)}(x)$ and $|p_{\pi(y)}{}^A(x) - p_\pi{}^A(x)| \leq \epsilon$ by definition. ∎

Proposition 4.13: A sufficient condition for a PA A to be quasidefinite is: For any $\epsilon > 0$, there is a number $k(\epsilon)$ such that for all x with $l(x) \geq k(\epsilon)$ and any two initial distributions π and ρ for A, $||\pi(x) - \rho(x)|| \leq \epsilon$. [If $\pi = (\pi_i)$ is a vector then $||\pi|| = \sum |\pi_i|$.]

Proof: If $||\pi(x) - \rho(x)|| \leq \epsilon$, then

$$|p_\pi(x) - p_\rho(x)| = |\pi(x)\eta^F - \rho(x)\eta^F|$$
$$= |(\pi(x) - \rho(x))\eta^F| \leq ||\pi(x) - \rho(x)|| \leq \epsilon$$

since the entries in η^F are either 0 or 1. ∎

Proposition 4.14: If and only if the condition specified in Proposition 4.13 holds for a PA A, then the corresponding system $(S, \{A(\sigma)\})$ is a weakly ergodic Markov system [see Definition 3.2 in Section II,A].

---

†For the purpose of this definition it is assumed that A does not have an a priori fixed initial distribution.

Proof: It follows from Proposition A, 1.4 in Chapter II that for any fixed word $x \in \Sigma^*$,

$$\|\pi(x) - \rho(x)\| = \|(\pi - \rho)A(x)\| \le \|\pi - \rho\|\delta(A(x)) \le 2\delta(A(x))$$

since $\|\pi - \rho\| \le 2$ for any two stochastic vectors π and ρ. On the other hand there are indices i_1 and i_2 such that $\delta(A(x)) = \sum_j (a_{i_1,j}(x) - a_{i_2,j}(x))^+$ and if π and ρ are the degenerate vectors having a 1 in the i_1 and i_2 entries respectively, then $\|(\pi - \rho)A(x)\| = \sum_j |a_{i_1,j}(x) - a_{i_2,j}(x)| = 2 \sum_j (a_{i_1,j}(x) - a_{i_2,j}(x))^+ = 2\delta(A(x))$ so that, for the specific vectors ρ and π as above, $\|\pi(x) - \rho(x)\| = 2\delta(A(x))$. It follows that $\lim_{l(x)\to\infty} \|\pi(x) - \rho(x)\| = 0$ not depending on the choice of π and ρ if and only if $\lim_{l(x)\to\infty} \delta(A(x)) = 0$. ∎

Remark 1: It is easy to verify that the condition of Proposition 4.13 is not a necessary condition for quasidefiniteness; on the other hand the condition is decidable, by Proposition 4.14 and Section II,A Corollary 4.6 and Theorem 4.7. More precisely we have the following:

Theorem 4.15: Let A be a PA. If for every ϵ there is a number $k = k(\epsilon)$ such that $\|\pi(x) - \rho(x)\| \le \epsilon$ for any distributions π and ρ and any $x \in \Sigma^*$ such that $l(x) \ge k(\epsilon)$, then the system $(S, \{A(\sigma)\})$ satisfies the condition H_2 of some order less or equal to $\frac{1}{2}(3^n - 2^{n+1} + 1)$ where $|S| = n$ [see Definition 4.4, Section II,A].

Remark 2: It is easily verified that the PA used in the proof of Theorem 3.1 is quasidefinite. This shows that the class of PCE which can be defined by quasidefinite PA is nondenumerable. The concept of quasidefiniteness is thus a proper generalization of the concept of definiteness.

We shall consider now quasidefinite PAs with isolated cut-point.

Theorem 4.16: If A is a quasidefinite PA and λ is an isolated cut-point for it, then $T(A, \lambda)$ is a definite [regular] event.

Proof: λ being an isolated cut-point, there is ϵ such that $|p^A(x) - \lambda| \ge \epsilon$ for all $x \in \Sigma^*$ and some $\epsilon > 0$. Since A is quasidefinite, there is a number $k = k(\epsilon/2)$ for the above $\epsilon > 0$ such that $|p(yx) - p(x)| \le \epsilon/2$ for all $x \in \Sigma^*$ with $l(x) \ge k(\epsilon/2)$ and all $y \in \Sigma^*$ [see Proposition 4.12]. We have therefore, for all x with $l(x) \ge k(\epsilon/2)$ and all $y \in \Sigma^*$, that $p(yx) > \lambda$ if and only if $p(x) > \lambda$. It follows that $T(A, \lambda) = U_1 \cup U_2$ where $U_1 = \{x : l(x) < k(\epsilon/2), p(x) > \lambda\}$ and $U_2 = \{x : x = yz, l(z) \ge k(\epsilon/2), p(z) > \lambda\}$. But U_1 is a finite set and therefore definite, and U_2 can be written in the form $U_2 = \Sigma^*V$ where V is the finite set $V = \{z : l(z) = k(\epsilon/2), p(z) > \lambda\}$. Thus U_2 is definite and, since definite events are closed under union, we have that also $T(A, \lambda)$ is definite. ∎

Remark: It is worth mentioning that the conditions of Theorem 4.16 may serve as a characterization of definite events, for the following converse of that theorem is also true.

Theorem 4.17: Any definite event E can be represented in the form $E = T(A, \lambda)$ where A is a quasidefinite PA and λ is an isolated cut-point for A.

Proof: Given the k-definite event $E = \Sigma^* U \cup V$ with U and V finite and length of all words in U equal to k [any definite event can be written in this form) we define the PA $A = (S, \pi, \{A(\sigma)\}, F]$ over the alphabet Σ as follows: Let $\Sigma' = \Sigma \cup b, b \notin \Sigma$, then

$$S = \{(\overbrace{b, \ldots, \sigma_1, \ldots, \sigma_r}^{k}) : \sigma_i \in \Sigma, 0 \leq r \leq k\}$$

i.e., the states are k-tuples of symbols in Σ' and only k-tuples of the above form are in S. If $|\Sigma| = m$, then $|S| = 1 + m + m^2 + \cdots + m^k = q$ and there is a 1-1 correspondence between the states in S in the words in Σ^* with length $\leq k$. The initial distribution π is the degenerate distribution having a 1 in the entry corresponding to the state $(b, \ldots, b)$. The set of final states F contains all the states corresponding to words in $U \cup V$. Finally, the transition matrices are defined as follows. If i is the state $(\tau_1, \ldots, \tau_k)$, then

$$a_{ij}(\sigma) = \begin{cases} 1 - \epsilon & \text{if } j = (\tau_2, \ldots, \tau_k \sigma) \\ \dfrac{\epsilon}{1 - q} & \text{otherwise} \end{cases}$$

If $x \in \Sigma^*$ is a word $x = \sigma_1 \cdots \sigma_r, r < k$ and i is the state $i = (b, \ldots, b)$, then $a_{ij}(\sigma_1 \cdots \sigma_r) = (1 - \epsilon)^r$ for $j = (b, \ldots, b, \sigma_1, \ldots, \sigma_r)$. If $x \in \Sigma^*$ is a word $x = \sigma_1 \cdots \sigma_k$ and i is any state then, $a_{ij}(\sigma_1 \cdots \sigma_k) = (1 - \epsilon)^k$ for $j = (\sigma_1, \ldots, \sigma_k)$. If $x, y \in \Sigma^*$ are words such that $x = \sigma_1 \cdots \sigma_k$, then for $j = (\sigma_1, \ldots, \sigma_k)$, and for any state i,

$$a_{ij}(yz) = \sum_{t=1}^{q} a_{it}(y)a_{tj}(x) = a_{tj}(x) \sum_{t=1}^{q} a_{it}(y) = (1 - \epsilon)^k \cdot 1 = (1 - \epsilon)^k$$

It follows that if $x \in E$ then $p^A(x) \geq (1 - \epsilon)^k$ [if $r < k$, then $(1 - \epsilon)^r > (1 - \epsilon)^k$] and we may choose ϵ so small as to have the value $(1 - \epsilon)^k$ as close to 1 as wanted [the number k is given a priori and depends on E only]. Let ϵ be such that $(1 - \epsilon)^k > \frac{3}{4}$ and let $\lambda = \frac{1}{2}$. For any word x, if $x \notin E$, then $p^A(x) < \frac{1}{4}$ [the machine will enter a state not in F with probability at least $\frac{3}{4}$ in this case] so that λ is isolated. Moreover, the above considerations show that $E = T(A, \lambda)$. Finally, all the entries in the matrices $A(\sigma)$ are positive and this implies that the set $(S, A(\sigma))$ is a quasidefinite set [the H_2 condition of order 1 is satisfied in this case]. ∎

EXERCISES

1. Prove by an example that the condition of the Proposition 4.13 is not necessary for quasidefiniteness.

2. Provide a full proof for Theorem 4.15.

3. Let $\bar{\lambda}$ be a vector all the entries of which are equal to λ, $0 \leq \lambda < 1$, and let A be a PA with number of states equal to the dimension of $\bar{\lambda}$. $\bar{\lambda}$ is an *isolated* vector for A if there is a number $\delta > 0$ such that

$$(A(x)\eta^F - \bar{\lambda})(A(x)\eta^F - \bar{\lambda}) \geq \delta^2$$

for all $x \in \Sigma^*$ where the product is the ordinary scalar product of vectors.

Prove: If λ is an isolated vector for a quasidefinite PA A, then the event $T(A, \lambda)$ is a definite [regular] event.

4. Prove that if A is a two state PA such that no matrix $A(\sigma)$ equals the matrix $\left[\begin{smallmatrix} 1 & 0 \\ 0 & 1 \end{smallmatrix}\right]$ or $\left[\begin{smallmatrix} 0 & 1 \\ 1 & 0 \end{smallmatrix}\right]$, then A is a quasidefinite PA.

5. Prove that if A is a PA such that all the entries in all the matrices $A(\sigma)$ are *positive*, then A is a quasidefinite PA.

5. Approximations

We know already that the cardinality of PCEs [over the real numbers] equals the cardinality of the continuum [Theorem 3.2] and therefore there must be PCEs which are not definable by any type of deterministic automaton [all deterministic machines, including Turing machines, are denumerable]. On the other hand we know also that if the cut-point λ is isolated, then the resulting PCE is regular [Theorem 2.3]. This raises the suspicion that probabilistic automata may reduce to deterministic automata when compared in a weaker form, allowing for approximations in the vicinity of the cut-point. To make this notion explicit we introduce the following:

Definition 5.1: Let A be a PA inducing the PE f over Σ^* and let B be any finite state machine [Turing machine, linear bounded, etc]. B *ϵ-approximates* A if there is a function ϕ with domain $B(s_0, x)$ [$B(s_0, x)$ denoting the configuration of B after the word x has been scanned from the initial state s_0] and real values such that

$$|f(x) - \phi(B(s_0, x))| \leq \epsilon$$

Definition 5.2: An event E [understood here as a subset of Σ^*] *ϵ-approximates* a PCE $T(A, \lambda)$ if

$$(E - T(A, \lambda)) \cup (\bar{E} - \overline{T(A, \lambda)}) \subseteq \{x : x \in \Sigma^*, |f(x) - \lambda| \leq \epsilon\}$$

where f is the event [here understood as a function] induced by A.

It is easy to prove that, in the above sense, PAs [the matrices and vectors defining A have real entries] are approximable by Turing machines, this being a consequence of the fact that Turing machines can "compute" within any preassigned ϵ the values of a function $f(x)$ induced by a PA. The above definitions will therefore enable us to compare the nondenumerable set of PAs [or cut-point events defined by them] with denumerable sets [e.g., Turing machine and events defined by them]. Some particular cases will be considered in the following subsections.

a. ϵ-Approximation by Finite Automata

Definition 5.3: Given a PE f and $\epsilon > 0$, an ϵ-cover induced by f is a finite set $\{C_i\}_{i=0}^{k}$ where the C_i are sets of points in the interval $[0, 1]$ satisfying the following requirements:

1. $\cup_{i=0}^{k} C_i = \{\xi : f(x) = \xi, x \in \Sigma^*\}$.

2. $\xi_1, \xi_2 \in C_i \Rightarrow |\xi_1 - \xi_2| < \epsilon$, $i = 0, 1, \ldots, k$.

3. For any i and z, there is j such that $C_i z \subseteq C_j$ where $C_i z$ is defined as the set $C_i z = \{\xi : f(xz) = \xi, f(x) \in C_i\}$.

Theorem 5.1: Given a PE f and $\epsilon > 0$, f is ϵ-approximable by a finite automaton B if and only if there exists a 2ϵ cover induced by f.

Proof: Let $\{C_i\}_{i=0}^{k}$ be an ϵ-cover for f. Define the deterministic automaton B as follows. The states of B are $C_0, \ldots, C_k$. Let C_0 be the first set such that $f(e) \in C_0$, then the initial state of B is C_0. The transition function of B is defined by the relation

$$B(C_i, \sigma) = C_j \qquad \text{if} \quad C_i \sigma \subseteq C_j$$

and j is the smallest index satisfying the relation. Finally, set $\phi(C_i) = \frac{1}{2}[\sup_{\xi \in C_i} \xi + \inf_{\xi \in C_i} \xi]$. We prove first, by induction, that for any $x \in \Sigma^*$, $f(x) \in B(s_0, x)$:

i. For $x = e$, the statement follows from the definition of B.

ii. Let x be a word with $l(x) = t$ and assume that $f(x) \in B(s_0, x) = C_i$. Then $f(x\sigma) \in C_i \sigma = B(s_0, x\sigma)$ by the definitions of $C_i \sigma$ and B, and this proves the statement. ∎

We have, therefore, that for any $x \in \Sigma^*$

$$|f(x) - \phi(B(s_0, x))| = |f(x) - \tfrac{1}{2}[\sup_{\xi \in C_i} \xi + \inf_{\xi \in C_i} \xi]| \leq \epsilon$$

by the fact that $f(x) \in B(s_0, x) = C_i$ and the second property of the ϵ cover. Assume now that f is ϵ-approximable by a deterministic automaton B with state set $S = \{s_0, \ldots, s_k\}$. Define the sets

$$C_i = \{\xi : f(x) = \xi, \quad B(s_0 x) = s_i\}$$

It is easily verified that the set C_i thus defined is a 2ϵ cover as required.

Definition 5.4: Given a PCE $E = T(A, \lambda)$, an ϵ-cover induced by the automaton A with cut-point λ is a finite set $\{C_i\}_{i=0}^k$ where the C_i are sets of points in the interval $[0, 1]$ satisfying the following requirements:

1. $\cup_{i=0}^k C_i = \{\xi : f^A(x) = \xi, x \in \Sigma^*\}$.

2. Either $C_i \subseteq \{\xi : \xi \geq \lambda - \epsilon\}$ or $C_i \subseteq \{\xi : \xi \leq \lambda + \epsilon\}$.

3. For any i and z, there is j such that $C_i z \subseteq C_j$ where $C_i z$ is defined as in Definition 5.3.

Theorem 5.2: A PCE $E = T(A, \lambda)$ is ϵ-approximable by a regular event $E' = T(B)$ if and only if there exists an ϵ-cover induced by the automaton A with cut-point λ.

Proof: The proof is similar to the proof of Theorem 5.1. The final states of B will be the C_i satisfying the relation

$$C_i \subseteq \{\xi : \xi \geq \lambda - \epsilon\} \quad \blacksquare$$

Proposition 5.3: Let f be a PE. If f is ϵ-approximable by some finite automaton B, then for any λ, the CPE $T(A, \lambda)$ is ϵ-approximable, where A is the PA defining f.

Proof: The final states of B will be defined to be the states s_i such that $\phi(s_i) > \lambda$ [see Definition 5.1]. For any $x \in \Sigma^*$, $|f(x) - \phi(B(s_0, x)| \leq \epsilon$ and if $\phi(B(s_0, x)) > \lambda$ meaning that $x \in T(B)$, then $f(x) > \lambda - \epsilon$. If $\phi(B(s_0, x)) \leq \lambda$ meaning that $x \notin T(B)$, then $f(x) \leq \lambda + \epsilon$. $\blacksquare$

Proposition 5.4: Let f be a PE defined by a PA A such that for any λ the CPE $T(A, \lambda)$ is ϵ-approximable by an event $T(B_\lambda)$ where B_λ is a finite [deterministic] automaton, then there exists a finite automaton B which ϵ-approximates A.

Proof: Divide the interval $[0, 1]$ into k equal parts by $k - 1$ points $\lambda_1, \ldots, \lambda_{k-1}$ $[\lambda_0 = 0, \lambda_k = 1]$ such that $\lambda_i - \lambda_{i-1} \leq \epsilon, i = 1, 2, \ldots, k$, and let B_{λ_i}, $i = 0, 1, \ldots, k - 1$ be the corresponding ϵ-approximating automaton for $T(A, \lambda_i)$. Define the machine B as follows. $B = (S, s_0, M)$ [F is immaterial here] with

$$S = \{(s_{i_1}(\lambda_0), s_{i_2}(\lambda_1), \ldots, s_{i_k}(\lambda_{k-1})): s_{i_t}(\lambda_j) \in S_{\lambda_j}\}$$
$$s_0 = (s_0(\lambda_0), \ldots, s_0(\lambda_{k-1}))$$
$$M((s_{i_1}(\lambda_0), s_{i_2}(\lambda_1), \ldots, s_{i_k}(\lambda_{k-1})), \sigma)$$
$$= (M_{\lambda_0}(s_{i_1}, \sigma), \ldots, M_{\lambda_{k-1}}(s_{i_k}, \sigma))$$

with $B_{\lambda_i} = (S_{\lambda_i}, s_0(\lambda_i), M_{\lambda_i}, F_{\lambda_i})$ and $S_{\lambda_i} = \{s_j(\lambda_i)\}$. Set

$$\phi(s) = \phi(s_{i_1}(\lambda_0), \ldots, s_{i_k}(\lambda_{k-1})) = \max_j \{\lambda_j : s_{i_{j-1}}(\lambda_j) \in F_{\lambda_j}\}$$

Thus, $\phi(B(s_0, x)) = \lambda_j$ implies that $x \in T(B_{\lambda_{j-1}})$ and $x \notin T(B_{\lambda_{j+1}})$ which implies that $f(x) > \lambda_j - \epsilon$ and $f(x) \leq \lambda_{j+1} + \epsilon \leq \lambda_j + 3\epsilon$. It follows that $|\phi(B(s_0, x)) - f(x)| \leq 2\epsilon$. $\blacksquare$

Remark: Any PE f induced by a PA A can be transformed into a PCE $T(A, \lambda)$ for a cut-point λ. It follows from the above two propositions that f is ϵ-approximable if and only if the derived PCEs $T(A, \lambda)$ are ϵ-approximable for *any* cut-point λ.

b. A Counterexample

Consider the following PA $A = (\pi, S, \{A(\sigma)\}, \eta^F)$ over $\Sigma = \{0, 1\}$ with $S = \{s_0 s_1 s_2 s_3\}$, $\pi = (1\ 0\ 0\ 0)$ and

$$
\eta^F = \begin{bmatrix} 1 \\ 0 \\ 0 \\ 0 \end{bmatrix}; \quad
A(0) = \begin{bmatrix} \frac{1}{2} & 0 & \frac{1}{2} & 0 \\ 0 & \frac{1}{2} & 0 & \frac{1}{2} \\ 0 & 0 & 1 & 0 \\ 0 & 0 & 0 & 1 \end{bmatrix}; \quad
A(1) = \begin{bmatrix} \frac{1}{2} & \frac{1}{2} & 0 & 0 \\ \frac{1}{2} & \frac{1}{2} & 0 & 0 \\ 1 & 0 & 0 & 0 \\ 0 & 1 & 0 & 0 \end{bmatrix}
$$

By straightforward computations one can prove the following relations:

$$
p(x) \begin{cases}
= (\frac{1}{2})^n & \text{if } x = 0^n, n = 0, 1, 2, \ldots, & [0^0 \text{ is the empty word.}] \\
= \frac{1}{2} & \text{if } x = 0^{n_1} 10^{n_2}, 1, \ldots, 0^{n_k} 1, & n_j \geq 0, j = 1, 2, \ldots, k \\
& \text{and there is } i \text{ with } n_i = 0 \\
> \frac{1}{2} & \text{if } x = 0^{n_1} 10^{n_2} 1, \ldots, 0^{n_k} 1, & n_j > 0, j = 1, 2, \ldots, k \\
< \frac{1}{2} & \text{if } x = 0^{n_1} 10^{n_2} 1, \ldots, 0^{n_k} 10^{n_{k+1}}, & n_j \geq 0, j = 1, 2, \ldots, k \\
& & n_{k+1} > 0
\end{cases}
$$

where $p(x)$ is the $(1, 1)$ entry in $A(x)$.

Consider now the PE defined by A, p^A, and let $T(A, \lambda)$ be the PCE, with $\lambda = \frac{1}{2}$.

We have that

$$
T((p^A, \lambda)) = \{x : p^A(x) > \tfrac{1}{2}\}
$$

It follows from the above inequalities that $T((A, \lambda))$ for $\lambda = \frac{1}{2}$ is the set of words x such that x is empty or x begins with a zero, ends with a one, and contains no subword of two or more consecutive ones. It is easily verified that this set of words is a regular set [there exists a finite automaton accepting it] and therefore it is ϵ-approximable [even for $\epsilon = 0$] by a finite automaton.

We shall show now that there is a λ such that $T(A, \lambda)$ is not ϵ-approximable by a finite automaton with the result that the function p^A is not approximable either, this following from Praposition 5.3.

Let x_n^m be the word $x_n^m = (0^n 1)^m$. One can prove, again using straight forward computation, that

$$
p^A(x_n^m) = \frac{1 + [1 - (\frac{1}{2})^n]^m}{2}
$$

Thus $\lim_{n\to\infty} p^A(x_n^m) = 1$ for fixed $m > 0$, while $\lim_{m\to\infty} p^A(x_n^m) = \frac{1}{2}$ for fixed $n > 0$. Now let λ be a real number $\frac{1}{2} < \lambda < 1$, say $\lambda = \frac{3}{4}$, and let ϵ be a real number $\epsilon < \frac{1}{4}$ and suppose that $T(A, \lambda)$ is ϵ-approximable for the given λ and ϵ. Let the approximating machine have k states. Choose n_0 so great that

$$p^A(x_{n_0}^m) > \lambda + \epsilon \qquad \text{for} \quad m = 1, 2, \ldots, k + 1$$

The first $k + 1$ applications of the input sequence x_{n_0} must send the approximating machine B through a sequence of states $s_0, s_1, \ldots, s_{k+1}$, which are all final states of B. But B has only k states so that $s_j = s_i$ for some $i < j \le k + 1$ so that all the tapes of the form $x_{n_0}^m, m = 1, 2, \ldots$ will be in $T(B)$. Thus B cannot ϵ-approximate p^A since there is m_0 with $p^A(x_{n_0}^{m_0}) < \lambda - \epsilon$, i.e.,

$$|p^A(x_{n_0}^{m_0}) - \lambda| > \epsilon$$

while $x_{n_0}^{m_0} \in T(B)$ and $x_{n_0}^{m_0} \notin T(A, \lambda)$. The following are direct consequences of the above example:

1. There is a PCE which is not approximable by a regular event.

2. There is a PE which is not approximable by a finite [deterministic] automaton [this follows from Proposition 5.3].

3. The PCE given in the above example with cut-point $\lambda = \frac{1}{2}$ is ϵ-approximable by a regular event, but the underlying PE, p^A is not ϵ-approximable. The two concepts of approximation are not equivalent.

4. The class of PCEs strictly includes the class of regular events even if comparison is based on ϵ-approximation and not strict equivalence.

5. There exists a PE f and ϵ such that there is no ϵ-cover induced by it.

6. There is a PCE, $T(A, \lambda)$ and ϵ such that there is no ϵ-cover induced by it.

6. Some Nonclosure and Unsolvability Results

The following notation will be used in this subsection:

An RPA is an PA such that all the entries in the vectors π and in the matrices $A(\sigma)$ are *rational numbers*.

An ISA is an SPA such that all the entries in the vectors π, η and in the matrices $A(\sigma)$ are *integers*.

A P-event is an event E which can be represented in the form $E = T(A, \lambda)$ where A is an RPA and λ is a rational number. Thus any P-event is a PCE.

An E-event is an event E which can be represented in the form

$$E = \{x : f^A(x) = f^B(x)\}$$

where A and B are RPA and f^A and f^B are the PEs induced by them.

A D-event is an event E which can be represented in the form

$$E = \{x : f^A(x) \neq f^B(x)\}$$

where A, B, f^A and f^B are as above.

Lemma 6.1: Every E-event can also be represented in the form

$$E = \{x : f^C(x) = \tfrac{1}{2}\}$$

where C is an RPA and every D-event is an exclusive PCE (see Section 4.a)

Proof: Set $f^C(x) = \tfrac{1}{2}f^A(x) + \tfrac{1}{2}\bar{f}^B(x) = \tfrac{1}{2} + \tfrac{1}{2}(f^A(x) - f^B(x))$, then use the construction in the proofs of Propositions 1.1, 1.2, and 1.5 in Section A to show that C can be chosen to be an RPA under the conditions of the lemma. ∎

Lemma 6.2: The set of P-events is equal to the set of events which can be represented in the form $T(A, \lambda)$ with A an ISA and λ an integer.

Proof: Any event of the form $T(A, \lambda)$ with A an ISA and λ an integer is a P-event. This follows from the construction involved in the proofs of Proposition 1.1 and of the propositions and theorems on which that proposition is based. To prove the converse let $E = T(A, \lambda)$ be a given P-event. One proves easily (using a construction similar to the one used in the proof of Theorem A.2.4) that E can be respresented also in the form $E = T(A', 0)$ where A' is an SPA but the entries in its matrices and vectors are still rational numbers. Let m be the absolute value of the smallest common multiple of all the denominators of all the entries in all the matrices and vectors of A' and let A'' be the SPA derived from A' by multiplying all its matrices and vectors by m. A'' is an ISA by construction and $f^A(x) > 0$ for every $x \in \Sigma^*$. Thus $T(A, \lambda) = T(A', 0) = T(A'', 0)$ as required. ∎

Theorem 6.3: The set of P-events is closed under complementation.

Proof: Let $E = T(A, \lambda)$ be a P-event. Then, as in the proof of the previous lemma, $E = T(A', 0)$ where A' is an ISA, i.e., the values $f^{A'}(x)$ are integers for every $x \in \Sigma^*$. Thus $E = \{x : f^{A'}(x) > 0\}$ and $\bar{E} = \{x : f^A(A) \leq 0\} = \{x : f^{A'}(x) < 1\}$ for the values $f^{A'}(x)$ are integers. If $A' = (S, \pi, \{A'(\sigma)\}, \eta)$, let $A'' = (S, \pi, \{A'(\sigma)\}, -\eta)$. A'' is an ISA and $\bar{E} = \{x : f^{A''}(x) > 1\}$ which is a P-event by Lemma 6.2. ∎

Corollary 6.4: The set of E-events is a proper subset of the set of P-events.

Proof: By Lemma 6.1 every E-event, E, can be represented in the form $E = \{x : f^A(x) = \tfrac{1}{2}\}$ with A an RPA. Thus $\bar{E} = \{x : f^A(x) \neq \tfrac{1}{2}\} = E'$. Now $E' = T_{\neq}(A, \tfrac{1}{2})$ is an exclusive PCE with A an RPA and using the construction used in the proof of Proposition 4.2 one proves that E' is a P-event so that, by Theorem 6.3, $\bar{E}' = E$ is also a P-event. That the inclusion is proper follows by an argument similar to the argument used in the proof of Proposition 4.2. This part of the proof is left to the reader. ∎

Lemma 6.5: Let $E_s = T(A, \lambda)$ be a PCE (not necessarily a P-event) and let $E_r = T(B, 0)$ be a regular event and let c be a symbol $c \notin \Sigma$. Then $E_r c E_s$ and $E_s c E_r$ are PCE.

Proof: Let $A = (S, \pi, \{A(\sigma)\}, \eta^{F_1})$ and let $B = (Q, \xi, \{B(\sigma)\}, \eta^{F_2})$, where the vector ξ and the matrices $B(\sigma)$ are degenerate stochastic. Let $|S| = m$ and $|Q| = n$. Construct the following PA, C, $C = (K, \zeta, \{C(\sigma)\}, \eta^{F_3})$ where $|K| = m + n + 1$

$$C(\sigma) = \begin{bmatrix} B(\sigma) & 0 & 0 \\ 0 & A(\sigma) & 0 \\ 0 & 0 & 1 \end{bmatrix}$$

$\zeta = (\xi \quad 0 \quad 0 \cdots 0)$, $\eta^{F_3} = (0 \cdots 0(\eta^{F_1})^T \ 0)^T$ and

$$C(c) = \begin{bmatrix} C_1(c) \\ \vdots \\ C_{m+n+1}(c) \end{bmatrix}$$

with

$$C_i(c) = \begin{matrix} (0 \cdots 0 \ \pi \ 0) & \text{if } s_i \in F_2 \\ (0 \cdots \quad 0 \ 1) & \text{otherwise} \end{matrix}$$

It is left for the reader to verify that $T(C, \lambda) = E_r \subset E_s$. Thus, $E_r \subset E_s$ is a PCE. In addition

$$E_s c E_r = \tilde{E}_r c \tilde{E}_s$$

which implies by Proposition 1.6 that $E_s \subset E_r$ is also a PCE. ∎

If E is a set of words, then E^* denotes the star closure of E and is defined as

$$E^* = \bigcup_{i=0}^{\infty} E^i \quad \text{with} \quad E^0 = \{e\}, \ E^i = E^{i-1} E.$$

Lemma 6.6: Let $\Sigma = \{a, b\}$. The set of words

$$E = \{a^\kappa \ b(a^* b)^* \ a^\kappa \ b : \kappa \geq 0\}$$

is a PCE.

Proof: Consider the following SPA $A = (S, \pi, \{A(\sigma)\}_{\sigma \in \Sigma}, \eta)$ with $S = \{s_1, \ldots, s_9\}$, $\pi = (\frac{1}{2} \ \frac{1}{2} \ 0 \cdots 0)$, $\eta = (0 \cdots 0 \ 1 - 1)^T$ and $A(\sigma) = [a_{ij}(\sigma)]$ with

$$a_{11}(a) = a_{17}(a) = a_{66}(a) = a_{67}(a) = \tfrac{1}{2}, \qquad a_{22}(a) = a_{55}(a) = \tfrac{1}{3}$$

$$a_{27}(a) = a_{57}(a) = \tfrac{2}{3}, \qquad a_{77}(a) = a_{87}(a) = a_{97}(a) = 1,$$

$a_{ij}(a) = 0$ in all other cases and

$$a_{13}(b) = a_{15}(b) = a_{24}(b) = a_{26}(b) = a_{33}(b) = a_{35}(b) = a_{44}(b) = a_{16}(b) = \tfrac{1}{2}$$
$$a_{58}(b) = a_{69}(b) = a_{77}(b) = a_{87}(b) = a_{97}(b) = 1$$

$a_{ij}(b) = 0$ in all other cases.

It is left for the reader to verify that the following relation holds

$$E_1 = \{x : f^A(x) = 0\}$$
$$= E_s \cup \overline{a^* b(a^*b)^* a^* b} = E_s \cup E_2$$

with E_2 a regular event.

Using an argument similar to the one used in the proof of Corollary 6.4 one can easily prove that E_1 is a *P*-event and therefore a CPE. By Proposition 1.5 E_s is also a CPE (since $E_s = E_1 - E_2$ and E_2 is regular). ▌

Lemma 6.7: Let E_s be defined as in Lemma 6.6. The events $E_s\Sigma^*$ and E_s^* are not CPEs.

Proof: If an event $E = T(A, \lambda)$ is a CPE, then, by Theorem 2.8 Section II, C, for every word $x \in \Sigma^*$ there are constants $C_0, \ldots, C_n$ such that for any $y \in \Sigma^*$ the following equations hold true

$$C_n f^A(x^n y) + C_{n-1} f^A(x^{n-1} y) + \cdots + C_0 f^A(y) = 0 \qquad (*)$$
$$C_n + C_{n-1} + \cdots + C_0 = 0 \qquad (**)$$

Assume now that $E_s\Sigma^*$ is a CPE $E_s\Sigma^* = T(A, \lambda)$. Then f^A satisfies the above property. Let $x = a$. For this x some of the coeficients in $(*)$ are positive and some are not. Let $C_{i_1}, C_{i_2}, \ldots, C_{i_k}$ be the positive coeficients, and let $y = ba^{i_1}ba^{i_2} \cdots ab^{i_{k_0}}$. Then $f^A(a^j y) > \lambda$ if and only if $a^j y \in E_s\Sigma^*$ i.e., if and only if j has one of the values $i_1, i_2, \ldots, i_k$.

Multiplying $(**)$ by λ and substracting from $(*)$ we get

$$C_n(f^A(x^n y) - \lambda) + \cdots + C_0(f^A(y) - \lambda) = 0 \qquad (***)$$

This leads to a contradiction since by the above argument, $f^A(x^j y) - \lambda > 0$ if and only if $C_j > 0$ which would imply that the left-hand side of $(***)$ is strictly positive. Thus $E_s\Sigma^*$ is not a CPE. The proof that E_s^* is not a CPE is similar, but $y = b(a^{i_1}b)(a^{i_2}b)^2 \cdots (a^{i_k}b)^2$ in this case. ▌

Definition 6.1: Let Σ and Δ be two alphabets and let Ψ be a mapping $\Psi : \Sigma \rightarrow \Delta^*$. The natural extension of Ψ of the form $\Psi(e) = e$ and for $x = \sigma_1 \cdots \sigma_\kappa \in \Sigma^*$, $\Psi(x) = \Psi(\sigma_1) \cdots \Psi(\sigma_\kappa) \in \Delta^*$ is called a homomorphism from Σ^* into Δ^*. Given a homomorphism $\Psi : \Sigma^* \rightarrow \Delta^*$ and an event $E \in \Sigma^*$, $\Psi(E)$ is the event $\Psi(E) = \{y \in \Delta^* : y = \Psi(x), x \in E\}$. (*e* here is the empty word.)

Theorem 6.8: The set of CPEs is closed neither under concatenation nor under concatenation closure nor under homomorphism.

Proof: E_s in Lemma 6.6 is a PCE and so is Σ^* (any regular event is a PCE) but by Lemma 6.7 $E_s\Sigma^*$ and E_s^* are not CPEs. This proves the first two statements of the theorem. Now, by Lemma 6.5 $E_sc\Sigma^*$ is a PCE. Consider the natural extension of the following homomorphism: $\Psi(a) = a$, $\Psi(b) = b$, $\Psi(c) = e$, Then $\Psi(E_sc\Sigma^*) = E_s\Sigma^*$ which is not a PCE. This completes the proof. ∎

Remark: It is well known that regular events are closed under the above operations.

Exercises 6.9: Let E be the event consisting of the set of all words $a^i b\, a^{\kappa_1} b\, a^{\kappa_2}$ $b \cdots a^{\kappa_r} b$ such that $i, \kappa_1, \ldots, \kappa_r$ are nonnegative integers and, for some t $(0 < t \leq r)$, $i = \kappa_1 + \kappa_2 \cdots \kappa_t$. Prove that E is context-free [see Ginzburg (1966)] but is not a CPE (compare with Theorem 1.10).

Definition 6.2: (Ginzburg, 1966) A generalized sequential machine (GSM) is a 6-tuple $A = (S, \Sigma, \Delta, s_0, M, N)$ where S, Σ, Δ are finite sets (representing the states, input, and output symbols, respectively) s_0 is an element of S (the initial state) M is a function $M : S \times \Sigma \to S$ (the next state function) and N is a function $N : S \times \Sigma \to \Delta^*$ (the output function).

The functions M and N are extended by induction to $S \times \Sigma^*$ by defining for every state s every word $x \in \Sigma^*$ and every $\sigma \in \Sigma$

$$M(s, e) = s, \qquad\qquad N(s, e) = e$$
$$M(s, x\sigma) = M(M(s, x), \sigma), \qquad N(s, x\sigma) = N(s, x)N(M(s, x),\sigma)$$

The mapping $\Psi^A : \Sigma^* \to \Delta^*$ defined by $\Psi^A(x) = N(s_0, x)$ where N is the output function of a given GSM is called as GSM mapping.

Theorem 6.10: Let Ψ^A be a GSM-mapping $\Psi^A : \Sigma^* \to \Delta^*$ and let f^B be a PE $f^B : \Delta^* \to [0, 1]$. The product $\Psi^A \circ f^B$ defined as $\Psi^A \circ f^B(x) = f^B(\Psi^A(x))$ for $x \in \Sigma^*$ is a PE, i.e. there exists a P A C such that $f^C = \Psi^A \circ f^B : \Sigma^* \to [0, 1]$. If B is an RPA, then C can be chosen to be an RPA.

Proof: Let $A = (S, \Sigma, \Delta, s_0, M, N)$ and $B = (Q, \pi, \{B(\delta)\}_{\delta \in \Delta}, \eta^F)$ with $|S| = m$ and $|Q| = n$. Define the PA $C = (K, \xi, \{C(\sigma)\}_{\sigma \in \Sigma}, \eta^{F_1})$ as follows:

$$K = S \times Q, \qquad |K| = m \times n, \qquad \xi = (\pi \underbrace{0\ 0 \cdots 0}_{(n-1)m})$$

η^{F_1} is a column vector consisting of n equal m-dimensional subvectors every such subvector equal to η^F. For each $\sigma \in \Sigma C(\sigma)$ is a square matrix of order $m \times n$ consisting of n^2 blocks $C_{pq}(\sigma)$, $p, q = 1, 2, \ldots, n$, each block $C_{pq}(\sigma)$ a square matrix of order m defined as follows:

$$C_{pq}(\sigma) = \begin{cases} B(\Psi^A(\sigma)) & \text{if } M(s_p, \sigma) = s_q \\ \text{a zero matrix of order } m & \text{otherwise} \end{cases}$$

If $\Psi^A(\sigma) = e$, then $B(\Psi^A(\sigma)) = B(e) = I =$ the unit matrix of order m. It is left to the reader to verify that C as defined above is a PA (and if B is an RPA, then so is C) and that it satisfies $f^C = \Psi^A \circ f^B$ as required. ∎

We are now able to establish some connections between CPEs and a certain type of context-free language. Familiarity with formal languages [e.g., Ginzburg (1966)] is a prerequisite for the following lemmas and theorems.

Definition 6.3: A context free grammar $G = (V, \Sigma, P, t)$(we use here the notation t for the start symbol, $t \in V - \Sigma$, instead of σ which stands for an element of Σ) is *deterministic linear* (DL) if the productions in P satisfy the following requirements.
(i) Each production has the form $v \to a\xi u$ or the form $v \to b$ with $v, \xi \in V - \Sigma$; $a, b \in \Sigma$, $u \in \Sigma^*$; (ii) if two productions $v_1 \to a_1 x$, $v_2 \to a_2 y$, $v_1, v_2 \in V - \Sigma$, $a_1, a_2 \in \Sigma$; $x, y \in \{e\} \cup (V - \Sigma\Sigma^*$ are such that $v_1 = v_2$ and $a_1 = a_2$, then also $x = y$.
A language $L \subset \Sigma^*$ is DL if it is generated by a DL grammar.

Lemma 6.11: Every DL language is an E-event and therefore a PCE.

Proof: Let L be a DL language generated by the grammar $G = (V, \Sigma, P, t)$. Let A_g be the GSM $A_g = (S, \Sigma, \Delta, t, M, N)$ such that $S = (V - \Sigma) \cup (f, d)$, $f, d \notin V$; $\Delta = \Sigma$ and the definitions of M and N are given by:

$$M(v, \sigma) = \begin{cases} \xi, & \text{if } v \to \sigma\xi u \in P \text{ for some } u \in \Sigma^* \\ f & \text{if } v \to \sigma \in P \text{ or if } v = f \\ d & \text{otherwise} \end{cases}$$

$$N(v, \sigma) = \begin{cases} \tilde{u} & \text{if } v \to \sigma\xi u \in P \text{ for some } u \in \Sigma^* \\ e & \text{otherwise} \end{cases}$$

Let A_G' be another GSM $A_G' = (S, \Sigma, \Delta, t, M, N')$ Thus A_G' differs from A_G only in the function N' which is defined as

$$N'(v, \sigma) = \begin{cases} \sigma & \text{if } v = f \\ e & \text{otherwise} \end{cases}$$

Let A_G'' be the finite automaton $A_G'' = (S, \Sigma, t, M, F)$ where $F = \{f\} \subset S$, and all the other elements are as in A_G.
Let $L_1 = T(A_G'', 0)$, L_1 is a regular event by definition. Let $x = x_1 x_2 \in L_1$ where x_1 is the subword of minimal length of x such that $x_1 \in L_1$. If $x_1 = \sigma_1 \sigma_2 \cdots \sigma_\kappa$ then, by the definition of M_1, the following productions are in P:

$$t \to \sigma_1 \xi_1 u_1, \qquad \xi_1 \to \sigma_2 \xi_2 u_2, \qquad \cdots, \qquad \xi_{\kappa-2} \to \sigma_{\kappa-1}\xi_{\kappa-1}, \qquad \xi_{\kappa-1} \to \sigma_\kappa$$

It follows that $x = x_1 x_2 \in L$ if and only if $x_2 = u_{\kappa-1}u_{\kappa-2} \cdots u_1$. In addition it follows from the definitions of N and N' that $\Psi^{AG}(x_1 x_2) = \tilde{u}_1 \tilde{u}_2 \cdots \tilde{u}_{\kappa-1}$ while $\Psi^{AG'}(x_1 x_2) = x_2$. Thus $x \in L_1$ implies that $x = x_1 x_2 \in L$ if and only if $\tilde{x}_2 = \tilde{u}_1 \cdots \tilde{u}_{\kappa-1}$ or $\Psi^{AG'}(x) = \Psi^{AG}(x)$. Let f^A be the RPE induced by the m-

adic, $m \geq 3$, PA (see Exercise 3.1) with $A(1) = A(a)$ and $A(2) = A(b)$ and all the other symbols in the alphabet of A are deleted.

Let $\tilde{f}^A$ be the reverse of f^A which is an RPE by the costruction in the proof of Proposition 1.6. It follows from Theorem 6.10 that $\Psi^{AG} \circ f^A \overset{\Delta}{=} g_1'$ and $\Psi^{AG'} \circ f^A \overset{\Delta}{=} g_2'$ are both RPEs. Moreover, it follows from the above considerations that if $x \in L_1$, then $x \in L$ if and only if $g_1'(x) = g_2'(x)$. It is clear, from the definition of A_G'' that if $x \in L_1$, then $x \in L$. Therefore, in order to complete the proof, one has to modify the functions g_1' and g_2' to g_1 and g_2 so that $g_i(x) = g_i'(x)$ if $x \in L_1$, $i = 1, 2$, but $g_1(x) \neq g_2(x)$ if $x \notin L_1$. Now L_1 is regular. Let h be the RPE such that $h(x) = 1$ if $x \in L_1$ and $h(x) = 0$ otherwise. Set $g_1 = g_1' \vee h$ and $g_2 = g_2' \wedge h$. By the construction in the proof of Proposition A.1.9, g_1 and g_2 are both RPEs. One verifies easily that g_1 and g_2 satisfy the above requirements and the proof is complete.

Lemma 6.12: Let E_1 and E_2 be two DL languages over the alphabets Σ_1 and Σ_2 respectively $\Sigma_1 \cap \Sigma_2 = \phi$. Let δ be a letter $\delta \notin \Sigma_1 \cup \Sigma_2$. Then $E_1 \delta E_2$ is an E event (and therefore a CPE).

Proof: We shall prove the Theorem for $\Sigma_1 = \{a, b\}$ and $\Sigma_2 = \{a', b'\}$. The proof for the general case is similar. By Lemma 6.11, we can construct two RPEs for E_1, g_1, and g_2 such that $x \in E_1$ if and only if $g_1(x) = g_2(x)$. Taking f^A in the proof of that lemma to be the RPE induced by the 9-adic PA will cause $g_1(x)$ and $g_2(x)$ to have the following properties:

   a. $g_1(x) = 1$ (if $x \in L_1$, where L_1 is as in the proof of Lemma 6.11 for the given DL language, including the case $x = e$)
       or

       $g_1(x) = . \epsilon_1 \epsilon_2 \cdots \epsilon_\kappa > 0$ with $\epsilon_i = 1$ or $\epsilon_i = 2$
       in any case $0 < g_1(x) \leq 1$.
   b. $g_2(x) = 0$ (if $x \notin L_1$ as above, including the case $x = e$)
       or

       $g_2(x) = . \epsilon_1 \cdots \epsilon_\kappa < 1$ with $\epsilon_i = 1$ or $\epsilon_i = 2$
       In any case $0 \leq g_2(x) < 1$.

Similarly we can construct two RPEs for E_2, g_1' and g_2' such that $x \in E_2$ if and only if $g_1'(x) = g_2'(x)$. We shall choose this time f^A to be the RPE induced by the 9-adic PA, but $A(a') = A(3)$ and $A(b') = A(6)$. g_1' and g_2' will have the properties:

   a. $g_1'(x') = 1$ or $g_1'(x') = . \epsilon_1 \cdots \epsilon_\kappa, \epsilon_i = 3$ or $\epsilon_i = 6$
       $0 < g_1'(x') \leq 1$
   b. $g_2'(x) = 0$ or $g_2'(x') = . \epsilon_1 \cdots \epsilon_\kappa, \epsilon_i = 3$ or $\epsilon_i = 6$
       $0 \leq g_2'(x') < 1$

We shall extend first the functions g_1g_2, $g_1'g_2'$ to the functions h_1, h_2, h_1', h_2' such that the domain of the new functions will be $(\Sigma \cup \Sigma' \cup \delta)^*$, by adding to the underlying PA of each function unit matrices of due dimension for all symbols not included in the original domain of the specific function.

We construct now the RPEs (Corollary A.1.7)$\frac{1}{2}(h_1 + h_1') = \psi_1$ and $\frac{1}{2}(h_2 + h_2') = \psi_2$. Finally, let χ be the characteristic function of the regular event $\Sigma^*\delta\Sigma'^* = E$ (i.e., $\chi(x) = 1$ if $x \in E$ and $\chi(x) = 0$ otherwise), and set $g = \psi_1 \vee \bar{\chi}$, $g' = \psi_2 \wedge \chi$. g and g' are RPEs [Proposition A.1.9] and $g(x) = g'(x)$ if and only if $x \in E$, i.e., if and only if x has the form $x = z\delta y$, $z \in \Sigma^*$, $y \in \Sigma'^*$ and $\psi_1(x) = \psi_2(x)$, which happens if and only if $h_1(z\delta y) + h_1'(z\delta y) = h_2(z\delta y) + h_2(z\delta y)$. This is equivalent to $g_1(z) + g_1'(y) = g_2(z) + g_2'(y)$ which is equivalent by properties (a), (b), (a'), and (b') to the equations $g_1(z) = g_2(z)$ and $g_1'(y) = g_2'(y)$ which hold true if and only if $z \in E_1$ and $y \in E_2$. Thus $x \in E_1\delta E_2$ if and only if $g(x) = g'(x)$ and $E_1\delta E_2$ is therefore an E-event. ∎

The lemmas proved above will be used now to prove some undecidability results for CPE. Some of the subsequent results and their proofs are similar to the ones used in the theory of context-free languages and will be omitted (see e.g., Ginsburg, 1966, Chapter 4).

Lemma 6.13: Consider the following languages:

For $\Sigma = \{a, b, c, a', b', c'\}$, if $x \in \{a, b, c\}^*$, let x' be the word derived from x by replacing every occurrence of a letter in x by its primed counterpart, thus $x' \in \{a', b', c'\}^*$.

Define $L_s = \{xcyd\tilde{y}'c\tilde{x}' : x, y \in \{a, b\}^*\}$. Let $\mathbf{x} = (x_1, \ldots, x_n)$ and $\mathbf{y} = (y_1, \ldots, y_n)$ denote n-tuples of nonempty words in $\{a, b\}^*$. Define

$$L(\mathbf{x}) = \{a^{i_\kappa}b \cdots a^{i_1}bcx_{i_1} \cdots x_{i_\kappa} : \kappa \geq 1, \quad 1 \leq ij \leq n\}$$
$$L(\mathbf{x}, \mathbf{y}) = L(\mathbf{x})\, dL(\mathbf{y}'), \qquad \mathbf{y}' = (y_1', \ldots, y_n')$$

All three languages, L_s, $L(\mathbf{x})$ and $L(\mathbf{x}, \mathbf{y})$ are E events for any given $\mathbf{x}$ and $\mathbf{y}$

Proof: L_s is generated by the DL grammar

$$G = (\{t, \xi, a, b, c, d, a', b', c'\}, \quad \{a, b, c, d, a', b', c'\}, \quad P, \quad t)$$

where $P = \{t \to ata', t \to btb', t \to c\xi c', \xi \to a\xi a', \xi \to b\xi b', \xi \to d\}$. Therefore, by Lemma 6.11, L_s is an E-event. $L(\mathbf{x})$ is generated by the DL grammar $G = (\{t, \xi_0, \ldots, \xi_n, a, b, c\}, \{a, b, c\}, P, t)$ where $P = \{t \to a\xi_1, \xi_0 \to a\xi_1, \xi_1 \to a\xi_2, \ldots, \xi_{n-1} \to a\xi_n, \xi_0 \to c, \xi_1 \to b\xi_0 x_1, \xi_2 \to b\xi_0 x_2, \ldots, \xi_n \to b\xi_0 x_n\}$ and therefore $L(\mathbf{x})$ is also an E event. As for the language $L(\mathbf{x}, \mathbf{y})$ one can use the same proof as the one used for Lemma 6.12 with f^A replaced by $\tilde{f}^A$ in the definition of the functions g_1' and g_2' in order to show that $L(\mathbf{x}, \mathbf{y})$ is an E-event as well.

Lemma 6.14: $L(\mathbf{x}, \mathbf{y}) \cap L_s$ is an E-event for given $\mathbf{x}$ and $\mathbf{y}$ and it contains no infinite constext-free language.

Proof: E-events are closed under intersection (see Exercise 4.a.3). The second statement is known (see Ginsburg, 1966). ∎

Lemma 6.15: Let τ be the homomorphism $\tau : \{a, b, c, d, a', b', c'\}^* \rightarrow \{a, b\}^*$ defined by $\tau(a) = ab$, $\tau(b) = a^2b$, $\tau(c) = a^3b$, $\tau(d) = a^4b$, $\tau(a') = a^5b$, $\tau(b') = a^6b$, $\tau(c') = a^7b$. Then $\tau(L(\mathbf{x}, \mathbf{y}) \cap L_s)$ for given $\mathbf{x}$ and $\mathbf{y}$ is a *P*-event and it contains no infinite context-free languages.

Proof: One can easily construct a GSM mapping $\Psi^A : \{a, b\}^* \rightarrow \{a, b, c, d, a'b'c'\}^*$ such that $\Psi^A(x) = y$ if $\tau(y) = x$ and $\Psi^A(x) = e$ otherwise. By Lemma 6.14, $L(\mathbf{x}, \mathbf{y}) \cap L_s$ is an *E*-event and therefore (by Corrollary 6.4), a *P*-event of the form $T(B, \lambda)$ with B an RPA. By Theorem 6.10, $g = \Psi^A \circ f^B$ is an RPE.† For $x \in \{a, b\}^*$, if $x = \tau(y)$ for some y then $g(x) = f^B(\Psi^A(x)) = f^B(y)$ so that $g(x) > \lambda$ if and only if $x \in \tau(L(\mathbf{x}, \mathbf{y}) \cap L_s)$. Let χ be the characteristic function of the regular event $\{ab, a^2b, \ldots, a^7b\}^*$ and set $g' = g \wedge \chi \cdot g'$ is an RPE having the property that $\tau(L(\mathbf{x}, \mathbf{y}) \cap L_s) = \tau(g', \lambda)$. The second statement of the lemma is well known (see Ginzburg, 1966). ∎

Lemma 6.16: Each of the following is recursively unsolvable for arbitrary $L(\mathbf{x}, \mathbf{y})$: (a) whether $L(\mathbf{x}, \mathbf{y}) \cap L_s$ is empty, (b) whether $\tau[L(\mathbf{x}, \mathbf{y}) \cap L_s]$ is empty where τ is as in Lemma 6.15.

Proof: This result is well known (see Ginzburg, 1966). ∎

Theorem 6.17: Let Σ contain at least two elements. It is recursively unsolvable to determine for arbitrary *P*-events $T(A, \lambda)$ over Σ (a) whether $T(A, \lambda)$ is empty (b) whether $T(A, \lambda) = \Sigma^*$ (c) whether $T(A, \lambda)$ is regular and (d) whether $T(A, \lambda)$ is context free.

Proof: By Lemma 6.15, $\tau(L(\mathbf{x}, \mathbf{y}) \cap L_s)$ is a *P*-event and it can be proved that it is either empty or infinite (see Ginzburg, 1966). Therefore Lemma 6.16 implies. (a). $\Sigma^* - \tau(L(\mathbf{x}, \mathbf{y}) \cap L_s)$ is a *P*-event (Theorem 6.3) which implies (b). Furthermore, $\tau(L(\mathbf{x}, \mathbf{y}) \cap L_s)$ is regular (and therefore also context free) if and only if it is empty, by Lemma 6.15. Therefore Lemma 6.16 implies also (c) and (d). ∎

Exercise

By Lemma 6.15, $\tau(L(\mathbf{x}, \mathbf{y}) \cap L_s)$ can be represented in the form $\tau(L(\mathbf{x}, \mathbf{y}) \cap L_s) = \{x : P(x) > \lambda\}$ for some RPE p. Let q be the RPE $q(x) = \frac{1}{2}$ for all $x \in \Sigma^*$. Prove: $p \wedge q$ and $p \vee q$ are RPEs if and only if $\tau(L(\mathbf{x}, \mathbf{y}) \cap L_s)$ is empty. (This implies that it is recursively unsolvable to determine, for arbitrary RPE's p and q over Σ^*, with $|\Sigma| \geq 2$ (1) whether $p \vee q$ is an RPE, (2) whether $p \wedge q$ is an RPE.)

---

†An RPE is a PE g^c such that the underlying PA, c, is an RPA.

EXERCISES

1. A word function f is called quasidefinite if it has the following property: For any ϵ, there exists an integer $k(\epsilon)$ such that for any x with $l(x) \geq k(\epsilon)$ the inequality $|f(x) - f(y)| \leq \epsilon$ holds, where y is the $k(\epsilon)$-suffix of x.

Prove that any quasidefinite function is ϵ-approximable by a finite automaton [for any given ϵ].

2. Let $A = (\pi, S, \{A(\sigma)\}, \eta^F)$ be a PA over $\Sigma = \{a, b\}$ with $S = \{s_0, s_1\}$, $\pi = (1\ 0)$ $= (\eta^F)^T$ and the transition matrices are

$$A(a) = \begin{bmatrix} 1 & 0 \\ 0 & 1 \end{bmatrix}, \qquad A(b) = \begin{bmatrix} \frac{1}{2} & \frac{1}{2} \\ 1 & 0 \end{bmatrix}$$

and let p^A be the PE defined by A.

Prove that A is not quasidefinite but p^A is ϵ-approximable for any $\epsilon > 0$ by a finite [deterministic] automaton.

3. Let f be a word function and consider a relation P_ϵ induced by f over Σ^*, as follows: $xP_\epsilon y$ if and only if for all $z \in \Sigma^*$ $|f(xz) - f(yz)| \leq \epsilon$ (thus $xP_\epsilon y$ implies that $|f(x) - f(y)| \leq \epsilon$).

a. Prove that P_ϵ is symmetric reflexive and right invariant.

b. Prove that any word function f which is ϵ-approximable by a finite automaton induces a $P_{2\epsilon}$ relation of finite index.

c. If the word function f is defined by a PA, then the relation P_ϵ is of finite index k with

$$k \leq \left(1 + \frac{1}{\epsilon}\right)^{n-1}$$

where n is the number of states of the PA defining f.

4. Let f be a word function and λ a cut-point. The relation R_ϵ induced by f and λ is defined as follows: $xR_\epsilon y$ if and only if for any $z \in \Sigma^*$ $|f(xz) - \lambda| > \epsilon$ and $|f(yz) - \lambda| > \epsilon$ implies that $f(xz) > \lambda$ if and only if $f(yz) > \lambda$.

Prove:

a. The relation P_ϵ defined in Exercise 3 above is a refinement of the relation R_ϵ here.

b. If f is induced by a PA, then for any λ and $\epsilon > 0$, R_ϵ is of finite index.

c. If the event $E = \{x : f(x) > \lambda\}$ is ϵ-approximable by a regular event then R_ϵ is of finite index.

5. A cut-point event $E = \{x : f(x) > \lambda\}$, where f is a word function, is quasidefinite if for any ϵ there is an integer $k(\epsilon)$ such that for any x with $l(x) \geq k(\epsilon)$ and any $y \in \Sigma^*$ we have that $x \in E$ implies that $f(yx) > \lambda - \epsilon$ and $x \notin E$ implies that $f(yx) \leq \lambda + \epsilon$.

a. Prove that if f is a quasidefinite function [see Exercise 1] then the cut-point event $E = \{x : f(x) > \lambda\}$ is quasidefinite for any λ.

b. Prove that the converse of the above statement is not true by considering the function induced by the PA $= (\pi, S, \{A(\sigma)\}, \eta^F)$ with $\pi = (1\ 0) = (\eta^F)^{\mathrm{T}}$ $\Sigma = \{a, b\}$ and

$$A(a) = \begin{bmatrix} 1 & 0 \\ 0 & 1 \end{bmatrix}, \qquad A(b) = \begin{bmatrix} \frac{3}{4} & \frac{1}{4} \\ \frac{1}{4} & \frac{3}{4} \end{bmatrix}$$

with $E = T(A, \frac{1}{2})$.

6. Prove that if f is a quasidefinite function [see Exercise 1] then any cut-point event of the form $E = \{x : f(x) > \lambda\}$ is ϵ-approximable by a regular event.

7. Prove that any quasidefinite cut-point event [see Exercise 5] is ϵ-approximable by a regular event.

OPEN PROBLEMS

1. Characterize the word functions which are ϵ-approximable by push down automata.

2. Characterize the events which are ϵ-approximable by context free languages.

3. Is the class of PCE ϵ-approximable by context free languages?

7. Bibliographical Notes

Probabilistic cut point events were introduced in the literature by Rabin (1963). Some subsequent and other ideas involved in the study of those events can be found also in the M.Sc. Thesis of Paz (1962) done in Jerusalem.

The source papers for the material given in this section is listed below. (It is to be mentioned here, however, that some of the theorems and many proof are new due to the unifying exposition.) Bukharaev (1964), [see also Bukharaev (1965, 1967, 1968)]: Theorems 1.8 and 1.9. [The above paper also includes an example for Theorem 1.10 but that example is much more complicated than the one given here and is mentioned there without proof. The author of this book was not able to convince himself that the example of Bukharaev actually works.]

Nasu and Honda (1968): Theorem 1.6, Exercises 1.5 and 2.2. [This paper also contains some generalizations of the topics included in Section 4,c]. Page (1966): Exercise 2.4 and the considerations concerning the impossibility of merging equivalent states in automata defining cut-point events (Figure 17). Page also introduced the generalization from PCEs to pseudo probabilistic cut-point events Paz (1966, 1967d, 1970a, c): Theorems (Lemmas, Corollaries) 1.5, 1.7, 1.10, 3.2, 3.4, 3.6, 3.7, 4.2, 4.8, 4.9, 4.10, 4.11, Sections 4,b and 4,c.

Exercises 1.2, 1.7, 1.8, 3.1, 3.12, 3.13, 4.2, 4.3. Rabin (1963): Teorems 1.2, 2.2, 2.3, 3.1, 3.3, 4.17 (private communication, Rabin proved also a weaker version of Theorem 4.16), Exercise 3.2 and our proposition 5.4 here is somewhat related to Theorem 5 in Rabin (1963). Salomaa (1965, 1966, 1967): Exercises 1.11, 3.5, 3.6, 3.7, 3.8, 3.9. Starke (1966a, c): Exercises 1.1, 1.3, 1.4, 2.1, 2.3. Turakainen (1968) Theorems 1.1, 1.4, 1.5, Section 4.a, Exercises 1.6, 3.10. The following are three additional recent works relevant to the subjects considered in this section: Flachs (1967), Yasui and Yajima (1969), and Turakainen (1969-b). See also: Rose and Ullian (1963), Even (1964), Kfoury and Liu (1969), Paz (1967c).

After a first example of a linear bounded language which is not a CPE has been found by the author of this book (Theorem 1.10) and distributed as a private communication (1969) Nasu and Honda used Paz's idea and gave another example of a context-free language which is not a CPE (their language is given here as Exercise 6.9 and was also distributed as a private communication (1970)). Using the language of Nasu and Honda as a starting point Turakainen (1970a, b) managed to prove the nonclosure properties of CPE given in section 6. Thus Section 6 up to and including Theorem 6.8 is based on the works of Turakainen (1969b, 1970a, 1970b). The rest of that section beginning from Exercise 6.9 and on is based on the work of Nasu and Honda (1970). See also Schützenberger (1962).

Chapter IV

Applications
and
Generalizations

INTRODUCTION

This part contains an extended survey of most known papers dealing with applications and generalizations of probabilistic automata theory.

There have been some attempts to apply the theory of probabilistics automata to other disciplines. These attempts are however still in the beginning stages. We choose therefore to supply the reader with an extended bibliography including explanatory remarks as to the nature or direction of the intended application or generalizations.

A. INFORMATION THEORY

One of the motivations for studying probabilistic sequential machines [see e.g. Carlyle (1963a)] was the fact that communication channels (Shannon and Weaver, 1968) can be represented as stochastic sequential machines. The topics studied in connection with the theory of information using probabilistic machines are: probability structure of channels-Carlyle (1963a, b), Onicescu and Guiasu (1965), Thomasian (1963), Wolfowitz (1963); encoding and decoding of finite state channels-Ott (1966a, b), Viterbi (1967), Guiasu (1968)

Viterbi and Odenwalder (1969). Other related references: Blackwell *et al.*
(1958) Huffman (1952) Fano (1961) Shannon (1957), Paz (1965), Souza,
et al. (1969).

B. RELIABILITY

When a deterministic automaton has some unreliable elements then its external
behavior is probabilistic, thus, another motivation for studying probabilistic
automata was the reliability problem. In connection with this aspect, the reader
is referred to Von Neuman (1956) and Rabin (1963). An additional interesting
reference can found in the book of Cowan and Winograd (1963). Many
authors working in reliability theory have attempted to construct reliable networks using unreliable components but the resulting network was always of
the "definite" type. Cowan and Winograd showed that this is not a coincidence.
They showed that, as a result of the axioms imposed on the network and the
unreliable behavior of its components, the resulting probabilistic automaton
satisfies the conditions of the Theorem 4.16 in Section III,B of Rabin and
therefore the reliable network *must* be definite. Additional relatted bibliography:
Arbib (1965) Harrison (1965) Tsertzvadze (1966) Germanov (1966).

C. LEARNING THEORY AND PATTERN RECOGNITION

Still another motivation for studying stochastic automata was the possibility of
using them as models of learning and pattern recognition systems [e.g. Tsetslin
(1961), Schreider (1962), Bruce and Fu (1963)]. The model used by Tsetslin
consists of a deterministic automaton subject to a probabilistic training
process. The input to the deterministic automaton is random and represents
the reaction of a medium ("teacher") to the performance of the automaton.
Two inputs are possible, 1 (representing a penalty) and 0 (representing a
nonpenalty) and the medium will insert its next input to the automaton in
a random way, the probability of a penalty or nonpenalty depending on the
present state. Let $\{s_i\}_{i=1}^n$ be the set of states of the (deterministic) automaton
and let p_i be the probability of receiving a penalty in state s_i. The automaton is called expedient if its expectation (in the long run) for receiving a
penalty is less than the average of the p_is. It is easy to see that the model
corresponding to the above description is a probabilistic automaton with a
single letter in the alphabet (the i-th row of its single transition matrix is the
convex combination of the i-th rows of the transition matrices of the deterministic automaton corresponding to the inputs 0 and 1 respectively, and the

coefficients of the combination are p_i and $1 - p_i$). Tsetslin who initiated the study of expediency (as explained above) of deterministic automata in random media was followed by many authors who extended and generalized its approach, allowing for changes in the transition probabilities induced by controlled learning, and using reinforcement algorithm: Bush and Mosteller (1955) Bruce and Fu (1963), Tsertsvadze (1963), Varshavskii and Vorontsova (1963), Fu and McMurtry (1965), Fu and McLaren (1965), Vorontzóva (1965), McMurtry and Fu (1966), and Fu and Wee (1967). Other related bibliography: Suppes and Atkinson (1960), Braines and Svechinsky (1962), Krulee and Kuick (1964), Vaisborg and Rosenstein (1965), Sklansky (1966), Fu (1966, 1967), Wee and Fu (1969), Gelenbe (1969b).

D. CONTROL

It occured to several authors that control systems [e.g. Eaton and Zadeh (1962)] can be modelized by stochastic machines, with input symbols representing commands, after some additional structure is added to take care of the costs associated with the transitions between the states. In this representation, a policy is a function associating commands to the states of the system and the policies are characterized by their expected costs. Some results in control theory, using this interpretation can be found in the works of Page (1965) and Arbib (1966). Other related bibliography: Zadeh (1963b); Screider (1962); Pospelov (1966), Kalman (1968), Kalman, *et al.* (1969).

E. OTHER APPLICATIONS

A connection between stochastic automata and the problem of time sharing in computer programming has been established by Kashiap (1966) and the theory of functions of Markov chains has been used by Fox and Rubin (1965) for statistical inference (for evaluating the cloud cover estimation of parameters and godness of fit based on Boston data). See also Lewis (1966).

F. EXTENSIONS AND CONNECTIONS TO OTHER THEORIES

Probabilistic extension of Turing machines have been studied by De Loeuw *et al.* (1956), Santos (1969), and Ellis (1969). Probabilistic extensions of context free languages have been considered by Salomaa (1969-b) and Ellis (1969). Probabilistic extension of time variant machine has been studied by Turakainen (1969a). Tree automata with a probabilistic structure have been studied by Magidor and Moran (1969), Paz (1968a), and Ellis (1969). Some properties of fuzzy automata similar to properties of probabilistic automata have been established by Santos and Wee (1968) and by Mizimoto *et al.* (1969), an approach to stochastic automata and systems, from the point of view of the theory of categories can be found in the works of Heller (1967) and Depeyrot (1968) finally, some connections with dynamical programming has been established by Feichtinger (1968) [see also Howard (1960)]. Additional references: Wing and Demetrious (1964), Warfield (1968), Tou (1968), Li and Fu (1969).

References

Abramson, N. (1963). "Information Theory and Coding." McGraw-Hill, New York.

Arbib, M. (1965). A Common framework for automata theory and control theory. *SIAM J. Control* **3**, 206-222.

Arbib, M. (1966). Automata theory and control theory-A rapprochement. *Automatica Internat. J. Automat. Control Automation* **3**, 161-189.

Arbib, M. (1967). Realization of stochastic systems. *IEEE Conf. Record Annu. Symp. Switching and Automata Theory, 7th, 1967*; *Ann. Math. Statist.* **38**, 927-933.

Arbib, M. (1969). "Theories of Abstract Automata." Prentice-Hall, Englewood Cliffs, New Jersey.

Areshyan, T. L., and Marangjyan, T. B. (1964). On some problems of the theory of stochastic automata. *Trudy Vycisl. Tsentra* **2**, 73-82.

Ash, R. (1965). "Information Theory." Wiley (Interscience), New York.

Ashby, R. W. (1958). "An Introduction to Cybernetics." Chapman & Hall, London.

Bacon, G. C. (1964). The decomposition of stochastic automata. *Information and Control* **7**, 320-339.

Bacon, G. C. (1966). Minimal state stochastic finite state systems. *IEEE Trans.* **PGCT-11**, 307-308.

Bernstein, S. N. (1936). Determination d'une limite inferieure de la dispersion des sommes de grandeurs liees en chain singuliere. *Mat. Sb.* **1(43)**, 29-38.

Bernstein, S. N. (1944). Extension of a limit theorem of the theory of probability to a sum of dependent variables. *Uspehi Mat. Nauk* **10**, 65-114.

Bernstein, S. N. (1946). "The Theory of Probability." Gostekhizdat, Moscow.

Blackwell, D., and Koopmans, L. (1957). On the identifiability problem for functions of finite Markov chains. *Ann. Math. Statist.* **28**, 1011-1015.

Blackwell, D., Breiman, L., and Thomasian, A. J. (1958). Proof of Shannon's transmission theorem for finite state indecomposable channels. *Ann. Math. Statist.* **29**, 1209-1220.

Blogovescensky, V. N. (1960). Ob ergodichnosti dlia schemi serii tzepii Markova konetznam cislom sostoianii, i, diskretnam vremenem. *Izv. Akad. Nauk USSR Ser. Fiz.-Ma.* No. 3, 7–15.

Booth, T. L. (1964). Random input automata. *ICMCI Conf. Tokyo, Japan, 1964.*

Booth, T. L. (1965). Random processes in sequential network. *Proc. IEEE Symp. Signal Transmission and Processing, 1965,* pp. 19–25.

Booth, T. L. (1966). Statistical properties of random digital sequences. *IEEE Conf. Record Ann. Symp. Switching and Automata Theory, 7th, 1966,* pp. 251–260.

Booth, T. L. (1967). "Sequential Machines and Automata." Wiley, New York.

Booth, T. L. (1969). Probabilistic representation of formal languages. *IEEE Conf. Record Ann. Symp. Switching and Automata Theory, 10th, 1969.*

Braines, S. N., and Svechinsky, V. B. (1962). Matrix structure in simulation of learning. *IRE Trans.* IT-S, No. 5. 186–190.

Bruce, G. D. and Fu, K. S. (1963). A model for finite state probabilistic systems. *Proc. Conf. Circuit and System Theory, Allerton, 1963,* Univ. of Michigan Press, Ann Arbor, Michigan.

Brzozowski, J. (1964). Derivates of regular expressions. *J. Assoc. Comput. Mach.* 11, No. 4, 481–494.

Bukharaev, R. G. (1964). Nekotorye ekivalentnosti v teorii verojatnostnykh avtomatov. *Kazan Gos. Univ. Ucen. Zap.* 124, 45–65.

Bukharaev, R. G. (1965). Kriterij predstavinosti sobytij v konechnykh verojatnostnykh automatakh. *Dokl. Akad. Nauk SSSR* 164, 289–291.

Bukharaev, R. G. (1967). Kriterij predstavinosti sobytij v konechnykh verojatnostnykh automatakh II. "Verojatnostii Methodi i Kibernetika," Vol. 5. Izd. Kazankovo Univ. [also in *Kibernetika* (Kiev) 1, 8–17 (1969)].

Bukharaev, R. G. (1968). Teoria veroiatnostykh automatakh. *Kibernetika* (Kiev) 2, 6–23.

Burke, C. J., and Rosenblatt, M. (1958). A Morkovian function of a Markov chain. *Ann. Math. Statist.* 29, 1112–1122.

Bush, R. R., and Mosteller, F. (1955). "Stochastic Models for Learning." Wiley, New York.

Carlyle, J. W. (1961). Equivalent stochastic sequential machines. Electron. Res. Lab. Ser. No. 60, Issue No. 415. Univ. of California, Berkeley, California.

Carlyle, J. W. (1963a). On the external probability structure of finite state channels. *Information and Control* 7, 167–175.

Carlyle, J. W. (1963b). Reduced forms for stochastic sequential machines. *J. Math. Anal. Appl.* 7, 167–175.

Carlyle, J. W. (1965). State calculable stochastic sequential machines, equivalences and events. *Proc. IEEE Ann. Symp. Switching Circuit Theory and Logical Des., 6th, 1965.*

Carlyle, J. W. (1967). Identification of state calculable functions of finite Markov chains. *Ann. Math. Statist.* 38, No. 1, 201–205.

Carlyle, J. W. (1969). Stochastic finite-state system theory. *In "System Theory"* (L. A. Zadeh and E. Polak, eds.), Chapter 10. McGraw-Hill, New York.

Carlyle, J. W., and Paz, A. (1970). Realizations by Stochastic finite automata. Tech. Rep. Dept. of System Sci., Univ. of California, Los Angeles, California.

Cleave, J. P. (1962). The synthesis of finite state homogeneous Markov chains. *Kybernetica* (Namur) 5, No. 1, 28–47.

Cowan, J. D., and Winograd, S. (1963). "Reliable Computation in the Presence of Noise." M.I.T. Press, Cambridge, Massachusetts.

Dantzig. A. B. (1963). "Linear Programming and Extensions." Princeton Univ. Press, Princeton, New Jersey.

Darling, D. A. and Robbins, H. (1968). Testing the sign of a mean. Rept. Univ. of California, Berkeley, California.

Davis, A. S. (1961). Markov chains as random input automata. *Amer. Math. Monthly* **68**, 264–267.

De Loeuw, K., Moore, E. F., Shannon, C. E., and Shapiro, N. (1956). Computability by probabilistic machines. *In "Automata Studies"* (C. E. Shannon and J. McCarthy, eds.). Princeton Univ. Press, Princeton, New Jersey.

Depeyrot, M. (1968). Operand investigation of stochastic systems. Thesis. Stanford Univ. Stanford, California.

Depeyrot, M. (1969a). Un algorithme rapide de decomposition. *Colloq. Internat. Systemes Logiques-Conception et Applications Brussells, 1969.*

Depeyrot, M. (1969b). Sur un example Numerique de realization d'un automate Stochastique. Rep. Centre d'automatique de l'Ecole Nationale Superieure des mines de Paris.

Dharmadhikari, S. W. (1963a). Functions of finite Markov chains. *Ann. Math. Statist.* **34**, 1022–1032.

Dharmadhikari, S. W. (1963b). Sufficient conditions for a stationary process to be a function of a finite Markov chain. *Ann. Math. Statist.* **34**, 1033–1041.

Dharmadhikari, S. W. (1965). A characterization of a class of functions of finite Markov chains, *Ann. Math. Statist.* **36**, 524–528.

Dharmadhikari, S. W. (1967). Some nonregular functions of finite Markov chains. Rep. No. RM-202 SD-2. Michigan State Univ.

Dobrushin, R. L. (1956). Central limit theorem for nonstationary Markov chains I, II. *Theor. Probability Appl.* **1**, 65–80, 298–383.

Doob, J. L. (1953). "Stochastic Processes." Wiley, New York.

Dynkin, E. B. (1954). On some limit theorems for Markov chains. *Ukrain. Mat. Z.* **6**, 21–27.

Eaton, J. H., and Zadeh, L. A. (1962). Optimal pursuit strategies in discrete state probabilistic systems. Trans. ASME, 23–29.

Elgot, C. C., and Mezei, J. (1965). On relations defined by generalized finite automata. *IBM J. Res. Develop.* **9**, 47–68.

Ellis, C. (1969). Probabilistic languages and automata, Ph.D. Thesis, Univ. of Illinois, Urbana, Illinois.

Even, S. (1964). Rational numbers and regular events, Sperry Rand Res. Rep., No. SRKC —PR—64—12; IEEE Trans. **EC-13**, 740–741.

Even, S. (1965). Comments on minimization of stochastic machines. *IEEE Trans.* **EC-14**, No. 4, 634–637.

Fano, R. M. (1961). "Transmission of Information," M. I. T. Press, Cambridge, Massachusetts and Wiley, New York.

Feichtinger, G. (1968). *Automaten theorie and dynamishe programming*, Elektron, *Informationsverarbeit. Kybernetik Sekt.* **4**, **6**, 347–352.

Feller, W. (1957). "An Introduction to Probability Theory and Its Applications," 2nd ed., Vol. I, Wiley, New York.

Feller, W. (1966). "An Introduction to Probability Theorem and Its Applications," Vol. II, Wiley, New York.

Fischer, K., Lindner, R, and Thiele, M. (1967). Stabile stochastische automaten. *Elektron, Informationsverarbeit. Kybernetik* **3**, 201–213.

Flachs, G. M. (1967). Stability and Cutpoints of Probabilistic Automata, Thesis, Michigan State Univ., East Lansing, Michigan.

Fox, M. (1959). Conditions under which a given process is a function of a Markov chain (abstract). *Ann. Math. Statist* **30**, 688-697.

Fox, M. and Rubin, H. (1965). A stochastic model for the evolution of cloud cover-estimation of parameters and goodness of fit based on Boston data, RM-132, Michigan State Univ.

Fox, M., and Rubin, H. (1967). Functions of processes with Markovian states, RM-193, Michigan State Univ.

Frazer, R. A., Duncan, W. G., and Collar, A. R. (1938). "Elementary Matrices." Cambridge Univ. Press, London and New York.

Frechet, M. (1938). "*Recherches Theoretiques Modernes Sur le Calcul Des Probabilities.* Vol. 2, Gauthier-Villars, Paris.

Fu K. S. (1966). Stochastic automata as models of learning systems. *Proc. Symp. Comput. Information Sci.*, Columbus, Ohio, 1966.

Fu, K. S. (1967). In "Computer and Information Sciences" (J. T. Tou, ed.,) Vol. II. Academic Press, New York.

Fu, K. S., and Li, T. J. (1969). Formulation of learning automata and automata games. *Information Sci.* **1**, 237-256.

Fu, K. S., and McLaren, R. W. (1965). An application of stochastic automata to the synthesis of learning systems, Tech. Rept. TR EE 65-17, School of Elec. Eng., Purdue Univ.

Fu, K. S., and Mc Murtry, G. J. (1965). A study of stochastic automata as models of addaptive and learning controllers. Rep. TR-E 65-65-17. Purdue Univ.

Fu, K. S., and Wee, G. W. (1967). On generalizations of adaptive algorithms and application of the fuzzy sets concept to pattern classification, *Tech. Rept. TR-EE 67-7.* School of Elec. Eng. 366, Purdue Univ.

Fujimoto, S., and Fukao, T. (1966). The decomposition of probabilistic automata, *Denki Shikenjo Iho* **30**, No. 8, 688-698.

Gantmacher, F. R. (1959). "The Theory of Matrices." Chelsea, New York.

Gelenbe, S. E. (1969a). On the loop-free decomposition of stochastic finite-state system. Rept. Polytech. Inst. of Brooklyn, New York.

Gelenbe, S. E. (1969b). On probabilistic automata with structural restrictions. *IEEE Conf. Record. Ann. Symp. Switching and Automata, Theory, 10th, 1969.*

Germanov, U. (1966). Can we look inside an unreliable automaton? *Res. Papers. Statist. Testchrift J. Neyman* pp. 107-123.

Gilbert, E. J. (1959). On the identifiability problem for functions of finite Markov chains. *Ann. Math. Statist,* **30**, 688-697.

Gill, A. (1962a). "Introduction to the Theory of Finite State Machines." McGraw-Hill, New York.

Gill, A. (1962b). Synthesis of probability transformers, *J. Franklin Inst.* **274**, No. 1, 1-19.

Gill, A. (1963). On a weight distribution problem, with application to the design of stochastic generators, Rep. No. 63-5 ERL. Univ. of California, Berkeley, California; *J. Assoc. Comput. Mach,* **10**, No. 1, 110-121.

Gill, A. (1966). Realization of input output relations by sequential Machines. *J. Assoc. Comput. Mach.* **13**, 33-42.

Ginsburg, S. (1963). "An Introduction to Mathematical Machine Theory." Addison-Wesley, Reading, Massachusetts.

Ginzburg, A., and Yeli, M. (1965). Products of automata and the problem of coverring. *Trans. Amer. Math. Soc.* **116**, 253-266.

Ginzburg, A. (1968). "Algebraic Theory of Automata." Academic Press, New York.

Gray, J. M., and Harrison, M. A. (1966). The theory of sequential relations. *Information and Control* **9**, 435-468.

Grunbaum, B. (1967). "Convex Polytopes." Wiley (Interscience), New York.

Guiasu, S. (1968). On codification in finite abstract random automata. *Information and Control* **12**, 277-283.

Gurkov, M. K. (1966a). On finite stochastic automata. *Vycisl. Tehn. Voprosy Programm.* **3**, 64-67.

Gurkov, M. K. (1966b). Stochastic automata and stochastic Mapping. *Diskret. Analiz.* **7**, 61-70.

Hajnal, J. (1956). The ergodic properties of non-homogeneous Markov chains, *Proc. Cambridge Philos. Soc.* **52**, 67-77.

Hajnal, J. (1958). Weak ergodicity in nonhomogeneous Markov chains. *Proc. Cambridge Philos. Soc.* **54**, 233-246.

Harris, T. E. (1955). On chains of infinite order. *Pacific J. Math.* **5**, 707-724.

Harrison, M. A. (1965). "Introduction to Switching and Automata Theory." McGraw-Hill, New York.

Hartmanis, J., and Stearns, R. E. (1966). Algebraic Structure Theory of Sequential Machines. Prentice-Hall, Englewood Cliffs, New Jersey.

Heller, A. (1965). On stochastic processes derived from Markov chains. *Ann. Math. Statist.* **36**, 1286-1291.

Heller, A. (1967). Probabilistic autonata and stochastic transformations. *Math. Systems Theory*, **1**, No. 3, 197-208.

Howard, R. A. (1960). "Dynamic Programming and Markov Processes." M. I. T. Press, Cambridge, Massachusetts and Wiley, New York.

Huffman, D. A. (1952). A method for the construction of minimum-redundancy codes. *Proc. IRE* **40**, 1098-1101.

Kalman, R. E. (1968). "Lectures on Controlability and Observability." Centre Internat. Mat. estivo.

Kalman, R. E., Falb, P. L., and Arbib, M. A., (1969). "Topics in Mathematical System Theory." McGraw-Hill, New York.

Kashyap, R. L. (1966). Optimization of stochastic finite state system. *IEEE Trans.* **AC-11**, No. 4, 685-692.

Kemeny, J. C. and Snell, J. L. (1960). "Finite Markov Chains." Van Nostrand, Princeton, New Jersey.

Kemeny, J. C., Snell, J. L., and Knapp, A. W. (1966). "Denumerable Markov Chains." Van Nostrand, New Jersey.

Kfoury, D. J. and Liu, C. L. (1969). Definite stochastic sequential machines and definite stochastic matrices." *IEEE Conf. Record Symp. Switching and Automata Theory, 10th, 1969.*

Kolmogorov, A. N. (1958). On analytical methods in the theory of probability. *Uspehi Mat. Nauk* **5**, 5-41.

Kovalenko, I. N. (1965). A note on the complexity of the representation of events in probabilistic and deterministic finite automata. *Kibernetika (Kiev)* No. 2, 35-36.

Kozniewska, J. (1958). Ergodicity of nonhomogeneous Markov chains with two-states. *Colloq. Math.* **5**, 208-215.

Kozniewska, J. (1962). Ergodicite et stationnerite des chaines de Markoff variables a un nombre fini d'etats possibles. *Colloq. Math.* **9**, 333-346.

Krohn, K. B., and Rhodes, J. L. (1963). Algebraic theory of machines. *Proc. Symp. Math. Theory of Automata, 1963*, pp. 341-384. Polytech. Press, Brooklyn. pp. 381-4.

Krulee, G. K., and Kuick, D. J. (1964). Finite state models for perception. *J. Mathematical Psychology* **6**, 316-335.

Kuich, W., and Walk, K. K. (1966). Block-stochastic matrices and associated finite-state languages. *Computing* **1**, 50-61.

Kuich, W. (1966). Quasi-block-stochastic matrices. Tech. Rep. TR 25063. IBM Labs, Vienna.

Larisse, J., and Schutzenberger M. (1966). Sur certaines chaines de Markov nonhomogenes. *In* "Automata Theory" (E. R. Caianello, ed.), pp. 239-250, Academic Press, New York.

Lewis, E. W. (1966). Stochastic sequential machines: Theory and applications. Ph. D. Thesis, Northwestern Univ., Suanston, Illinois.

Li, T. J. and Fu, K. S. (1969). Automa games, stochastic automata and formal languages. Rep. TR-EE, 69-1. Purdue Univ.

Linnik, Yu. V. (1948). Inhomogeneous Markov chains. *Dokl. Akad. Nauk SSSR Ser. Mat.* LX 1, 21-24.

Linnik, Yu. V. (1949). "On the Theory of Inhomogeneous Markov Chains" *Izv. Akad. Nauk SSSR Ser. Mat.* XIII, 1, 65-94.

Linnik, Yu. V., and Sapogov, N. A. (1949). Multidimensional Integral and local laws for inhomogeneous Markov chains. *Izv. Akad Nauk SSSR Ser. Mat.* XIII, 6, 533-566.

Lovell, B. W. (1969). The incompletely specified finite state stochastic sequential machine equivalence and reduction. *IEEE Conf. Record Ann. Symp. Switching and Automata Theory, 10th, 1969.*

McCluskey, E. J. (1965). "Introduction of the Theory of Switching Circuits." McGraw-Hill, New York.

MacDufee, C. C. (1964). "Vectors and Matrices." Math. Assoc. Amer.

McMurtry, G. J., and Fu, K. S. (1966). A variable structure automation used as a multy modal searching technique. *IEEE Trans.* AC11.

Magidor, M., and Moran G. (1969). Finite automata over finite trees. Tec. Rep. No. 30, U. S. Office of Naval Res. Information System Branch, Hebrew Univ., Jerusalem.

Marik, J., and Ptak, V. (1960). Norms, spectra and combinatorial properties of matrices. *Czechoslovak Math. J.* 10, (85). 181-195.

Markov, A. (1913). "Calculus of Probabilities." Moscow.

Markov, A. (1951). Isledovanee obctzero slutzara ispatanaii sviaganah v tzepi. *Izv. Trudy Moscov.*

Mizimoto, M., Toyoda, J., and Tanaka, K. (1969). Some considerations on fuzzy automata. *J. Comput. System Sci.* 3, 111-124.

Moore, E. E., ed. (1964), "Sequential Machines" Addison-Wesley, Reading, Massachusetts.

Moot, J. L. (1957), Conditions for the ergodicity of nonhomogeneous Markov chains, *Proc. Roy. Soc. Edinburgh, Sect. A*64, 369-380.

Mott, G. L. S., and Schneider, H. (1957). Matrix norms applied to weakly ergodic Markov chains, *Arch. Math.* 8, 331-333.

Narbrotzki, K. (1967), Eine bemerkung uber reduktion von stochastichen automaten, *Elektron. Informations verarbeit. Kybernetik*

Nasu, M. and Honda, N. (1969). Mappings induced by PGSM—mappings and some recursively unsolvable problems of finite probabilisitic automata. *Information and Control* 15, 250-273.

Nasu, M., and Honda, N. (1968), Fuzzy events realized by finite probabilistic automata, *Information and Control* 12, 248-303.

Nieh, T. T. (1967), Orderings of stochastic sequential machines, D. Sc. Thesis U.C.L.A.

Nieh, T. T., and Carlyle, J. W. (1968), On the deterministic realization of stochastic finite-state machines, *Proc. Ann. Conf. Information Sci. Systems, 2nd, Princeton, 1968.*

Niven, I. (1956), Irrational Numbers, Math. Assoc. Amer.

Onicescu, O., and Guiasu, S (1965). Finite abstract random automata. *Z. Wahrscheinlichkeitstheorie und Verw. Geqiete* 3, 279-285.

Ott, G. (1966a). Theory and applications of stochastic sequential machines, Rep. No. SREC-RR-66-39. Sperry Rand. Res. Center.

Ott, G. (1966b). Reconsider the state minimization problem for stochastic finite state. systems. *IEEE Conf. Record Ann. Syuup. Switching Theory and Automata Theory, 7th, 1966.*

Page, C. V. (1965). Equivalences between probabilistic sequential machines. D. Sc. Thesis. Tech. Rep. Univ. of Michigan.

Page, C. V. (1966). Equivalences between probabilistic and deterministic machines. *Information and Control* 9, 469-520.

Paz, A. (1962). Finite Automata. M. Sc. Thesis sumbitted to the Hebrew Univ. Jerusalem (unpublished).

Paz, A. (1963). Graph—Theoretical and algebraic characterisation of some Markov processes. *Israel J. Math.* 1, No. 3, 169-180.

Paz, A. (1964). Finite probabilistic automata. D. Sc. Thesis submitted to the Technion IIT, Haifa (unpublished).

Paz, A. (1965). Definite and quasidefinite sets of stochastic matrices. *Proc. Amer Math. Soc.* 16, No. 4, 634-641.

Paz, A. (1966). Some aspects of probabilistic automata. *Informotion and Control* 9, No. 1, 26-60.

Paz, A. (1967a). Minimization theorems and techniques for sequential stochastic machines, *Information and Control* 11, 155-166.

Paz, A. (1967b). A Finite set of $n \times n$ stochastic matrices generating all n-dimensional probability vectors whose coordinates have finite binary expansion. *J. SIAM J. Control* 5, 545-554.

Paz, A. (1967c). Fuzzy star functions, probabilities automa and the relation to nonprobabilistic automata. *IEEE Conf. Record Ann. Symp. Switching and automata Theory, 8th, 1967,* pp 280-290; *J. Comput System Sci.* 1, 371-389.

Paz, A. (1967d). Homomorphisms between stochastic sequential machines aud related topics. Mem. No. ERL-M221. College of Engi. Univ. of California, Berkeley, California; *Math· Systems Theory* 2, No. 3, 223-245.

Paz, A. (1968a). Probabilistic arrays. *Proc. Ann. Conf. Information Sci. Systems, 2nd, Princeton, 1968.*

Paz, A. (1968b). Infinite state probabilistic transition tables and chains. Ergodic properties. *IEEE Conf. Record Ann. Symp. Switching and Automata Theory, 9th 1968.*

Paz, A. (1970a). Regular events in stochastic sequential machines. *IEEE Trans. Electronic Computers* Vol C-19, 5, 456-457.

Paz, A. (1970b). *Whirl decomposition of stochastic automata.* Technical Rept. No. 8, Technion Dept. of Computer Science.

Paz, A. (1970c). Formal series, finiteness properties and decision problems. Technical Rept. No. 4, Technion Dept. of Computer Science.

Paz, A. (1970d). Ergodic theorems for infinite probabilistic tables. *Ann. Math. Statist.* 41, 539-550.

Paz, A. and Reichaw, M. (1967). Ergodic theorems for sequences of infinite stochastic matrices *Proc. Cambridge Philos. Soc.* 63, 777-786.

Perles, M., Rabin, M. O., and Shamir, E. (1963). The theory of derinite automata. *IRE Trans.* EC12, No. 3, 230-245.

Pospelov, D. A. (1966). "Games and Automata." Izd. Energia, Moscow.

Rabin, M. O. (1963). Probabilistic automata. *Information and Control* 6, No. 3, 230-245; Also *In* "Sequential Machines" (E. F. Moore, ed.). Addison-Wesley, Reading, Massachusetts. (1964)

Rabin, M. O. (1966). Lectures on classical and probabilistic automata. *In* "Automata Theory" (E. R. Caianiello, ed.). Academic Press, New York.

Rabin, M. O. (1967). Mathematical theory of automata. *Proc. of symposia in Applied Mathematics Vol. 19, Amer. Math. Soc.*

Rabin, M. O., and Scott, D. (1959). Finite automata and their decision problem. *In* "Sequential Machines" (E. F. Moore, ed.). Addison-Wesley, Reading, Massachusetts. (1964)

Raney, G. N. (1958). Sequential Functions. *J. Assoc. Comput. Mach.* **5**, 177-180.

Rose, G. F., and Ullian, J. S. (1963). Approximations of functions on the integers. *Pacific J. Math.* **13**, No. 2, 693-701.

Rosenblatt, D. (1957). On the graphs and asymptotic forms of finite Boolean relation matrices and stochastic matrices. *Naval Res. Logist. Quart.* **4**, No. 2, 151-167.

Salomaa, A. (1965). On probabilistic automata with one-input letter. *Ann. Univ. Turku. Ser. A1*, p. 85.

Salomaa, A. (1966). On events represented by probabilistic automata of different types. *Canad. J. Math.* **20**, 242-251.

Salomaa, A. (1967). On m-Adic probabilistic automata. *Information and Control* **10**, 215-219.

Salomaa, A. (1968). On languages accepted by probabilistic and time variant automata. *Proc. Ann. Conf. Information Sci. Systems, 2nd, Princeton, 1968.*

Salomaa, A. (1969a). "Theory of Automata." Pergamon, New York.

Salomaa, A. (1969b). Probabilistic and wighted grammars. Sci. Rep. Univ. of Turku, Finland.

Santos, E. S. and Wee, W. G. (1968). General formulation of sequential machines. *Information and Control* **12**, 5-10.

Santos, E. S. (1968). Maximin automata. *Information and Control* **13**, 363-377.

Santos, E. S. (1969). Probabilistic Turing machines and computability. *Proc. Amer. Math. Soc.* **22**, 704-710.

Sapogov, N. A. (1949). Multidimensional inhomogeneous Markov chains. *Dokl. Akad. Nauk SSSR* LXIX, 2, 133-135.

Sapogov, N. A. (1950). The iterated logarithm law for sums of dependent variables. *Uch. Zap. Leningrad Univ. Ser. Mat.* **19**, 160-179.

Sapogov, N. A. (1967). The Laplace-Lyapunov limit theorem for a singular Markov chain. *Dokl. Akad. Nauk SSSR*, LVIII, 9, 1905-1908.

Sarymsakov, T. A. (1952). The ergodic principle for inhomogeneous Markov chains. *Dokl. Akad. Nauk SSSR*, XC, 1, 25-28.

Sarymsakov, T. A. (1956). The theory of inhomogeneous Markov chains. *Dokl. Akad. Nauk Uz. SSSR* **8**, 3-7.

Sarymsakov, T. A. (1958). Inhomogeneous Markov chains. *Dokl. Akad. Nauk SSSR* CXX, 3, 465-468.

Sarymsakov, T. A. (1961). Inhomogeneous Markov chains. *Teor Verojatnost i Primenen* **6**, 194-201.

Sarymsakov, T. A. and Mustafin Kh. A. (1957). To the ergodic theorem for inhomogeneous Markov chains. *Taskent, Tr. Gredneoziatsk. Gos. Univ.* 74, *Fig.-Mat. Nauk,* **15**, 1-38.

Schreider, J. A. (1962). Learning models and control systems. In "Stochastic Models for Learning" Bush and Mosteller, Russian. Mos.

Schützenberger, M. P. (1961). On the definition of a family of automata. *Information and Control* **4**, 245-270.

Shannon, C. E. (1957). Certain results in coding theory for noisy channels. *Information and Control* **1**, 6-25.

Shannon, C. E., and Weaver, W. (1948). "The Mathematical Theory of Communication." Univ. of Illinois Press, Urbana, Illinois.

Sheng, C. L. (1965). Threshold elements used as a probability transformer. *J. Assoc. Comput. Mach.* **12**, No. 2, 203-276.

Sirazdinov, S. H. (1950). The principle of ergodicity for nonhomogeneous Markov chains. *Dokl. Asud. Nauk. SSSR* **71**, 821-836.

Sklansky, J. (1966). Learning systems for automatic control. *IEEE Trans.* **AC-11**, No. 1, 6-19.

Sklansky, J., and Kaplan, K. R. (1963). Transients in probabilistic machines. *IEEE Trans. Electronic Computers* EC-12, No. 6, 921-922.

Souza, C., de Renna, E. (1968). On notions of equivalence for stochastic finite state systems. *Proc. Ann. Conf. Information Sci. Systems, 2nd, Princeton, 1968.*

Souza, C. de Renna, E., and Leake, R. J. (1969). Relationship among distinct models and notions of equivalence for stochastic finite state systems. *IEEE Trans.* **EC-18**, No. 7, 633-641.

Starke, P. H. (1965). Theorie stochastischer automaten I, II. *Elektron. Informationsverarbeit. Kybernetik* **1**, 5-32, 71-98.

Starke, P. H. (1966 a). Stochastische Eriginsse and Wortmengen. *Z. Math. Logik Grundlagen Math.* **12**, 61-68.

Starke, P. H. (1966 b). Theory of stochastic automata, *Kybernetika Prague* 2, 6 475-482.

Starke, P. H. (1966 c). Stochastische Ereignisse und Stochastische Operatore. *Elektron. Informationsverarbeit. Kybernetik* **2**, 177-190.

Starke, P. H, (1969). "Abstracte Automaten" Deut. Verlag. Wiss. Berlin.

Starke, P. H., and Thiele, H. (1967). Zu Fallige Zustande Stochastichen Automaten, *Elektron. Informationsverarbeit. Kybernetik* **3**, 25-37.

Suppes, P., and Atkinson, R. C. (1960). Markov learning models for multiperson interactions, In Stanford Mathematical Studies in the Social Sciences, Vol. V.

Tal. H. A. (1966). Questionnaire language and abstract synthesis of minimal sequential machines, *Avtomat. i Telemeh.* **25**, 946-962.

Thomasian, A. J. (1963), A finite criterion for indecomposable channels. *Ann. Math. Statist.* **34**, 337-338.

Thrall, R. M., and Tornheim, L. (1957), "Vector Spaces and Matrices," Wiley New York.

Tou, J. T. (1968), Stochastic automata and discrete systems theory. In Applied "Automata Theory" (J. T. Tou, ed.). Academic Press New York.

Tsertzvadze, G. N. (1963). Certain properties of stachastic automata and certain methods for synthesizing them, *Avtomat. i Telemeh.* **24**, No. 3, 341-352.

Tsertzvadze, G. N. (1966). Stochastic automata and the problem of constructing reliable automata from Unreliable elements I, II. *Avtomat. i Telemeh.* **25**, 213-226, 492-499.

Tsetslin, M. L. (1961). On the behaviour of finite automata in random media. *Automat. Remote Control* **22**, 1345-1354.

Turakainen, P. (1966). On regular events representable in probabilistic automata with one-input letter. *Ann. Univ. Turku. Ser. A*1 **90**.

Turakainen, P. (1968). On stochastic languages. *Ann. Acad. Sci. Fenn. Ser. AI* **429**; Also *Information and Control* **12**, 304-313.

Turakainen, P. (1969 a). *On variant probabilistic automata with monitors.* Sci. Rep. Univ. of Turku Finland.

Turakainen, P. (1969 b). On languages representable in rational probabilistic automata. *Ann. Acad. Sci. Fenn. AI* **439**.

Turakainen, P. (1970a). The family of stochastic languages is closed neither under catenation nor under homomoprphism, *Am. Univ. Turku. Ser. Al* **133**.

Turakainen, P. (1970b). Some closure properties of the family of stochastic languages. Technical Rept., University of Turku, Dept. of Mathematics, Finland.

Turnbull, H. W., and Aitken, A. C. (1932). "An Introduction to the Theory of Canonical Matrices." Blackie, London and Glasgow.

Vaisborg, E. M.. and Rosenstein, G. S. (1965). On the time of living of stochastic automata, *Izv. Akad. Nauk SSSR Tehn. Kibernet;* **4,** 52–59.

Vajda, S. (1961). "Mathematical Programming." Addison-Wesley, Reading, Massachusetts.

Varshaviskii, V. I., and Vorontsova, I. P. (1963). On the behaviour of stochastic automata with a variable structure, *Atomat. i Telemeh.* **24,** No. 3, 353–360.

Viterbi, A. J. (1967). Error bounds for convolutional codes and an asymptotically optimum decoding algorithm. *IEEE Trans.* **IT-13,** No. 2, 260–269.

Viterbi, A. J., and Odenwalder, J. P. (1969). Further results on optimal decoding of convolutional codes. Sci. Rep. Dept. of Eng. U.C.L.A., Los Angels, California.

Von Neuman, J. (1956). Probabilistic logics and the synthesis of reliable organisms from unreliable components, *Ann. Math. Studies* **34,** 43–98.

Vorontzówa, I. P. (1965). Algorithms of changing the transition probabilities of stochastic automata. *Problemy Peredaci Informacii* **31,** 122–126.

Warfield, J. N. (1965). Synthesis of switching circuits to yield prescribed probability relations. *IEEE Conf. Record Switching, Circuit Theory and Logical Design.*

Warfield, J. N. (1968). Switching networks as models of discrete stochastic processes. In "Applied Automata Theory" J. T. Tou, ed. Academic Press New York.

Wee, W. G., and Fu, K. S. (1969). A formulation of fuzzy automata and its application as a model of learning systems. *IEEE Trans.* **SSC-5,** No. 3, 215–223.

Wing, O. and Demetrious, P. (1964). Analysis of probabilistic network, *IEEE Trans.* **CT-12,** No. 3, 38–49.

Wolfowitz, J. (1963). Products of indecomposable, aperiodic. stochastic matrices. *Proc. Amer. Math. Soc.* **14,** No. 5, 733–737.

Yarovitzkii, N. V. (1966). Stochastic automata as models for discrete systems, *Kibernetika,* *(Kiev)* **5,** 35–43 (in Russian).

Yasui, T., and Yajima, S. (1969). Some algebraic properties of sets of stochastic matrices. *Information and Control* **14,** 319–357.

Zadeh, L. A. (1963 a). The general identification problem. *Proc. Conf. Identification Problems Communication and Control Systems, Princeton Univ., 1963.* Princeton, New Jersey.

Zadeh, L. A. (1963 b). Stochastic finite state systems in control theory. *Proc. Symp. Optimal Control Nonlinear Systems,* pp. 123–132. Faculte des Sci. Paris.

Zadeh, L. A. (1965). Fuzzy sets. *Inform Control* **6,** 230–245.

Zadeh, L. A., and Polak, E., ed. (1968). System Theory. McGraw-Hill, New York.

Answers and Hints to Selected Exercises

SECTION I, A.1

1.a.

$$A(v|u) = \begin{bmatrix} \frac{1}{8} & \frac{1}{8} \\ \frac{3}{8} & \frac{1}{8} \end{bmatrix}, \qquad \eta(v|u) = \begin{bmatrix} \frac{1}{4} \\ \frac{1}{2} \end{bmatrix}$$

$$\pi(v|u) = (\tfrac{3}{8}, \tfrac{1}{8}), \qquad \bar\pi(v|u) = (\tfrac{3}{4}, \tfrac{1}{4}), \qquad p_\pi(v, u) = \tfrac{1}{2}$$

1.b.

$$A(v|u) = \begin{bmatrix} \frac{1}{4} & 0 \\ 0 & 0 \end{bmatrix}, \qquad (v|u) = \begin{bmatrix} \frac{1}{4} \\ 0 \end{bmatrix}$$

$$\pi(v|u) = (0, 0) \qquad \bar\pi(v|u)\text{—not defined}, \qquad p_\pi(v|u) = 0 = p_\pi(aba|100)$$

5.a. 9/16

5.b. 87/128

6. $A(a|1)$ has negative entries.
   $A(b|1)$ has entries bigger than 1.
   $A(a|0) + A(b|0)$ is not a stochastic matrix.

SECTION I, A.2

5.a. $p_{s_1}(abb|010) = 0$.

5.b. $q(a|011, bb) = 1/4m + 1/2n$, where (m, n) is the initial distribution.

5.c. $r(a|1101) = \frac{13}{16}m + \frac{5}{8}n$.

7.

$$A(a) = \begin{bmatrix} \frac{3}{4} & \frac{1}{4} \\ \frac{1}{2} & \frac{1}{2} \end{bmatrix}, \qquad I(0|a) = \begin{bmatrix} \frac{1}{3} & 0 \\ 0 & \frac{2}{3} \end{bmatrix}, \qquad I(1|a) = \begin{bmatrix} \frac{2}{3} & 0 \\ 0 & \frac{1}{3} \end{bmatrix}$$

SECTION I, A.3

2.

$$A(0) = \frac{1}{2}\begin{bmatrix} 0 & 1 & 0 \\ 0 & 0 & 1 \\ 1 & 0 & 0 \end{bmatrix} + \frac{1}{4}\begin{bmatrix} 1 & 0 & 0 \\ 0 & 1 & 0 \\ 0 & 0 & 1 \end{bmatrix} + \frac{1}{6}\begin{bmatrix} 0 & 1 & 0 \\ 0 & 0 & 1 \\ 0 & 0 & 1 \end{bmatrix} + \frac{1}{12}\begin{bmatrix} 1 & 0 & 0 \\ 0 & 0 & 1 \\ 0 & 0 & 1 \end{bmatrix}$$

$$A(1) = \frac{5}{8}\begin{bmatrix} 1 & 0 & 0 \\ 0 & 1 & 0 \\ 0 & 0 & 1 \end{bmatrix} + \frac{1}{4}\begin{bmatrix} 0 & 0 & 1 \\ 1 & 0 & 0 \\ 1 & 0 & 0 \end{bmatrix} + \frac{1}{8}\begin{bmatrix} 1 & 0 & 0 \\ 0 & 1 & 0 \\ 0 & 1 & 0 \end{bmatrix}$$

$|Z| = 6$

$$A = \begin{bmatrix} \frac{1}{2} & \frac{1}{4} & \frac{1}{6} & \frac{1}{12} & 0 & 0 \\ 0 & \frac{5}{8} & 0 & 0 & \frac{1}{4} & \frac{1}{8} \end{bmatrix}, \qquad \text{etc.}$$

4. $|w^{M_1}| = 10; \qquad |w^{M_2}| = 5$.

SECTION I, B.1

2.

$$\begin{bmatrix} 1 & \frac{2}{3} & 1 \\ 1 & \frac{2}{3} & 0 \\ 1 & \frac{1}{3} & \frac{1}{4} \\ 1 & \frac{1}{3} & \frac{3}{4} \end{bmatrix}$$

3. Hint: Let M be a machine over an input alphabet X with $|X| = m - 1$ where m is the number of colums in the given matrix H, and output alphabet $|Y| = 2$, define the matrices $A(y|x)$ as follows: $A(y_1|x_i)$ has its first column equal to the ith column of H all its other entries being zero and $A(y_2|x_i)$ has

its first column such that with all the entries in the other columns zero $A(y_1|x_i) + A(y_2|x_i)$ is stochastic.

SECTION I, B.2

1. Reduced form:

$$A(y_1|x) = \begin{bmatrix} \frac{1}{4} & \frac{1}{2} & 0 \\ \frac{1}{6} & \frac{1}{3} & 0 \\ \frac{1}{12} & \frac{1}{6} & 0 \end{bmatrix}, \qquad A(y_2|x) = \begin{bmatrix} 0 & \frac{1}{8} & \frac{1}{8} \\ 0 & \frac{1}{4} & \frac{1}{4} \\ 0 & \frac{3}{8} & \frac{3}{8} \end{bmatrix}$$

Minimal form:

$$A(y_1|x) = \begin{bmatrix} \frac{1}{2} & \frac{1}{4} \\ \frac{1}{6} & \frac{1}{12} \end{bmatrix}, \qquad A(y_2|x) = \begin{bmatrix} \frac{1}{6} & \frac{3}{16} \\ \frac{3}{16} & \frac{9}{16} \end{bmatrix}$$

$(\frac{9}{16} \ 0 \ 0 \ \frac{7}{16})$ is a distribution which is equivalent to the distribution $(\frac{1}{4} \ \frac{1}{2} \ \frac{1}{8} \ \frac{1}{8})$.

5. Given that $f_i = \sum_{j=1}^{k} a_j f_j, \ \sum_{j=1}^{k} a_j = 1, a_j \geq 0$ we have that $f_i(1 - a_i) = \sum_{j \neq i} a_j f_j$ or $f_i = \sum_{j \neq i} [a_j/(1 - a_i)]f_j$ [since f_i is not extremal $0 < 1 - a_i < 1$] and

$$\sum_{j \neq i} \frac{a_j}{1 - a_i} = 1, \quad \frac{a_j}{1 - a_i} \geq 0$$

11.a. Hint: Let F denote the given flat and let a_0 be an element of F; prove that the set $L^F = \{a - a_0: a \in F\}$ is a linear space.

   b. Hint: Define the equivalence R over $\mathscr{P}_n^-$ $\pi R \rho \Leftrightarrow \pi H^M = \rho H^M$ where $\pi, \rho \in \mathscr{P}_n^-$. Show that R is right invariant and the set of equivalence classes is closed under convex combinations. Show also that each equivalence class is closed under convex combination of its elements. The rest of the proof is straightforward.

SECTION I, B.3

1. All the rows of H^M are different vertices of the $|S|$-cube and no vertex of the cube is a convex combination of other vertices.

3. $M^* \geq M, M \not\geq M^*$.

8. Let v_i represent the ith row in H^M, then the faces are: $\{v_1, v_2\}, \{v_2, v_3\}, \{v_3, v_4\},$ $\{v_5, v_1\}, \{v_5, v_2\}, \{v_5, v_3\}, \{v_5, v_4\}, \{v_1, v_2, v_5\}, \{v_1, v_4, v_5\}, \{v_4, v_3, v_5\}, \{v_2, v_3, v_5\},$ $\{v_1, v_2, v_3, v_4\}, \{v_1, v_2, v_3, v_5\}$. The faces containing two or three vertices above are simplexes.

11. H^M has two columns one of them having all its entries equal to 1; therefore, there are two rows in H^M such that all the other rows are convexly dependent on those two rows. The theorem follows from Theorem 2.8 in the previous section.

SECTION I, B.4

3. $M^* \geq M$, $M \not\geq M^*$.

SECTION I, B.6

2. Yes.

3.

$$
H^M = \begin{bmatrix} 1 & 1 & 1 & 1 \\ 1 & 1 & 1 & 0 \\ 1 & 1 & 0 & 0 \\ 1 & 0 & 0 & 0 \end{bmatrix}
$$

3.b. The trivial machine M^* with a single state and such that $A^*(0|0) = A^*(0|1) = A^*(0|2) = 1$, $A^*(1|0) = A^*(1|1) = A^*(1|2) = 0$ satisfies the conditions.

5. Proof: Let $h_{i_1}, \ldots, h_{i_m}$ be m linearly independent rows of H^M. As rank $H^M = m$, all the other rows of H^M are linearly dependent on $h_{i_1}, \ldots, h_{i_m}$. Let $\xi(y|x)$ be a row in a matrix of M. There is a vector $\xi'(y|x)$ having nonzero entries only in columns corresponding to the indexes $i_1, \ldots, i_m$ [the entries in $\xi'(y|x)$ may assume now negative values or values bigger than 1] and such that $\xi(y|x)H^M = \xi'(y|x)H^M$, since $\xi(y|x)H^M$ is a vector which represents a linear combination of the rows of H^M.

   Using an argument similar to the one used in the proof of Theorem 2.3 we see that the machine M', defined as the machine derived from M by replacing all vectors $\xi(y|x)$ in the matrices $A(y|x)$ by the corresponding vectors $\xi'(y|x)$, is state equivalent to M and all the columns in the matrices $A'(y|x)$ corresponding to indexes other than $i_1, \ldots, i_m$ are zero columns. The machine M' can now be reduced to an equivalent m-state machine M'' for only the states corresponding to the indexes $i_1, \ldots, i_m$ are accessible in M'.

SECTION I, B.7

1.a.

$$G^{(M,\pi)} = \begin{bmatrix} \frac{1}{8} & 0 & \frac{7}{8} & 0 \\ \frac{1}{2} & \frac{1}{2} & 0 & 0 \\ \frac{1}{4} & \frac{1}{4} & \frac{1}{2} & 0 \\ \frac{1}{4} & 0 & \frac{1}{2} & \frac{1}{4} \end{bmatrix}, \qquad H^{(H,\pi)} = \begin{bmatrix} 1 & \frac{7}{8} & \frac{7}{8} \\ 1 & \frac{1}{2} & 0 \\ 1 & \frac{3}{4} & \frac{1}{2} \\ 1 & \frac{1}{2} & \frac{3}{4} \end{bmatrix}$$

2. Consider formula (28). The number of linearly independent rows in $[K^{(M,\pi)}]$ equals rank $H^{(M,\pi)}$ therefore there must be at least that many rows in K^{M^*} so that rank $M^* \geq$ rank $H^{(M,\pi)}$.

4. $\pi^* = (\frac{1}{2}, \frac{1}{2})$

$$A^*(0|0) = \begin{bmatrix} \frac{1}{2} & 0 \\ \frac{3}{4} & 0 \end{bmatrix}, \qquad A^*(1|0) = \begin{bmatrix} \frac{1}{2} & 0 \\ \frac{1}{4} & 0 \end{bmatrix}$$

$$A^*(0|1) = \begin{bmatrix} 0 & \frac{1}{2} \\ 0 & \frac{3}{4} \end{bmatrix}, \qquad A^*(1|1) = \begin{bmatrix} 0 & \frac{1}{2} \\ 0 & \frac{1}{4} \end{bmatrix}$$

5.

$$A^*(0|0) = \begin{bmatrix} 0 & 0 & 0 \\ \frac{1}{2} & \frac{1}{2} & 0 \\ 0 & 0 & 0 \end{bmatrix}, \qquad A^*(1|0) = \begin{bmatrix} \frac{1}{2} & \frac{1}{2} & 0 \\ 0 & 0 & 0 \\ \frac{1}{2} & \frac{1}{2} & 0 \end{bmatrix}$$

$$A^*(0|1) = \begin{bmatrix} 0 & 0 & 0 \\ \frac{1}{4} & \frac{3}{4} & 0 \\ \frac{1}{4} & \frac{3}{4} & 0 \end{bmatrix}, \qquad A^*(1|1) = \begin{bmatrix} \frac{1}{4} & \frac{3}{4} & 0 \\ 0 & 0 & 0 \\ 0 & 0 & 0 \end{bmatrix}$$

$$\pi^* = \begin{bmatrix} \frac{1}{4} & 0 & \frac{3}{4} \end{bmatrix}$$

No further reduction is possible in this case.

6.

$$H^M = \begin{bmatrix} 1 & 1 & 1 \\ 1 & 1 & 0 \\ 1 & 0 & 1 \\ 1 & 0 & 0 \end{bmatrix} = H^{(M,\pi)}$$

and there is no convex polygon inside the unit cube with less than four vertices in two dimensional plane which covers the unit cube [the rows of H^M, ignoring the first coordinate].

SECTION I, C.2

1. By definition $p(\lambda|\lambda) = 1$ and any compound sequence determinant of order 2 is equal to zero. Thus

$$\begin{vmatrix} p(\lambda|\lambda) & p(v'|u') \\ p(v|u) & p(vv'|uu') \end{vmatrix} = 0$$

or $p(vv'|uu') = p(v|u)p(v'|u')$.

SECTION I, C.3

3.

$$p = \begin{bmatrix} 1 & \frac{7}{10} \\ \frac{3}{10} & \frac{1}{10} \end{bmatrix}, \qquad Q = \begin{bmatrix} \frac{3}{10} & \frac{7}{10} \\ \frac{1}{4} & \frac{1}{20} \end{bmatrix}$$

$$\pi = [\frac{3}{10} \quad \frac{7}{10}], \qquad A^M(0) = \begin{bmatrix} \frac{5}{6} & \frac{1}{6} \\ 0 & 0 \end{bmatrix}, \qquad A^M(1) = \begin{bmatrix} 0 & 0 \\ \frac{1}{2} & \frac{1}{2} \end{bmatrix}$$

4.b. It is easily seen that $A^M(v)$, for any $v \in Y^*$ has the form

$$\begin{bmatrix} a & 0 & 0 \\ - & - & - \\ - & - & - \end{bmatrix}$$

where $a \geq 0$ so that $\eta^M(v) = A^M(v) \eta$ is a column vector whose first entry has a *positive* and ≤ 1 value for any $v \in Y^*$. As the sum of the matrices $A^M(0) + A^M(1)$ has row sums equal to 1, this is true also for the sums

$$\sum_{v:l(v)=k} A^M(v) \qquad \text{so that} \qquad \sum_{v:l(v)=k} p_\pi{}^M(\sigma) = 1.$$

The required statement is proved now by induction on the length of v. For $l(v) = 1$, the proof results from straightforward computation. We consider now $p_\pi{}^M(1v)$ and $p_\pi{}^M(0v)$ for $l(v) = k$.

$$p_\pi{}^M(1v) = \pi A(1)\eta(v) = [\frac{4}{5} \quad \frac{1}{10} \quad \frac{1}{10}] \begin{bmatrix} \frac{1}{2} & 0 & 0 \\ \frac{4}{3} & 0 & 0 \\ \frac{5}{4} & 0 & 0 \end{bmatrix} \begin{bmatrix} a(v) \\ b(v) \\ c(v) \end{bmatrix}$$

$$= a(v)[\frac{4}{5} \quad \frac{1}{10} \quad \frac{1}{10}] \begin{bmatrix} \frac{1}{2} \\ \frac{4}{3} \\ \frac{5}{4} \end{bmatrix}$$

thus, $0 \le p_\pi^M(1v) \le p_\pi^M(1) \le 1$. Considering now the value $p_\pi^M(0v)$, we have that

$$p_\pi^M(0v) = \begin{bmatrix} \frac{4}{5} & \frac{1}{10} & \frac{1}{10} \end{bmatrix} \begin{bmatrix} \frac{1}{2} & 0 & 0 \\ 0 & -\frac{1}{3} & 0 \\ 0 & 0 & -\frac{1}{4} \end{bmatrix} \begin{bmatrix} a(v) \\ b(v) \\ c(v) \end{bmatrix}$$

$$= \tfrac{4}{5} \tfrac{1}{2} a(v) - \tfrac{1}{10} \tfrac{1}{3} b(v) - \tfrac{1}{10} \tfrac{1}{4} c(v)$$

It is clear from the definitions of the matrices that either both $b(v)$ and $c(v)$ are > 0 or both values are < 0. In the second case, $p_\pi^M(0v) > 0$. In the first case $p_\pi^M(v) = \tfrac{4}{5} a(v) - \tfrac{1}{10} b(v) - \tfrac{1}{10} c(v) > 0$ by the induction hypothesis. Therefore,

$$\tfrac{4}{5} a(v) > \tfrac{1}{10} b(v) + \tfrac{1}{10} c(v)$$

or

$$\tfrac{1}{2} \tfrac{4}{5} a(v) > \tfrac{1}{2} \tfrac{1}{10} b(v) + \tfrac{1}{2} \tfrac{1}{10} c(v) > \tfrac{1}{3} \tfrac{1}{10} b(v) + \tfrac{1}{4} \tfrac{1}{10} c(v)$$

or

$$p_\pi^M(0v) > 0$$

It follows that $p_\pi^M(0v) > 0$ and $p_\pi^M(1v) > 0$. But $\sum_v p_\pi^M(0v) + p_\pi^M(1v) = 1$; and, therefore, both values are also ≤ 1.

4.c. Hint: Use eigenvalue considerations.

9. Hint: Use the nulity laws of Sylvester and the fact that the ranks of the spaces of the vectors $\pi(v|u)$ and $\eta(v|u)$ grow strictly when $l(v, u)$ grows or else the ranks do not grow any more.

10. Hint: Use Exercise 9.

SECTION II, A.1

4.d. Let $P = (p_{ij})$ be the matrix such that $p_{ij} = \tfrac{1}{2}$ if $j = i$ or $j = i + 2$ and $p_{ij} = 0$ otherwise. Show that $\delta(P^n) = 1$ for $n = 1, 2, \ldots$ but $\lim_{n \to \infty} d(P^n) = 0$.

4.e. $d(P) = 0$ implies that P is constant.

6. Let E be the matrix all the rows of which are equal to some row of P then $Q = P - E = P - RP$ where R is a matrix having a column of ones all the other columns being zero columns. Now use Corollary 1.5.

11. Use induction. If $n = 2$, then

$$\|A_1 A_2 - \bar{A}_1 \bar{A}_2\| \le \|A_1 A_2 - \bar{A}_1 A_2\| + \|\bar{A}_1 A_2 - \bar{A}_1 \bar{A}_2\| = \|(A_1 - \bar{A}_1) A_2\|$$
$$+ \|\bar{A}_1 (A_2 - \bar{A}_2)\| \le \|A_1 - \bar{A}_1\| \|A_2\| + \|\bar{A}_1\| \|A_2 - \bar{A}_2\| \le 2\epsilon$$

by Exercise 10 and by the assumption.

12. $||\bar{P} - \bar{P}_{i_0}|| = ||P - RP|| \le 2\delta(P)$ by Corollary 1.5 where R is a matrix whose i_0 column is a column of ones, the other columns being zero columns. Thus $\delta(P) \ge \frac{1}{2}||P - \bar{P}_{i_0}||$. On the other hand $2\delta(P) = \sup_{i_0} ||P - \bar{P}_{i_0}||$ which proves the second part of the exercise.

13.a. $\delta(P) = 0$ implies that P is constant and an infinite constant matrix cannot be doubly stochastic.

13.b. A matrix P is doubly stochastic if and only if A and A^{T} are both stochastic. If P and Q are doubly stochastic, then PQ is stochastic and $(PQ)^{\mathrm{T}} = Q^{\mathrm{T}}P^{\mathrm{T}}$ is a stochastic matrix because Q^{T} and P^{T} are stochastic.

13.c. One proves easily that $EP^n = E$ thus $||P^n - E|| = ||P^n - EP^n|| \le \delta(P^n) \to 0$.

13.d. If the statement is not true, then for some $0 < \epsilon < \frac{1}{2}$ there is n such that $\delta(P^n) < \epsilon < \frac{1}{2}$. There is k such that for given i_0, $\sum_{j=1}^{k} p_{i_0 j}^{(n)} > 1 - \epsilon$. But for any i_0, and i

$$|\sum_{j=1}^{k} p_{i_0 j}^{(n)} - p_{ij}^{(n)}| \le \delta(P^n) < \epsilon$$

This implies that $\sum_{j=1}^{k} p_{ij}^{(n)} \ge 1 - 2\epsilon, i = 1, 2, \dots$ or

$$\sum_{i=1}^{\infty} \sum_{j=1}^{k} p_{ij}^{(n)} = \infty \quad \text{but} \quad \sum_{i=1}^{\infty} \sum_{j=1}^{k} p_{ij}^{(n)} = k,$$

a contradiction.

14. Use the fact that if $Q = \lim_{n \to \infty} P^n$ then $PQ = QP = Q$.

SECTION II, A.2

3.

$$||\pi P_n - \pi|| \le ||\pi H_{mn} - \pi|| + ||\pi H_{mn} - \pi P_n||$$
$$||\pi H_{mn} - \pi P_n|| = ||\pi H_{m,n-1} P_n - \pi P_n||$$
$$= ||(\pi H_{m,n-1} - \pi)P_n|| \le ||\pi H_{m,n-1} - \pi||$$

Thus,

$$||\pi P_n - \pi|| \le ||\pi H_{mn} - \pi|| + ||\pi H_{m,n-1} - \pi|| \to 0$$

4.

$$||\bar{P}_n P_n \bar{P}_{n-1} P_{n-1} \cdots \bar{P}_1 P_1 - \bar{P}_{n-1} P_{n-1} \cdots \bar{P}_1 P_1||$$
$$\le \delta(\bar{P}_{n-1} P_{n-1} \cdots \bar{P}_1 P_1) \le \delta(P_{n-1})\delta(P_{n-1}) \cdots \delta(P_1) \to 0.$$

This implies that $\lim_{n \to \infty} \bar{P}_n P_n \bar{P}_{n-1} P_{n-1} \cdots \bar{P}_1 P_1 = S$ exists [since the infinite

sequence of products is bounded]. That S is constant follows from the fact that
$$\delta(S) = \lim_{n \to \infty} \delta(\bar{P}_n P_n \bar{P}_{n-1} \cdots \bar{P}_1 P_1) \le \lim_{n \to \infty} \delta(P_n P_{n-1} \cdots P_1) = 0$$

5. See Exercise 4.d in Section II, A.1.

6. See Exercise 4.a in Section II, A.1.

13. Hint: Use Exercise 4 in this section.

SECTION II, A.4

4. $S = \{s_1, \ldots, s_n\}$, $s_i \Gamma = s_{i+1}$ for $i = 1, 2, \ldots, n - 2$ and $s_{n-1}\Gamma = \{s_n, s_1\}$, $s_n \Gamma = s_1$.

9. Hint: Show that at most 2^n states can have a common consequent of order n.

10. Let P be defined as follows: $P = [p_{ij}]$ with $p_{n1} = 1/n$, $p_{nn} = 1 - (1/n)$, $p_{ij} = 0$ otherwise. It is easy to see that $\gamma(P) = \lim_{n \to \infty} p_{n1} = 0$, but the first column of P has all its entries different from zero.

11. See Exercise 4.d in Section II, A.1.

12. The matrices $(1/n) \sum_{m=1}^{n} P^m$ are stochastic and any sequence of stochastic [therefore bounded] matrices has a convergent subsequence. It suffices to show that all the convergent subsequences have the same limit. Let $n_1, n_2, \ldots, n_j$ be a subsequence of integers such that $Q = \lim_{n_j \to \infty} (1/n_j) \sum_{m=1}^{n_j} P^m$ exists. Then $QP = PQ = \lim (1/n) \sum_{m=2}^{n_j+1} P^m$ and the two limits are equal, since they differ by the terms P^{n_j+1}/n_j, P/n_j which tend to zero when $n_j \to \infty$. Similarly, for any n, $Q = QP^n = P^nQ$ which implies that $Q = QR = RQ$ for any limit R of another subsequence of averages of matrices. Using the same argument one finds that $R = QR = RQ$ or $R = Q$.

15. See Exercise 12 above.

17. By Exercise 16, the equations
$$(x_1 \cdots x_n)[I - P] = 0; \qquad \sum x_i = 1 \qquad\qquad (*)$$
have a unique solution. Thus $\det [I - P] = 0$ and $[I - P]$ has rank $n - 1$. The system of equations $(*)$ can be shown to be equivalent to the system
$$(x_1 \cdots x_n)[I - [P - \eta\xi_r]] = \xi_r$$
where η denotes a column vector with all its entries equal to 1 and ξ_r is the rth row of P. Thus $\det [I - [P - \eta\xi_r]] \ne 0$ and both parts of the exercise follow.

18.

$$\begin{bmatrix} \frac{2}{5} & \frac{1}{5} & \frac{2}{5} \\ \frac{2}{5} & \frac{1}{5} & \frac{2}{5} \\ \frac{2}{5} & \frac{1}{5} & \frac{2}{5} \end{bmatrix}$$

21. Let $Q = \lim_{n \to \infty} P^n$. Then Q is constant and $QP^k = 0$ for all k. Let $\pi = (\pi_i)$ be a row of Q, then $\pi \eta_r{}^k = \pi_r$. Thus the vectors $\eta_r{}^k$ all satisfy the equation of the $(n-1)$-dimensional hyperplane $\pi_1 x_1 + \pi_2 x_2 + \cdots + \pi_n x_n = \pi_r$.

22a.

$$A = \begin{bmatrix} \frac{1}{2} & 0 & 0 & \frac{1}{2} \\ 0 & \frac{1}{2} & \frac{1}{2} & 0 \\ 0 & \frac{1}{2} & \frac{1}{2} & 0 \\ \frac{1}{2} & 0 & 0 & \frac{1}{2} \end{bmatrix}, \qquad B = \begin{bmatrix} \frac{1}{2} & \frac{1}{2} & 0 & 0 \\ \frac{1}{2} & \frac{1}{2} & 0 & 0 \\ 0 & 0 & \frac{1}{2} & \frac{1}{2} \\ 0 & 0 & \frac{1}{2} & \frac{1}{2} \end{bmatrix}$$

b.

$$\gamma(AB) = 1 > 0, \qquad \gamma(A^k) = \gamma(B^k) = 0$$

$$A = \begin{bmatrix} \frac{1}{2} & \frac{1}{2} & 0 & 0 \\ 0 & \frac{1}{2} & \frac{1}{2} & 0 \\ 0 & 0 & 0 & 1 \\ 0 & 0 & 0 & 1 \end{bmatrix}, \qquad B = \begin{bmatrix} \frac{1}{2} & \frac{1}{2} & 0 & 0 \\ \frac{1}{2} & \frac{1}{2} & 0 & 0 \\ \frac{1}{2} & \frac{1}{2} & 0 & 0 \\ 0 & 0 & \frac{1}{2} & \frac{1}{2} \end{bmatrix}$$

$$\gamma(AB) = 0, \qquad \gamma(A^3) > 0, \qquad \gamma(B^2) > 0$$

23. It follows from the assumption that $PQ^n \sim P$. There is n such that Q^n is scrambling so that also PQ^n is scrambling and also P is scrambling.

25. Let $Q_x = \lim_{n \to \infty} A(x^n)$, then

$$\begin{aligned}
&\|A(yx) - Q_x\| \\
&\leq \|A(yx) - A(x)\| + \|A(x) - Q_x\| \\
&= \|A(y)A(x) - A(x)\| + \|A(x) - Q_x A(x)\| \\
&\leq 2\delta(A(x)) + 2\delta(A(x))
\end{aligned}$$

which tends to zero with n.

26. If $P = [p_{ij}]$ is a matrix of order n such that $p_{ij} \neq 0$ for $j = i$ and $j = i + 1$ only then P satisfies H_2 of order $n - 1$, which is minimal.

28. Use Exercise 4.

29. Use Theorem 4.9.

30. Use Exercise 4.9.

31. Use Exercise 4.10.

SECTION II, A.5

6. Hint: Use Exercise 5 and induction on the length of x.

7. For any 2-state matrix $P(\sigma) = [P_{ij}(\sigma)]$, one can prove that

$$P(\sigma) = \begin{bmatrix} u_1(\sigma) & u_2(\sigma) \\ u_1(\sigma) & u_2(\sigma) \end{bmatrix} + \lambda^P \begin{bmatrix} u_2(\sigma) & -u_2(\sigma) \\ -u_1(\sigma) & u_2(\sigma) \end{bmatrix}$$

where $u_1(\sigma) = P_{21}(\sigma)/(P_{12}(\sigma) + P_{21}(\sigma))$, $u_2(\sigma) = 1 - u_1(\sigma)$. Under the assumptions $u_1(\sigma)$ and $u_2(\sigma)$ are independent of σ and therefore,

$$P(\sigma_1\sigma_2) = \begin{bmatrix} u_1 & u_2 \\ u_1 & u_2 \end{bmatrix} + \lambda^{P(\sigma_1)} \lambda^{P(\sigma_2)} \begin{bmatrix} u_2 & -u_2 \\ -u_1 & u \end{bmatrix}$$

since $\lim_{k\to\infty} \lambda^{P(\sigma_1)} \lambda^{P(\sigma_2)} \cdots \lambda^{P(\sigma_k)} = 0$, the limiting matrix is

$$\begin{bmatrix} u_1 & u_2 \\ u_1 & u_2 \end{bmatrix}$$

9. As in Exercise 8, we have that the limiting matrix is

$$\begin{bmatrix} u_1 & u_2 \\ u_1 & u_2 \end{bmatrix} + \lim \pi\lambda^{P_i} \begin{bmatrix} u_2 & -u_2 \\ u_1 & -u_1 \end{bmatrix}$$

SECTION II, B.1

6. Using the ordinary probability laws, resolve first the probability of the state of the whole system, given the present and past, into the probabilities of the next states of the separate systems A and B given the same, then use the Markov property of the two systems to eliminate the dependence on the past, and then combine back, proving that the resulting probability for the whole system depends only on its present situation.

SECTION II, B.2

1.b. The matrix VU has stochastic submatrices in its diagonal parts with rows and columns corresponding to the same block π_i of π and, because of the lumpability condition, every column in the matrix $A(\sigma)V$ has all the entries corresponding to the same block π_i equal one to the other. This implies that $VUA(\sigma)V = A(\sigma)V$.

1.c. Use the property 2.1.b proved above.

1.d. As in 2.1.b the matrix VU has stochastic submatrices in its diagonal parts with rows and columns corresponding to the same block π_i of π, moreover the rows of those submatrices are equal. This fact together with the condition that $VUA(\sigma)V = A(\sigma)V$ implies that all the entries in a column of $A(\sigma)V$ corresponding to the same block π_i of π are equal one to the other which implies the lumpability condition.

2.

$$U = \begin{bmatrix} \frac{1}{2} & \frac{1}{2} & 0 & 0 \\ 0 & 0 & \frac{1}{2} & \frac{1}{2} \end{bmatrix}, \qquad V = \begin{bmatrix} 1 & 0 \\ 1 & 0 \\ 0 & 1 \\ 0 & 1 \end{bmatrix}$$

$$\hat{A}(a) = \begin{bmatrix} 0.5 & 0.5 \\ 0.3 & 0.7 \end{bmatrix}, \qquad \hat{A}(b) = \begin{bmatrix} 0.4 & 0.6 \\ 0.75 & 0.25 \end{bmatrix}$$

3. The system A is equivalent to the cascade product of the two systems

$$B = (\pi, \{B(\sigma)\}) \text{ and } C = (\tau, \{C(i, \sigma))$$

with

$$B(a) = \begin{bmatrix} 0.4 & 0.6 \\ 0.5 & 0.5 \end{bmatrix}, \qquad B(b) = \begin{bmatrix} 0.3 & 0.7 \\ 0.2 & 0.8 \end{bmatrix}$$

and

$$C(1, a) = \begin{bmatrix} 0.5 & 0.5 \\ 0 & 1 \end{bmatrix}, \qquad C(2, a) = \begin{bmatrix} 0.8 & 0.2 \\ 0.5 & 0.5 \end{bmatrix}$$

$$C(1, b) = \begin{bmatrix} 1 & 0 \\ 0 & 1 \end{bmatrix}, \qquad C(2, b) = \begin{bmatrix} 0.4 & 0.6 \\ 0.3 & 0.7 \end{bmatrix}$$

4. The system A is equivalent to the cascade product of the systems $B = (T_1\{B(\sigma)\})$ and $C = (T_2\{C(s, \sigma)\})$ with $T_1 = \{s_1 s_2\}$, $T_2 = \{s_1' s_2'\}$ when the states $(s_1 s_2')$ and (s_2, s_1') of the composite system are merged at the output and the transition matrices of B and C are defined as follows

$$B(a) = \begin{bmatrix} 0.4 & 0.6 \\ 0.75 & 0.25 \end{bmatrix}, \qquad B(b) = \begin{bmatrix} 0.3 & 0.7 \\ 0.2 & 0.8 \end{bmatrix}, \qquad C(s_1, b) = \begin{bmatrix} 1 & 0 \\ 0.2 & 0.8 \end{bmatrix}$$

$$C(s_1, a) = \begin{bmatrix} 0.5 & 0.5 \\ 0.75 & 0.25 \end{bmatrix}, \qquad C(s_2, a) = \begin{bmatrix} 0.4 & 0.6 \\ 0.6 & 0.4 \end{bmatrix}, \qquad C(s_2, b) = \begin{bmatrix} 0.3 & 0.7 \\ 0.7 & 0.3 \end{bmatrix}$$

SECTION II, C.1

5. Let P_σ be a compound sequence matrix of maximal rank for f. The entries in P_σ are of the form $f(v_i \sigma v_j')$: Assume that there is some δ in v_i and let $v_i = w_i \delta \sigma^{k_i}$ where k_i is some integer [including 0 in which case $\sigma^0 = \lambda$] and w_i is a word. Then, $f(v_i \sigma v_j') = f(w_i \delta \sigma^{k_i} v_j') = (f(w_i \delta)/f(\delta))f(\delta \sigma^{k_i} \sigma v_j')$ [by (22)] one can replace therefore the sequence v_i by the sequence $\delta \sigma^{k_i}$ without affecting the nonsingularity of the compound sequence matrix [the factor $f(w_i \delta)/f(\delta)$ multiplies all the entries in the ith row of P and it is assumed that $f(\delta) \neq 0$]. If there is no symbol δ in v_i, then $v_i = \sigma^{k_i}$. To complete the exercise one uses a similar argument for the columns of P_σ.

6. Let σ_i, considered as a block of the partition $\sum$ over S contain the states $s_{i_1}, s_{i_2}, \ldots, s_{i_{k(i)}}$ where $k(i)$ is the rank of σ_i. Consider the partition $\sum'$ which is the same as $\sum$, but the block σ_i of $\sum$ is split into $k(i)$ blocks containing the states s_{i_j} as their single elements. Let f' be the function corresponding to the new partition $\sum'$. Then $f(v\sigma_i v') = \sum_{j=1}^{k(i)} f'(vs_{i_j} v')$. But the compound sequence matrices whose elements are of the form $f'(vs_{i_j} v')$ are of rank $1 = r(s_{i_j})$.

7. As in Example 16 one can always find a nonsingular diagonal matrix X satisfying the condition $\bar{\eta}' = X\bar{\eta}$ and then define $A' = XAX^{-1}$ $\pi' = \pi X^{-1}$ with $\pi' \bar{\eta}' = \pi X^{-1} X\bar{\eta} = \pi\bar{\eta} = 1$ and $A'\bar{\eta}' = A'X\eta = XA\bar{\eta} = X\bar{\eta} = \bar{\eta}'$.

8. Let G, H, G', H' be the G and H [see the proof of Theorem 1.12 for definitions) matrices corresponding to $\mathcal{M}$ and $\mathcal{M}'$ respectively. $\mathcal{M}$ and $\mathcal{M}'$ being equivalent we have that $GH = G'H'$ and $GAH = G'A'H'$. But rank $f = |S|$ and therefore G and H are nonsingular so that $A = G^{-1}G'A'H'H^{-1}$ and $G^{-1}G'H'H^{-1} = G^{-1}GHH^{-1} = I$. Let now $B = G^{-1}G'$ and $C = HH^{-1}$.

9. Prove that the conditions in Example 17 are satisfied for this case.

12. Use Exercise 9 above.

SECTION II, C.2

7.c. It follows from Corollary 2.13 that $XA(\sigma) = A'(\sigma)X$ for a nonsingular matrix X. If ϵ is an eigenvalue for $A(\sigma)$ then $A(\sigma)\xi^T = \epsilon\xi^T$ for some vector ξ and therefore $A'(\sigma)X\xi^T = XA(\sigma)\xi^T = \epsilon X\xi^T$ which proves that ϵ is an eigenvalue for $A'(\sigma)$ with eigenvector $X\xi^T$. Similarly, if ϵ is an eigenvalue for $A'(\sigma)$ with row eigenvector ξ, then $\xi XA(\sigma) = \xi A'(\sigma)X = \epsilon\xi X$ so that ξX is a row eigenvector for $A(\sigma)$ with same eigenvalue.

8. Use the Sylvester inequalities for matrices.

10. Let X be the unity matrix with an additional all zero row. Show that the conditions of Theorem 2.15 are satisfied for this matrix X under the conditions of the exercise.

11. Let X be the matrix whose rows are all $2^{|S|}$ vectors of dimension $|S|$ with entries zero or one. Show that the conditions of Theorem 2.15 are satisfied for this matrix X under the conditions of the exercise.

12. See Exercise 2.7.c.

13. Let t be the maximal absolute value of the eigenvalues of a matrix AA^T. It can be shown that t satisfies the inequality $(\xi A, \xi A) \leq |t|(\xi, \xi)$ where ξ is any row vector and (ξ, ζ) denotes the scalar product of ξ by ζ. Let X in Theorem 2.15 be the matrix with $2^{|S|}$ rows, its rows being all possible $|S|$-dimensional vectors with entries either 0 or 1. Let ξ be a row of X, then $(\xi A, \xi A) \leq (1/|S|)(\xi, \xi) \leq 1$, for $(\xi, \xi) \leq |S|$. This proves that the conditions of Theorem 2.15 are satisfied.

SECTION III, A.2

1. $h = \frac{1}{2} f + \frac{1}{2} \bar{g} = \frac{1}{2} + \frac{1}{2}(f - g)$.

5. Change the matrices $A(\sigma)$ into $(|S| + 1) \times (|S| + 1)$ matrices with first column an all zero column and first row of form $(0, \pi)$, the remaining $|S| \times |S|$ diagonal submatrix of $A'(\sigma)$ being equal to the matrix $A(\sigma)$.

9. Express $|f - g|$ in terms of the operations "$\vee$" and "$\wedge$" and use *Proposition 2.3*.

SECTION III, B

5. Use Exercise 1 in Section III, A.2.

7. Let $u = \sigma_1 \cdots \sigma_n$, $u' = \sigma_1' \cdots \sigma_m'$ and define the following equivalence relation R: uRu' if and only if (1) $\pi A(\sigma_1 \cdots \sigma_{n-1}) = \pi A(\sigma_1' \cdots \sigma_{m-1}')$; (2) $A(y|\sigma_n) = A(y|\sigma_m')$ for all $y \in Y$. R is right invariant, of finite index and $P^M(y|u) > \lambda$ if and only if $P^M(y|u') > \lambda$.

The reader will find additional hints and answers by consulting the bibliographical notes associated with each section.

Author Index

Subject Index